Friendship! Lifelong friends
are important.
Energy! Morning jogs are nice.
Victory! I'd rather be a
winner, not a loser.
Take that advice to heart!

—Tsugumi Ohba

I had a classmate who was very
good at drawing. Whenever he drew
a face, he'd draw a cross so that
the eyes and nose looked balanced.
How cool! It had a huge impact on
me, and I've been drawing crosses
on faces ever since.

—Takeshi Obata

Tsugumi Ohba

**Born in Tokyo, Tsugumi Ohba is the author of the hit series *Death Note*.
His current series *Bakuman₀* is serialized in *Weekly Shonen Jump*.**

Takeshi Obata

**Takeshi Obata was born in 1969 in Niigata, Japan, and is the artist of
the wildly popular SHONEN JUMP title *Hikaru no Go*, which won the
2003 Tezuka Osamu Cultural Prize: Shinsei "New Hope" award and
the 2000 Shogakukan Manga award. Obata is also the artist of *Arabian
Majin Bokentan Lamp Lamp*, *Ayatsuri Sakon*, *Cyborg Jichan G.*, and the
smash hit manga *Death Note*. His current series *Bakuman₀* is serialized**

BAKUMAN.

Volume 8

SHONEN JUMP Manga Edition

Story by **TSUGUMI OHBA**
Art by **TAKESHI OBATA**

Translation | **Tetsuichiro Miyaki**
English Adaptation | **Hope Donovan**
Touch-up Art & Lettering | **James Gaubatz**
Design | **Fawn Lau**
Editor | **Alexis Kirsch**

BAKUMAN. © 2008 by Tsugumi Ohba, Takeshi Obata
All rights reserved.
First published in Japan in 2008 by SHUEISHA Inc., Tokyo.
English translation rights arranged by SHUEISHA Inc.

The rights of the author(s) of the work(s) in this publication to be
so identified have been asserted in accordance with the Copyright,
Designs and Patents Act 1988. A CIP catalogue record for this book
is available from the British Library.

Printed in the U.S.A.

Published by VIZ Media, LLC
P.O. Box 77010
San Francisco, CA 94107

10 9 8 7 6 5 4 3 2 1
First printing, December 2011

PARENTAL ADVISORY
BAKUMAN. is rated T for Teen
and is recommended for ages
13 and up. This volume contains
suggestive themes.
ratings.viz.com

www.viz.com

www.shonenjump.com

BAKUMAN。

8

PANTY SHOT and SAVIOR

STORY BY
TSUGUMI OHBA

ART BY
TAKESHI OBATA

SHONENJUMP MANGA

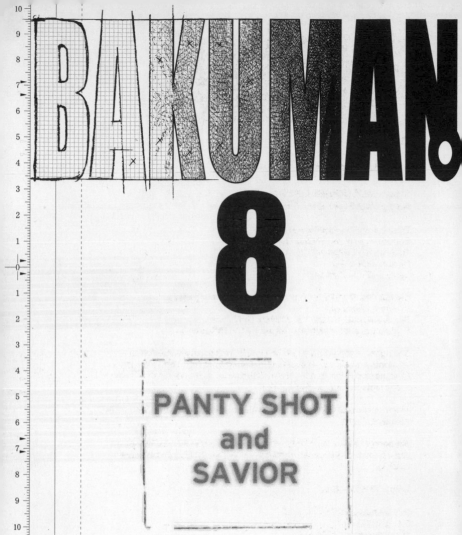

UMAN。

バクマン。 vol. 8

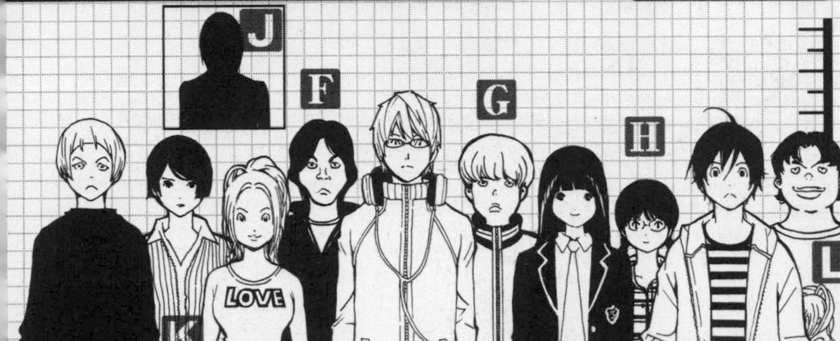

L
H
G
F
J
LOVE
K

EIJI
Nizuma

A manga prodigy and Tezuka Award winner at the age of 15. One of the most popular creators in *Jump*.

Age: 19

KAYA
Miyoshi

Miho's friend and Akito's girlfriend. A nice girl who actively works as the interceder between Moritaka and Azuki.

Age: 18

AKITO
Takagi

Manga writer. An extremely smart guy who gets the best grades in his class. A cool guy who becomes very passionate when it comes to manga.

Age: 18

MIHO
Azuki

A girl who dreams of becoming a voice actress. She promised to marry Moritaka under the condition that they not see each other until their dreams come true.

Age: 18

MORITAKA
Mashiro

Manga artist. An extreme romantic who believes that he will marry Miho Azuki once their dreams come true.

Age: 18

*These ages are from June 2012.

STORY In order to attain the glory that only a handful of people can, two young men decide to walk the rough "path of manga" and become professional manga creators. This is the story of a great artist, Moritaka Mashiro, a talented writer, Akito Takagi, and their quest to become manga legends!

WEEKLY SHONEN JUMP
Editorial Office

1 Editor in Chief Sasaki	Age: 49
2 Deputy Editor in Chief Heishi	Age: 43
3 Soichi Aida	Age: 36
4 Yujiro Hattori	Age: 30
5 Akira Hattori	Age: 32
6 Koji Yoshida	Age: 34
7 Goro Miura	Age: 25
8 Masakazu Yamahisa	Age: 25

THE MANGA ARTISTS

A SHINTA FUKUDA	Age: 21
B TAKURO NAKAI	Age: 36
C KO AOKI	Age: 22
D KOJI MAKAINO	Age: 32
E KAZUYA HIRAMARU	Age: 28
J RYU SHIZUKA	Age: 18
K AIKO IWASE	Age: 19
L ISHIZAWA	Age: 19

F Ogawa **G** Takahama **H** Kato **I** Yasuoka

Vol. BAKUMAN。8

CONTENTS

(PANTY SHOT) (AND SAVIOR)

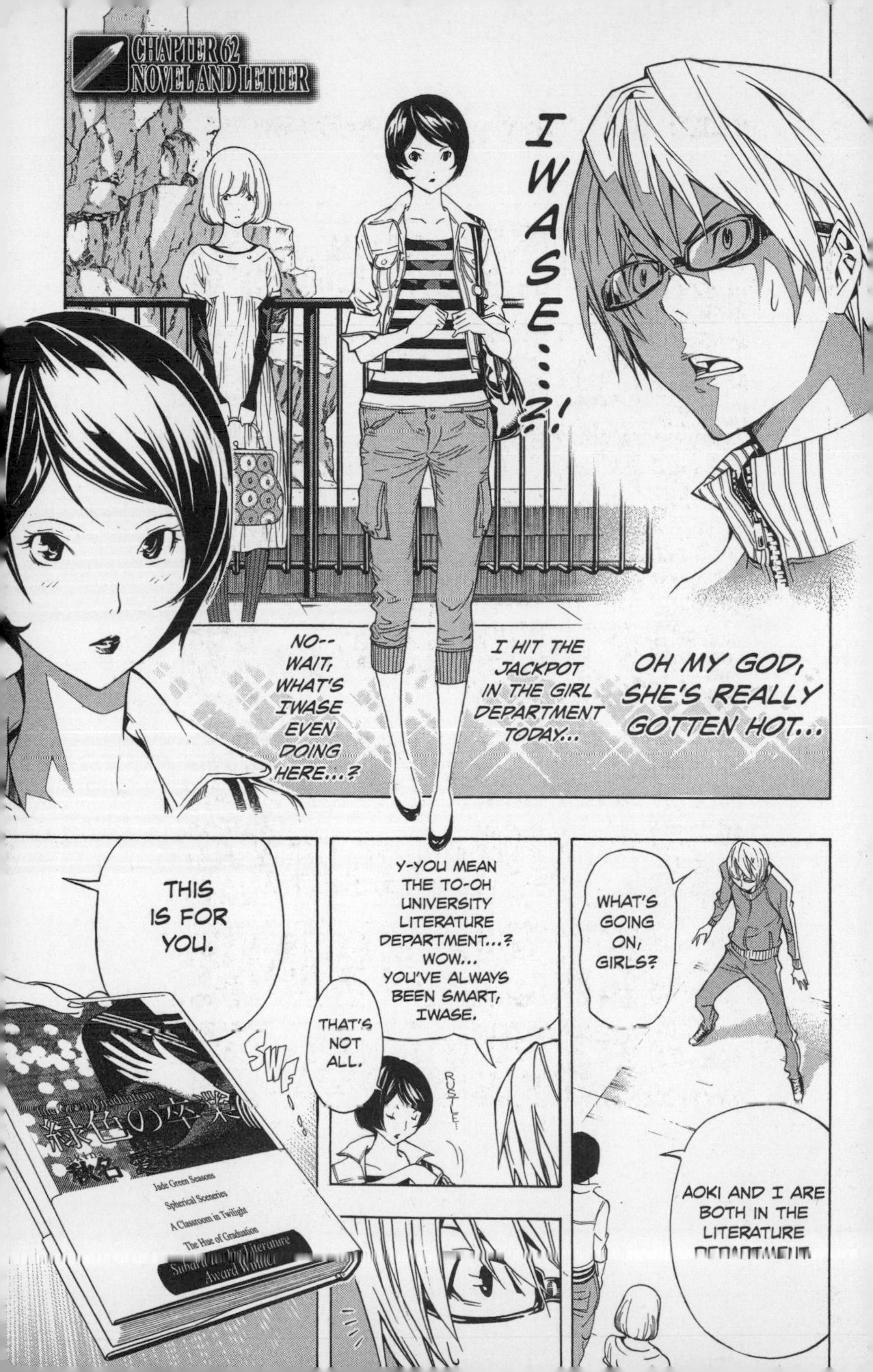
CHAPTER 62
NOVEL AND LETTER
IWASE...?!
OH MY GOD, SHE'S REALLY GOTTEN HOT...
I HIT THE JACKPOT IN THE GIRL DEPARTMENT TODAY...
NO-- WAIT, WHAT'S IWASE EVEN DOING HERE...?
WHAT'S GOING ON, GIRLS?
AOKI AND I ARE BOTH IN THE LITERATURE
Y-YOU MEAN THE TO-OH UNIVERSITY LITERATURE DEPARTMENT...? WOW... YOU'VE ALWAYS BEEN SMART, IWASE.
THAT'S NOT ALL.
RUSTLE...
SWF
THIS IS FOR YOU.
The Green Graduation
緑色の卒業
Jade Green Seasons
Spherical Sceneries
A Classroom in Twilight
The Hue of Graduation
Award Winner

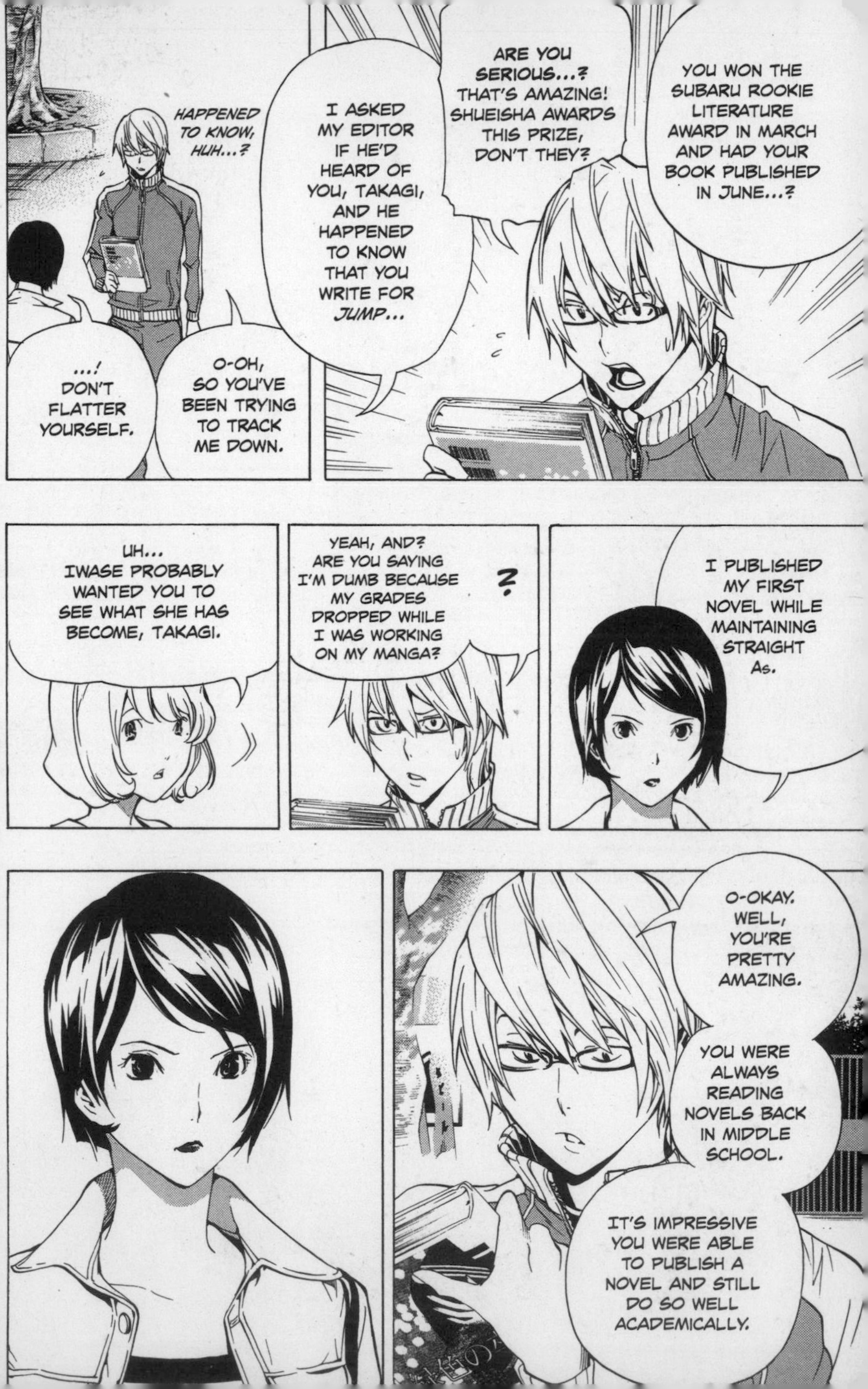
YOU WON THE SUBARU ROOKIE LITERATURE AWARD IN MARCH AND HAD YOUR BOOK PUBLISHED IN JUNE...?
ARE YOU SERIOUS...? THAT'S AMAZING! SHUEISHA AWARDS THIS PRIZE, DON'T THEY?
I ASKED MY EDITOR IF HE'D HEARD OF YOU, TAKAGI, AND HE HAPPENED TO KNOW THAT YOU WRITE FOR *JUMP*...
HAPPENED TO KNOW, HUH...?
O-OH, SO YOU'VE BEEN TRYING TO TRACK ME DOWN.
...! DON'T FLATTER YOURSELF.
I PUBLISHED MY FIRST NOVEL WHILE MAINTAINING STRAIGHT As.
?
YEAH, AND? ARE YOU SAYING I'M DUMB BECAUSE MY GRADES DROPPED WHILE I WAS WORKING ON MY MANGA?
UH... IWASE PROBABLY WANTED YOU TO SEE WHAT SHE HAS BECOME, TAKAGI.
O-OKAY. WELL, YOU'RE PRETTY AMAZING.
YOU WERE ALWAYS READING NOVELS BACK IN MIDDLE SCHOOL.
IT'S IMPRESSIVE YOU WERE ABLE TO PUBLISH A NOVEL AND STILL DO SO WELL ACADEMICALLY.

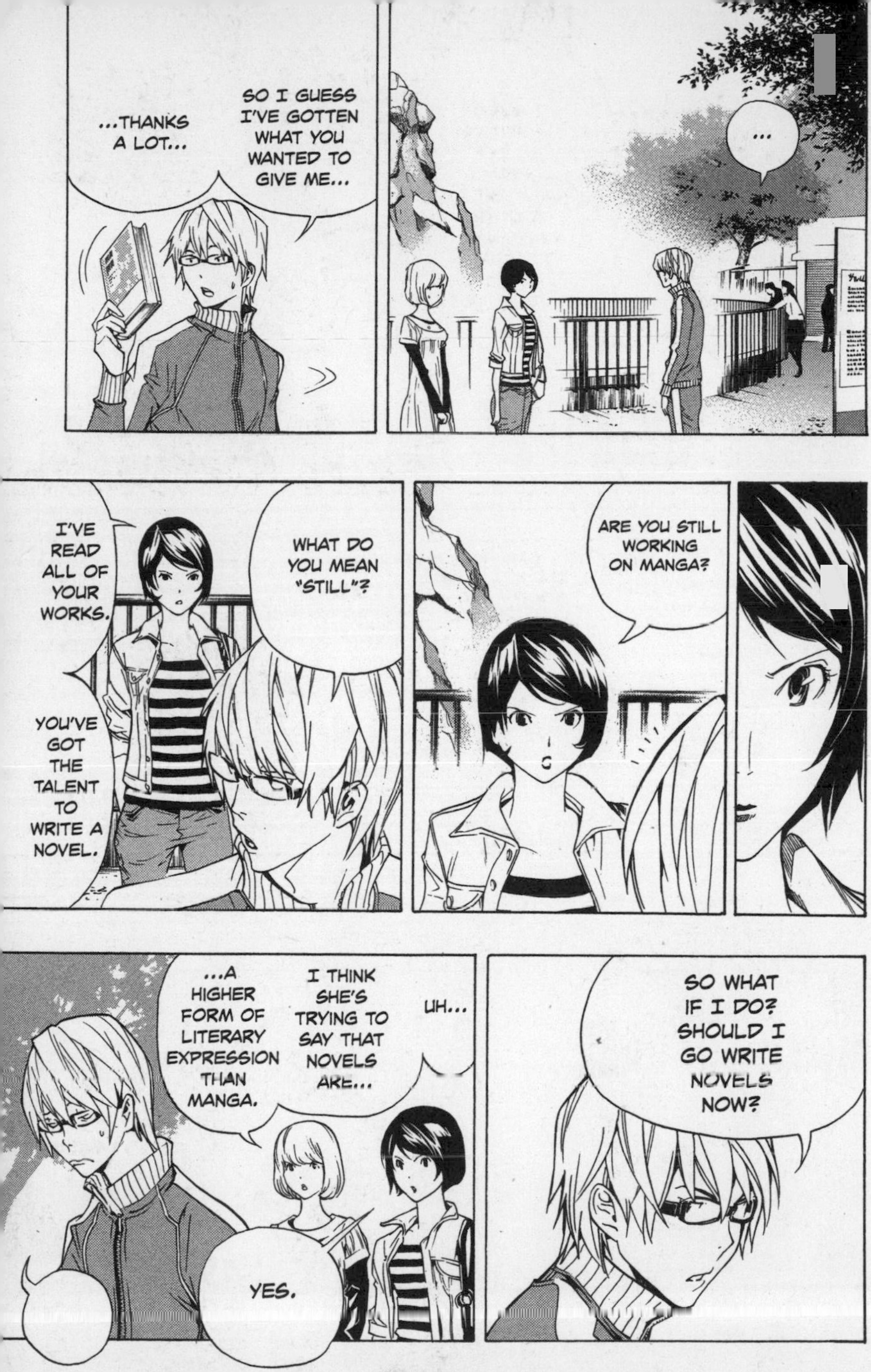
...
SO I GUESS I'VE GOTTEN WHAT YOU WANTED TO GIVE ME...
...THANKS A LOT...
ARE YOU STILL WORKING ON MANGA?
WHAT DO YOU MEAN "STILL"?
I'VE READ ALL OF YOUR WORKS.
YOU'VE GOT THE TALENT TO WRITE A NOVEL.
SO WHAT IF I DO? SHOULD I GO WRITE NOVELS NOW?
UH...
I THINK SHE'S TRYING TO SAY THAT NOVELS ARE...
...A HIGHER FORM OF LITERARY EXPRESSION THAN MANGA.
YES.

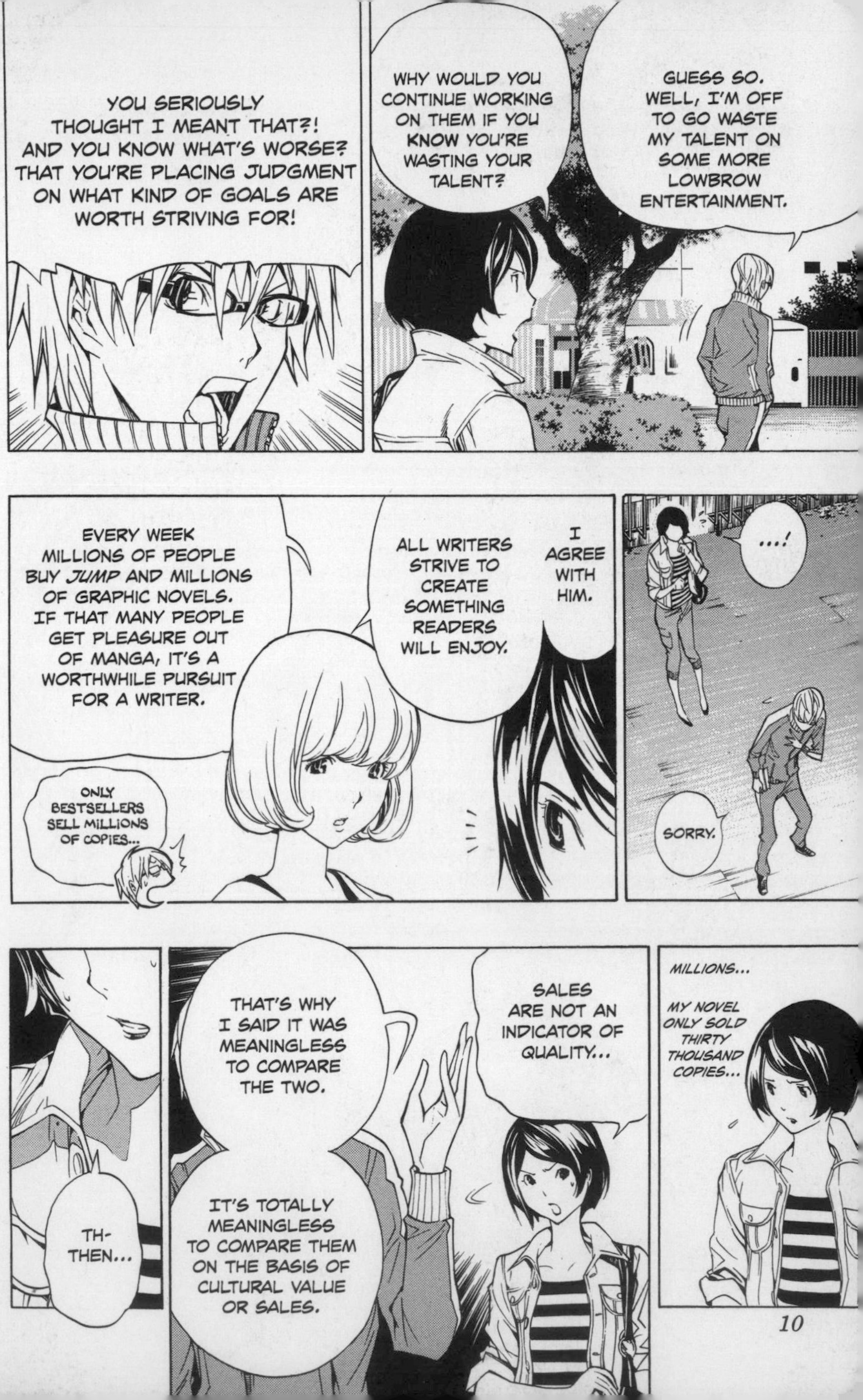
WHY WOULD YOU CONTINUE WORKING ON THEM IF YOU KNOW YOU'RE WASTING YOUR TALENT?
GUESS SO. WELL, I'M OFF TO GO WASTE MY TALENT ON SOME MORE LOWBROW ENTERTAINMENT.
YOU SERIOUSLY THOUGHT I MEANT THAT?! AND YOU KNOW WHAT'S WORSE? THAT YOU'RE PLACING JUDGMENT ON WHAT KIND OF GOALS ARE WORTH STRIVING FOR!
...!
SORRY.
I AGREE WITH HIM.
ALL WRITERS STRIVE TO CREATE SOMETHING READERS WILL ENJOY.
EVERY WEEK MILLIONS OF PEOPLE BUY *JUMP* AND MILLIONS OF GRAPHIC NOVELS. IF THAT MANY PEOPLE GET PLEASURE OUT OF MANGA, IT'S A WORTHWHILE PURSUIT FOR A WRITER.
ONLY BESTSELLERS SELL MILLIONS OF COPIES...
MILLIONS...
MY NOVEL ONLY SOLD THIRTY THOUSAND COPIES...
SALES ARE NOT AN INDICATOR OF QUALITY...
THAT'S WHY I SAID IT WAS MEANINGLESS TO COMPARE THE TWO.
IT'S TOTALLY MEANINGLESS TO COMPARE THEM ON THE BASIS OF CULTURAL VALUE OR SALES.
TH- THEN...

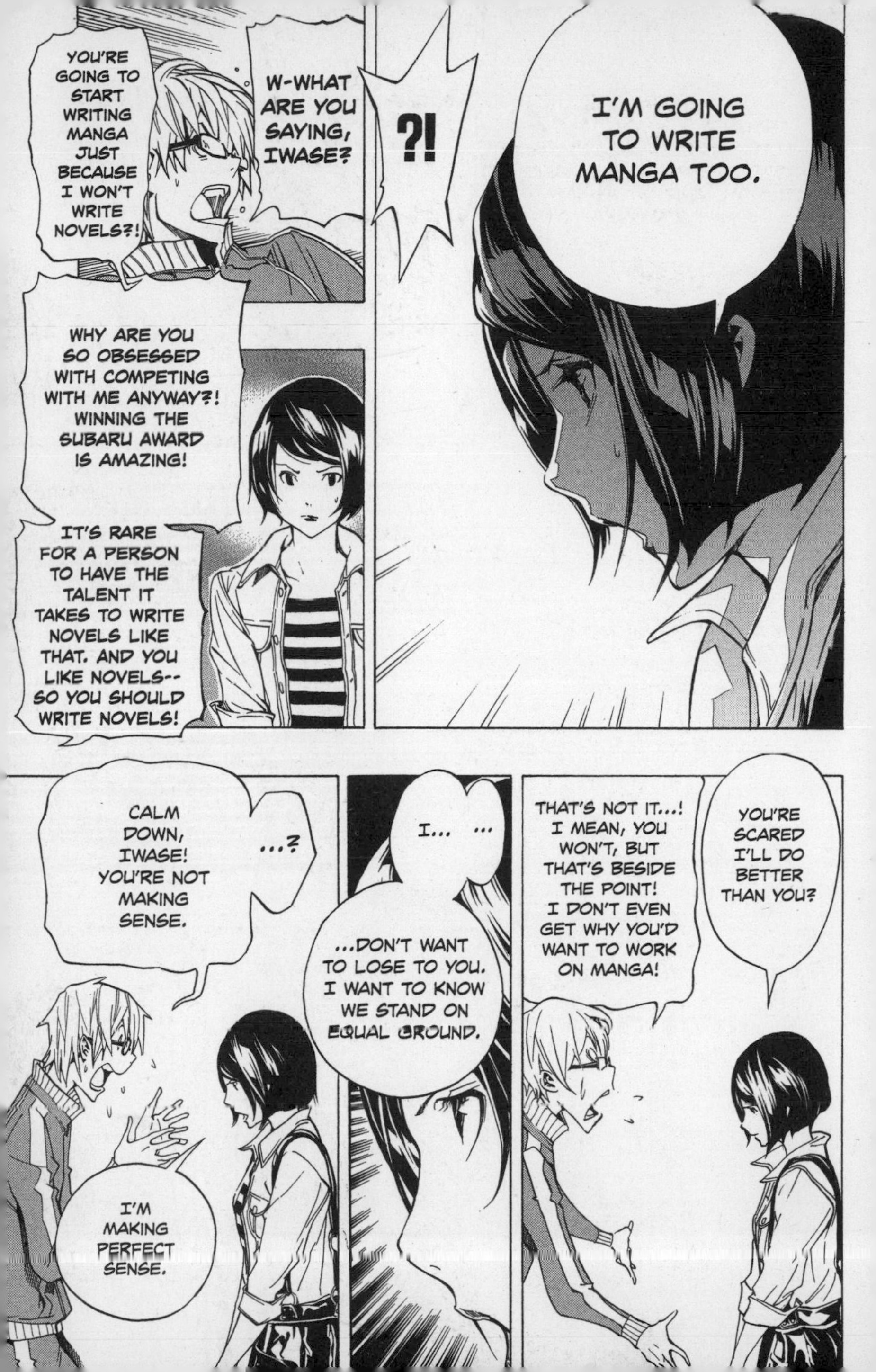
I'M GOING TO WRITE MANGA TOO.
?!
W-WHAT ARE YOU SAYING, IWASE?
YOU'RE GOING TO START WRITING MANGA JUST BECAUSE I WON'T WRITE NOVELS?!
WHY ARE YOU SO OBSESSED WITH COMPETING WITH ME ANYWAY?! WINNING THE SUBARU AWARD IS AMAZING!
IT'S RARE FOR A PERSON TO HAVE THE TALENT IT TAKES TO WRITE NOVELS LIKE THAT. AND YOU LIKE NOVELS--SO YOU SHOULD WRITE NOVELS!
YOU'RE SCARED I'LL DO BETTER THAN YOU?
THAT'S NOT IT...! I MEAN, YOU WON'T, BUT THAT'S BESIDE THE POINT! I DON'T EVEN GET WHY YOU'D WANT TO WORK ON MANGA!
I... ...
...DON'T WANT TO LOSE TO YOU. I WANT TO KNOW WE STAND ON EQUAL GROUND.
...?
CALM DOWN, IWASE! YOU'RE NOT MAKING SENSE.
I'M MAKING PERFECT SENSE.

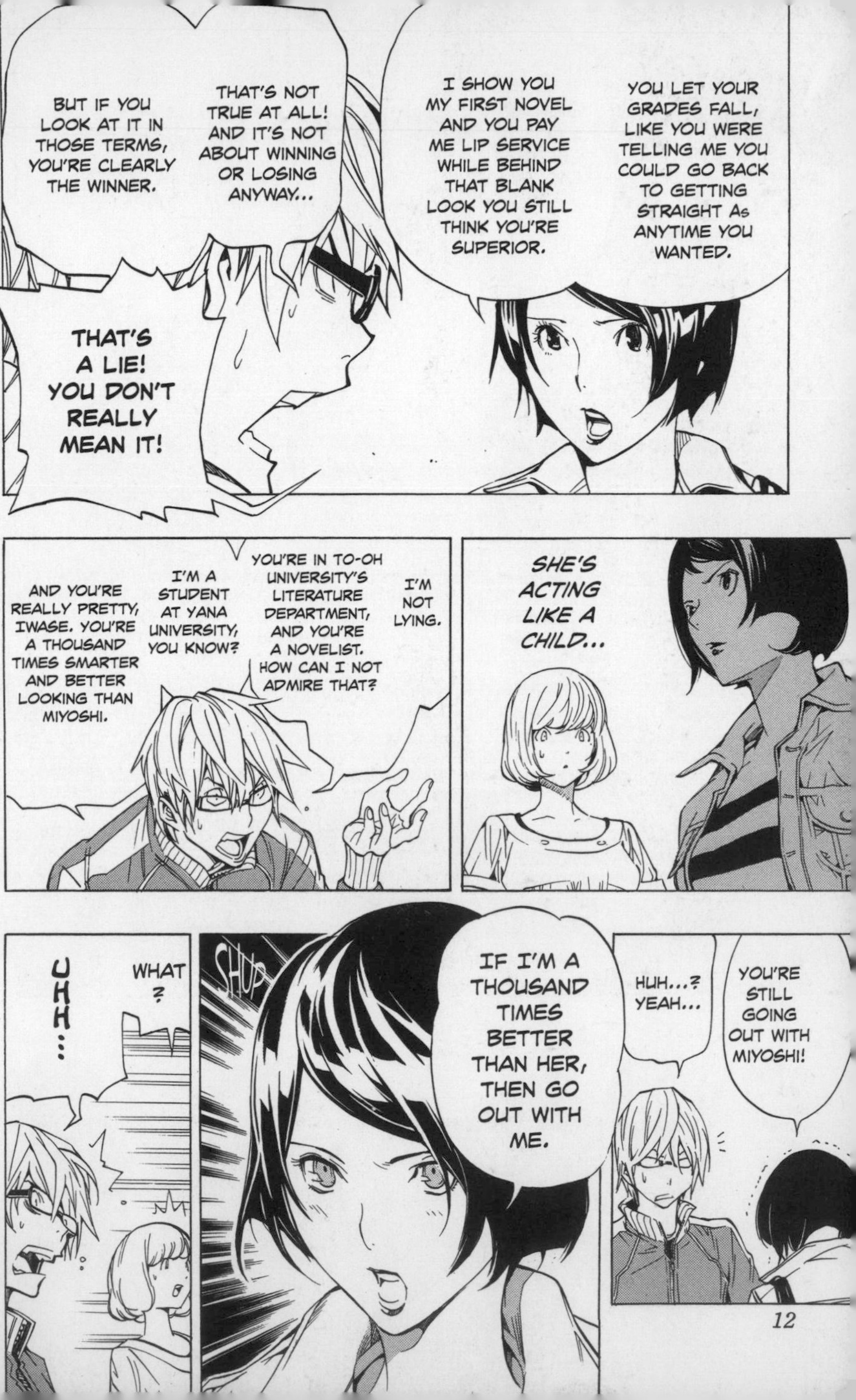
YOU LET YOUR GRADES FALL, LIKE YOU WERE TELLING ME YOU COULD GO BACK TO GETTING STRAIGHT As ANYTIME YOU WANTED.
I SHOW YOU MY FIRST NOVEL AND YOU PAY ME LIP SERVICE WHILE BEHIND THAT BLANK LOOK YOU STILL THINK YOU'RE SUPERIOR.
THAT'S NOT TRUE AT ALL! AND IT'S NOT ABOUT WINNING OR LOSING ANYWAY...
BUT IF YOU LOOK AT IT IN THOSE TERMS, YOU'RE CLEARLY THE WINNER.
THAT'S A LIE! YOU DON'T REALLY MEAN IT!
SHE'S ACTING LIKE A CHILD...
I'M NOT LYING.
YOU'RE IN TO-OH UNIVERSITY'S LITERATURE DEPARTMENT, AND YOU'RE A NOVELIST. HOW CAN I NOT ADMIRE THAT?
I'M A STUDENT AT YANA UNIVERSITY, YOU KNOW?
AND YOU'RE REALLY PRETTY, IWASE. YOU'RE A THOUSAND TIMES SMARTER AND BETTER LOOKING THAN MIYOSHI.
YOU'RE STILL GOING OUT WITH MIYOSHI!
HUH...? YEAH...
SHUP
IF I'M A THOUSAND TIMES BETTER THAN HER, THEN GO OUT WITH ME.
WHAT?
UHH...

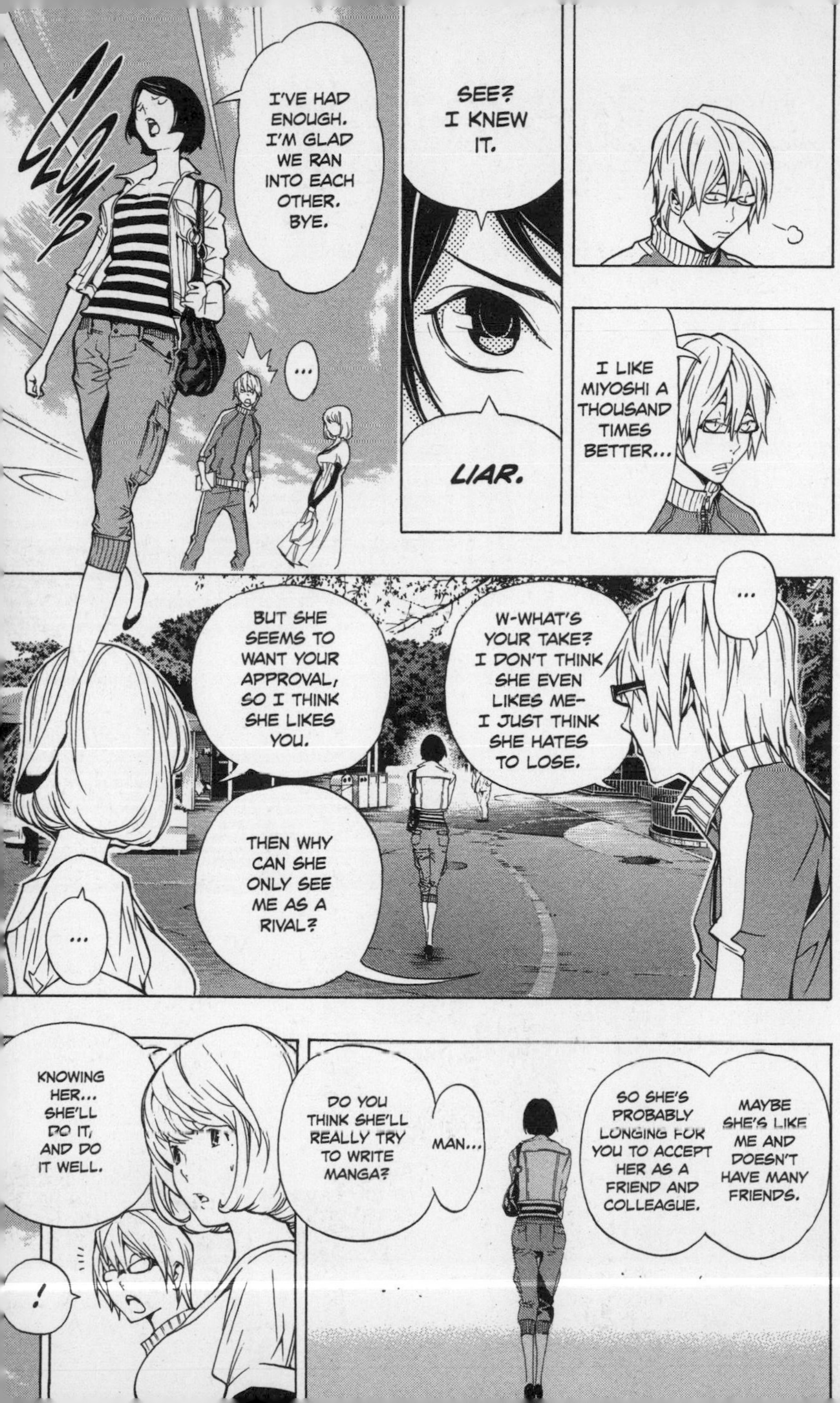
I LIKE MIYOSHI A THOUSAND TIMES BETTER...
SEE? I KNEW IT.
LIAR.
I'VE HAD ENOUGH. I'M GLAD WE RAN INTO EACH OTHER. BYE.
CLOMP
...
...
W-WHAT'S YOUR TAKE? I DON'T THINK SHE EVEN LIKES ME- I JUST THINK SHE HATES TO LOSE.
BUT SHE SEEMS TO WANT YOUR APPROVAL, SO I THINK SHE LIKES YOU.
THEN WHY CAN SHE ONLY SEE ME AS A RIVAL?
...
MAYBE SHE'S LIKE ME AND DOESN'T HAVE MANY FRIENDS.
SO SHE'S PROBABLY LONGING FOR YOU TO ACCEPT HER AS A FRIEND AND COLLEAGUE.
MAN...
DO YOU THINK SHE'LL REALLY TRY TO WRITE MANGA?
KNOWING HER... SHE'LL DO IT, AND DO IT WELL.
!

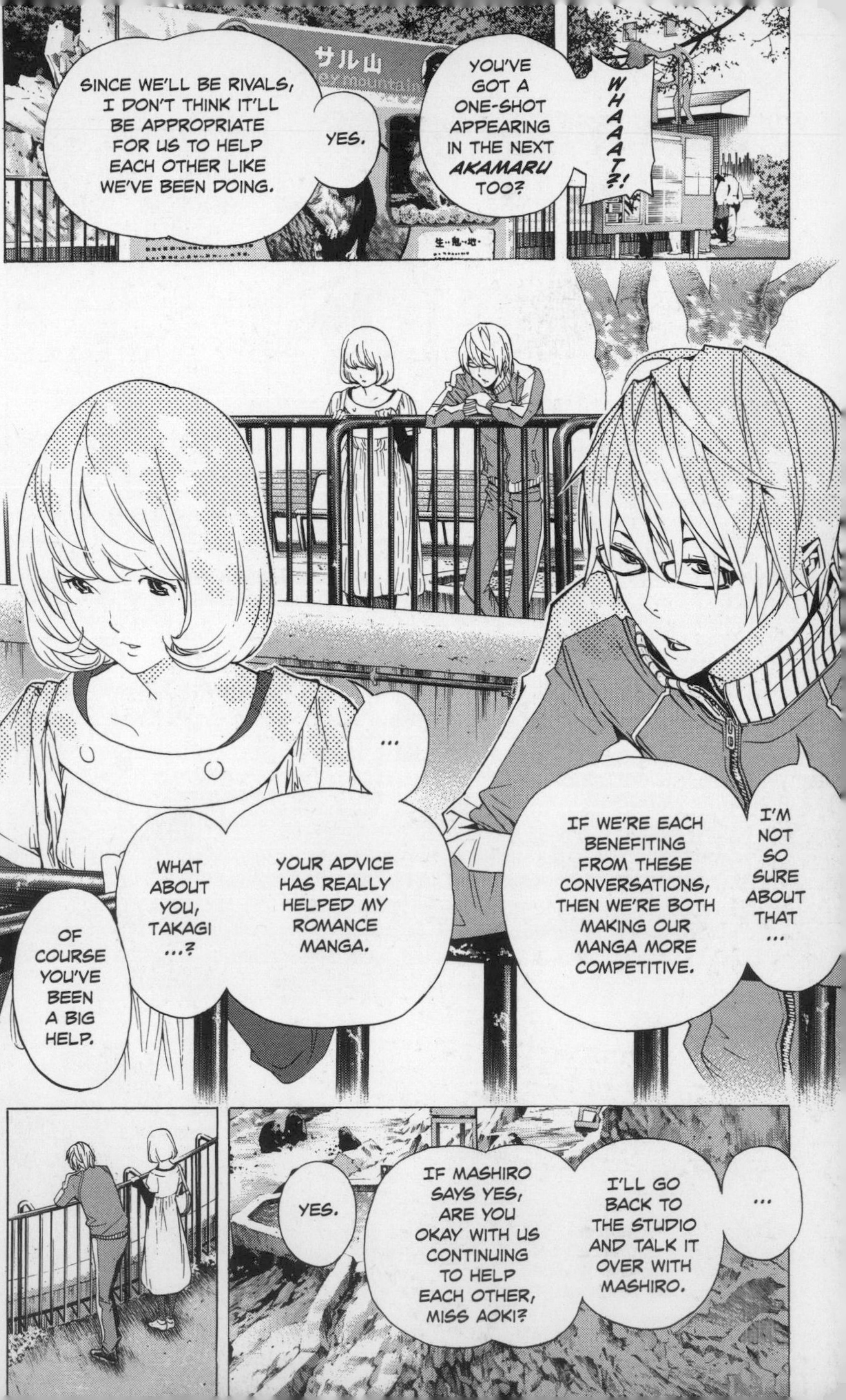
YOU'VE GOT A ONE-SHOT APPEARING IN THE NEXT *AKAMARU* TOO?
WHAAAAT?!
YES.
SINCE WE'LL BE RIVALS, I DON'T THINK IT'LL BE APPROPRIATE FOR US TO HELP EACH OTHER LIKE WE'VE BEEN DOING.
I'M NOT SO SURE ABOUT THAT...
IF WE'RE EACH BENEFITING FROM THESE CONVERSATIONS, THEN WE'RE BOTH MAKING OUR MANGA MORE COMPETITIVE.
...
YOUR ADVICE HAS REALLY HELPED MY ROMANCE MANGA.
WHAT ABOUT YOU, TAKAGI...?
OF COURSE YOU'VE BEEN A BIG HELP.
...
I'LL GO BACK TO THE STUDIO AND TALK IT OVER WITH MASHIRO.
IF MASHIRO SAYS YES, ARE YOU OKAY WITH US CONTINUING TO HELP EACH OTHER, MISS AOKI?
YES.

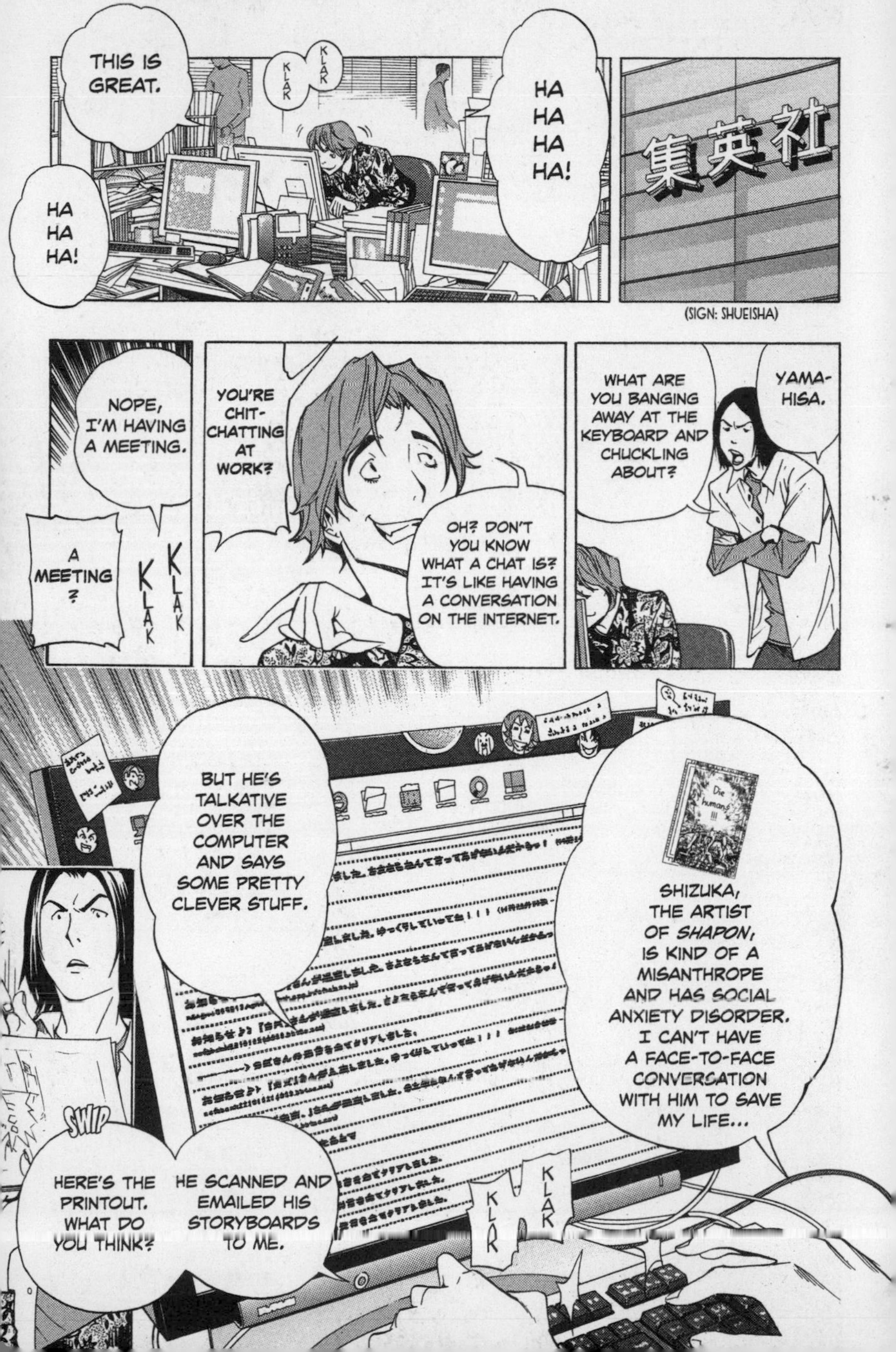
集英社
(SIGN: SHUEISHA)
HA HA HA HA!
KLAK KLAK
THIS IS GREAT.
HA HA HA!
YAMA-HISA.
WHAT ARE YOU BANGING AWAY AT THE KEYBOARD AND CHUCKLING ABOUT?
OH? DON'T YOU KNOW WHAT A CHAT IS? IT'S LIKE HAVING A CONVERSATION ON THE INTERNET.
YOU'RE CHIT-CHATTING AT WORK?
NOPE, I'M HAVING A MEETING.
KLAK KLAK
A MEETING?
Die humans!!!
SHIZUKA, THE ARTIST OF *SHAPON*, IS KIND OF A MISANTHROPE AND HAS SOCIAL ANXIETY DISORDER. I CAN'T HAVE A FACE-TO-FACE CONVERSATION WITH HIM TO SAVE MY LIFE...
BUT HE'S TALKATIVE OVER THE COMPUTER AND SAYS SOME PRETTY CLEVER STUFF.
KLAK
KLAK
HE SCANNED AND EMAILED HIS STORYBOARDS TO ME.
SWIP
HERE'S THE PRINTOUT. WHAT DO YOU THINK?

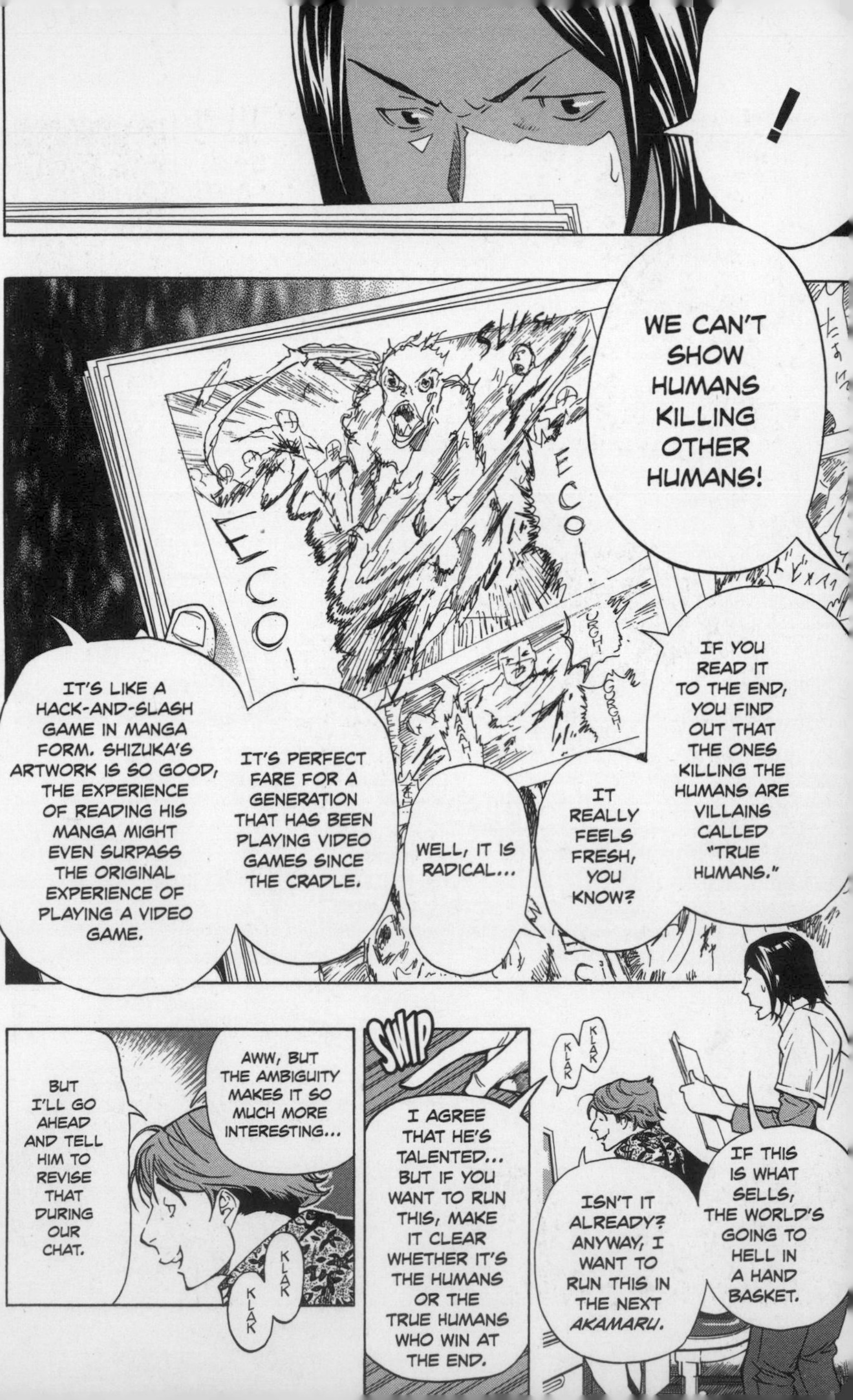
!
WE CAN'T SHOW HUMANS KILLING OTHER HUMANS!
IF YOU READ IT TO THE END, YOU FIND OUT THAT THE ONES KILLING THE HUMANS ARE VILLAINS CALLED "TRUE HUMANS."
ECO!
ECO!
URGH!
GURGH!
AAAH!
IT REALLY FEELS FRESH, YOU KNOW?
WELL, IT IS RADICAL...
IT'S PERFECT FARE FOR A GENERATION THAT HAS BEEN PLAYING VIDEO GAMES SINCE THE CRADLE.
IT'S LIKE A HACK-AND-SLASH GAME IN MANGA FORM. SHIZUKA'S ARTWORK IS SO GOOD, THE EXPERIENCE OF READING HIS MANGA MIGHT EVEN SURPASS THE ORIGINAL EXPERIENCE OF PLAYING A VIDEO GAME.
IF THIS IS WHAT SELLS, THE WORLD'S GOING TO HELL IN A HAND BASKET.
KLAK KLAK
ISN'T IT ALREADY? ANYWAY, I WANT TO RUN THIS IN THE NEXT *AKAMARU*.
SWIP
I AGREE THAT HE'S TALENTED... BUT IF YOU WANT TO RUN THIS, MAKE IT CLEAR WHETHER IT'S THE HUMANS OR THE TRUE HUMANS WHO WIN AT THE END.
AWW, BUT THE AMBIGUITY MAKES IT SO MUCH MORE INTERESTING...
BUT I'LL GO AHEAD AND TELL HIM TO REVISE THAT DURING OUR CHAT.
KLAK KLAK

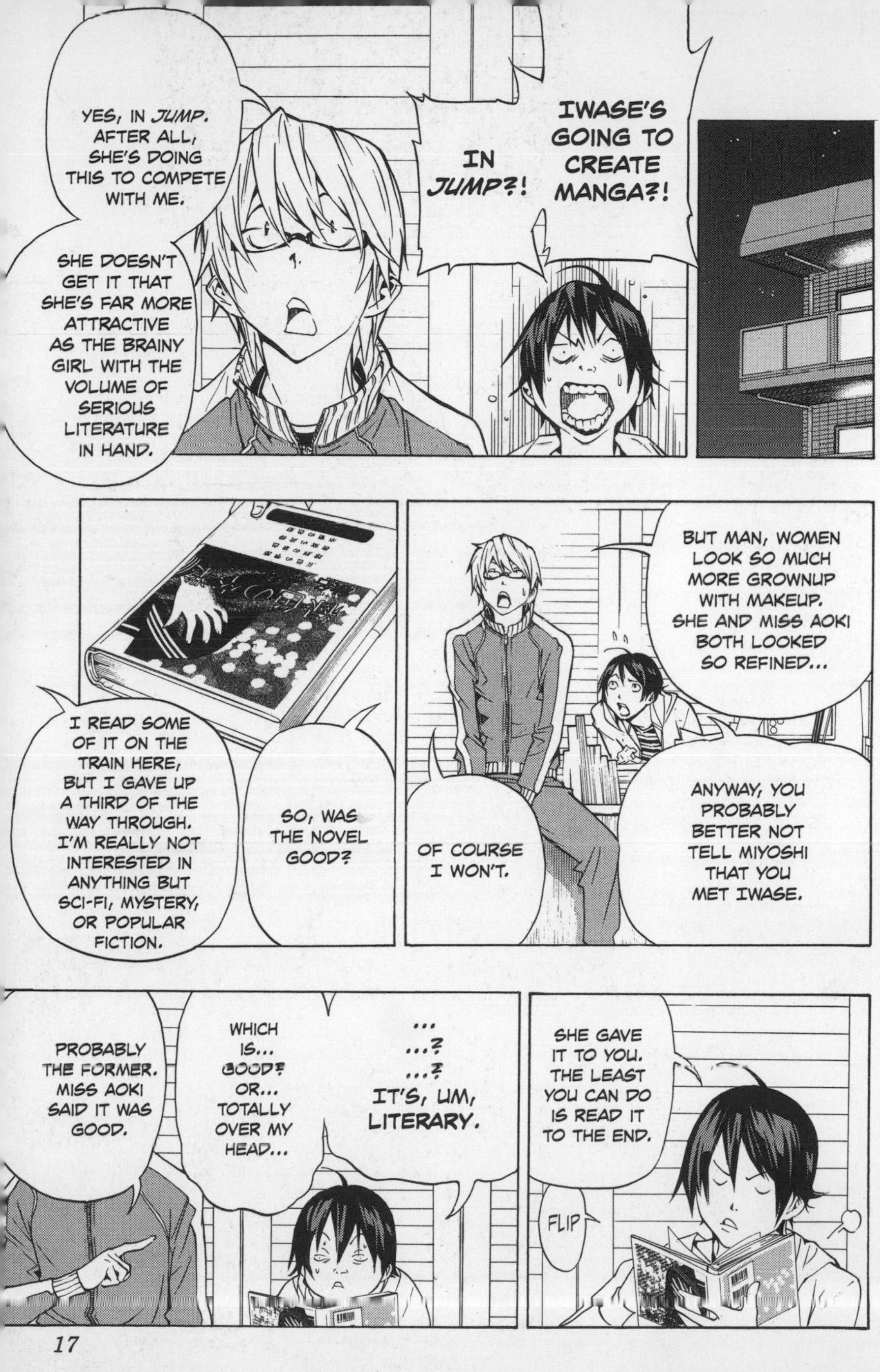

IWASE'S GOING TO CREATE MANGA?!
IN *JUMP*?!
YES, IN *JUMP*. AFTER ALL, SHE'S DOING THIS TO COMPETE WITH ME.
SHE DOESN'T GET IT THAT SHE'S FAR MORE ATTRACTIVE AS THE BRAINY GIRL WITH THE VOLUME OF SERIOUS LITERATURE IN HAND.
BUT MAN, WOMEN LOOK SO MUCH MORE GROWNUP WITH MAKEUP. SHE AND MISS AOKI BOTH LOOKED SO REFINED...
ANYWAY, YOU PROBABLY BETTER NOT TELL MIYOSHI THAT YOU MET IWASE.
OF COURSE I WON'T.
SO, WAS THE NOVEL GOOD?
I READ SOME OF IT ON THE TRAIN HERE, BUT I GAVE UP A THIRD OF THE WAY THROUGH. I'M REALLY NOT INTERESTED IN ANYTHING BUT SCI-FI, MYSTERY, OR POPULAR FICTION.
SHE GAVE IT TO YOU. THE LEAST YOU CAN DO IS READ IT TO THE END.
FLIP
... ...? ...? IT'S, UM, LITERARY.
WHICH IS... GOOD? OR... TOTALLY OVER MY HEAD...
PROBABLY THE FORMER. MISS AOKI SAID IT WAS GOOD.

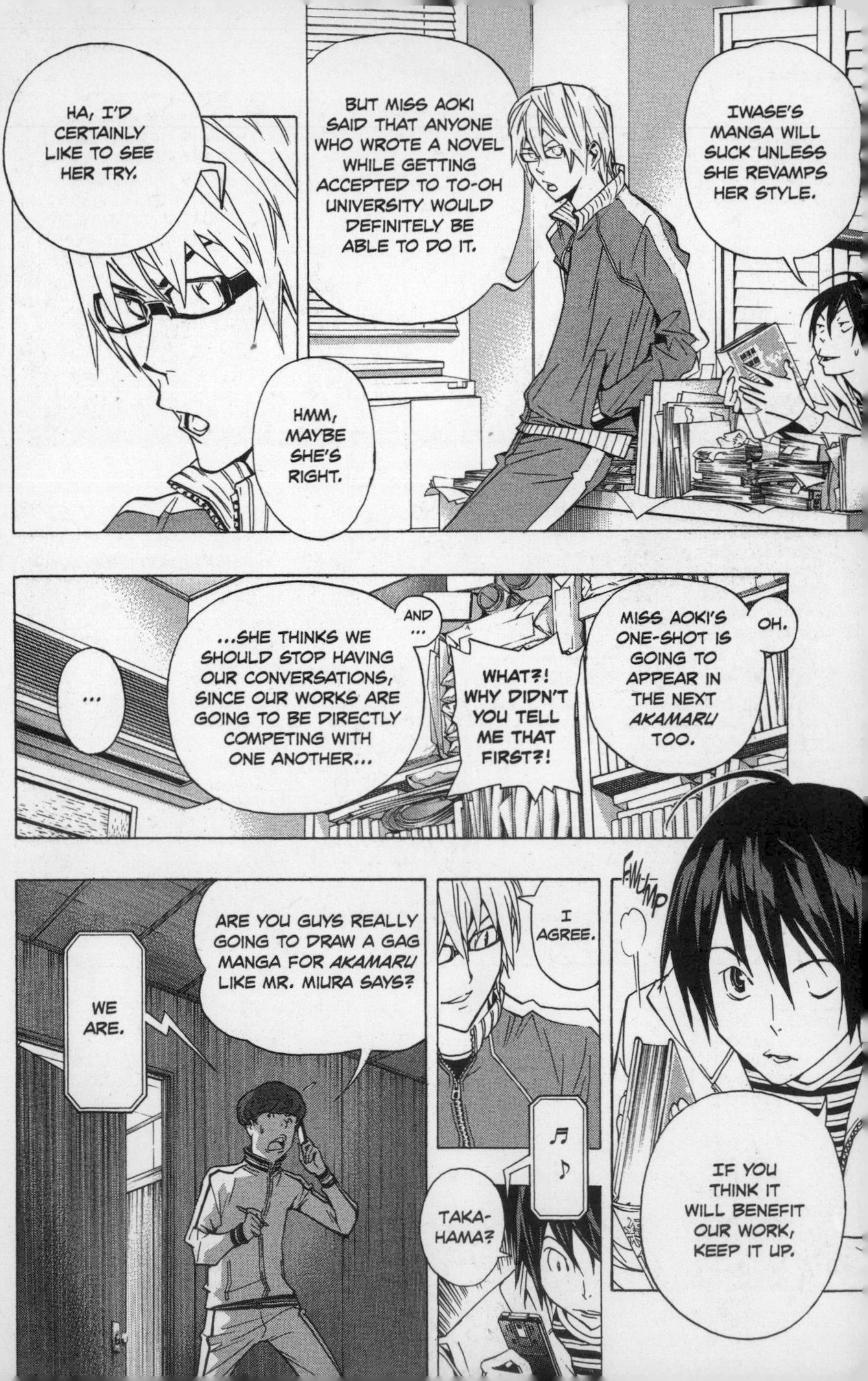
IWASE'S MANGA WILL SUCK UNLESS SHE REVAMPS HER STYLE.
BUT MISS AOKI SAID THAT ANYONE WHO WROTE A NOVEL WHILE GETTING ACCEPTED TO TO-OH UNIVERSITY WOULD DEFINITELY BE ABLE TO DO IT.
HMM, MAYBE SHE'S RIGHT.
HA, I'D CERTAINLY LIKE TO SEE HER TRY.
OH.
MISS AOKI'S ONE-SHOT IS GOING TO APPEAR IN THE NEXT *AKAMARU* TOO.
WHAT?! WHY DIDN'T YOU TELL ME THAT FIRST?!
AND ...
...SHE THINKS WE SHOULD STOP HAVING OUR CONVERSATIONS, SINCE OUR WORKS ARE GOING TO BE DIRECTLY COMPETING WITH ONE ANOTHER...
...
FWUMP
IF YOU THINK IT WILL BENEFIT OUR WORK, KEEP IT UP.
I AGREE.
♬ ♪
TAKA-HAMA?
ARE YOU GUYS REALLY GOING TO DRAW A GAG MANGA FOR *AKAMARU* LIKE MR. MIURA SAYS?
WE ARE.

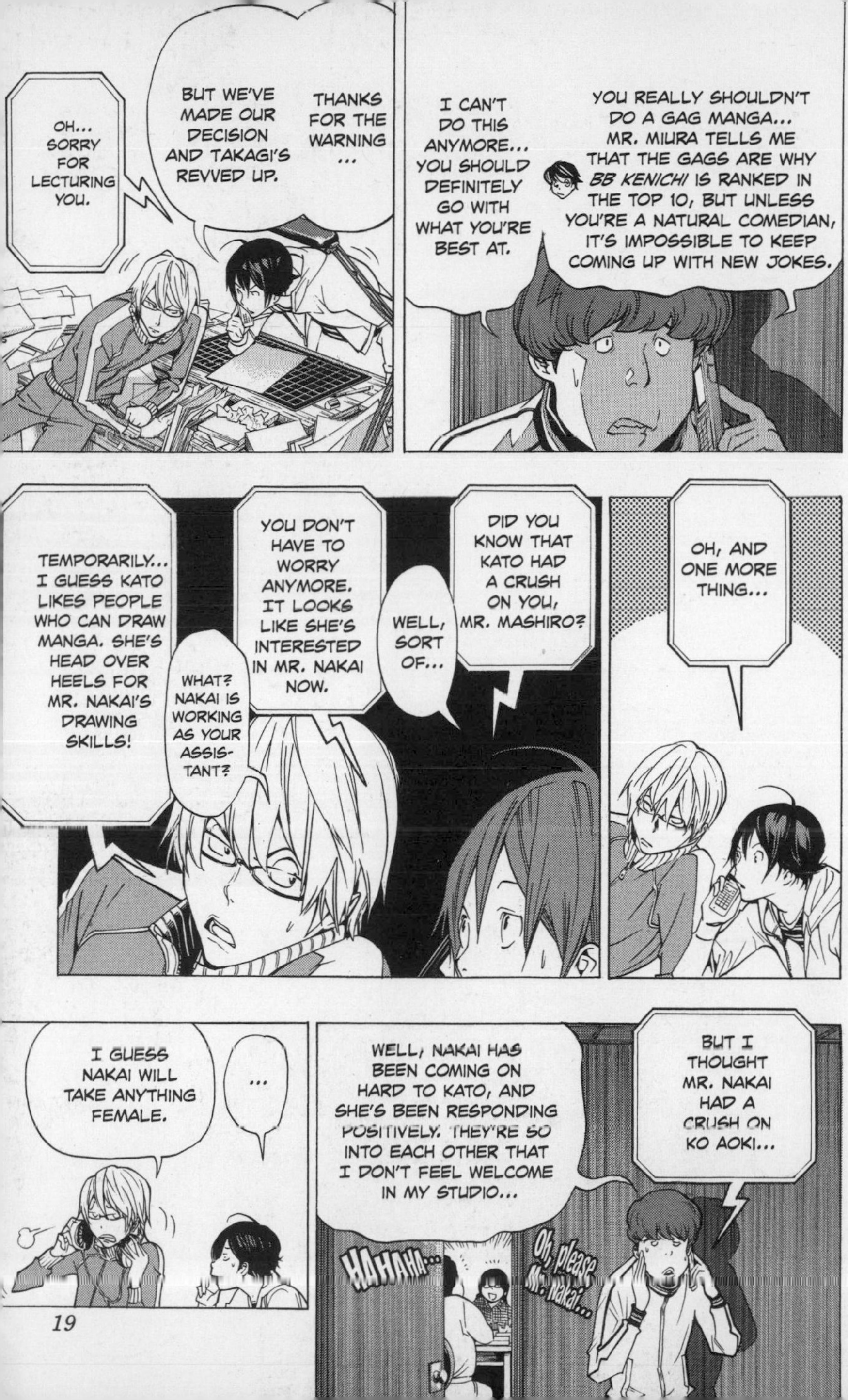
YOU REALLY SHOULDN'T DO A GAG MANGA... MR. MIURA TELLS ME THAT THE GAGS ARE WHY *BB KENICHI* IS RANKED IN THE TOP 10, BUT UNLESS YOU'RE A NATURAL COMEDIAN, IT'S IMPOSSIBLE TO KEEP COMING UP WITH NEW JOKES.
I CAN'T DO THIS ANYMORE... YOU SHOULD DEFINITELY GO WITH WHAT YOU'RE BEST AT.
THANKS FOR THE WARNING ...
BUT WE'VE MADE OUR DECISION AND TAKAGI'S REVVED UP.
OH... SORRY FOR LECTURING YOU.
OH, AND ONE MORE THING...
DID YOU KNOW THAT KATO HAD A CRUSH ON YOU, MR. MASHIRO?
WELL, SORT OF...
YOU DON'T HAVE TO WORRY ANYMORE. IT LOOKS LIKE SHE'S INTERESTED IN MR. NAKAI NOW.
WHAT? NAKAI IS WORKING AS YOUR ASSIS-TANT?
TEMPORARILY... I GUESS KATO LIKES PEOPLE WHO CAN DRAW MANGA. SHE'S HEAD OVER HEELS FOR MR. NAKAI'S DRAWING SKILLS!
BUT I THOUGHT MR. NAKAI HAD A CRUSH ON KO AOKI...
WELL, NAKAI HAS BEEN COMING ON HARD TO KATO, AND SHE'S BEEN RESPONDING POSITIVELY. THEY'RE SO INTO EACH OTHER THAT I DON'T FEEL WELCOME IN MY STUDIO...
Oh, please Mr. Nakai...
HAHAHA...
...
I GUESS NAKAI WILL TAKE ANYTHING FEMALE.

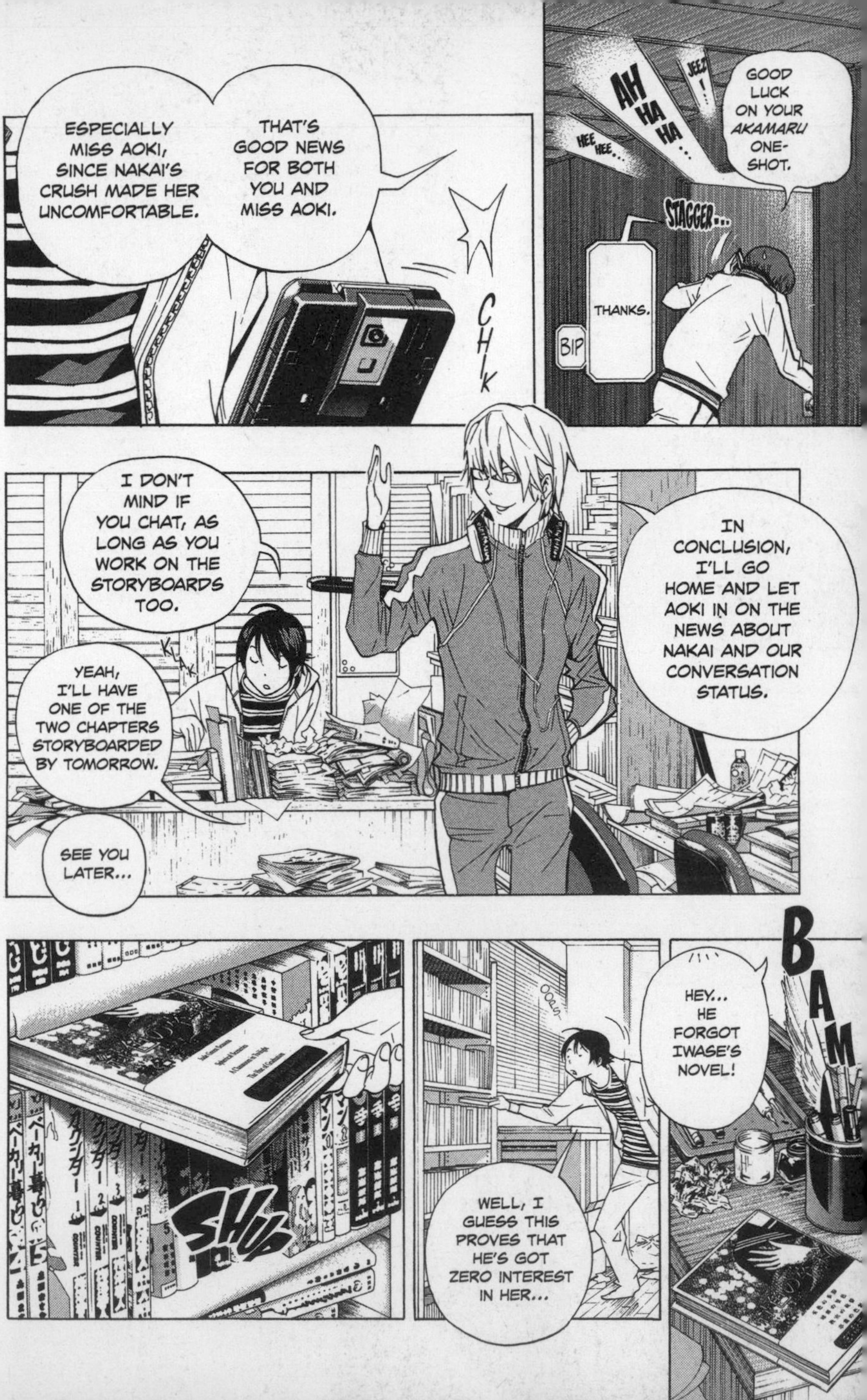
GOOD LUCK ON YOUR AKAMARU ONE-SHOT.
JEEZ!...
AH HA HA...
HEE HEE...
STAGGER...
THANKS.
BIP
THAT'S GOOD NEWS FOR BOTH YOU AND MISS AOKI.
ESPECIALLY MISS AOKI, SINCE NAKAI'S CRUSH MADE HER UNCOMFORTABLE.
CHIK
IN CONCLUSION, I'LL GO HOME AND LET AOKI IN ON THE NEWS ABOUT NAKAI AND OUR CONVERSATION STATUS.
I DON'T MIND IF YOU CHAT, AS LONG AS YOU WORK ON THE STORYBOARDS TOO.
KLAK
YEAH, I'LL HAVE ONE OF THE TWO CHAPTERS STORYBOARDED BY TOMORROW.
SEE YOU LATER...
BAM
HEY... HE FORGOT IWASE'S NOVEL!
OOPS
WELL, I GUESS THIS PROVES THAT HE'S GOT ZERO INTEREST IN HER...
SHUP

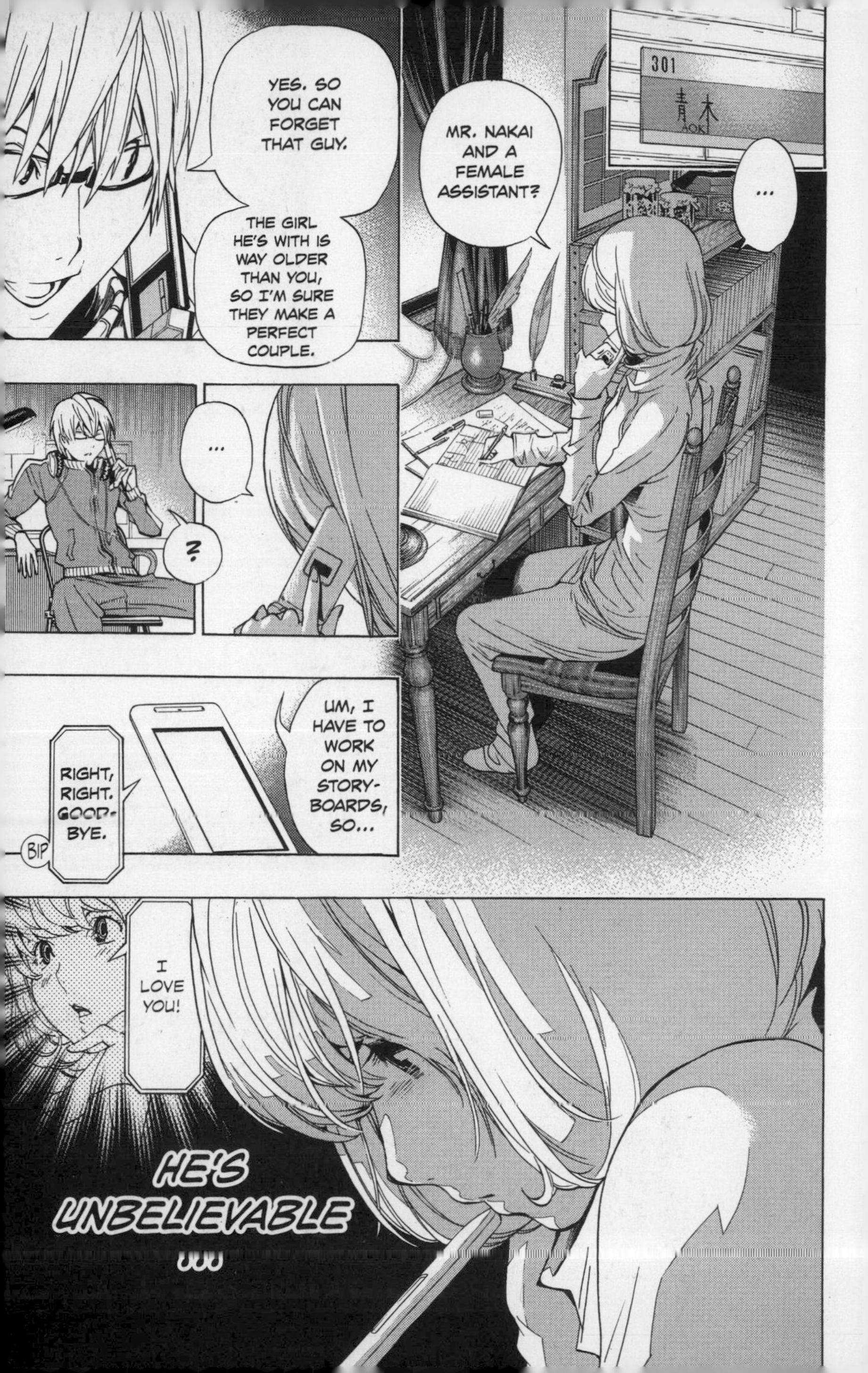
301
青木
AOKI
MR. NAKAI AND A FEMALE ASSISTANT?
...
YES. SO YOU CAN FORGET THAT GUY.
THE GIRL HE'S WITH IS WAY OLDER THAN YOU, SO I'M SURE THEY MAKE A PERFECT COUPLE.
...
?
UM, I HAVE TO WORK ON MY STORY-BOARDS, SO...
RIGHT, RIGHT. GOOD-BYE.
BIP
I LOVE YOU!
HE'S UNBELIEVABLE...

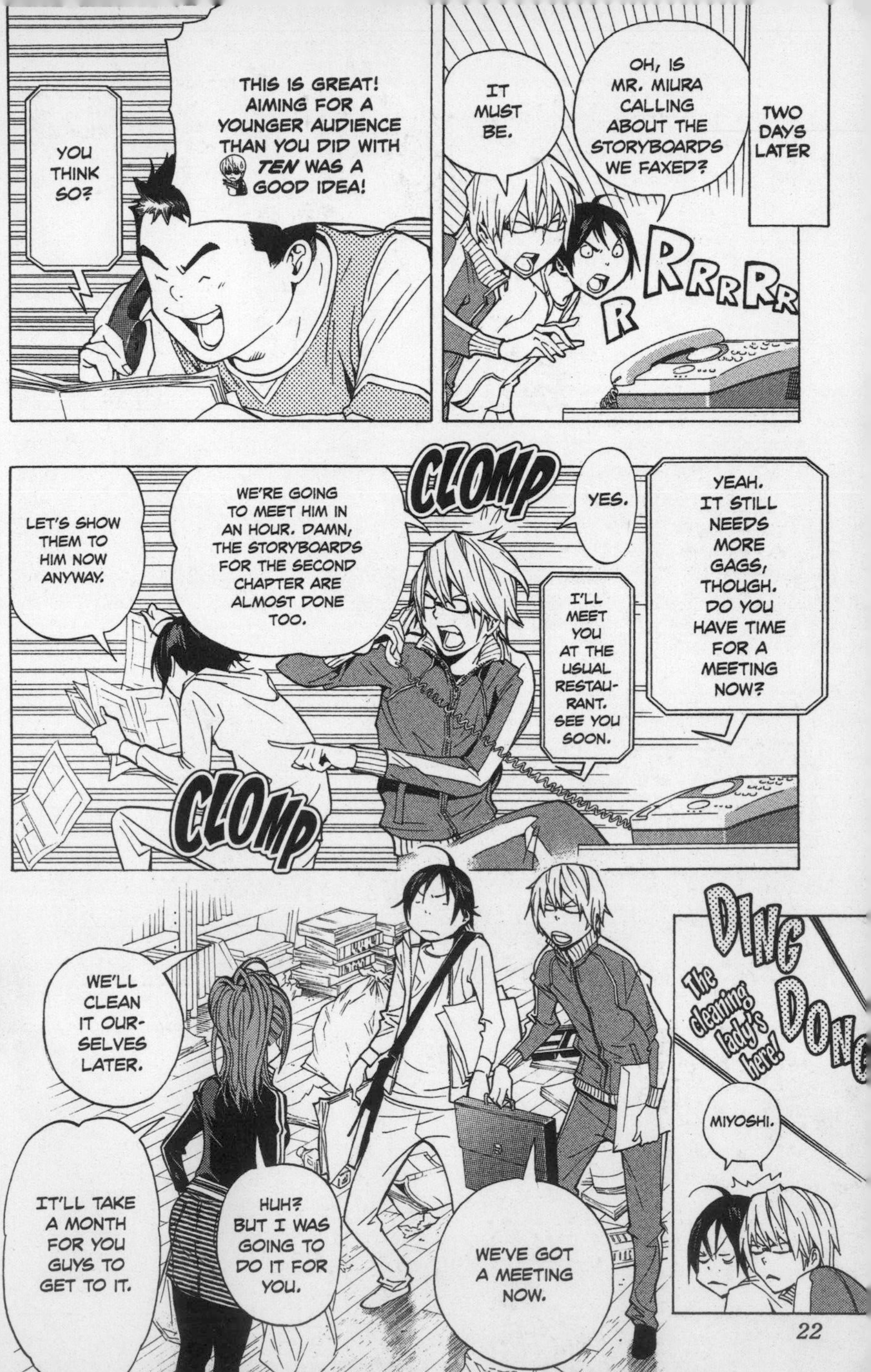
TWO DAYS LATER
OH, IS MR. MIURA CALLING ABOUT THE STORYBOARDS WE FAXED?
IT MUST BE.
RRRRRRR
THIS IS GREAT! AIMING FOR A YOUNGER AUDIENCE THAN YOU DID WITH *TEN* WAS A GOOD IDEA!
YOU THINK SO?
YEAH. IT STILL NEEDS MORE GAGS, THOUGH. DO YOU HAVE TIME FOR A MEETING NOW?
YES.
I'LL MEET YOU AT THE USUAL RESTAU-RANT. SEE YOU SOON.
CLOMP
WE'RE GOING TO MEET HIM IN AN HOUR. DAMN, THE STORYBOARDS FOR THE SECOND CHAPTER ARE ALMOST DONE TOO.
LET'S SHOW THEM TO HIM NOW ANYWAY.
CLOMP
DING DONG
The cleaning lady's here!
MIYOSHI.
WE'VE GOT A MEETING NOW.
HUH? BUT I WAS GOING TO DO IT FOR YOU.
WE'LL CLEAN IT OUR-SELVES LATER.
IT'LL TAKE A MONTH FOR YOU GUYS TO GET TO IT.

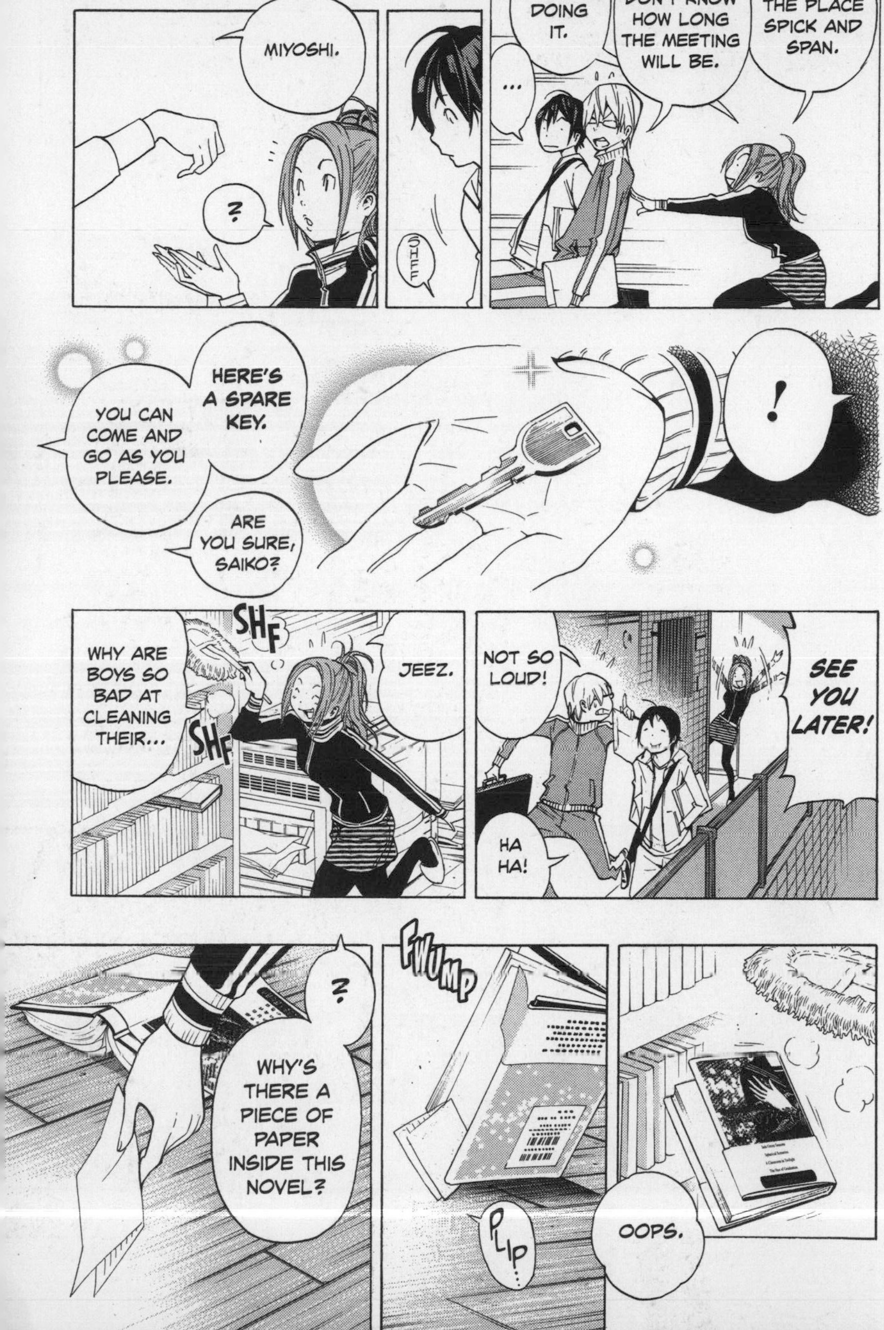
I'LL MAKE THE PLACE SPICK AND SPAN.
BUT WE DON'T KNOW HOW LONG THE MEETING WILL BE.
I'M DOING IT.
...
SHFF
MIYOSHI.
?
!
HERE'S A SPARE KEY.
YOU CAN COME AND GO AS YOU PLEASE.
ARE YOU SURE, SAIKO?
SEE YOU LATER!
NOT SO LOUD!
HA HA!
JEEZ.
SHF
WHY ARE BOYS SO BAD AT CLEANING THEIR...
SHF
OOPS.
FWUMP
PLIP...
?
WHY'S THERE A PIECE OF PAPER INSIDE THIS NOVEL?

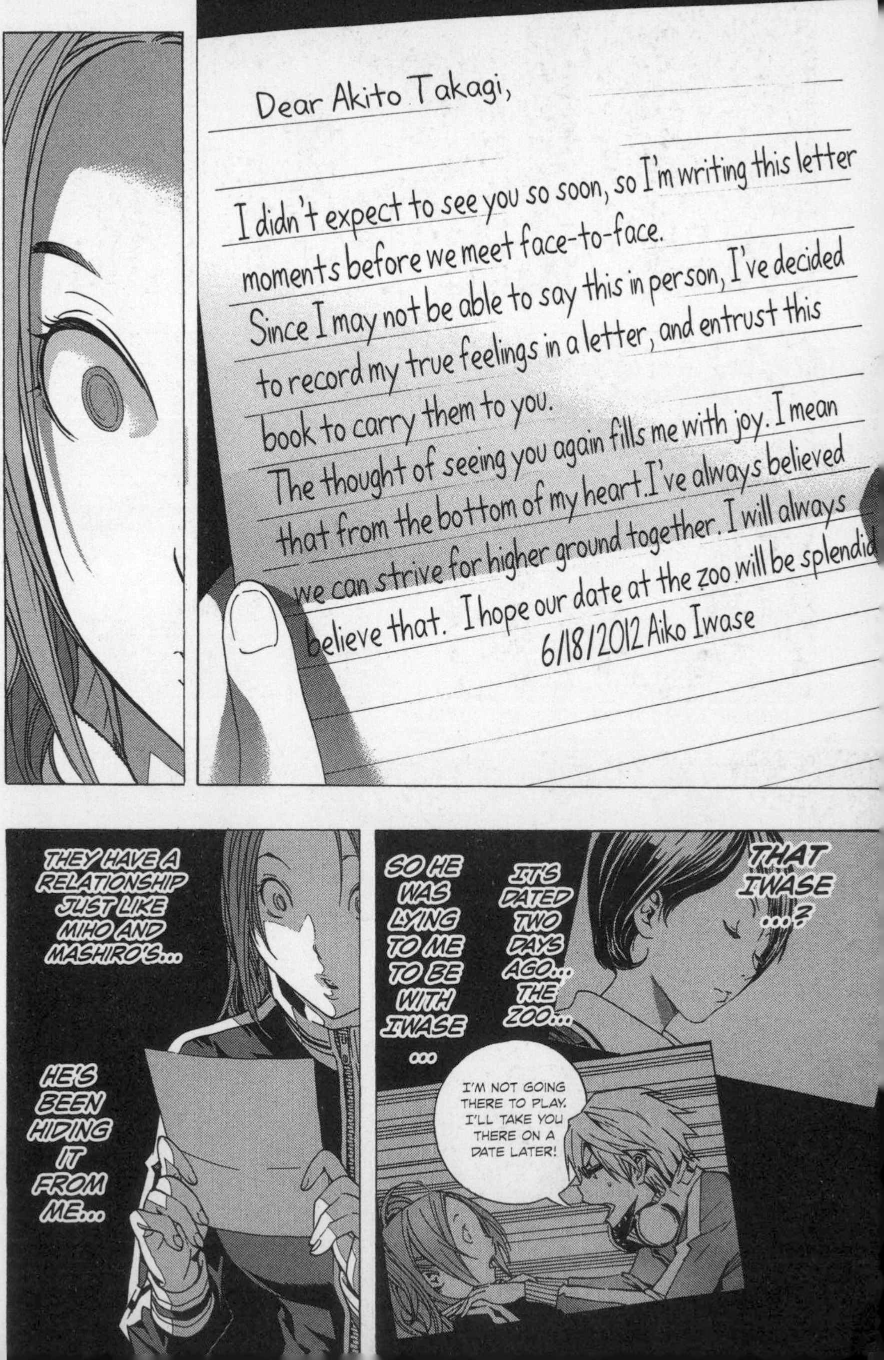
Dear Akito Takagi,
I didn't expect to see you so soon, so I'm writing this letter moments before we meet face-to-face.
Since I may not be able to say this in person, I've decided to record my true feelings in a letter, and entrust this book to carry them to you.
The thought of seeing you again fills me with joy. I mean that from the bottom of my heart. I've always believed we can strive for higher ground together. I will always believe that. I hope our date at the zoo will be splendid
6/18/2012 Aiko Iwase
THAT IWASE ...?
IT'S DATED TWO DAYS AGO... THE ZOO...
SO HE WAS LYING TO ME TO BE WITH IWASE ...
I'M NOT GOING THERE TO PLAY. I'LL TAKE YOU THERE ON A DATE LATER!
THEY HAVE A RELATIONSHIP JUST LIKE MIHO AND MASHIRO'S...
HE'S BEEN HIDING IT FROM ME...

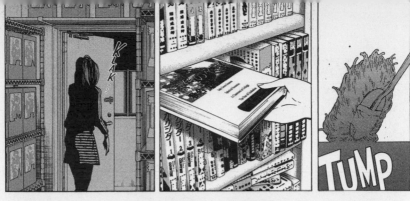

KLAK...

TUMP

CHIK...

CHIK

CHIK

CHIK

901

906

KRCHK..

...

NNGH ...UNGH ...

I WON'T CRY UNTIL I GET HOME.

I-I WON'T CRY...

OHBA'S STORYBOARD

62話サブタイ　プライドと手紙
60話　サブタイ　男性と女性
61話サブタイ　同盟と同級　でどうでしょう？

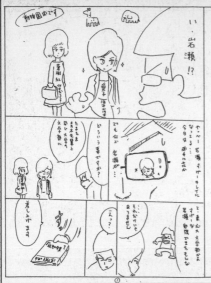

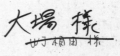

#62 title Pride & Letter
#60 title Men & Women
#61 title Alliance & Classmate
What do you think?

次の目次コメント
空気清浄機を買いましたが部屋が無菌状態だと外に出られなくなるのでは？（つぐみ）

Author comments for the magazine:
I bought an air sanitizer but if my room is now germ free, doesn't that mean I can't go outside anymore? -Tsugumi

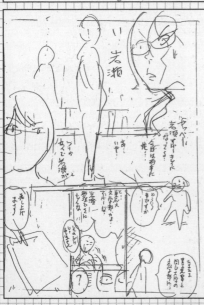

OBATA'S STORYBOARD

大場様
~~相田様~~

To Ohba
~~To Aida~~

チャットの画面
プリントしたものが
欲しいです。

See printout for what to make the computer screen look like.

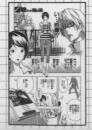

COMPLETE!

*CREATOR STORYBOARDS AND FINISHED PAGES IN JAPANESE

BAKUMAN。 vol.8
"Until the Final Draft Is Complete"
Chapter 62, pp. 7

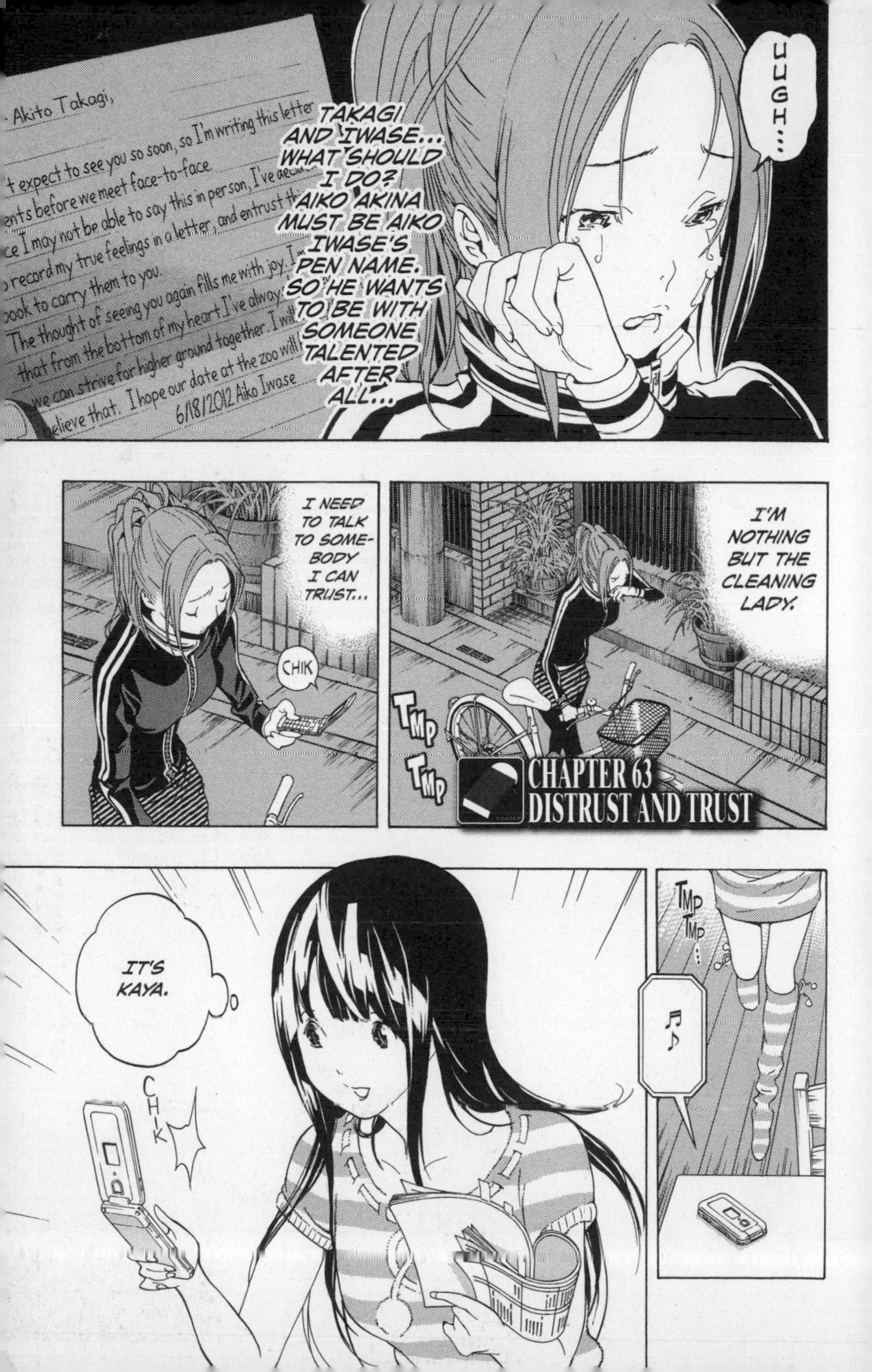
UUGH...
TAKAGI AND IWASE... WHAT SHOULD I DO? AIKO AKINA MUST BE AIKO IWASE'S PEN NAME. SO HE WANTS TO BE WITH SOMEONE TALENTED AFTER ALL...
Akito Takagi,
t expect to see you so soon, so I'm writing this letter
ents before we meet face-to-face.
ce I may not be able to say this in person, I've
o record my true feelings in a letter, and entrust
ook to carry them to you.
The thought of seeing you again fills me with joy.
that from the bottom of my heart. I've alway
we can strive for higher ground together. I wil
believe that. I hope our date at the zoo will
6/18/2012 Aiko Iwase
I'M NOTHING BUT THE CLEANING LADY.
TMP
TMP
CHAPTER 63
DISTRUST AND TRUST
I NEED TO TALK TO SOMEBODY I CAN TRUST...
CHIK
TMP TMP...
♪
IT'S KAYA.
CHIK

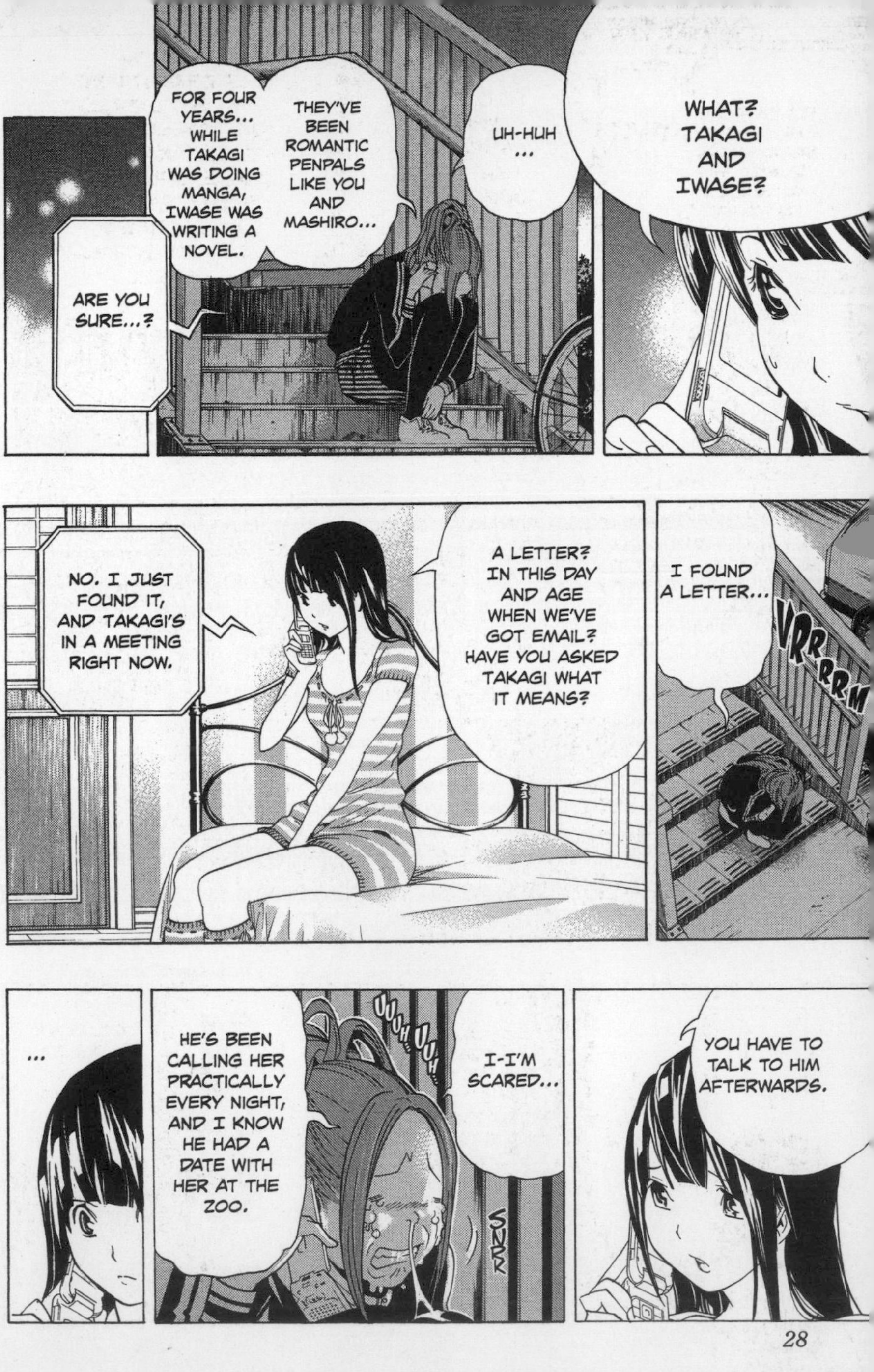
WHAT? TAKAGI AND IWASE?
UH-HUH ...
THEY'VE BEEN ROMANTIC PENPALS LIKE YOU AND MASHIRO...
FOR FOUR YEARS... WHILE TAKAGI WAS DOING MANGA, IWASE WAS WRITING A NOVEL.
ARE YOU SURE...?
I FOUND A LETTER...
VRRRRM
A LETTER? IN THIS DAY AND AGE WHEN WE'VE GOT EMAIL? HAVE YOU ASKED TAKAGI WHAT IT MEANS?
NO. I JUST FOUND IT, AND TAKAGI'S IN A MEETING RIGHT NOW.
YOU HAVE TO TALK TO HIM AFTERWARDS.
I-I'M SCARED...
UUH UUH
SNRK
HE'S BEEN CALLING HER PRACTICALLY EVERY NIGHT, AND I KNOW HE HAD A DATE WITH HER AT THE ZOO.
...

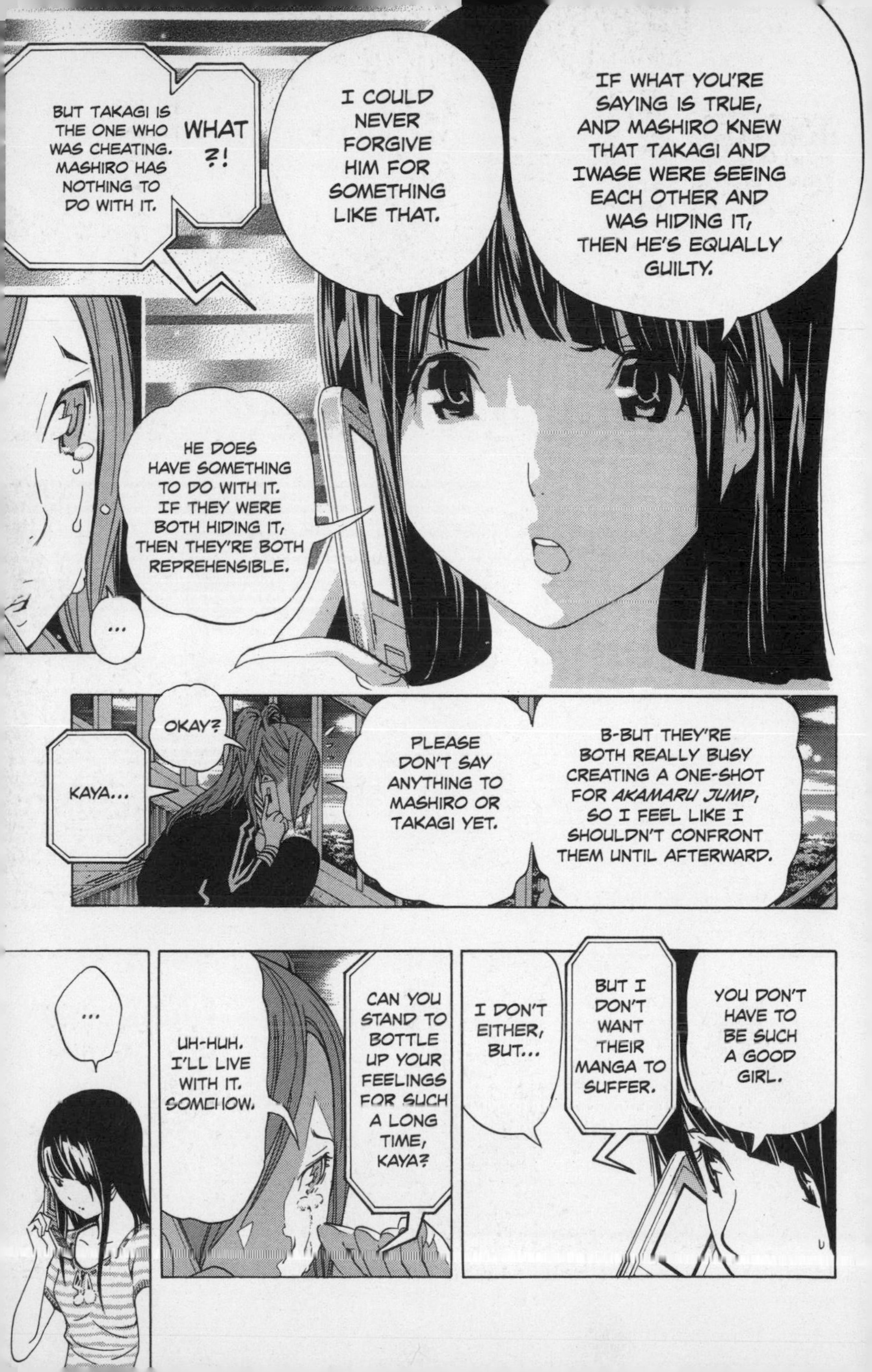
IF WHAT YOU'RE SAYING IS TRUE, AND MASHIRO KNEW THAT TAKAGI AND IWASE WERE SEEING EACH OTHER AND WAS HIDING IT, THEN HE'S EQUALLY GUILTY.
I COULD NEVER FORGIVE HIM FOR SOMETHING LIKE THAT.
WHAT ?!
BUT TAKAGI IS THE ONE WHO WAS CHEATING. MASHIRO HAS NOTHING TO DO WITH IT.
HE DOES HAVE SOMETHING TO DO WITH IT. IF THEY WERE BOTH HIDING IT, THEN THEY'RE BOTH REPREHENSIBLE.
...
B-BUT THEY'RE BOTH REALLY BUSY CREATING A ONE-SHOT FOR *AKAMARU JUMP*, SO I FEEL LIKE I SHOULDN'T CONFRONT THEM UNTIL AFTERWARD.
PLEASE DON'T SAY ANYTHING TO MASHIRO OR TAKAGI YET.
OKAY?
KAYA...
YOU DON'T HAVE TO BE SUCH A GOOD GIRL.
BUT I DON'T WANT THEIR MANGA TO SUFFER.
I DON'T EITHER, BUT...
CAN YOU STAND TO BOTTLE UP YOUR FEELINGS FOR SUCH A LONG TIME, KAYA?
UH-HUH. I'LL LIVE WITH IT. SOMEHOW.
...

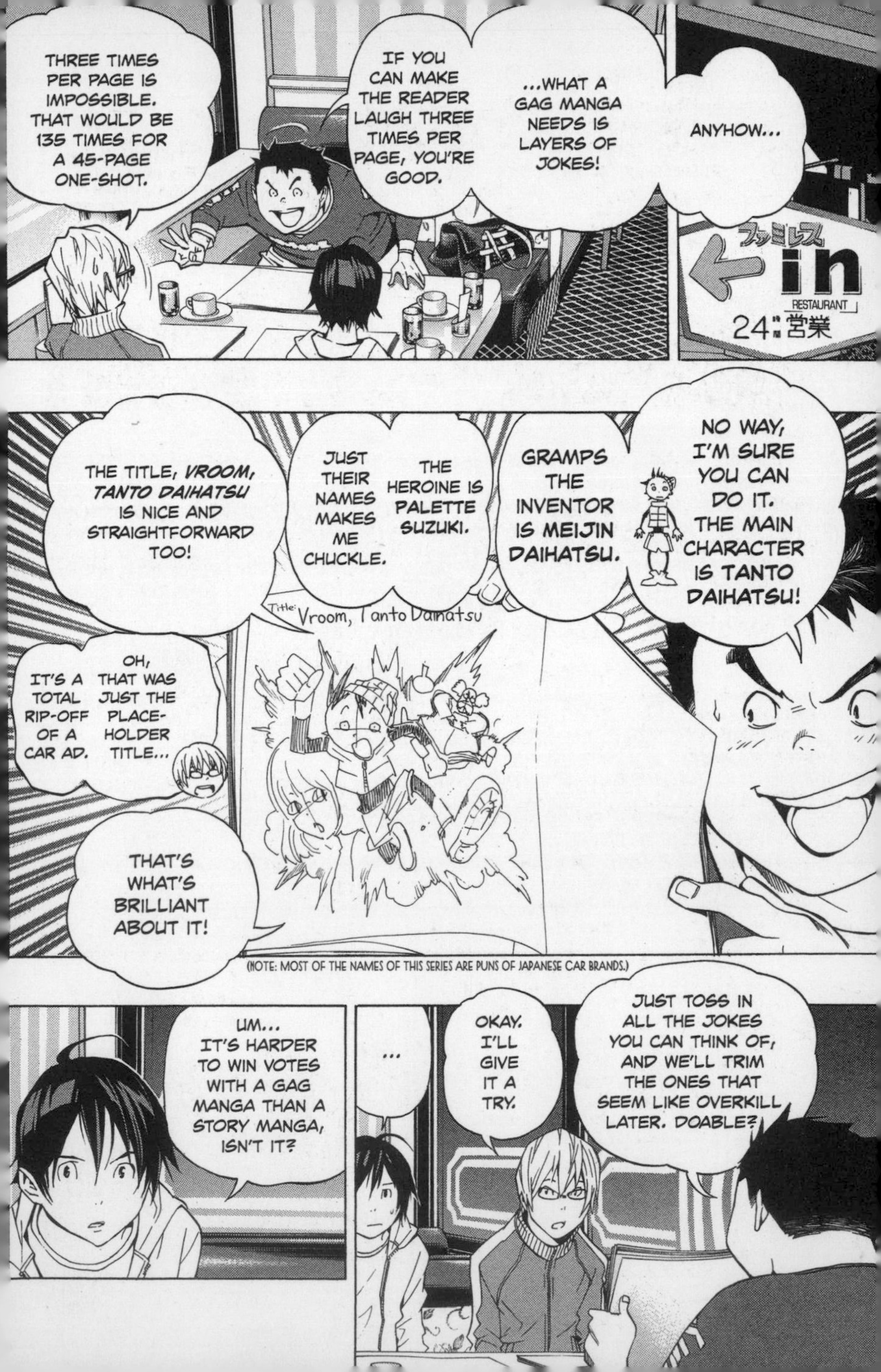
ANYHOW...
ファミレス in RESTAURANT 24時間営業
...WHAT A GAG MANGA NEEDS IS LAYERS OF JOKES!
IF YOU CAN MAKE THE READER LAUGH THREE TIMES PER PAGE, YOU'RE GOOD.
THREE TIMES PER PAGE IS IMPOSSIBLE. THAT WOULD BE 135 TIMES FOR A 45-PAGE ONE-SHOT.
NO WAY, I'M SURE YOU CAN DO IT. THE MAIN CHARACTER IS TANTO DAIHATSU!
GRAMPS THE INVENTOR IS MEIJIN DAIHATSU.
THE HEROINE IS PALETTE SUZUKI.
JUST THEIR NAMES MAKES ME CHUCKLE.
THE TITLE, *VROOM, TANTO DAIHATSU* IS NICE AND STRAIGHTFORWARD TOO!
Title: Vroom, Tanto Daihatsu
OH, THAT WAS JUST THE PLACE-HOLDER TITLE...
IT'S A TOTAL RIP-OFF OF A CAR AD.
THAT'S WHAT'S BRILLIANT ABOUT IT!
(NOTE: MOST OF THE NAMES OF THIS SERIES ARE PUNS OF JAPANESE CAR BRANDS.)
JUST TOSS IN ALL THE JOKES YOU CAN THINK OF, AND WE'LL TRIM THE ONES THAT SEEM LIKE OVERKILL LATER. DOABLE?
OKAY. I'LL GIVE IT A TRY.
...
UM... IT'S HARDER TO WIN VOTES WITH A GAG MANGA THAN A STORY MANGA, ISN'T IT?

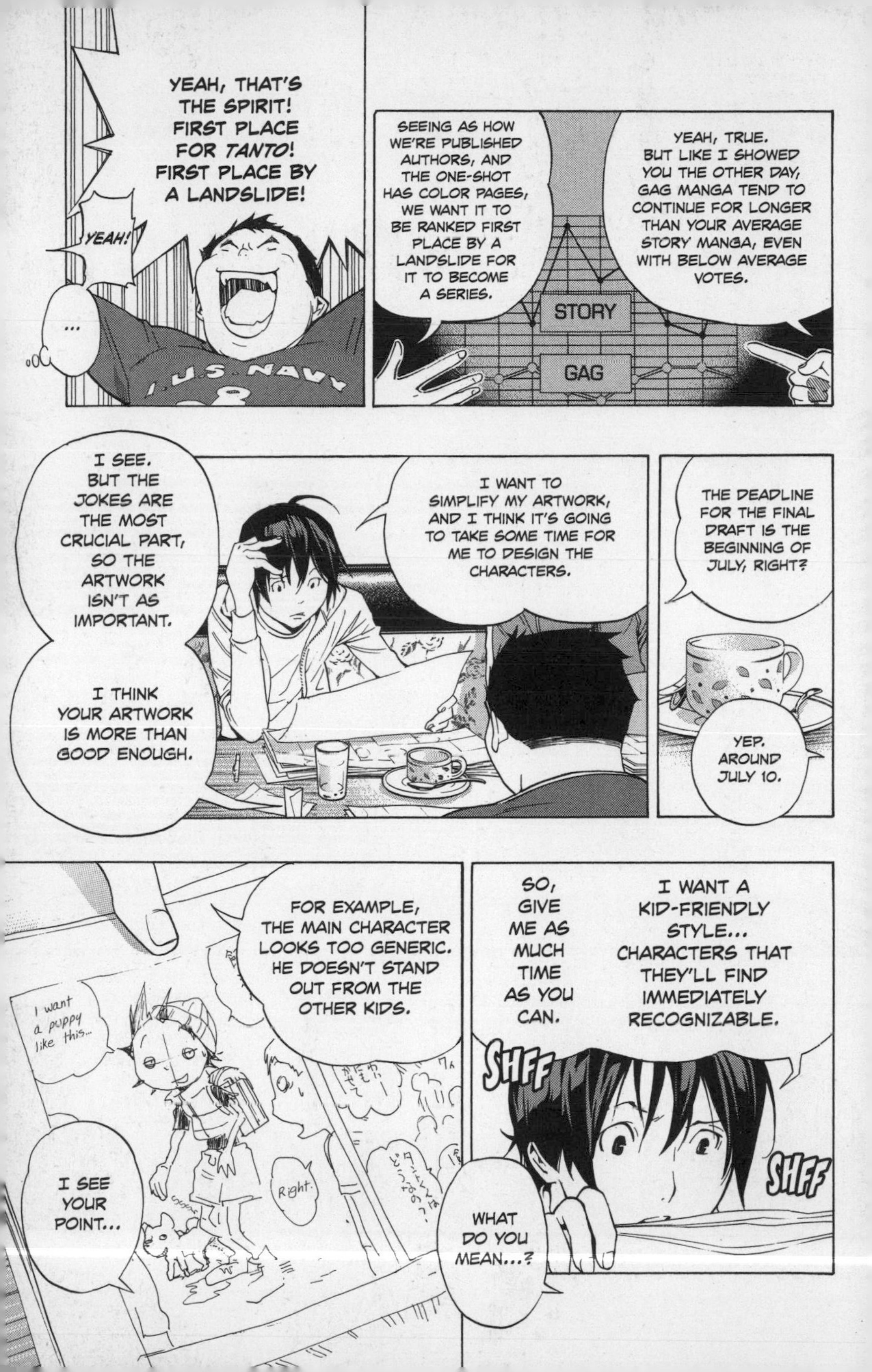
YEAH, TRUE. BUT LIKE I SHOWED YOU THE OTHER DAY, GAG MANGA TEND TO CONTINUE FOR LONGER THAN YOUR AVERAGE STORY MANGA, EVEN WITH BELOW AVERAGE VOTES.
SEEING AS HOW WE'RE PUBLISHED AUTHORS, AND THE ONE-SHOT HAS COLOR PAGES, WE WANT IT TO BE RANKED FIRST PLACE BY A LANDSLIDE FOR IT TO BECOME A SERIES.
STORY
GAG
YEAH, THAT'S THE SPIRIT! FIRST PLACE FOR *TANTO*! FIRST PLACE BY A LANDSLIDE!
YEAH!
...
THE DEADLINE FOR THE FINAL DRAFT IS THE BEGINNING OF JULY, RIGHT?
YEP. AROUND JULY 10.
I WANT TO SIMPLIFY MY ARTWORK, AND I THINK IT'S GOING TO TAKE SOME TIME FOR ME TO DESIGN THE CHARACTERS.
I SEE. BUT THE JOKES ARE THE MOST CRUCIAL PART, SO THE ARTWORK ISN'T AS IMPORTANT.
I THINK YOUR ARTWORK IS MORE THAN GOOD ENOUGH.
I WANT A KID-FRIENDLY STYLE... CHARACTERS THAT THEY'LL FIND IMMEDIATELY RECOGNIZABLE.
SO, GIVE ME AS MUCH TIME AS YOU CAN.
SHFF
SHFF
WHAT DO YOU MEAN...?
FOR EXAMPLE, THE MAIN CHARACTER LOOKS TOO GENERIC. HE DOESN'T STAND OUT FROM THE OTHER KIDS.
I want a puppy like this...
Right.
I SEE YOUR POINT...

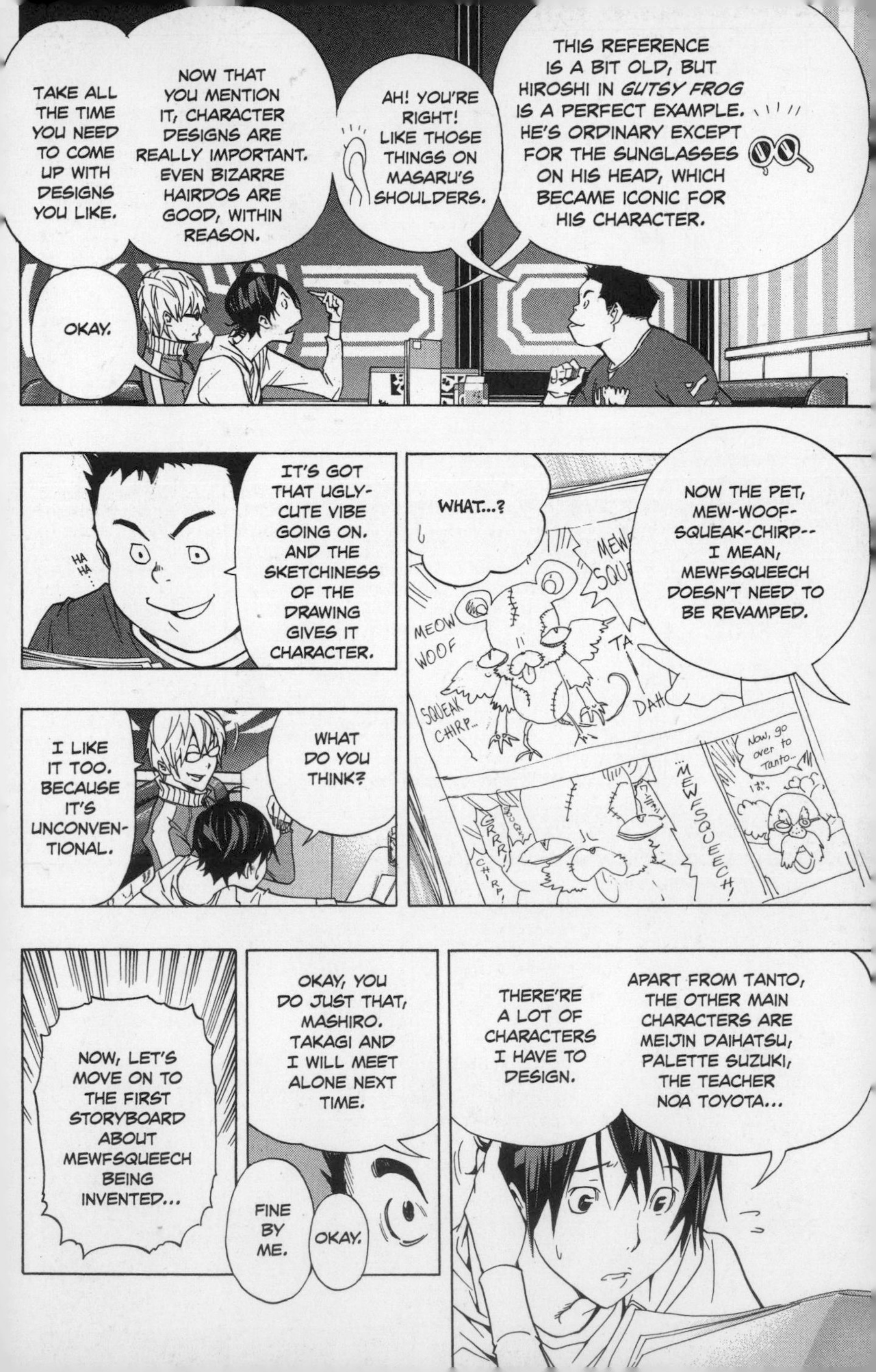
THIS REFERENCE IS A BIT OLD, BUT HIROSHI IN *GUTSY FROG* IS A PERFECT EXAMPLE. HE'S ORDINARY EXCEPT FOR THE SUNGLASSES ON HIS HEAD, WHICH BECAME ICONIC FOR HIS CHARACTER.
AH! YOU'RE RIGHT! LIKE THOSE THINGS ON MASARU'S SHOULDERS.
NOW THAT YOU MENTION IT, CHARACTER DESIGNS ARE REALLY IMPORTANT. EVEN BIZARRE HAIRDOS ARE GOOD, WITHIN REASON.
TAKE ALL THE TIME YOU NEED TO COME UP WITH DESIGNS YOU LIKE.
OKAY.
NOW THE PET, MEW-WOOF-SQUEAK-CHIRP-- I MEAN, MEWFSQUEECH DOESN'T NEED TO BE REVAMPED.
WHAT...?
MEOW WOOF
SQUEAK CHIRP...
TA DAH
Now, go over to Tanto...
MEWFSQUEECH!
IT'S GOT THAT UGLY-CUTE VIBE GOING ON. AND THE SKETCHINESS OF THE DRAWING GIVES IT CHARACTER.
HA HA...
WHAT DO YOU THINK?
I LIKE IT TOO. BECAUSE IT'S UNCONVENTIONAL.
APART FROM TANTO, THE OTHER MAIN CHARACTERS ARE MEIJIN DAIHATSU, PALETTE SUZUKI, THE TEACHER NOA TOYOTA...
THERE'RE A LOT OF CHARACTERS I HAVE TO DESIGN.
OKAY, YOU DO JUST THAT, MASHIRO. TAKAGI AND I WILL MEET ALONE NEXT TIME.
OKAY.
FINE BY ME.
NOW, LET'S MOVE ON TO THE FIRST STORYBOARD ABOUT MEWFSQUEECH BEING INVENTED...

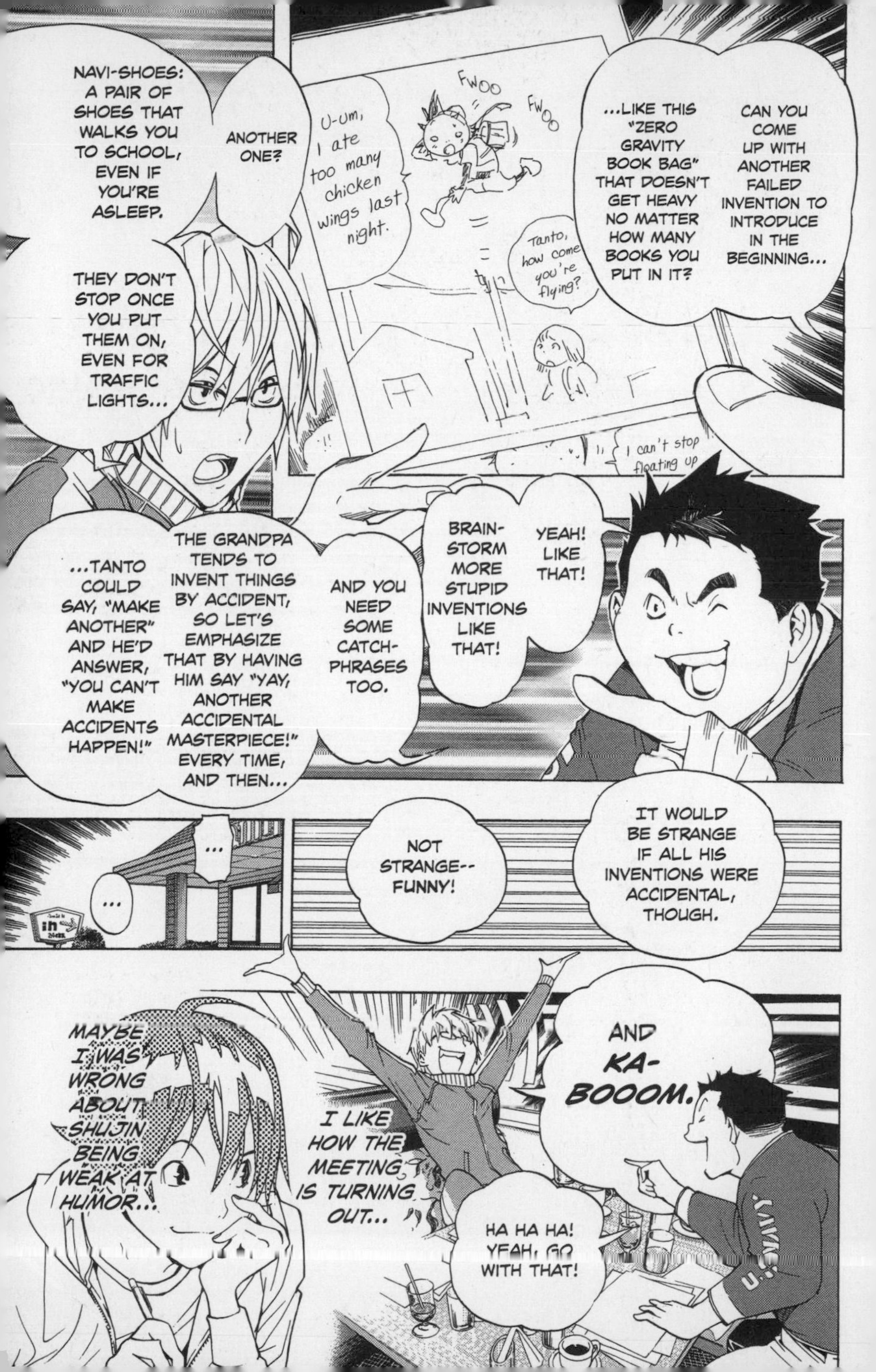
CAN YOU COME UP WITH ANOTHER FAILED INVENTION TO INTRODUCE IN THE BEGINNING...
...LIKE THIS "ZERO GRAVITY BOOK BAG" THAT DOESN'T GET HEAVY NO MATTER HOW MANY BOOKS YOU PUT IN IT?
FWOO
FWOO
U-um, I ate too many chicken wings last night.
Tanto, how come you're flying?
I can't stop floating up
ANOTHER ONE?
NAVI-SHOES: A PAIR OF SHOES THAT WALKS YOU TO SCHOOL, EVEN IF YOU'RE ASLEEP.
THEY DON'T STOP ONCE YOU PUT THEM ON, EVEN FOR TRAFFIC LIGHTS...
YEAH! LIKE THAT!
BRAIN-STORM MORE STUPID INVENTIONS LIKE THAT!
AND YOU NEED SOME CATCH-PHRASES TOO.
THE GRANDPA TENDS TO INVENT THINGS BY ACCIDENT, SO LET'S EMPHASIZE THAT BY HAVING HIM SAY "YAY, ANOTHER ACCIDENTAL MASTERPIECE!" EVERY TIME, AND THEN...
...TANTO COULD SAY, "MAKE ANOTHER" AND HE'D ANSWER, "YOU CAN'T MAKE ACCIDENTS HAPPEN!"
IT WOULD BE STRANGE IF ALL HIS INVENTIONS WERE ACCIDENTAL, THOUGH.
NOT STRANGE--FUNNY!
...
...
AND KA-BOOOM.
HA HA HA! YEAH, GO WITH THAT!
I LIKE HOW THE MEETING IS TURNING OUT...
MAYBE I WAS WRONG ABOUT SHUJIN BEING WEAK AT HUMOR...

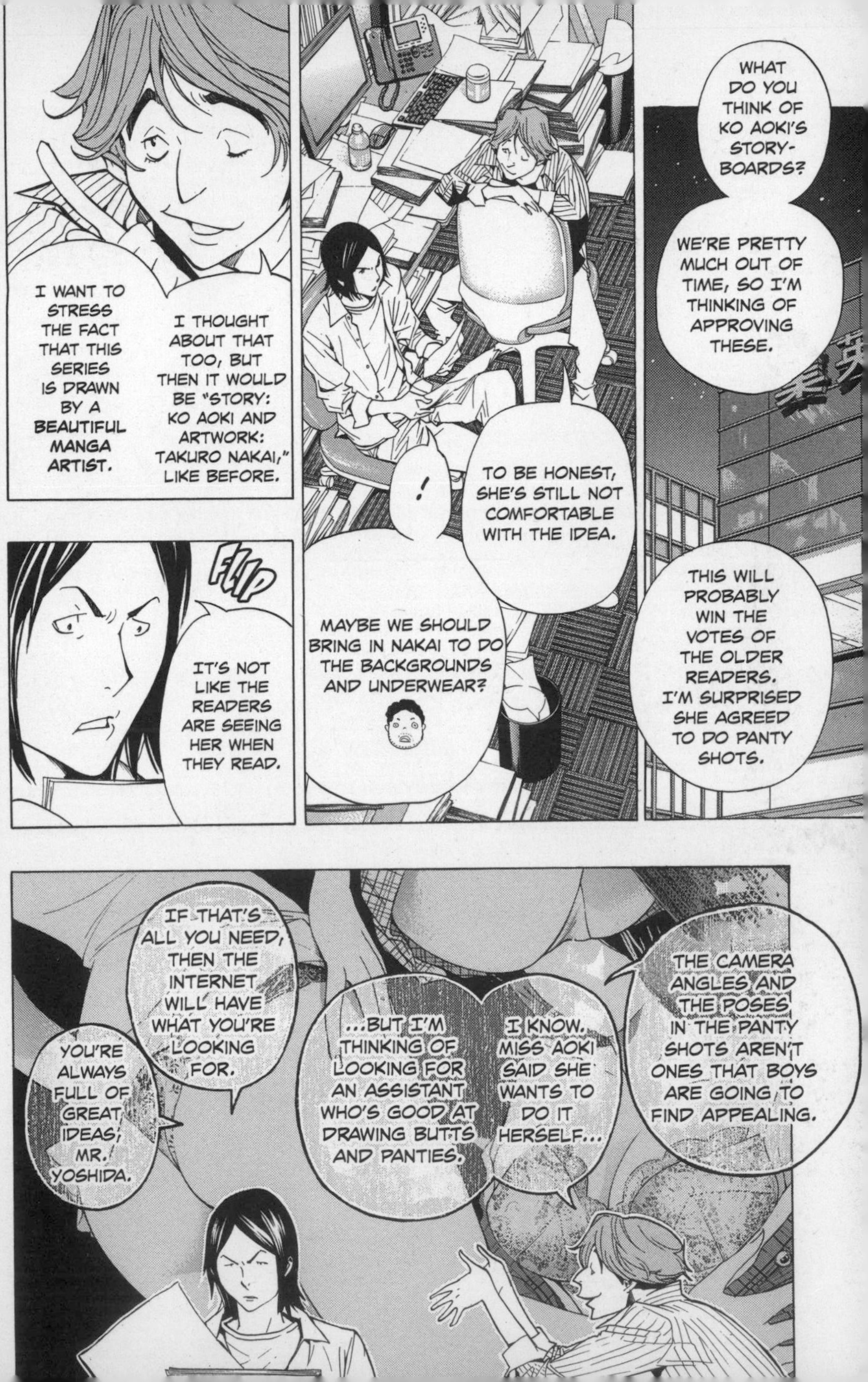
WHAT DO YOU THINK OF KO AOKI'S STORY-BOARDS?
WE'RE PRETTY MUCH OUT OF TIME, SO I'M THINKING OF APPROVING THESE.
THIS WILL PROBABLY WIN THE VOTES OF THE OLDER READERS. I'M SURPRISED SHE AGREED TO DO PANTY SHOTS.
TO BE HONEST, SHE'S STILL NOT COMFORTABLE WITH THE IDEA.
!
MAYBE WE SHOULD BRING IN NAKAI TO DO THE BACKGROUNDS AND UNDERWEAR?
I THOUGHT ABOUT THAT TOO, BUT THEN IT WOULD BE "STORY: KO AOKI AND ARTWORK: TAKURO NAKAI," LIKE BEFORE.
I WANT TO STRESS THE FACT THAT THIS SERIES IS DRAWN BY A BEAUTIFUL MANGA ARTIST.
FLIP
IT'S NOT LIKE THE READERS ARE SEEING HER WHEN THEY READ.
THE CAMERA ANGLES AND THE POSES IN THE PANTY SHOTS AREN'T ONES THAT BOYS ARE GOING TO FIND APPEALING.
I KNOW. MISS AOKI SAID SHE WANTS TO DO IT HERSELF...
...BUT I'M THINKING OF LOOKING FOR AN ASSISTANT WHO'S GOOD AT DRAWING BUTTS AND PANTIES.
IF THAT'S ALL YOU NEED, THEN THE INTERNET WILL HAVE WHAT YOU'RE LOOKING FOR.
YOU'RE ALWAYS FULL OF GREAT IDEAS, MR. YOSHIDA.

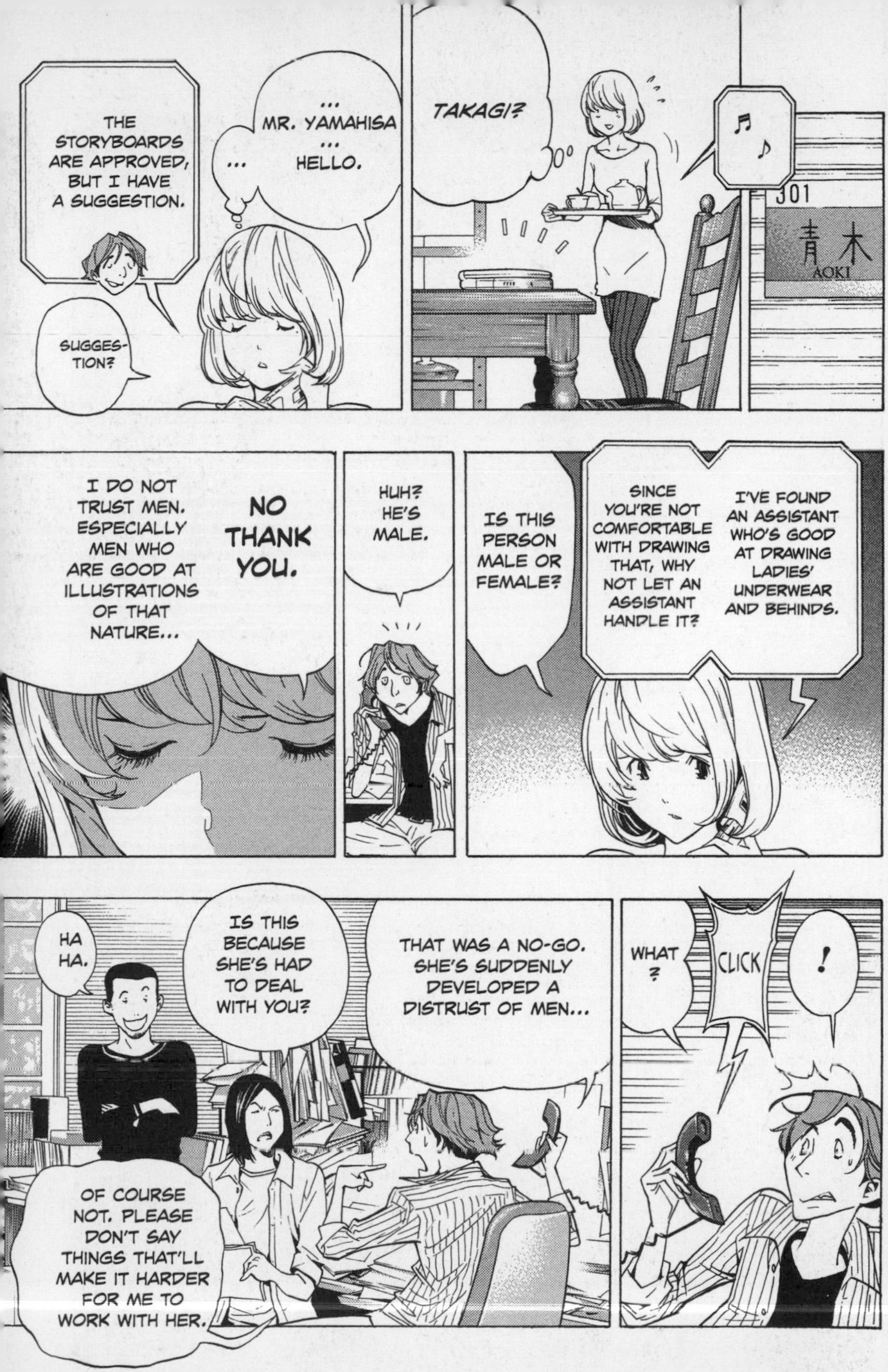
♪ ♪
301
青木
AOKI
TAKAGI?
... MR. YAMAHISA ... HELLO.
...
THE STORYBOARDS ARE APPROVED, BUT I HAVE A SUGGESTION.
SUGGES-TION?
I'VE FOUND AN ASSISTANT WHO'S GOOD AT DRAWING LADIES' UNDERWEAR AND BEHINDS.
SINCE YOU'RE NOT COMFORTABLE WITH DRAWING THAT, WHY NOT LET AN ASSISTANT HANDLE IT?
IS THIS PERSON MALE OR FEMALE?
HUH? HE'S MALE.
NO THANK YOU.
I DO NOT TRUST MEN. ESPECIALLY MEN WHO ARE GOOD AT ILLUSTRATIONS OF THAT NATURE...
!
CLICK
WHAT?
THAT WAS A NO-GO. SHE'S SUDDENLY DEVELOPED A DISTRUST OF MEN...
IS THIS BECAUSE SHE'S HAD TO DEAL WITH YOU?
HA HA.
OF COURSE NOT. PLEASE DON'T SAY THINGS THAT'LL MAKE IT HARDER FOR ME TO WORK WITH HER.

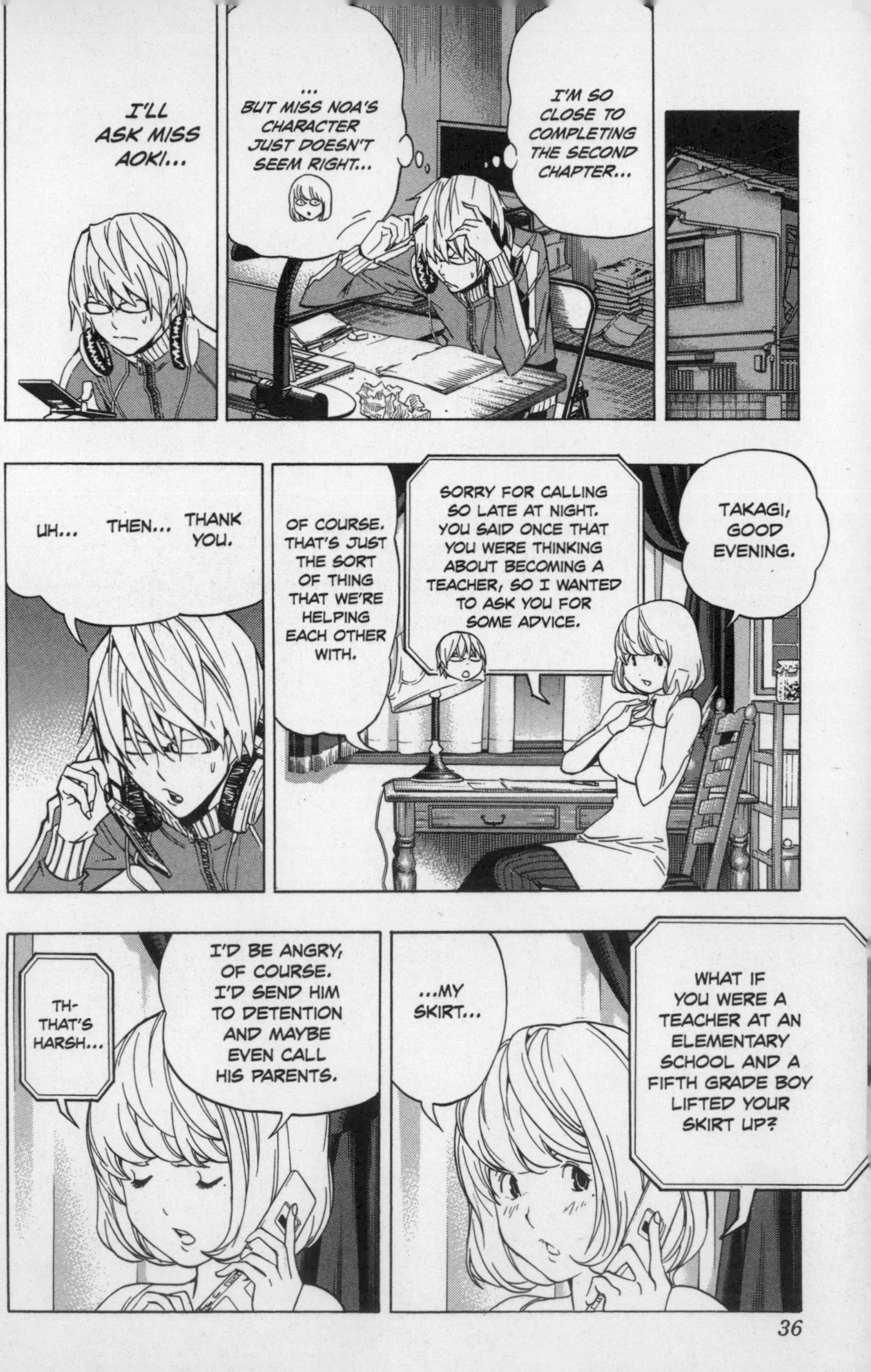
I'M SO CLOSE TO COMPLETING THE SECOND CHAPTER...
... BUT MISS NOA'S CHARACTER JUST DOESN'T SEEM RIGHT...
I'LL ASK MISS AOKI...
TAKAGI, GOOD EVENING.
SORRY FOR CALLING SO LATE AT NIGHT. YOU SAID ONCE THAT YOU WERE THINKING ABOUT BECOMING A TEACHER, SO I WANTED TO ASK YOU FOR SOME ADVICE.
OF COURSE. THAT'S JUST THE SORT OF THING THAT WE'RE HELPING EACH OTHER WITH.
UH... THEN... THANK YOU.
WHAT IF YOU WERE A TEACHER AT AN ELEMENTARY SCHOOL AND A FIFTH GRADE BOY LIFTED YOUR SKIRT UP?
...MY SKIRT...
I'D BE ANGRY, OF COURSE. I'D SEND HIM TO DETENTION AND MAYBE EVEN CALL HIS PARENTS.
TH-THAT'S HARSH...

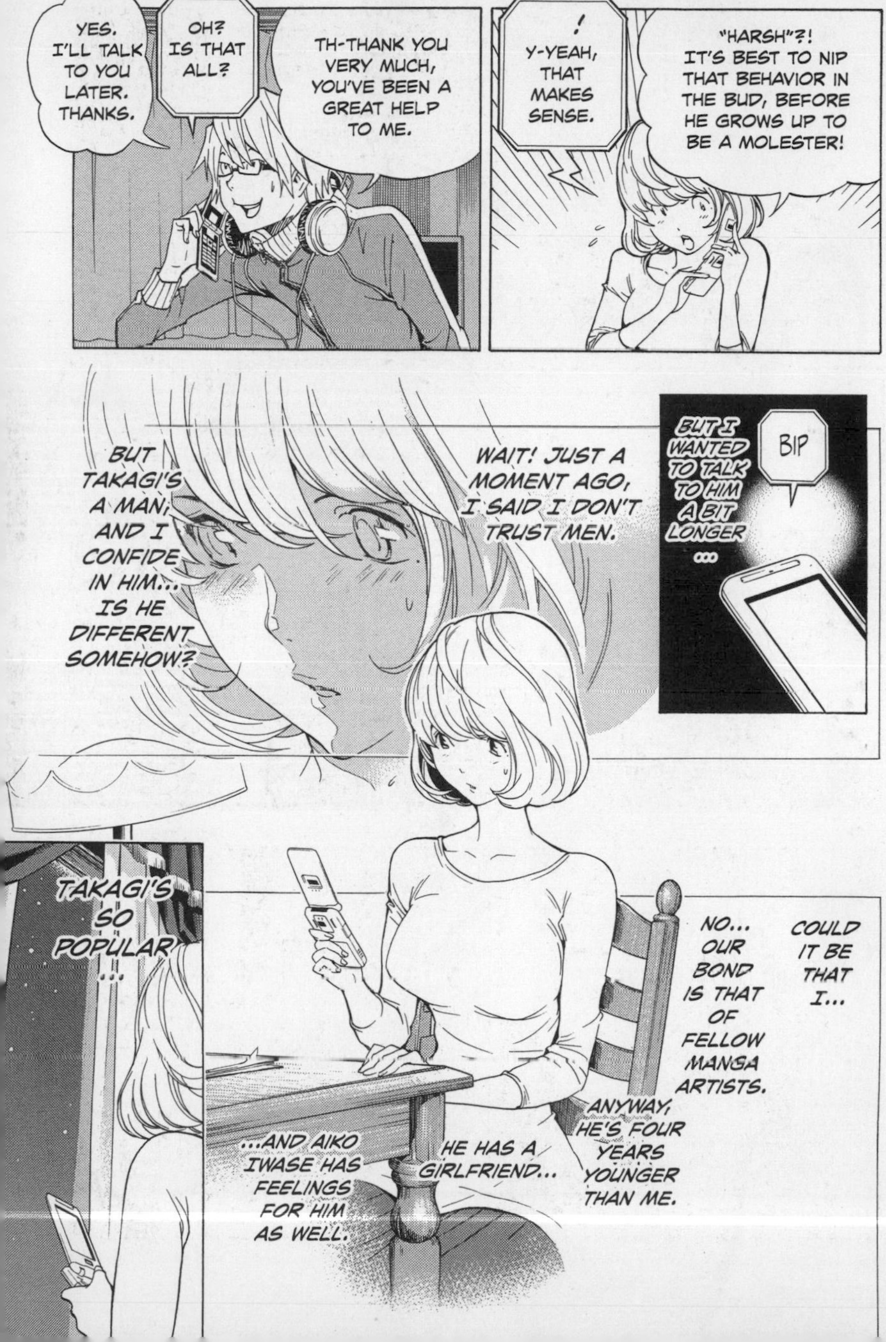
"HARSH"?! IT'S BEST TO NIP THAT BEHAVIOR IN THE BUD, BEFORE HE GROWS UP TO BE A MOLESTER!
! Y-YEAH, THAT MAKES SENSE.
TH-THANK YOU VERY MUCH, YOU'VE BEEN A GREAT HELP TO ME.
OH? IS THAT ALL?
YES. I'LL TALK TO YOU LATER. THANKS.
BIP
BUT I WANTED TO TALK TO HIM A BIT LONGER...
WAIT! JUST A MOMENT AGO, I SAID I DON'T TRUST MEN.
BUT TAKAGI'S A MAN, AND I CONFIDE IN HIM... IS HE DIFFERENT SOMEHOW?
COULD IT BE THAT I...
NO... OUR BOND IS THAT OF FELLOW MANGA ARTISTS.
ANYWAY, HE'S FOUR YEARS YOUNGER THAN ME.
HE HAS A GIRLFRIEND...
...AND AIKO IWASE HAS FEELINGS FOR HIM AS WELL.
TAKAGI'S SO POPULAR...

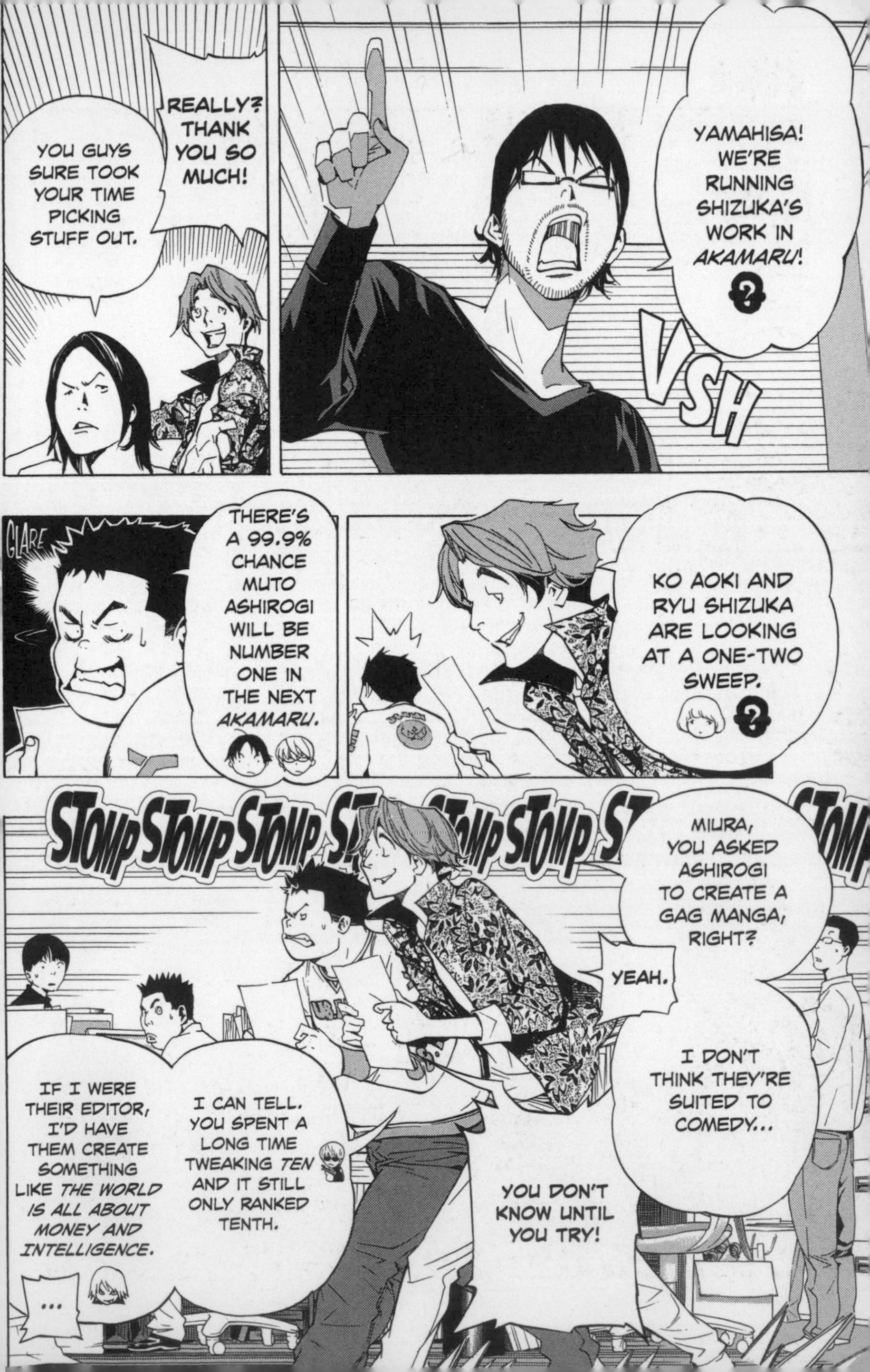
YAMAHISA! WE'RE RUNNING SHIZUKA'S WORK IN *AKAMARU*!
VSH
REALLY? THANK YOU SO MUCH!
YOU GUYS SURE TOOK YOUR TIME PICKING STUFF OUT.
KO AOKI AND RYU SHIZUKA ARE LOOKING AT A ONE-TWO SWEEP.
THERE'S A 99.9% CHANCE MUTO ASHIROGI WILL BE NUMBER ONE IN THE NEXT *AKAMARU*.
GLARE
STOMP STOMP STOMP ST STOMP STOMP ST STOMP
MIURA, YOU ASKED ASHIROGI TO CREATE A GAG MANGA, RIGHT?
YEAH.
I DON'T THINK THEY'RE SUITED TO COMEDY...
YOU DON'T KNOW UNTIL YOU TRY!
I CAN TELL. YOU SPENT A LONG TIME TWEAKING *TEN* AND IT STILL ONLY RANKED TENTH.
IF I WERE THEIR EDITOR, I'D HAVE THEM CREATE SOMETHING LIKE *THE WORLD IS ALL ABOUT MONEY AND INTELLIGENCE*.
...

READ THIS WAY

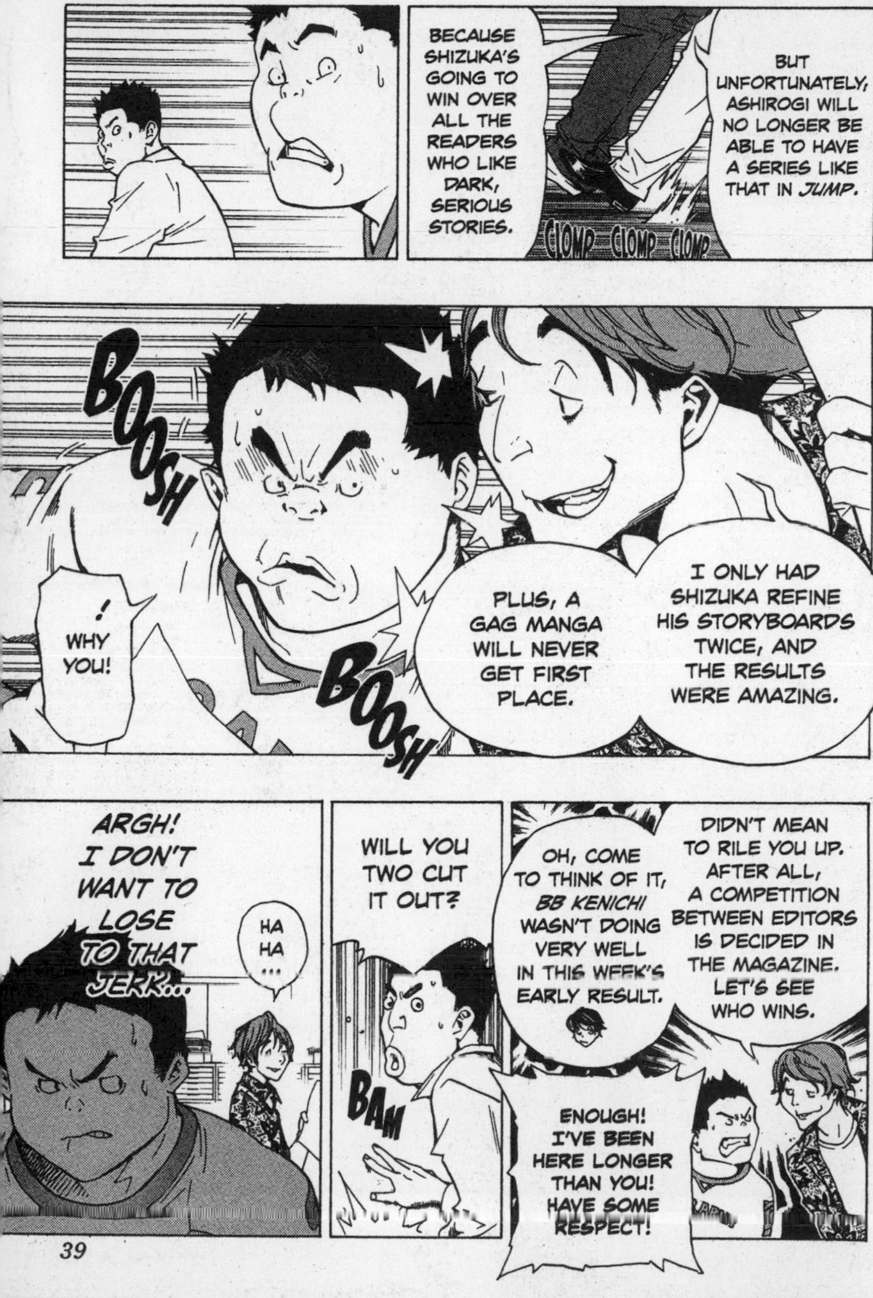
BUT UNFORTUNATELY, ASHIROGI WILL NO LONGER BE ABLE TO HAVE A SERIES LIKE THAT IN *JUMP*.
BECAUSE SHIZUKA'S GOING TO WIN OVER ALL THE READERS WHO LIKE DARK, SERIOUS STORIES.
CLOMP CLOMP CLOMP
I ONLY HAD SHIZUKA REFINE HIS STORYBOARDS TWICE, AND THE RESULTS WERE AMAZING.
PLUS, A GAG MANGA WILL NEVER GET FIRST PLACE.
BOOSH
BOOSH
! WHY YOU!
DIDN'T MEAN TO RILE YOU UP. AFTER ALL, A COMPETITION BETWEEN EDITORS IS DECIDED IN THE MAGAZINE. LET'S SEE WHO WINS.
OH, COME TO THINK OF IT, *BB KENICHI* WASN'T DOING VERY WELL IN THIS WEEK'S EARLY RESULT.
ENOUGH! I'VE BEEN HERE LONGER THAN YOU! HAVE SOME RESPECT!
WILL YOU TWO CUT IT OUT?
BAM
ARGH! I DON'T WANT TO LOSE TO THAT JERK...
HA HA ...

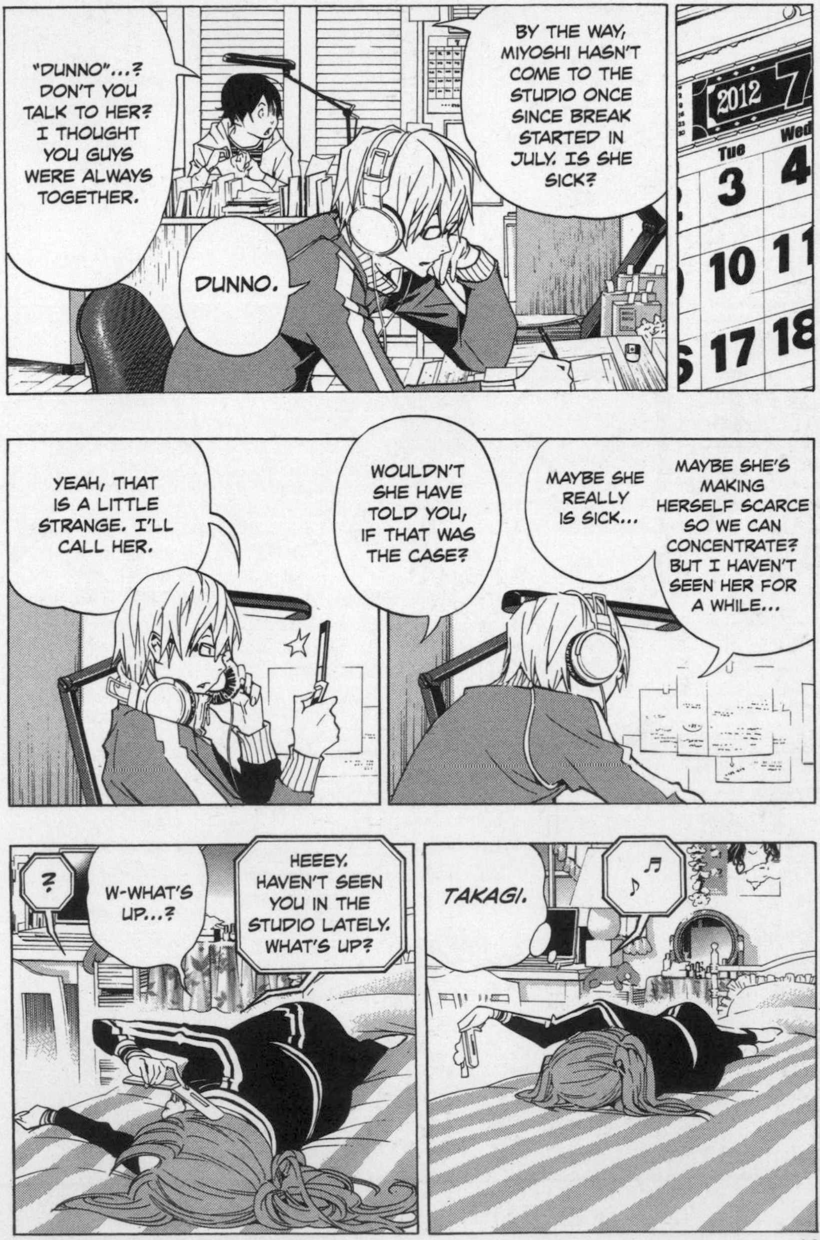
2012 7
Tue Wed
3 4
10 11
17 18
BY THE WAY, MIYOSHI HASN'T COME TO THE STUDIO ONCE SINCE BREAK STARTED IN JULY. IS SHE SICK?
DUNNO.
"DUNNO"...? DON'T YOU TALK TO HER? I THOUGHT YOU GUYS WERE ALWAYS TOGETHER.
MAYBE SHE'S MAKING HERSELF SCARCE SO WE CAN CONCENTRATE? BUT I HAVEN'T SEEN HER FOR A WHILE...
MAYBE SHE REALLY IS SICK...
WOULDN'T SHE HAVE TOLD YOU, IF THAT WAS THE CASE?
YEAH, THAT IS A LITTLE STRANGE. I'LL CALL HER.
♪
TAKAGI.
HEEEY. HAVEN'T SEEN YOU IN THE STUDIO LATELY. WHAT'S UP?
W-WHAT'S UP...?
?

READ THIS WAY

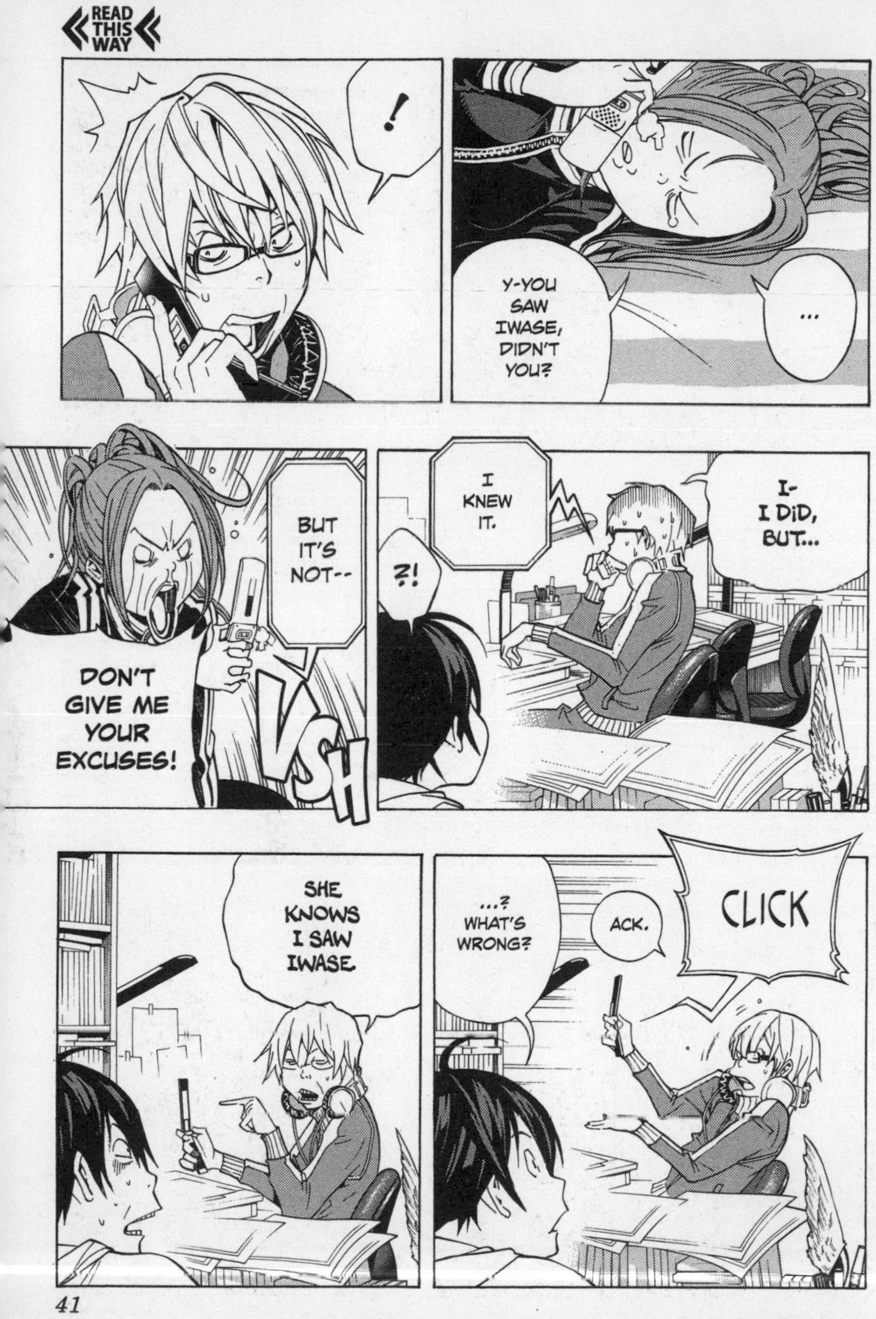
...
Y-YOU SAW IWASE, DIDN'T YOU?
!
I- I DID, BUT...
I KNEW IT.
?!
BUT IT'S NOT--
DON'T GIVE ME YOUR EXCUSES!
VSH
CLICK
ACK.
...? WHAT'S WRONG?
SHE KNOWS I SAW IWASE

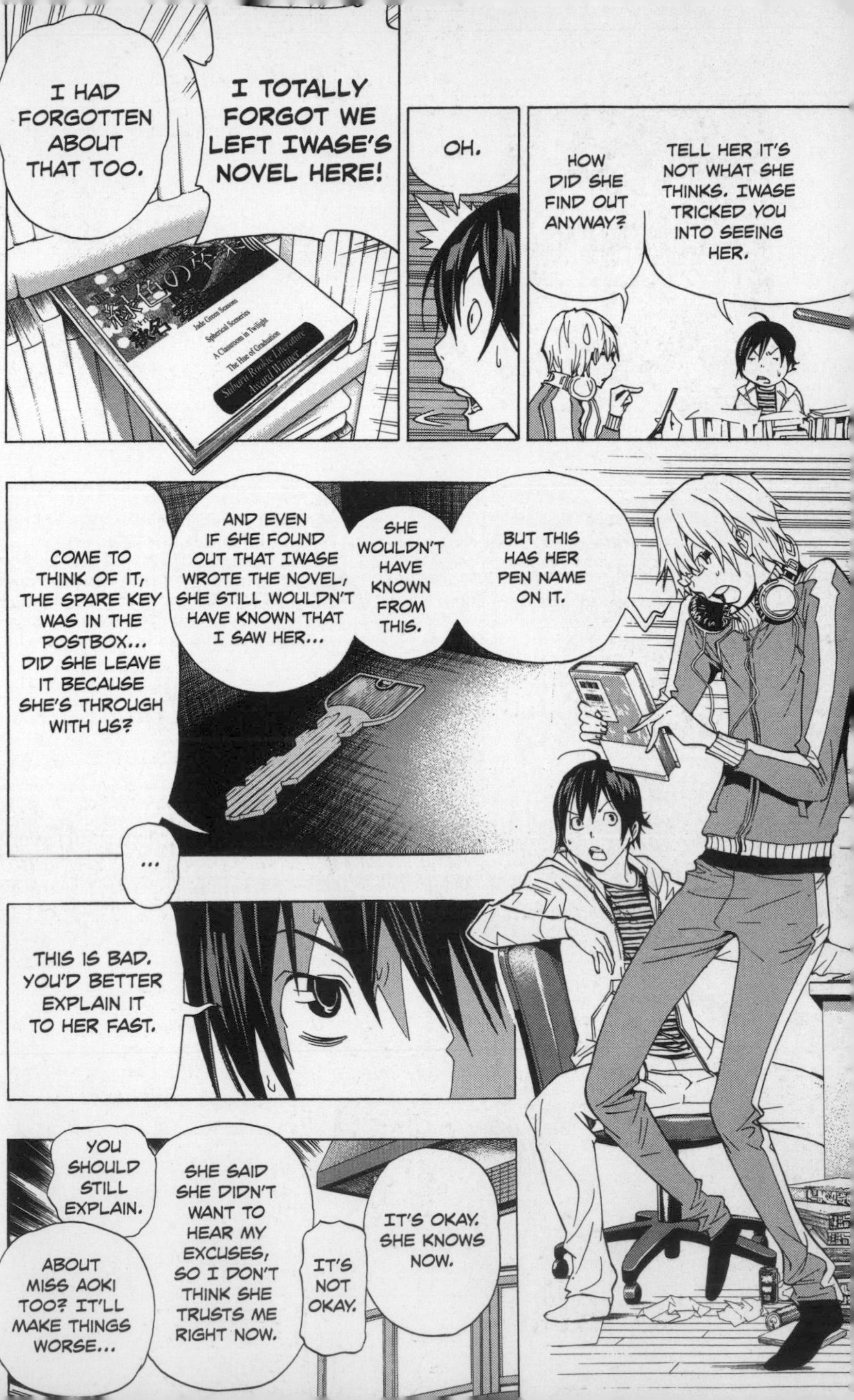
TELL HER IT'S NOT WHAT SHE THINKS. IWASE TRICKED YOU INTO SEEING HER.
HOW DID SHE FIND OUT ANYWAY?
OH.
I TOTALLY FORGOT WE LEFT IWASE'S NOVEL HERE!
I HAD FORGOTTEN ABOUT THAT TOO.
The Green Graduation
Jade Green Seasons
Spherical Sceneries
A Classroom in Twilight
The Hue of Graduation
Subaru Rookie Literature Award Winner
BUT THIS HAS HER PEN NAME ON IT.
SHE WOULDN'T HAVE KNOWN FROM THIS.
AND EVEN IF SHE FOUND OUT THAT IWASE WROTE THE NOVEL, SHE STILL WOULDN'T HAVE KNOWN THAT I SAW HER...
COME TO THINK OF IT, THE SPARE KEY WAS IN THE POSTBOX... DID SHE LEAVE IT BECAUSE SHE'S THROUGH WITH US?
...
THIS IS BAD. YOU'D BETTER EXPLAIN IT TO HER FAST.
IT'S OKAY. SHE KNOWS NOW.
IT'S NOT OKAY.
SHE SAID SHE DIDN'T WANT TO HEAR MY EXCUSES, SO I DON'T THINK SHE TRUSTS ME RIGHT NOW.
YOU SHOULD STILL EXPLAIN.
ABOUT MISS AOKI TOO? IT'LL MAKE THINGS WORSE...

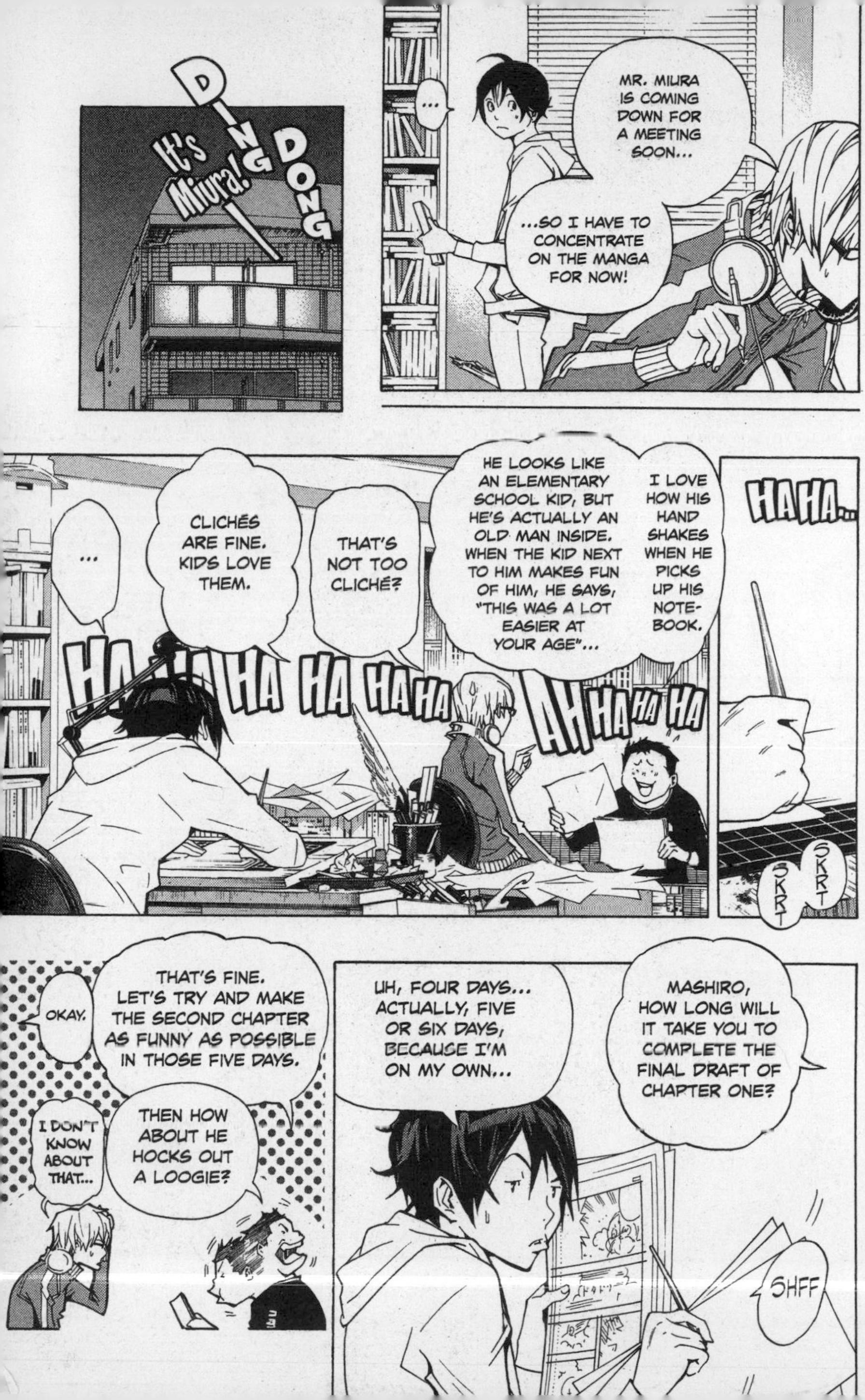
MR. MIURA IS COMING DOWN FOR A MEETING SOON...
...SO I HAVE TO CONCENTRATE ON THE MANGA FOR NOW!
...
DING DONG
It's Miura!
HAHA...
SKRT SKRT
I LOVE HOW HIS HAND SHAKES WHEN HE PICKS UP HIS NOTE-BOOK.
HE LOOKS LIKE AN ELEMENTARY SCHOOL KID, BUT HE'S ACTUALLY AN OLD MAN INSIDE. WHEN THE KID NEXT TO HIM MAKES FUN OF HIM, HE SAYS, "THIS WAS A LOT EASIER AT YOUR AGE"...
THAT'S NOT TOO CLICHÉ?
CLICHÉS ARE FINE. KIDS LOVE THEM.
...
AHHAHAHA HA
HAHAHA HA HAHA
MASHIRO, HOW LONG WILL IT TAKE YOU TO COMPLETE THE FINAL DRAFT OF CHAPTER ONE?
UH, FOUR DAYS... ACTUALLY, FIVE OR SIX DAYS, BECAUSE I'M ON MY OWN...
SHFF
THAT'S FINE. LET'S TRY AND MAKE THE SECOND CHAPTER AS FUNNY AS POSSIBLE IN THOSE FIVE DAYS.
OKAY.
THEN HOW ABOUT HE HOCKS OUT A LOOGIE?
I DON'T KNOW ABOUT THAT...

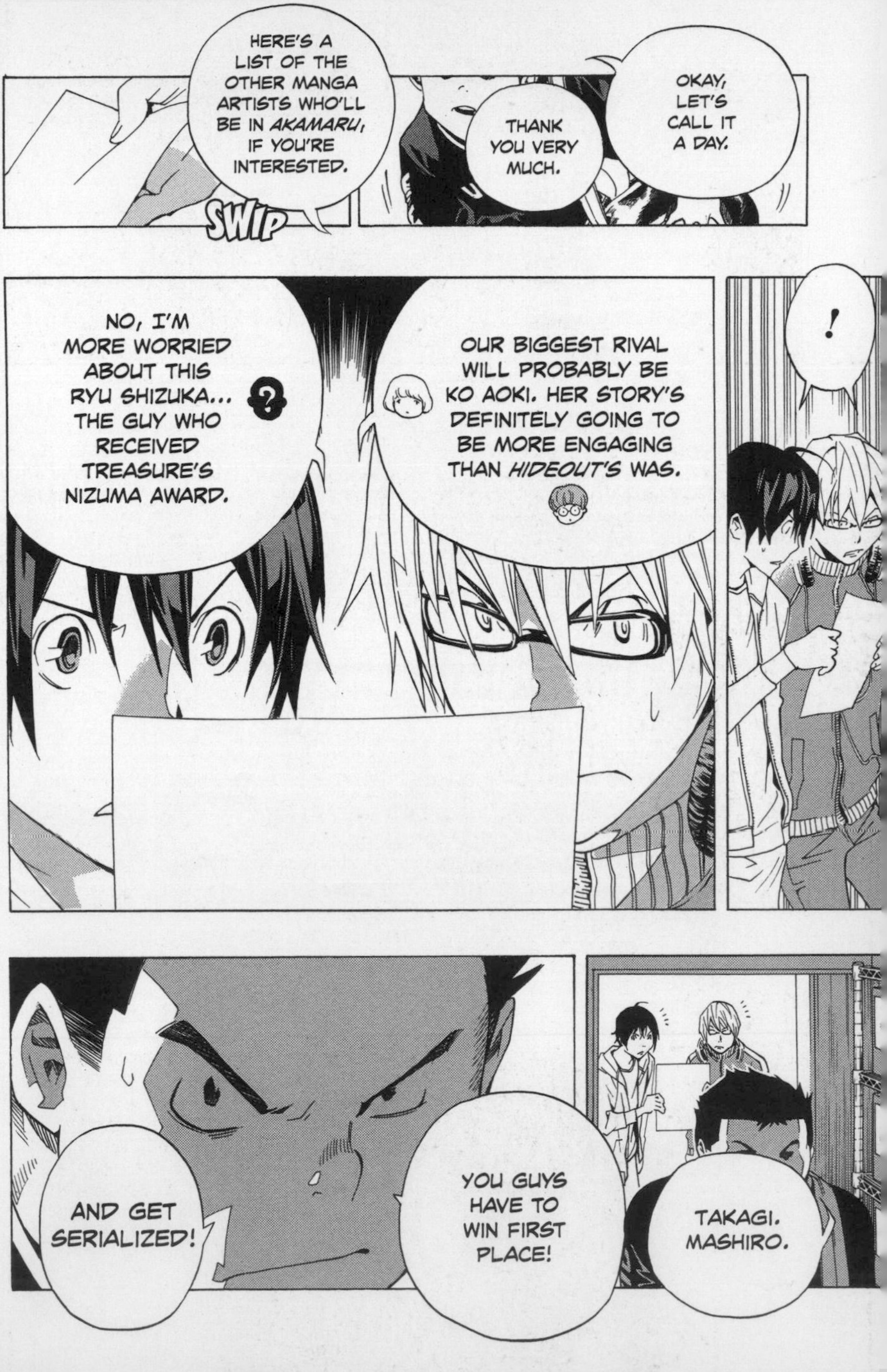
OKAY, LET'S CALL IT A DAY.
THANK YOU VERY MUCH.
HERE'S A LIST OF THE OTHER MANGA ARTISTS WHO'LL BE IN *AKAMARU*, IF YOU'RE INTERESTED.
SWIP
!
OUR BIGGEST RIVAL WILL PROBABLY BE KO AOKI. HER STORY'S DEFINITELY GOING TO BE MORE ENGAGING THAN *HIDEOUT'S* WAS.
NO, I'M MORE WORRIED ABOUT THIS RYU SHIZUKA... THE GUY WHO RECEIVED TREASURE'S NIZUMA AWARD.
?
TAKAGI. MASHIRO.
YOU GUYS HAVE TO WIN FIRST PLACE!
AND GET SERIALIZED!

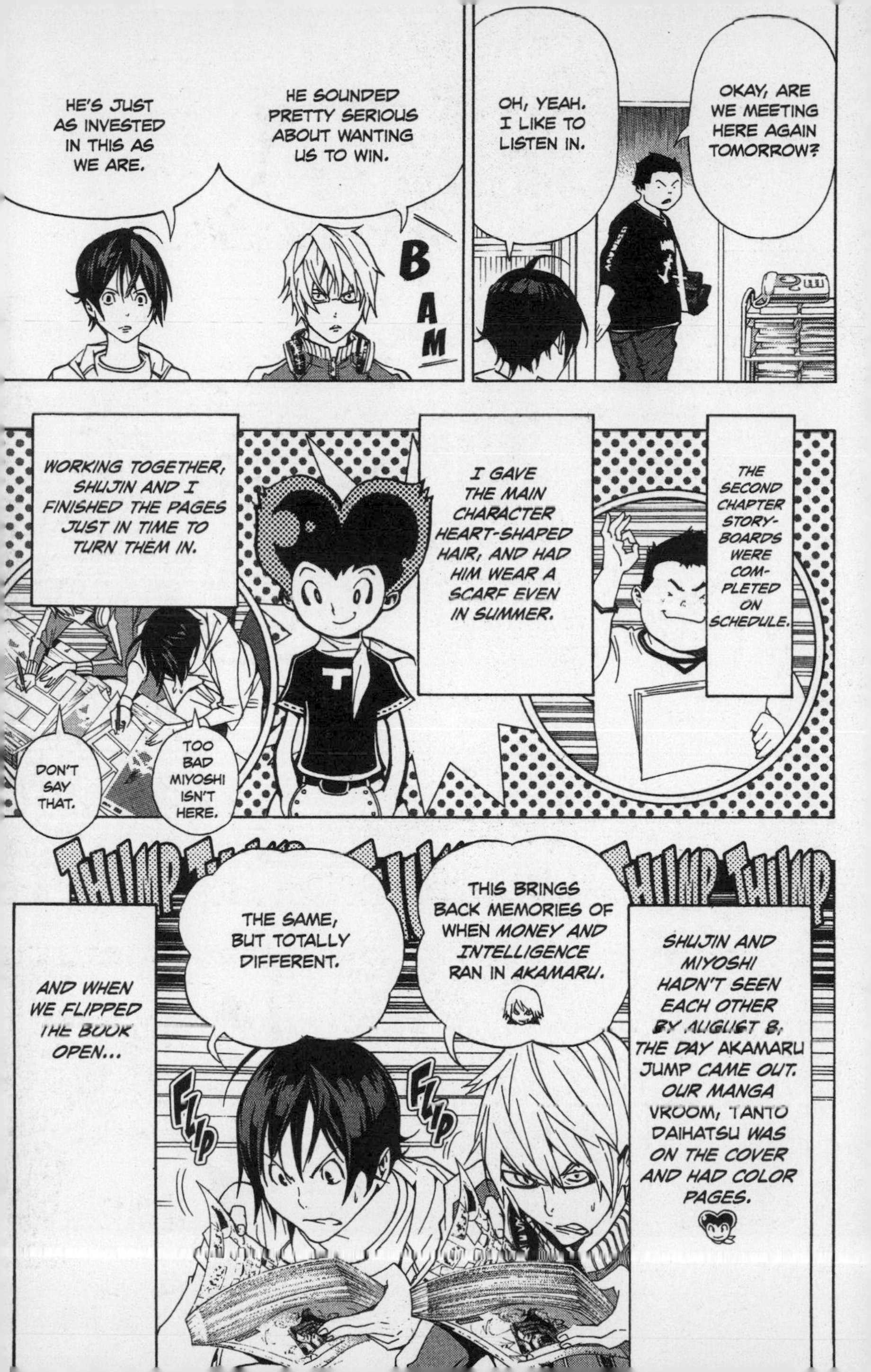
OKAY, ARE WE MEETING HERE AGAIN TOMORROW?
OH, YEAH. I LIKE TO LISTEN IN.
BAM
HE SOUNDED PRETTY SERIOUS ABOUT WANTING US TO WIN.
HE'S JUST AS INVESTED IN THIS AS WE ARE.
THE SECOND CHAPTER STORY-BOARDS WERE COM-PLETED ON SCHEDULE.
I GAVE THE MAIN CHARACTER HEART-SHAPED HAIR, AND HAD HIM WEAR A SCARF EVEN IN SUMMER.
WORKING TOGETHER, SHUJIN AND I FINISHED THE PAGES JUST IN TIME TO TURN THEM IN.
TOO BAD MIYOSHI ISN'T HERE.
DON'T SAY THAT.
THUMP THUMP
SHUJIN AND MIYOSHI HADN'T SEEN EACH OTHER BY AUGUST 8, THE DAY AKAMARU JUMP CAME OUT. OUR MANGA VROOM, TANTO DAIHATSU WAS ON THE COVER AND HAD COLOR PAGES.
THIS BRINGS BACK MEMORIES OF WHEN MONEY AND INTELLIGENCE RAN IN AKAMARU.
THE SAME, BUT TOTALLY DIFFERENT.
FLIP
FLIP
AND WHEN WE FLIPPED THE BOOK OPEN...

OHBA'S STORYBOARD

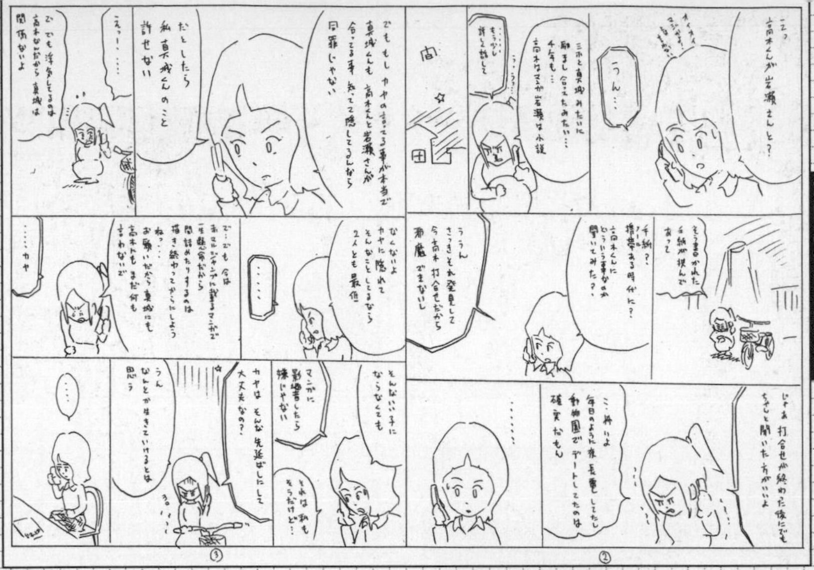

エッ? 高木くんが岩瀬さんと?
うん…
三木と真城みたいに励まし合ってたみたい… 千年も… 高木はマンガ 岩瀬は小説
もう少し詳しく話して
手紙?
携帯ある時代に? 高木くんにどういう事なのか聞いてみた?
ううん さっきそれ発見して 今高木打合せだから 邪魔できないし
じゃあ打合せが終わった後にでも ちゃんと聞いた方がいいよ
動物園でデートしてたのは 確実なもん
……
でももしカヤの言ってる事が本当で 真城くんも高木くんと岩瀬さんが合ってる事知ってて隠してるんなら 同罪じゃない
だとしたら 私 真城くんのこと 許せない
えっ…、……
で でも浮気してるのは 高木なんだから 真城は関係ないよ
なくないよ カヤに隠れて そんなことしてるなら 2人とも最低
……
お願いだから 真城にも 高木にも まだ何も 言わないで
……カヤ
そんないい子にならなくても
それは 私も そうだけど…
マンガに影響したら嫌じゃない
カヤは そんな先延ばしにして 大丈夫なの?
……

OBATA'S STORYBOARD

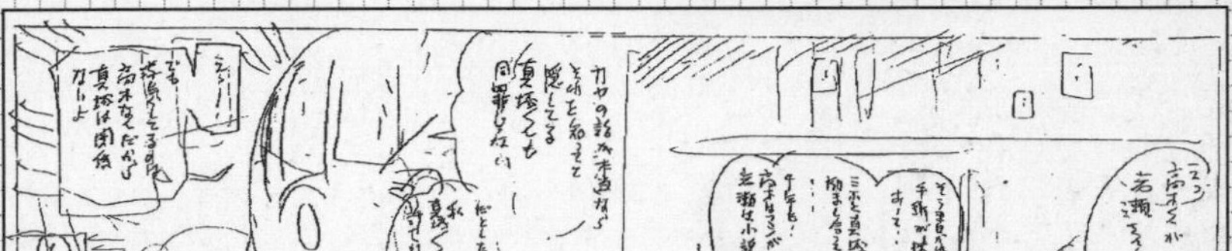

COMPLETE!

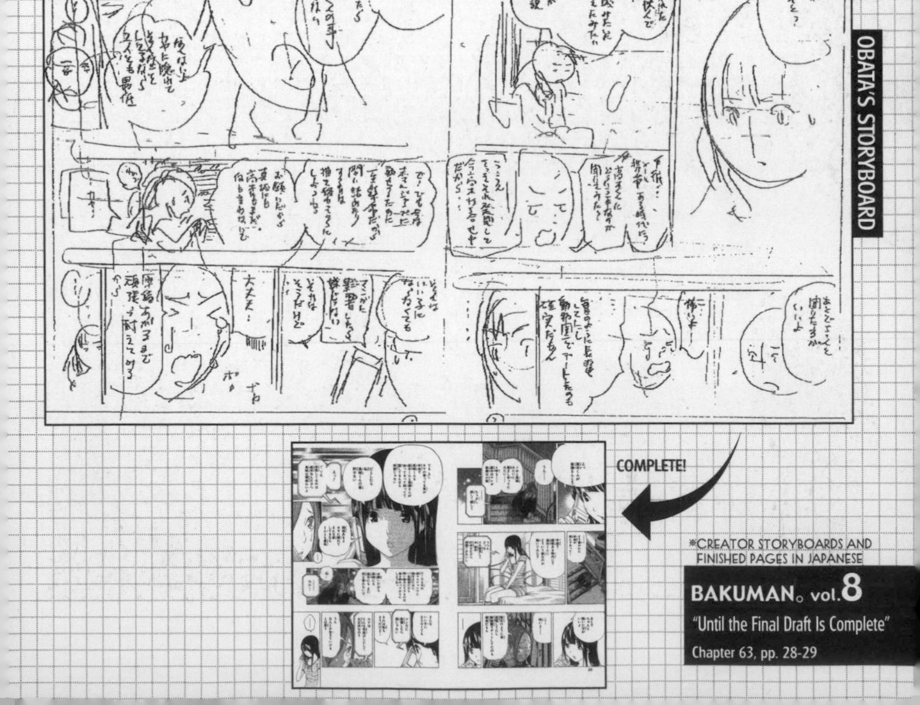

*CREATOR STORYBOARDS AND FINISHED PAGES IN JAPANESE

BAKUMAN。 vol.8

"Until the Final Draft Is Complete"

Chapter 63, pp. 28-29

CHAPTER 64
JUST SO AND SECRET

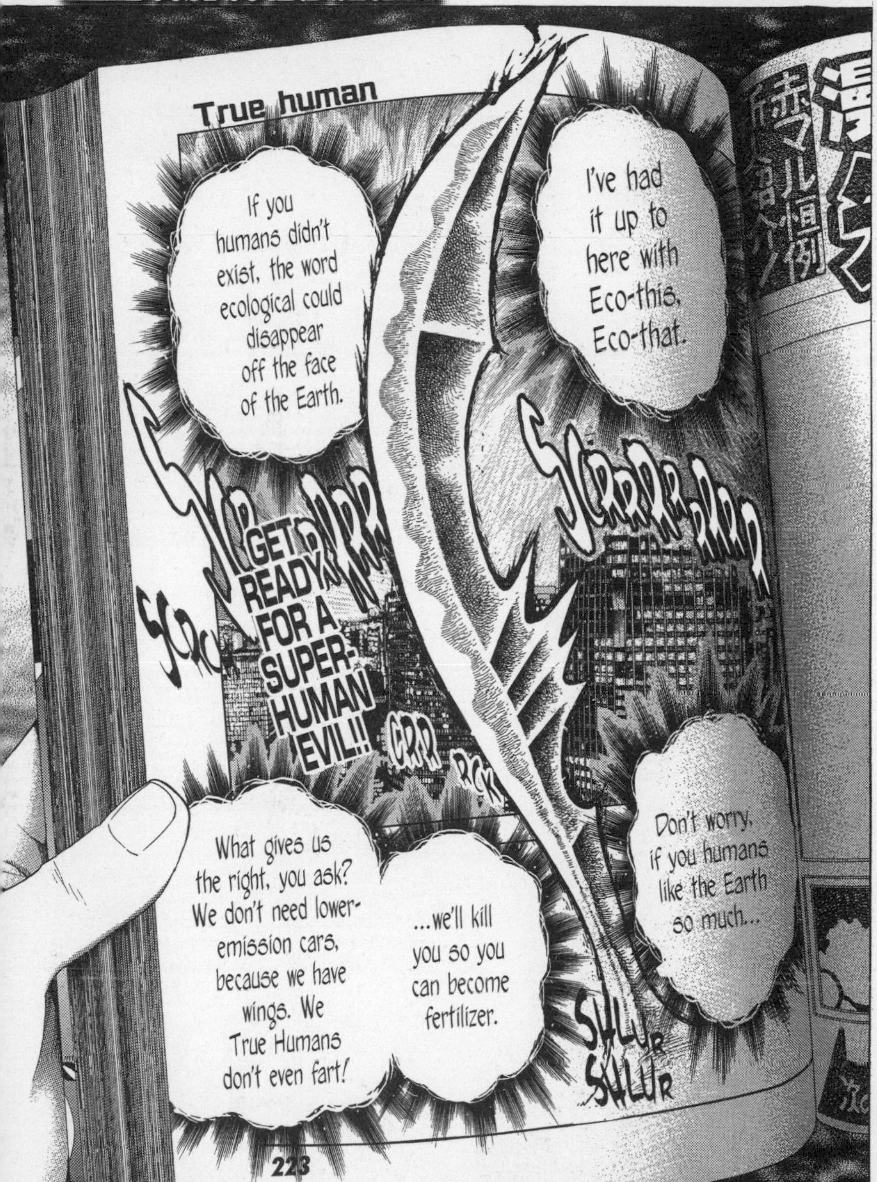

True human
I've had it up to here with Eco-this, Eco-that.
If you humans didn't exist, the word ecological could disappear off the face of the Earth.
GET READY FOR A SUPER-HUMAN EVIL!!
Don't worry, if you humans like the Earth so much...
...we'll kill you so you can become fertilizer.
What gives us the right, you ask? We don't need lower-emission cars, because we have wings. We True Humans don't even fart!
SHLUR SHLUR
223

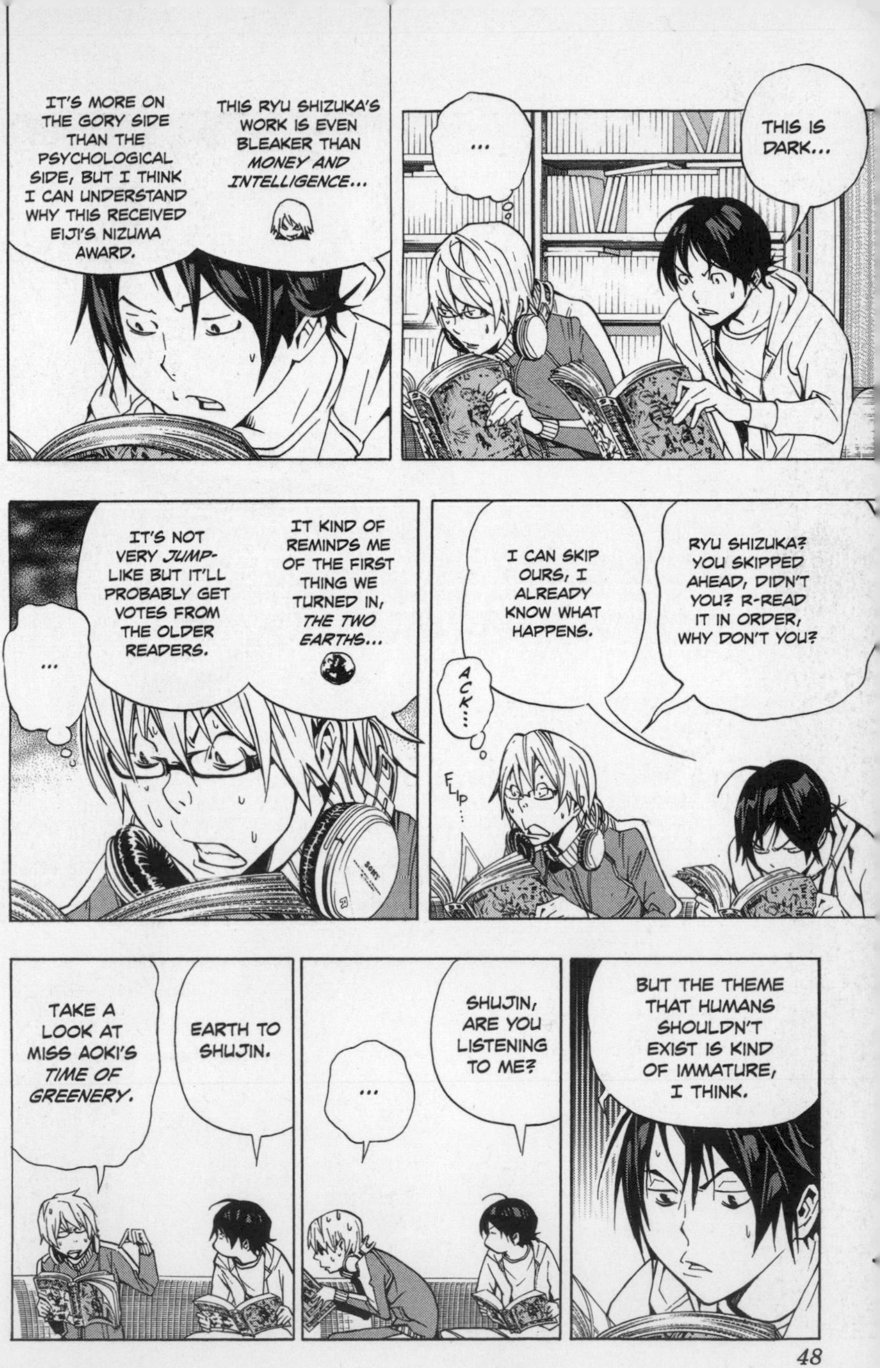
THIS IS DARK...
...
THIS RYU SHIZUKA'S WORK IS EVEN BLEAKER THAN *MONEY AND INTELLIGENCE*...
IT'S MORE ON THE GORY SIDE THAN THE PSYCHOLOGICAL SIDE, BUT I THINK I CAN UNDERSTAND WHY THIS RECEIVED EIJI'S NIZUMA AWARD.
RYU SHIZUKA? YOU SKIPPED AHEAD, DIDN'T YOU? R-READ IT IN ORDER, WHY DON'T YOU?
I CAN SKIP OURS, I ALREADY KNOW WHAT HAPPENS.
ACK...
FLIP...
IT KIND OF REMINDS ME OF THE FIRST THING WE TURNED IN, *THE TWO EARTHS*...
IT'S NOT VERY *JUMP*-LIKE BUT IT'LL PROBABLY GET VOTES FROM THE OLDER READERS.
...
BUT THE THEME THAT HUMANS SHOULDN'T EXIST IS KIND OF IMMATURE, I THINK.
SHUJIN, ARE YOU LISTENING TO ME?
...
EARTH TO SHUJIN.
TAKE A LOOK AT MISS AOKI'S *TIME OF GREENERY*.

READ THIS WAY

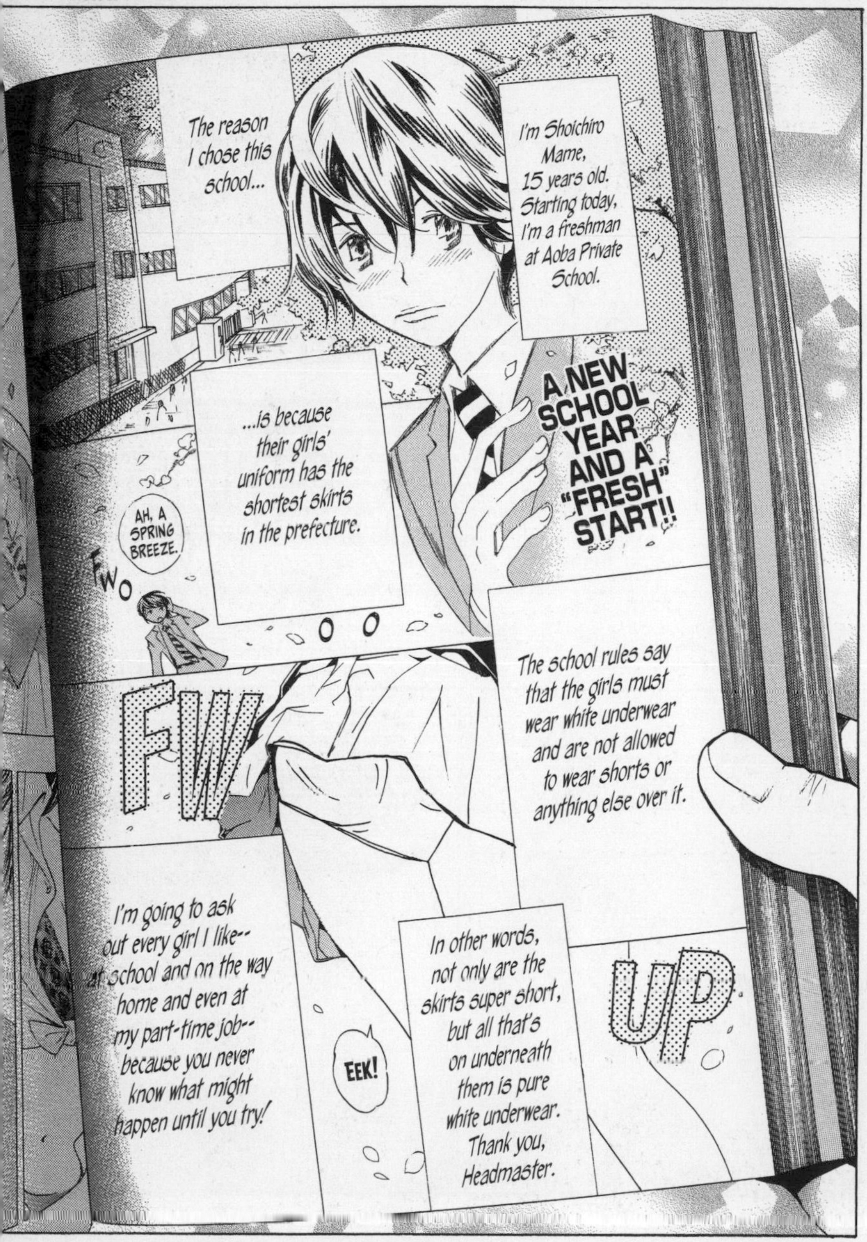
A NEW SCHOOL YEAR AND A "FRESH START"!!
I'm Shoichiro Mame, 15 years old. Starting today, I'm a freshman at Aoba Private School.
The reason I chose this school...
...is because their girls' uniform has the shortest skirts in the prefecture.
AH, A SPRING BREEZE.
FWO
O O
The school rules say that the girls must wear white underwear and are not allowed to wear shorts or anything else over it.
FW
UP
In other words, not only are the skirts super short, but all that's on underneath them is pure white underwear. Thank you, Headmaster.
EEK!
I'm going to ask out every girl I like--at school and on the way home and even at my part-time job--because you never know what might happen until you try!

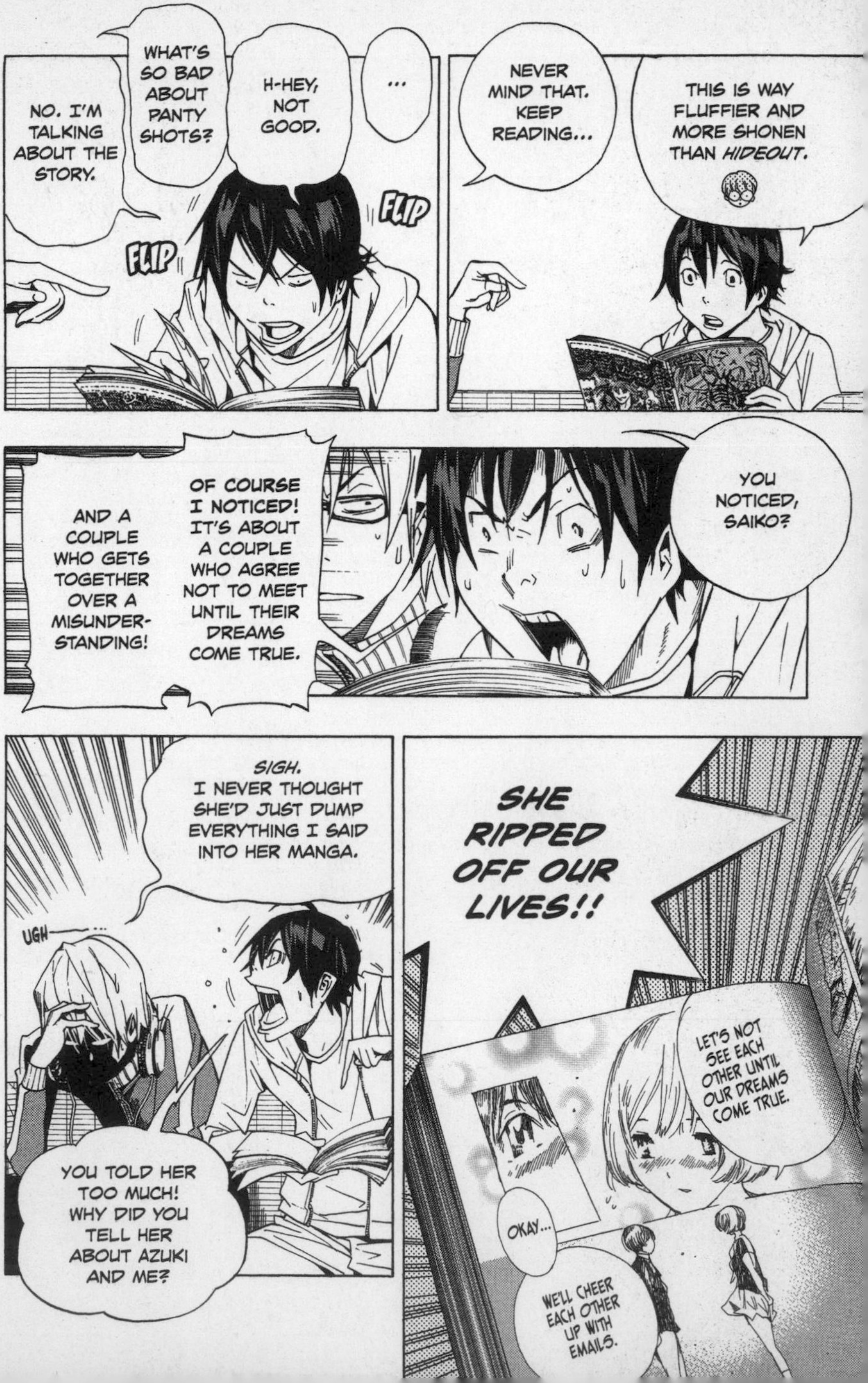

THIS IS WAY FLUFFIER AND MORE SHONEN THAN *HIDEOUT*.
NEVER MIND THAT. KEEP READING...
FLIP
...
H-HEY, NOT GOOD.
WHAT'S SO BAD ABOUT PANTY SHOTS?
NO. I'M TALKING ABOUT THE STORY.
FLIP
YOU NOTICED, SAIKO?
OF COURSE I NOTICED! IT'S ABOUT A COUPLE WHO AGREE NOT TO MEET UNTIL THEIR DREAMS COME TRUE.
AND A COUPLE WHO GETS TOGETHER OVER A MISUNDERSTANDING!
SHE RIPPED OFF OUR LIVES!!
LET'S NOT SEE EACH OTHER UNTIL OUR DREAMS COME TRUE.
OKAY...
WE'LL CHEER EACH OTHER UP WITH EMAILS.
SIGH. I NEVER THOUGHT SHE'D JUST DUMP EVERYTHING I SAID INTO HER MANGA.
UGH—...
YOU TOLD HER TOO MUCH! WHY DID YOU TELL HER ABOUT AZUKI AND ME?

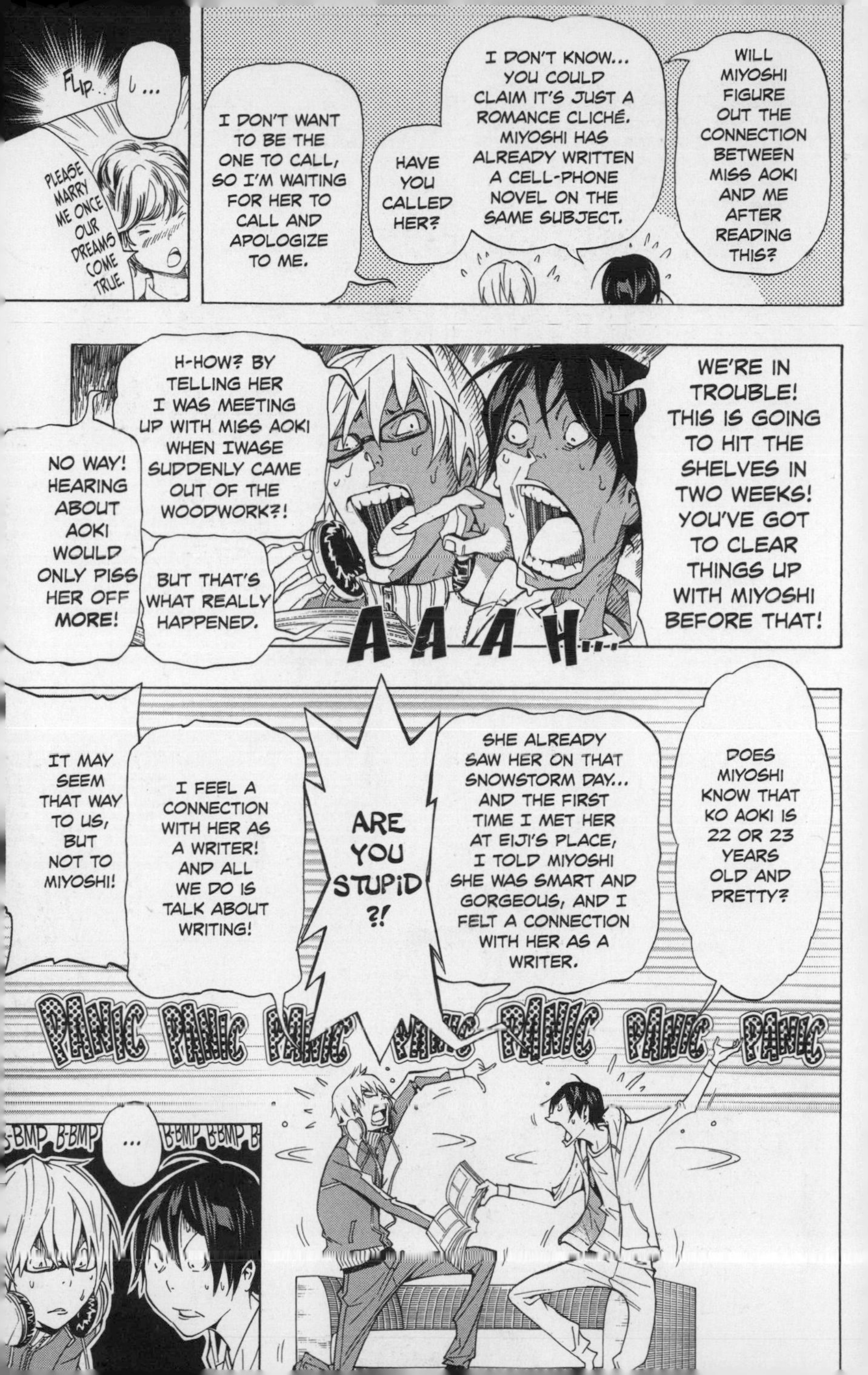
WILL MIYOSHI FIGURE OUT THE CONNECTION BETWEEN MISS AOKI AND ME AFTER READING THIS?
I DON'T KNOW... YOU COULD CLAIM IT'S JUST A ROMANCE CLICHÉ. MIYOSHI HAS ALREADY WRITTEN A CELL-PHONE NOVEL ON THE SAME SUBJECT.
HAVE YOU CALLED HER?
I DON'T WANT TO BE THE ONE TO CALL, SO I'M WAITING FOR HER TO CALL AND APOLOGIZE TO ME.
FLIP...
I ...
PLEASE MARRY ME ONCE OUR DREAMS COME TRUE.
WE'RE IN TROUBLE! THIS IS GOING TO HIT THE SHELVES IN TWO WEEKS! YOU'VE GOT TO CLEAR THINGS UP WITH MIYOSHI BEFORE THAT!
H-HOW? BY TELLING HER I WAS MEETING UP WITH MISS AOKI WHEN IWASE SUDDENLY CAME OUT OF THE WOODWORK?!
NO WAY! HEARING ABOUT AOKI WOULD ONLY PISS HER OFF MORE!
BUT THAT'S WHAT REALLY HAPPENED.
AAAH....
DOES MIYOSHI KNOW THAT KO AOKI IS 22 OR 23 YEARS OLD AND PRETTY?
SHE ALREADY SAW HER ON THAT SNOWSTORM DAY... AND THE FIRST TIME I MET HER AT EIJI'S PLACE, I TOLD MIYOSHI SHE WAS SMART AND GORGEOUS, AND I FELT A CONNECTION WITH HER AS A WRITER.
ARE YOU STUPID ?!
I FEEL A CONNECTION WITH HER AS A WRITER! AND ALL WE DO IS TALK ABOUT WRITING!
IT MAY SEEM THAT WAY TO US, BUT NOT TO MIYOSHI!
PANIC PANIC PANIC PANIC PANIC PANIC PANIC
B-BMP B-BMP B-BMP B-BMP B-
...

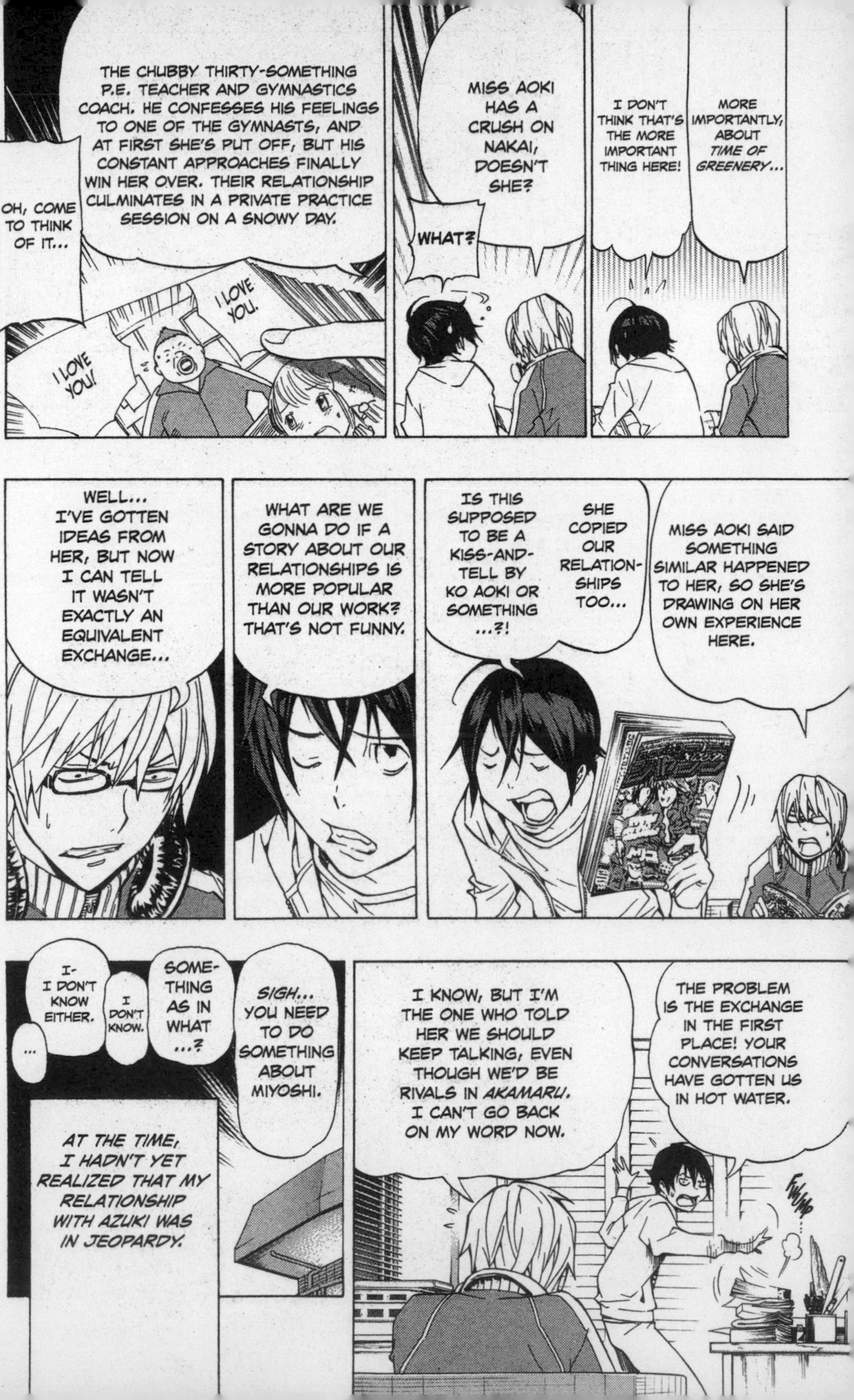
MORE IMPORTANTLY, ABOUT *TIME OF GREENERY*...
I DON'T THINK THAT'S THE MORE IMPORTANT THING HERE!
MISS AOKI HAS A CRUSH ON NAKAI, DOESN'T SHE?
WHAT?
THE CHUBBY THIRTY-SOMETHING P.E. TEACHER AND GYMNASTICS COACH. HE CONFESSES HIS FEELINGS TO ONE OF THE GYMNASTS, AND AT FIRST SHE'S PUT OFF, BUT HIS CONSTANT APPROACHES FINALLY WIN HER OVER. THEIR RELATIONSHIP CULMINATES IN A PRIVATE PRACTICE SESSION ON A SNOWY DAY.
OH, COME TO THINK OF IT...
I LOVE YOU.
I LOVE YOU!
MISS AOKI SAID SOMETHING SIMILAR HAPPENED TO HER, SO SHE'S DRAWING ON HER OWN EXPERIENCE HERE.
SHE COPIED OUR RELATION-SHIPS TOO...
IS THIS SUPPOSED TO BE A KISS-AND-TELL BY KO AOKI OR SOMETHING ...?!
WHAT ARE WE GONNA DO IF A STORY ABOUT OUR RELATIONSHIPS IS MORE POPULAR THAN OUR WORK? THAT'S NOT FUNNY.
WELL... I'VE GOTTEN IDEAS FROM HER, BUT NOW I CAN TELL IT WASN'T EXACTLY AN EQUIVALENT EXCHANGE...
THE PROBLEM IS THE EXCHANGE IN THE FIRST PLACE! YOUR CONVERSATIONS HAVE GOTTEN US IN HOT WATER.
I KNOW, BUT I'M THE ONE WHO TOLD HER WE SHOULD KEEP TALKING, EVEN THOUGH WE'D BE RIVALS IN *AKAMARU*. I CAN'T GO BACK ON MY WORD NOW.
FWUMP
SIGH... YOU NEED TO DO SOMETHING ABOUT MIYOSHI.
SOME-THING AS IN WHAT ...?
I DON'T KNOW.
I- I DON'T KNOW EITHER.
...
AT THE TIME, I HADN'T YET REALIZED THAT MY RELATIONSHIP WITH AZUKI WAS IN JEOPARDY.

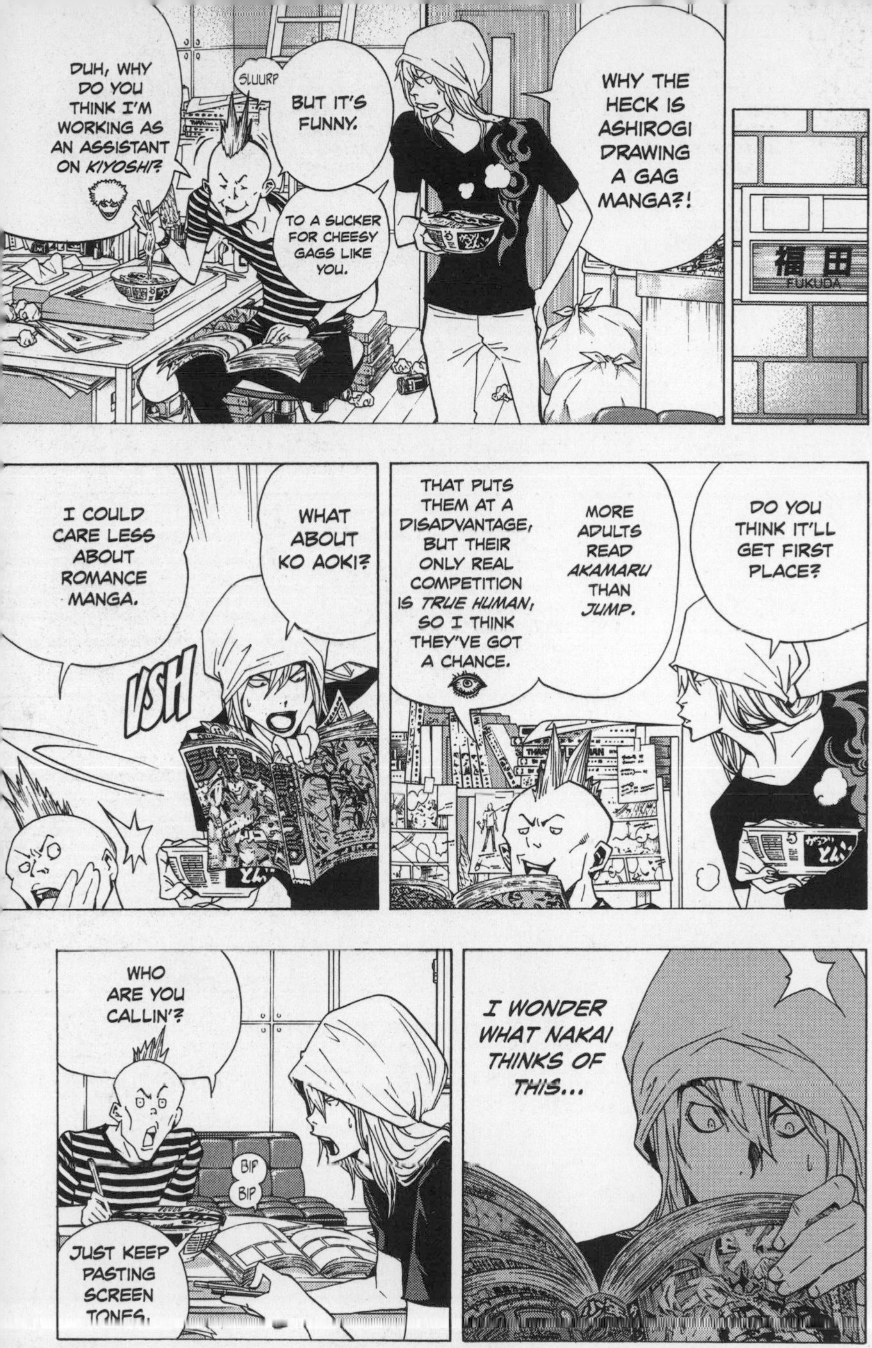
福田
FUKUDA
WHY THE HECK IS ASHIROGI DRAWING A GAG MANGA?!
BUT IT'S FUNNY.
TO A SUCKER FOR CHEESY GAGS LIKE YOU.
SLUURP
DUH, WHY DO YOU THINK I'M WORKING AS AN ASSISTANT ON *KIYOSHI*?
DO YOU THINK IT'LL GET FIRST PLACE?
MORE ADULTS READ *AKAMARU* THAN *JUMP*.
THAT PUTS THEM AT A DISADVANTAGE, BUT THEIR ONLY REAL COMPETITION IS *TRUE HUMAN*, SO I THINK THEY'VE GOT A CHANCE.
WHAT ABOUT KO AOKI?
I COULD CARE LESS ABOUT ROMANCE MANGA.
VSH
I WONDER WHAT NAKAI THINKS OF THIS...
WHO ARE YOU CALLIN'?
BIP
BIP
JUST KEEP PASTING SCREEN TONES.

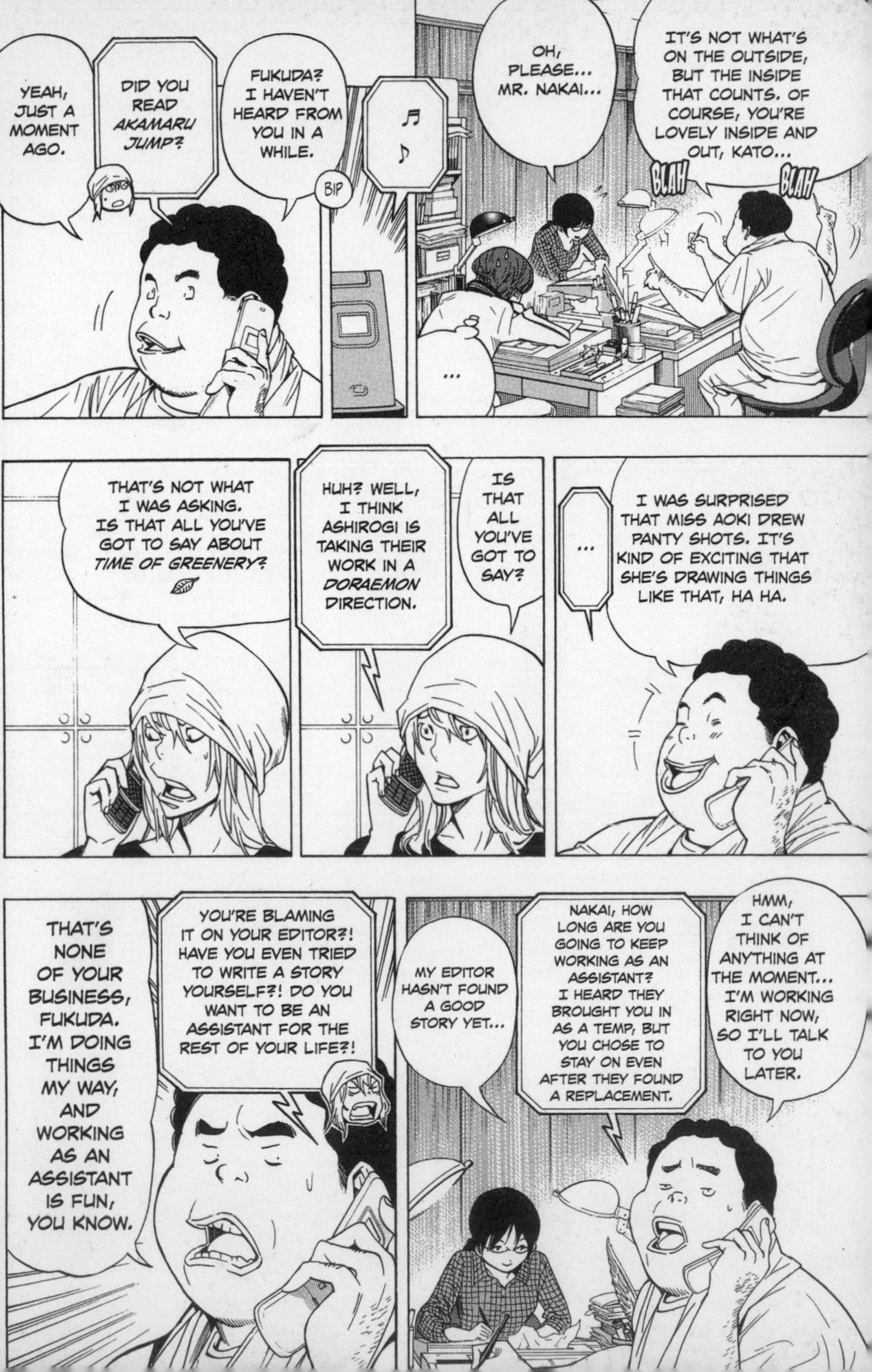

IT'S NOT WHAT'S ON THE OUTSIDE, BUT THE INSIDE THAT COUNTS. OF COURSE, YOU'RE LOVELY INSIDE AND OUT, KATO...
BLAH
BLAH
OH, PLEASE... MR. NAKAI...
...
♬ ♪
BIP
FUKUDA? I HAVEN'T HEARD FROM YOU IN A WHILE.
DID YOU READ *AKAMARU JUMP*?
YEAH, JUST A MOMENT AGO.
I WAS SURPRISED THAT MISS AOKI DREW PANTY SHOTS. IT'S KIND OF EXCITING THAT SHE'S DRAWING THINGS LIKE THAT, HA HA.
...
IS THAT ALL YOU'VE GOT TO SAY?
HUH? WELL, I THINK ASHIROGI IS TAKING THEIR WORK IN A *DORAEMON* DIRECTION.
THAT'S NOT WHAT I WAS ASKING. IS THAT ALL YOU'VE GOT TO SAY ABOUT *TIME OF GREENERY*?
HMM, I CAN'T THINK OF ANYTHING AT THE MOMENT... I'M WORKING RIGHT NOW, SO I'LL TALK TO YOU LATER.
NAKAI, HOW LONG ARE YOU GOING TO KEEP WORKING AS AN ASSISTANT? I HEARD THEY BROUGHT YOU IN AS A TEMP, BUT YOU CHOSE TO STAY ON EVEN AFTER THEY FOUND A REPLACEMENT.
MY EDITOR HASN'T FOUND A GOOD STORY YET...
YOU'RE BLAMING IT ON YOUR EDITOR?! HAVE YOU EVEN TRIED TO WRITE A STORY YOURSELF?! DO YOU WANT TO BE AN ASSISTANT FOR THE REST OF YOUR LIFE?!
THAT'S NONE OF YOUR BUSINESS, FUKUDA. I'M DOING THINGS MY WAY, AND WORKING AS AN ASSISTANT IS FUN, YOU KNOW.

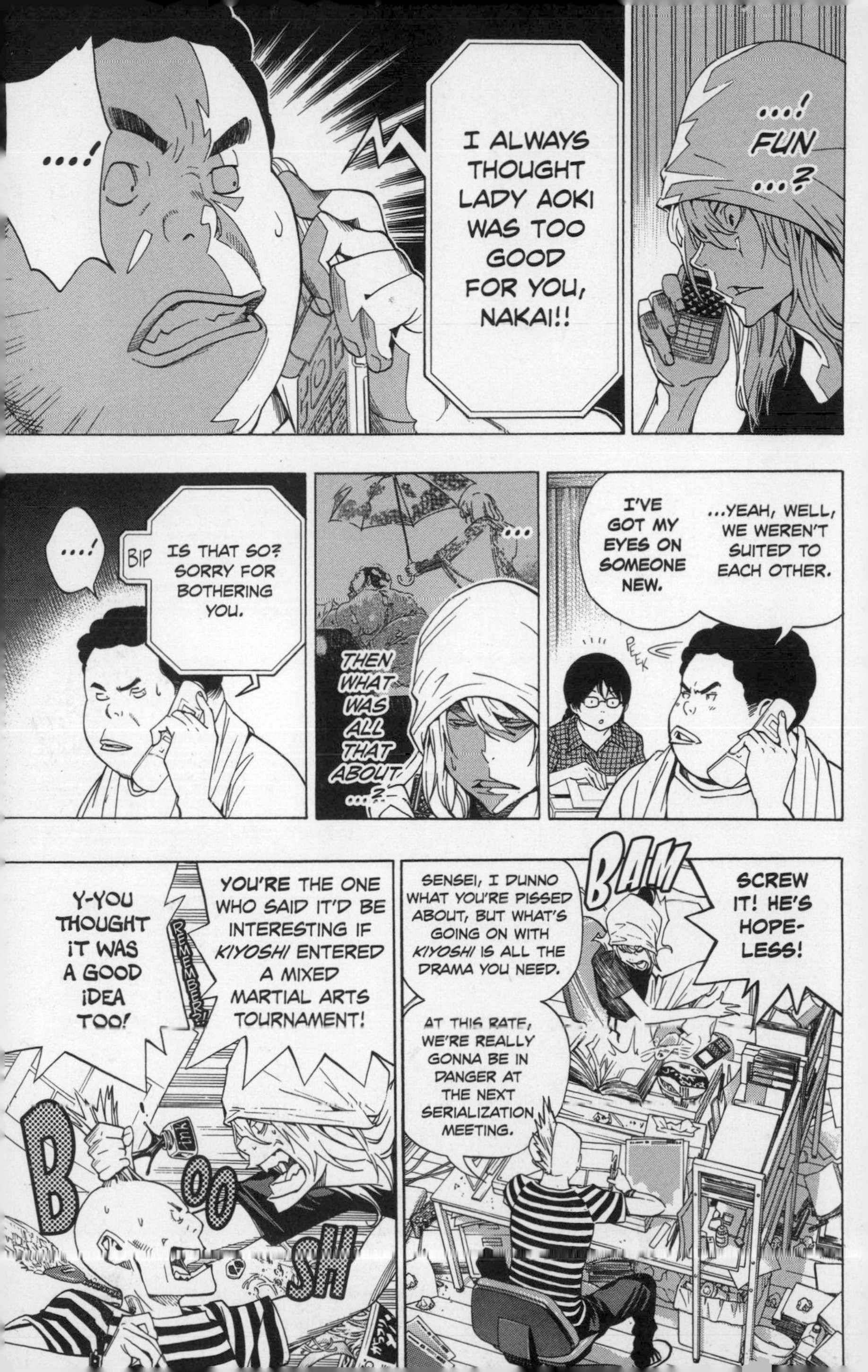
...! FUN ...?
I ALWAYS THOUGHT LADY AOKI WAS TOO GOOD FOR YOU, NAKAI!!
...!
...YEAH, WELL, WE WEREN'T SUITED TO EACH OTHER.
I'VE GOT MY EYES ON SOMEONE NEW.
PEEK
...
THEN WHAT WAS ALL THAT ABOUT ...?
BIP
IS THAT SO? SORRY FOR BOTHERING YOU.
...!
BAM
SCREW IT! HE'S HOPE-LESS!
SENSEI, I DUNNO WHAT YOU'RE PISSED ABOUT, BUT WHAT'S GOING ON WITH KIYOSHI IS ALL THE DRAMA YOU NEED.
AT THIS RATE, WE'RE REALLY GONNA BE IN DANGER AT THE NEXT SERIALIZATION MEETING.
YOU'RE THE ONE WHO SAID IT'D BE INTERESTING IF KIYOSHI ENTERED A MIXED MARTIAL ARTS TOURNAMENT!
REMEMBER?!
Y-YOU THOUGHT IT WAS A GOOD IDEA TOO!
BOOSH

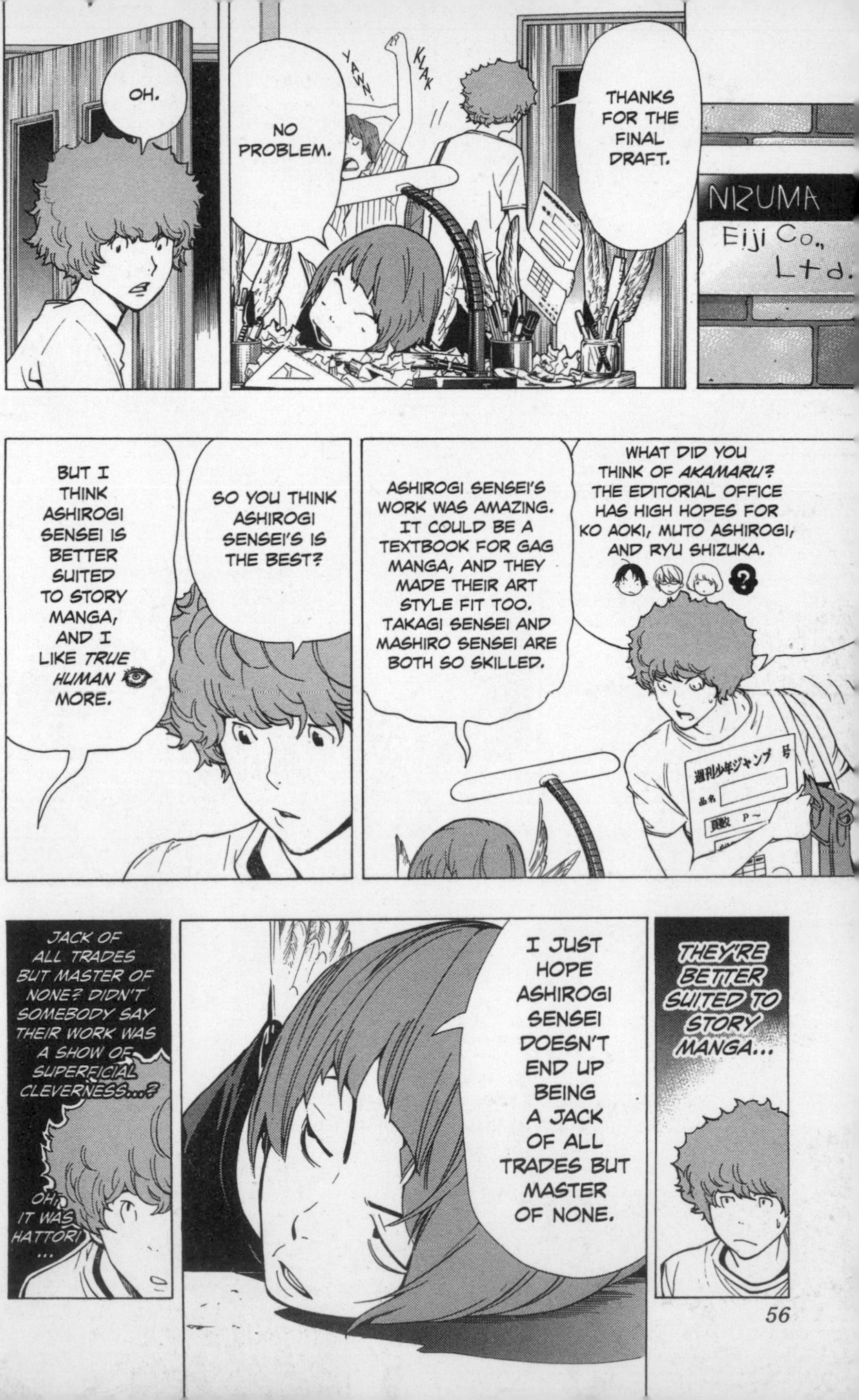
NIZUMA Eiji Co., Ltd.
THANKS FOR THE FINAL DRAFT.
KLAK
YAWN
NO PROBLEM.
OH.
WHAT DID YOU THINK OF *AKAMARU*? THE EDITORIAL OFFICE HAS HIGH HOPES FOR KO AOKI, MUTO ASHIROGI, AND RYU SHIZUKA.
ASHIROGI SENSEI'S WORK WAS AMAZING. IT COULD BE A TEXTBOOK FOR GAG MANGA, AND THEY MADE THEIR ART STYLE FIT TOO. TAKAGI SENSEI AND MASHIRO SENSEI ARE BOTH SO SKILLED.
週刊少年ジャンプ 号
品名
頁数 P~
SO YOU THINK ASHIROGI SENSEI'S IS THE BEST?
BUT I THINK ASHIROGI SENSEI IS BETTER SUITED TO STORY MANGA, AND I LIKE *TRUE HUMAN* MORE.
THEY'RE BETTER SUITED TO STORY MANGA...
I JUST HOPE ASHIROGI SENSEI DOESN'T END UP BEING A JACK OF ALL TRADES BUT MASTER OF NONE.
JACK OF ALL TRADES BUT MASTER OF NONE? DIDN'T SOMEBODY SAY THEIR WORK WAS A SHOW OF SUPERFICIAL CLEVERNESS...?
OH, IT WAS HATTORI...

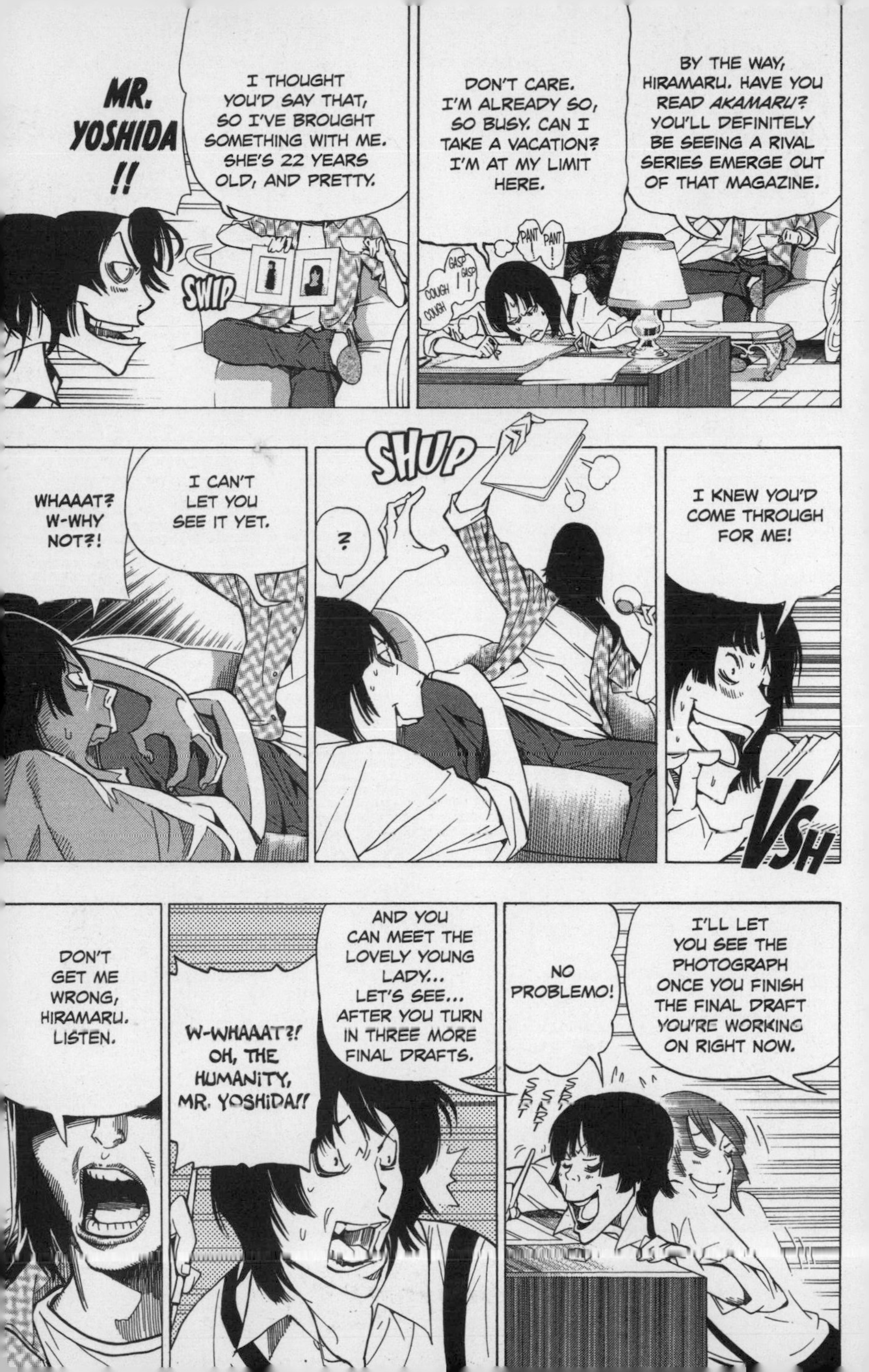
BY THE WAY, HIRAMARU. HAVE YOU READ *AKAMARU*? YOU'LL DEFINITELY BE SEEING A RIVAL SERIES EMERGE OUT OF THAT MAGAZINE.
PANT PANT
DON'T CARE. I'M ALREADY SO, SO BUSY. CAN I TAKE A VACATION? I'M AT MY LIMIT HERE.
GASP GASP
COUGH COUGH
I THOUGHT YOU'D SAY THAT, SO I'VE BROUGHT SOMETHING WITH ME. SHE'S 22 YEARS OLD, AND PRETTY.
MR. YOSHIDA!!
SWIP
I KNEW YOU'D COME THROUGH FOR ME!
VSH
SHUP
?
I CAN'T LET YOU SEE IT YET.
WHAAAT? W-WHY NOT?!
I'LL LET YOU SEE THE PHOTOGRAPH ONCE YOU FINISH THE FINAL DRAFT YOU'RE WORKING ON RIGHT NOW.
NO PROBLEMO!
SKRT SKRT SKRT
AND YOU CAN MEET THE LOVELY YOUNG LADY... LET'S SEE... AFTER YOU TURN IN THREE MORE FINAL DRAFTS.
W-WHAAAT?! OH, THE HUMANITY, MR. YOSHIDA!!
DON'T GET ME WRONG, HIRAMARU. LISTEN.

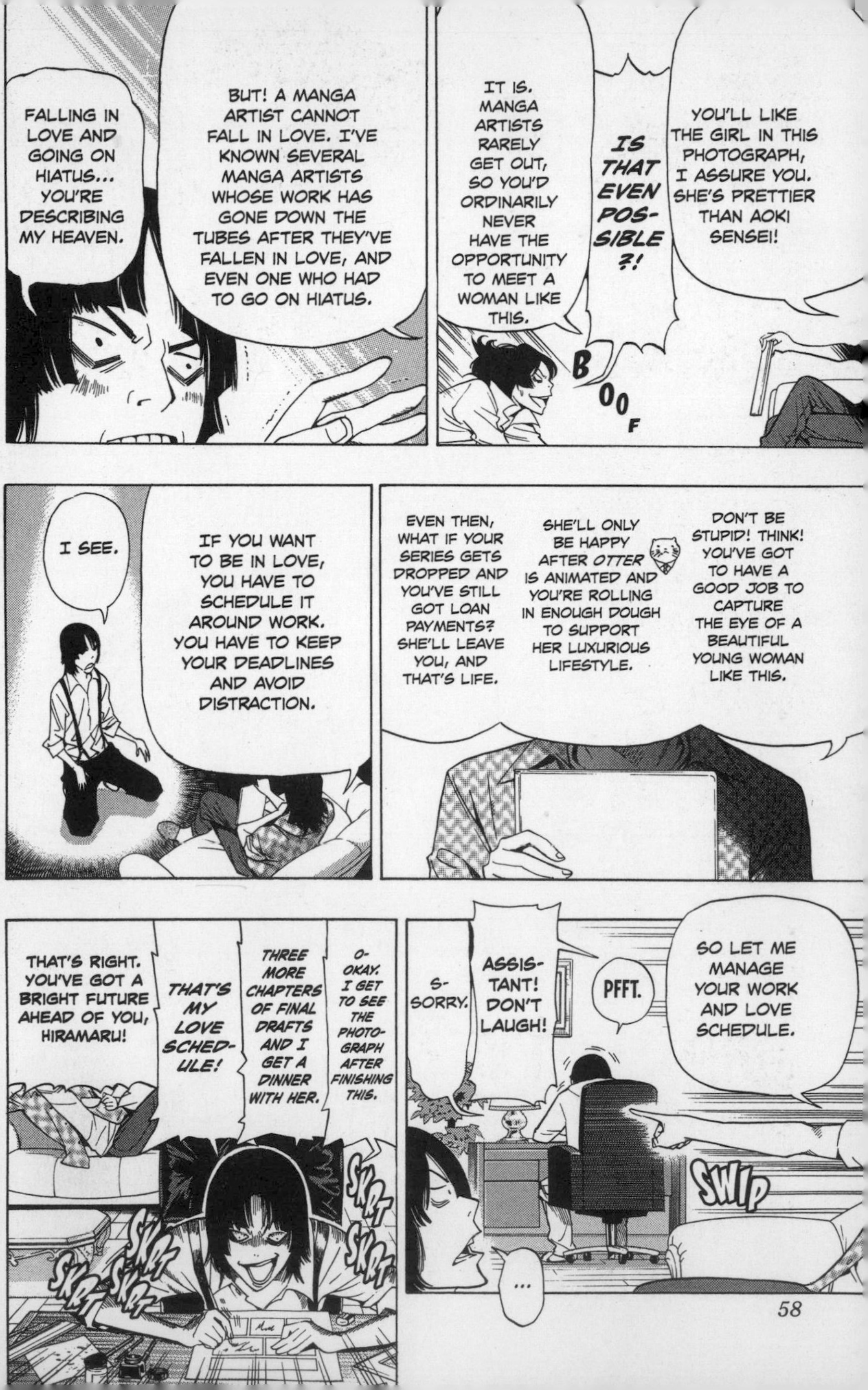

YOU'LL LIKE THE GIRL IN THIS PHOTOGRAPH, I ASSURE YOU. SHE'S PRETTIER THAN AOKI SENSEI!
IS THAT EVEN POS-SIBLE ?!
IT IS. MANGA ARTISTS RARELY GET OUT, SO YOU'D ORDINARILY NEVER HAVE THE OPPORTUNITY TO MEET A WOMAN LIKE THIS.
BOOF
BUT! A MANGA ARTIST CANNOT FALL IN LOVE. I'VE KNOWN SEVERAL MANGA ARTISTS WHOSE WORK HAS GONE DOWN THE TUBES AFTER THEY'VE FALLEN IN LOVE, AND EVEN ONE WHO HAD TO GO ON HIATUS.
FALLING IN LOVE AND GOING ON HIATUS... YOU'RE DESCRIBING MY HEAVEN.
DON'T BE STUPID! THINK! YOU'VE GOT TO HAVE A GOOD JOB TO CAPTURE THE EYE OF A BEAUTIFUL YOUNG WOMAN LIKE THIS.
SHE'LL ONLY BE HAPPY AFTER OTTER IS ANIMATED AND YOU'RE ROLLING IN ENOUGH DOUGH TO SUPPORT HER LUXURIOUS LIFESTYLE.
EVEN THEN, WHAT IF YOUR SERIES GETS DROPPED AND YOU'VE STILL GOT LOAN PAYMENTS? SHE'LL LEAVE YOU, AND THAT'S LIFE.
IF YOU WANT TO BE IN LOVE, YOU HAVE TO SCHEDULE IT AROUND WORK. YOU HAVE TO KEEP YOUR DEADLINES AND AVOID DISTRACTION.
I SEE.
SO LET ME MANAGE YOUR WORK AND LOVE SCHEDULE.
PFFT.
ASSIS-TANT! DON'T LAUGH!
S-SORRY.
SWIP
...
O-OKAY. I GET TO SEE THE PHOTO-GRAPH AFTER FINISHING THIS.
THREE MORE CHAPTERS OF FINAL DRAFTS AND I GET A DINNER WITH HER.
THAT'S MY LOVE SCHED-ULE!
THAT'S RIGHT. YOU'VE GOT A BRIGHT FUTURE AHEAD OF YOU, HIRAMARU!
SKRT SKRT SKRT SKRT SKRT SKRT

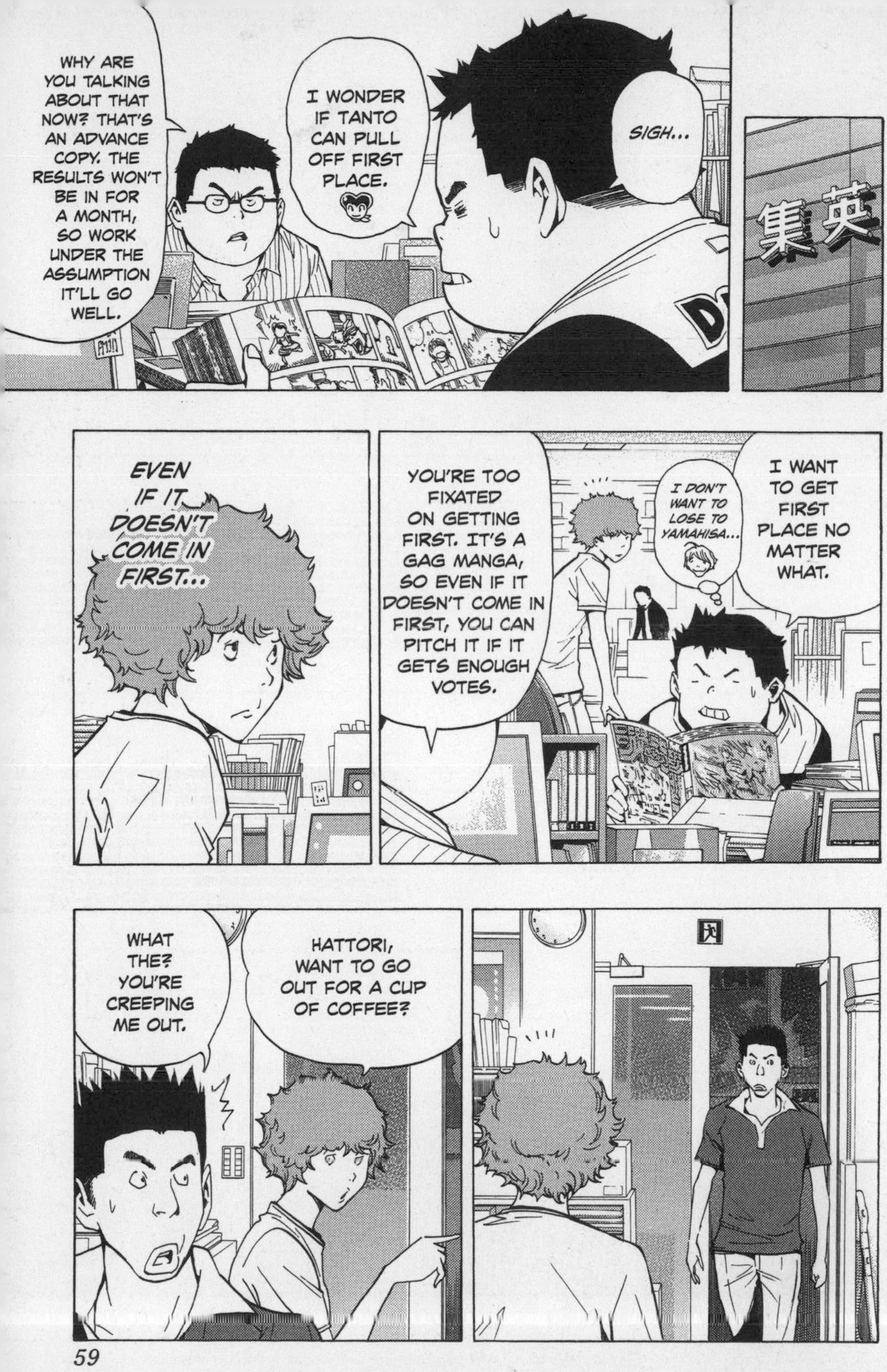
集英
SIGH...
I WONDER IF TANTO CAN PULL OFF FIRST PLACE.
WHY ARE YOU TALKING ABOUT THAT NOW? THAT'S AN ADVANCE COPY. THE RESULTS WON'T BE IN FOR A MONTH, SO WORK UNDER THE ASSUMPTION IT'LL GO WELL.
I WANT TO GET FIRST PLACE NO MATTER WHAT.
I DON'T WANT TO LOSE TO YAMAHISA...
YOU'RE TOO FIXATED ON GETTING FIRST. IT'S A GAG MANGA, SO EVEN IF IT DOESN'T COME IN FIRST, YOU CAN PITCH IT IF IT GETS ENOUGH VOTES.
EVEN IF IT DOESN'T COME IN FIRST...
HATTORI, WANT TO GO OUT FOR A CUP OF COFFEE?
WHAT THE? YOU'RE CREEPING ME OUT.

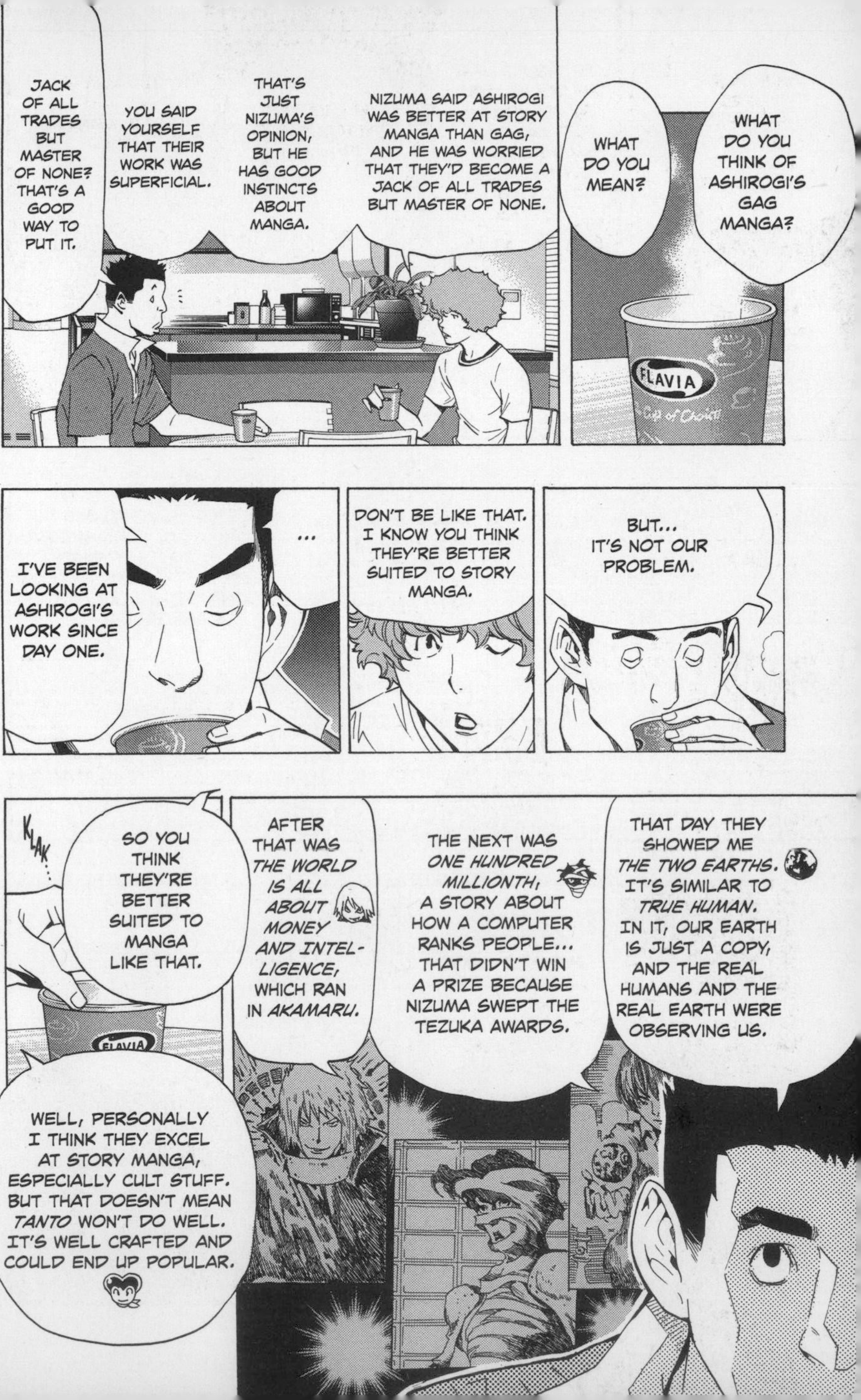
WHAT DO YOU THINK OF ASHIROGI'S GAG MANGA?
WHAT DO YOU MEAN?
NIZUMA SAID ASHIROGI WAS BETTER AT STORY MANGA THAN GAG, AND HE WAS WORRIED THAT THEY'D BECOME A JACK OF ALL TRADES BUT MASTER OF NONE.
THAT'S JUST NIZUMA'S OPINION, BUT HE HAS GOOD INSTINCTS ABOUT MANGA.
YOU SAID YOURSELF THAT THEIR WORK WAS SUPERFICIAL.
JACK OF ALL TRADES BUT MASTER OF NONE? THAT'S A GOOD WAY TO PUT IT.
BUT... IT'S NOT OUR PROBLEM.
DON'T BE LIKE THAT. I KNOW YOU THINK THEY'RE BETTER SUITED TO STORY MANGA.
...
I'VE BEEN LOOKING AT ASHIROGI'S WORK SINCE DAY ONE.
THAT DAY THEY SHOWED ME *THE TWO EARTHS*. IT'S SIMILAR TO *TRUE HUMAN*. IN IT, OUR EARTH IS JUST A COPY, AND THE REAL HUMANS AND THE REAL EARTH WERE OBSERVING US.
THE NEXT WAS *ONE HUNDRED MILLIONTH*, A STORY ABOUT HOW A COMPUTER RANKS PEOPLE... THAT DIDN'T WIN A PRIZE BECAUSE NIZUMA SWEPT THE TEZUKA AWARDS.
AFTER THAT WAS *THE WORLD IS ALL ABOUT MONEY AND INTELLIGENCE*, WHICH RAN IN *AKAMARU*.
SO YOU THINK THEY'RE BETTER SUITED TO MANGA LIKE THAT.
KLAK
WELL, PERSONALLY I THINK THEY EXCEL AT STORY MANGA, ESPECIALLY CULT STUFF. BUT THAT DOESN'T MEAN *TANTO* WON'T DO WELL. IT'S WELL CRAFTED AND COULD END UP POPULAR.

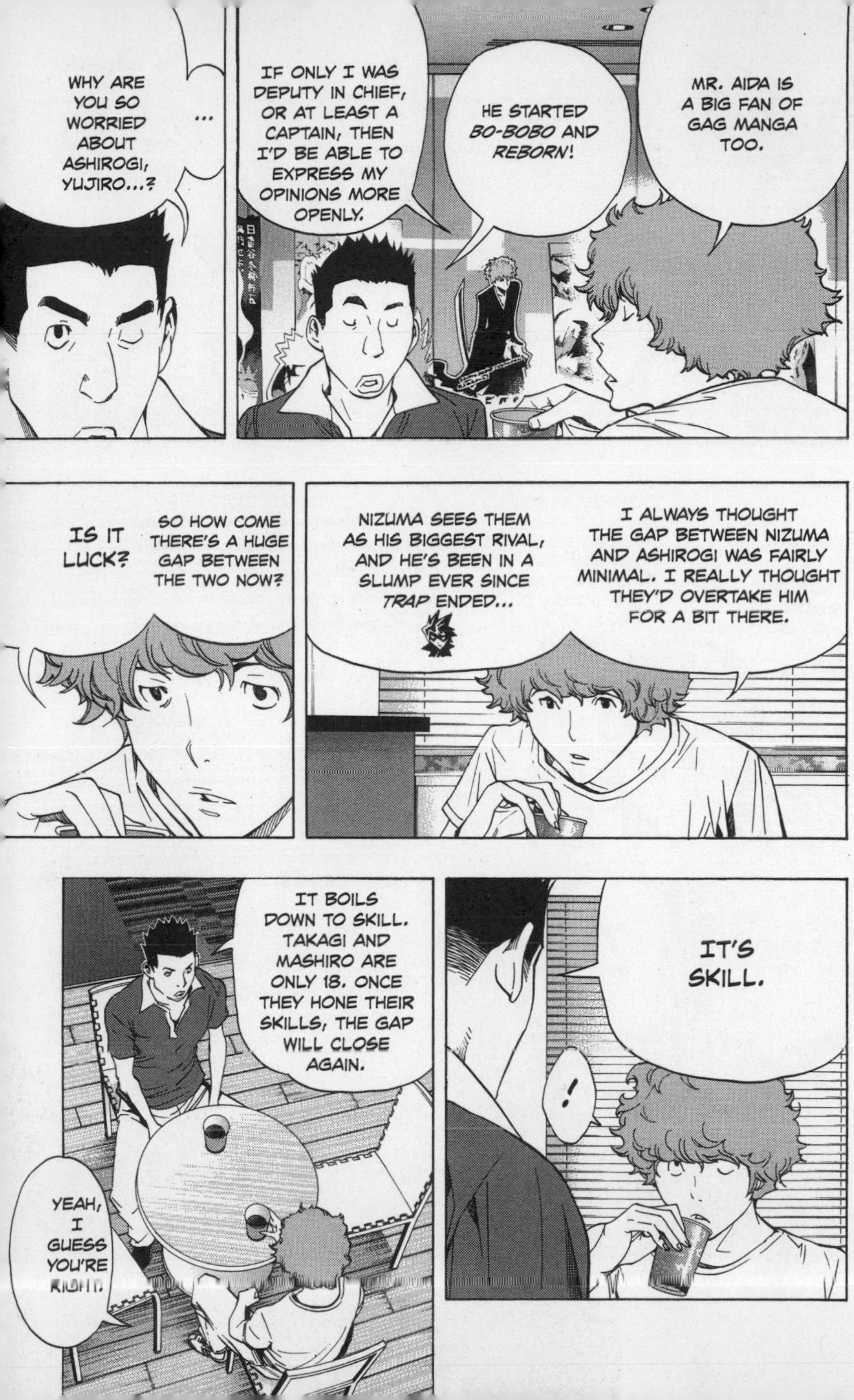
MR. AIDA IS A BIG FAN OF GAG MANGA TOO.
HE STARTED *BO-BOBO* AND *REBORN*!
IF ONLY I WAS DEPUTY IN CHIEF, OR AT LEAST A CAPTAIN, THEN I'D BE ABLE TO EXPRESS MY OPINIONS MORE OPENLY.
...
WHY ARE YOU SO WORRIED ABOUT ASHIROGI, YUJIRO...?
I ALWAYS THOUGHT THE GAP BETWEEN NIZUMA AND ASHIROGI WAS FAIRLY MINIMAL. I REALLY THOUGHT THEY'D OVERTAKE HIM FOR A BIT THERE.
NIZUMA SEES THEM AS HIS BIGGEST RIVAL, AND HE'S BEEN IN A SLUMP EVER SINCE *TRAP* ENDED...
SO HOW COME THERE'S A HUGE GAP BETWEEN THE TWO NOW?
IS IT LUCK?
IT'S SKILL.
!
IT BOILS DOWN TO SKILL. TAKAGI AND MASHIRO ARE ONLY 18. ONCE THEY HONE THEIR SKILLS, THE GAP WILL CLOSE AGAIN.
YEAH, I GUESS YOU'RE RIGHT.

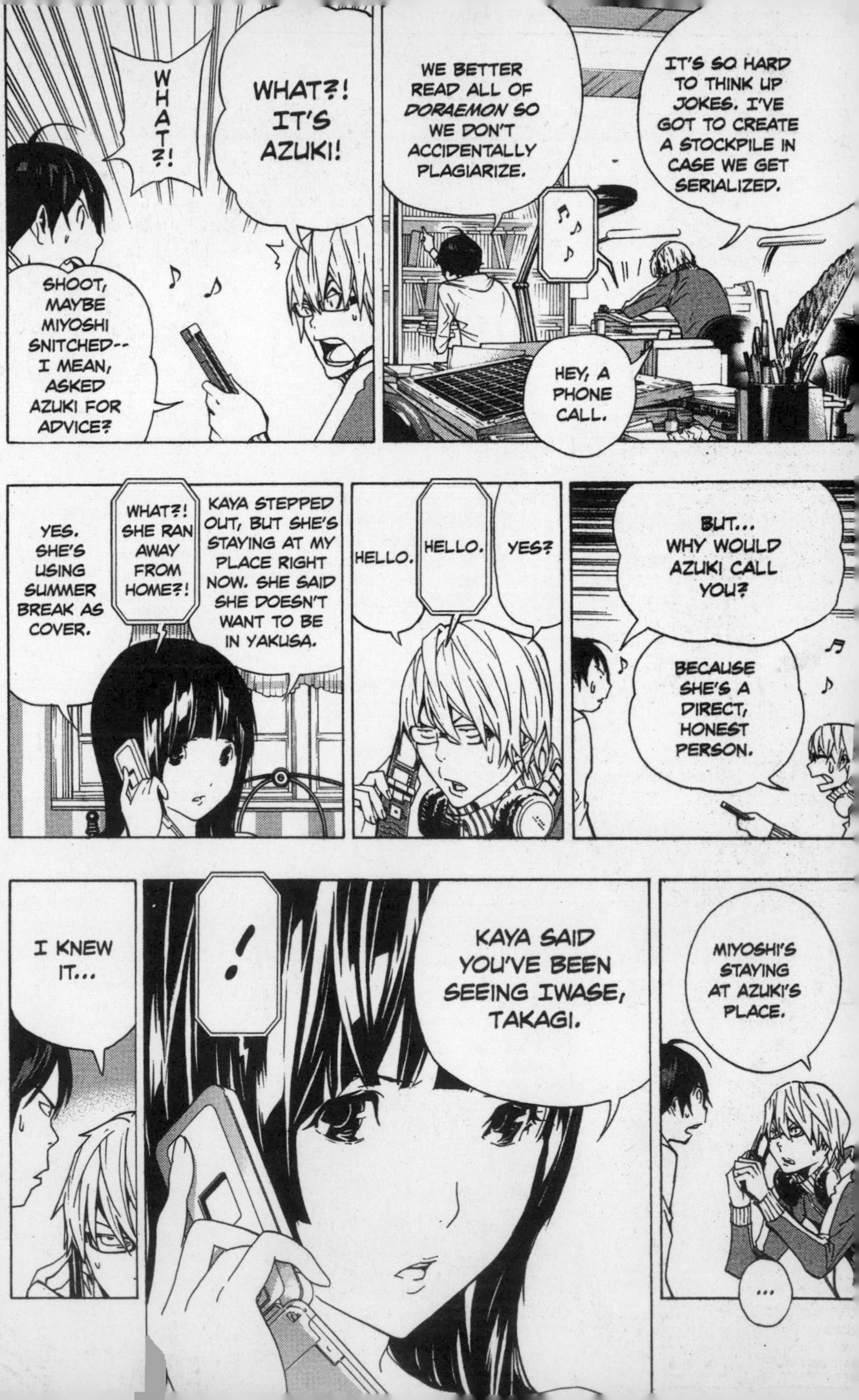
IT'S SO HARD TO THINK UP JOKES. I'VE GOT TO CREATE A STOCKPILE IN CASE WE GET SERIALIZED.
WE BETTER READ ALL OF *DORAEMON* SO WE DON'T ACCIDENTALLY PLAGIARIZE.
HEY, A PHONE CALL.
WHAT?! IT'S AZUKI!
WHAT?!
SHOOT, MAYBE MIYOSHI SNITCHED-- I MEAN, ASKED AZUKI FOR ADVICE?
BUT... WHY WOULD AZUKI CALL YOU?
BECAUSE SHE'S A DIRECT, HONEST PERSON.
YES?
HELLO.
HELLO.
KAYA STEPPED OUT, BUT SHE'S STAYING AT MY PLACE RIGHT NOW. SHE SAID SHE DOESN'T WANT TO BE IN YAKUSA.
WHAT?! SHE RAN AWAY FROM HOME?!
YES. SHE'S USING SUMMER BREAK AS COVER.
MIYOSHI'S STAYING AT AZUKI'S PLACE.
...
KAYA SAID YOU'VE BEEN SEEING IWASE, TAKAGI.
!
I KNEW IT...

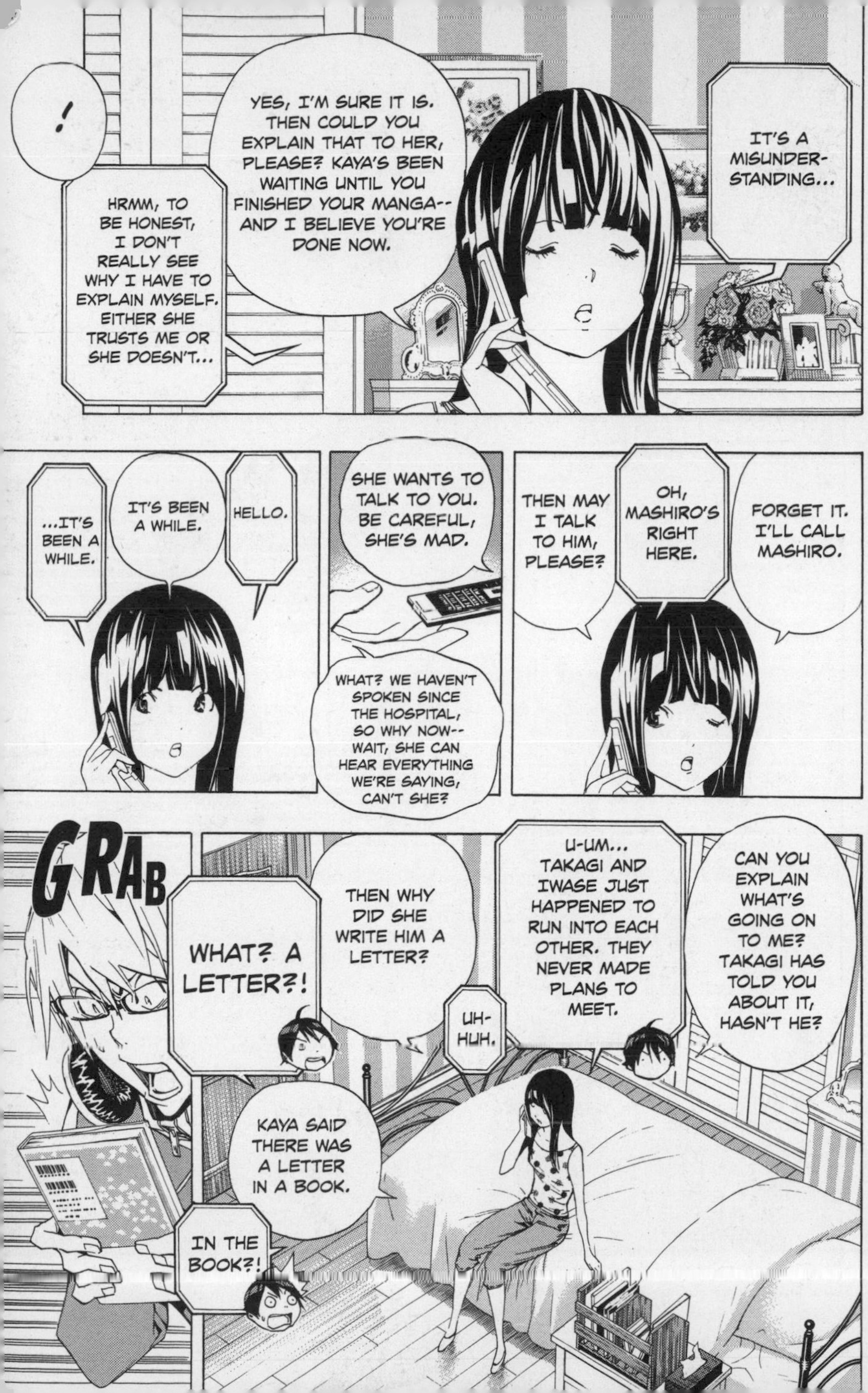
IT'S A MISUNDER-STANDING...
YES, I'M SURE IT IS. THEN COULD YOU EXPLAIN THAT TO HER, PLEASE? KAYA'S BEEN WAITING UNTIL YOU FINISHED YOUR MANGA-- AND I BELIEVE YOU'RE DONE NOW.
!
HRMM, TO BE HONEST, I DON'T REALLY SEE WHY I HAVE TO EXPLAIN MYSELF. EITHER SHE TRUSTS ME OR SHE DOESN'T...
FORGET IT. I'LL CALL MASHIRO.
OH, MASHIRO'S RIGHT HERE.
THEN MAY I TALK TO HIM, PLEASE?
SHE WANTS TO TALK TO YOU. BE CAREFUL, SHE'S MAD.
WHAT? WE HAVEN'T SPOKEN SINCE THE HOSPITAL, SO WHY NOW-- WAIT, SHE CAN HEAR EVERYTHING WE'RE SAYING, CAN'T SHE?
HELLO.
IT'S BEEN A WHILE.
...IT'S BEEN A WHILE.
CAN YOU EXPLAIN WHAT'S GOING ON TO ME? TAKAGI HAS TOLD YOU ABOUT IT, HASN'T HE?
U-UM... TAKAGI AND IWASE JUST HAPPENED TO RUN INTO EACH OTHER. THEY NEVER MADE PLANS TO MEET.
UH-HUH.
THEN WHY DID SHE WRITE HIM A LETTER?
KAYA SAID THERE WAS A LETTER IN A BOOK.
GRAB
WHAT? A LETTER?!
IN THE BOOK?!

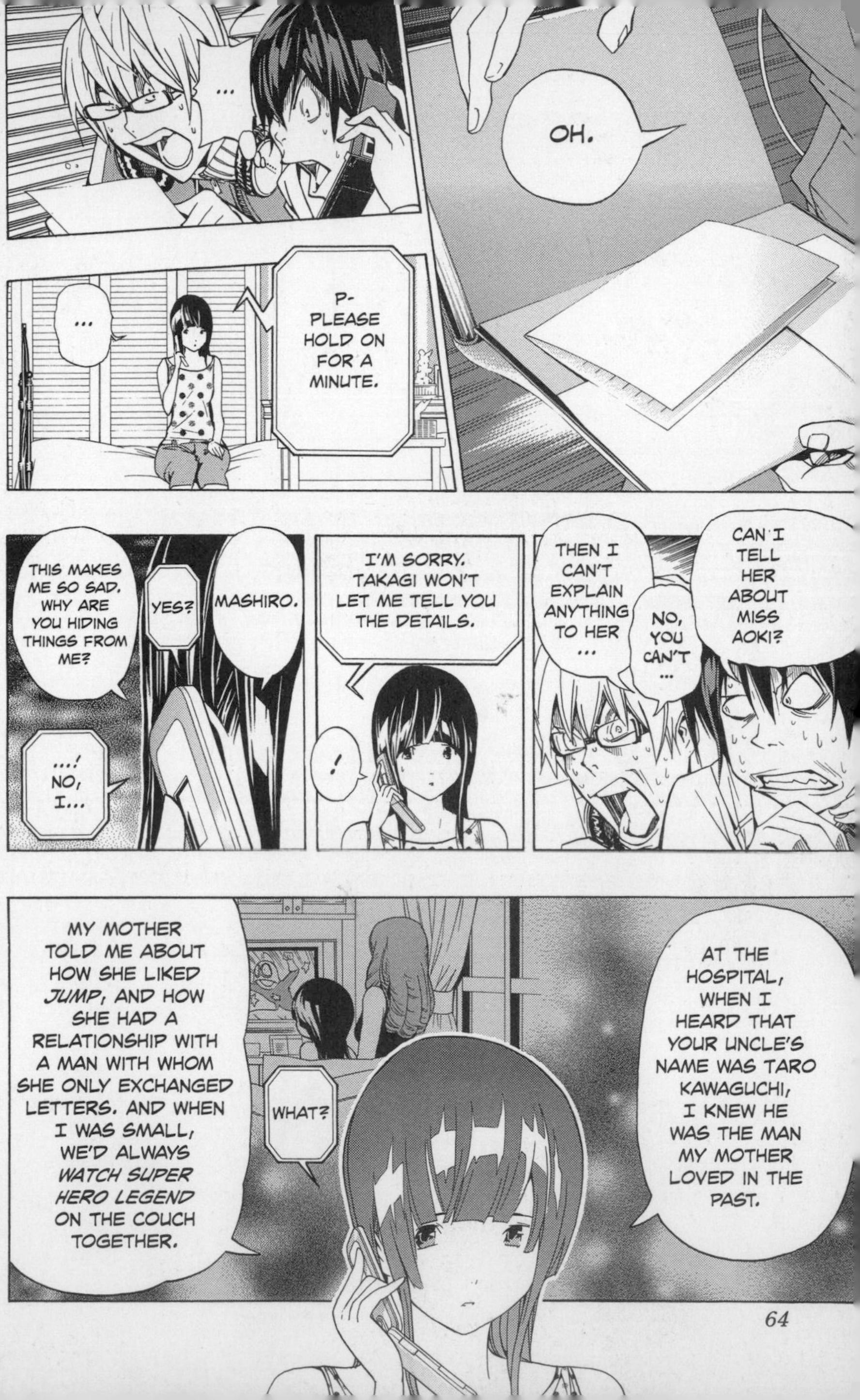
OH.
...
P- PLEASE HOLD ON FOR A MINUTE.
...
CAN I TELL HER ABOUT MISS AOKI?
THEN I CAN'T EXPLAIN ANYTHING TO HER ...
NO, YOU CAN'T ...
I'M SORRY. TAKAGI WON'T LET ME TELL YOU THE DETAILS.
!
MASHIRO.
YES?
THIS MAKES ME SO SAD. WHY ARE YOU HIDING THINGS FROM ME?
...! NO, I...
AT THE HOSPITAL, WHEN I HEARD THAT YOUR UNCLE'S NAME WAS TARO KAWAGUCHI, I KNEW HE WAS THE MAN MY MOTHER LOVED IN THE PAST.
WHAT?
MY MOTHER TOLD ME ABOUT HOW SHE LIKED *JUMP*, AND HOW SHE HAD A RELATIONSHIP WITH A MAN WITH WHOM SHE ONLY EXCHANGED LETTERS. AND WHEN I WAS SMALL, WE'D ALWAYS WATCH *SUPER HERO LEGEND* ON THE COUCH TOGETHER.

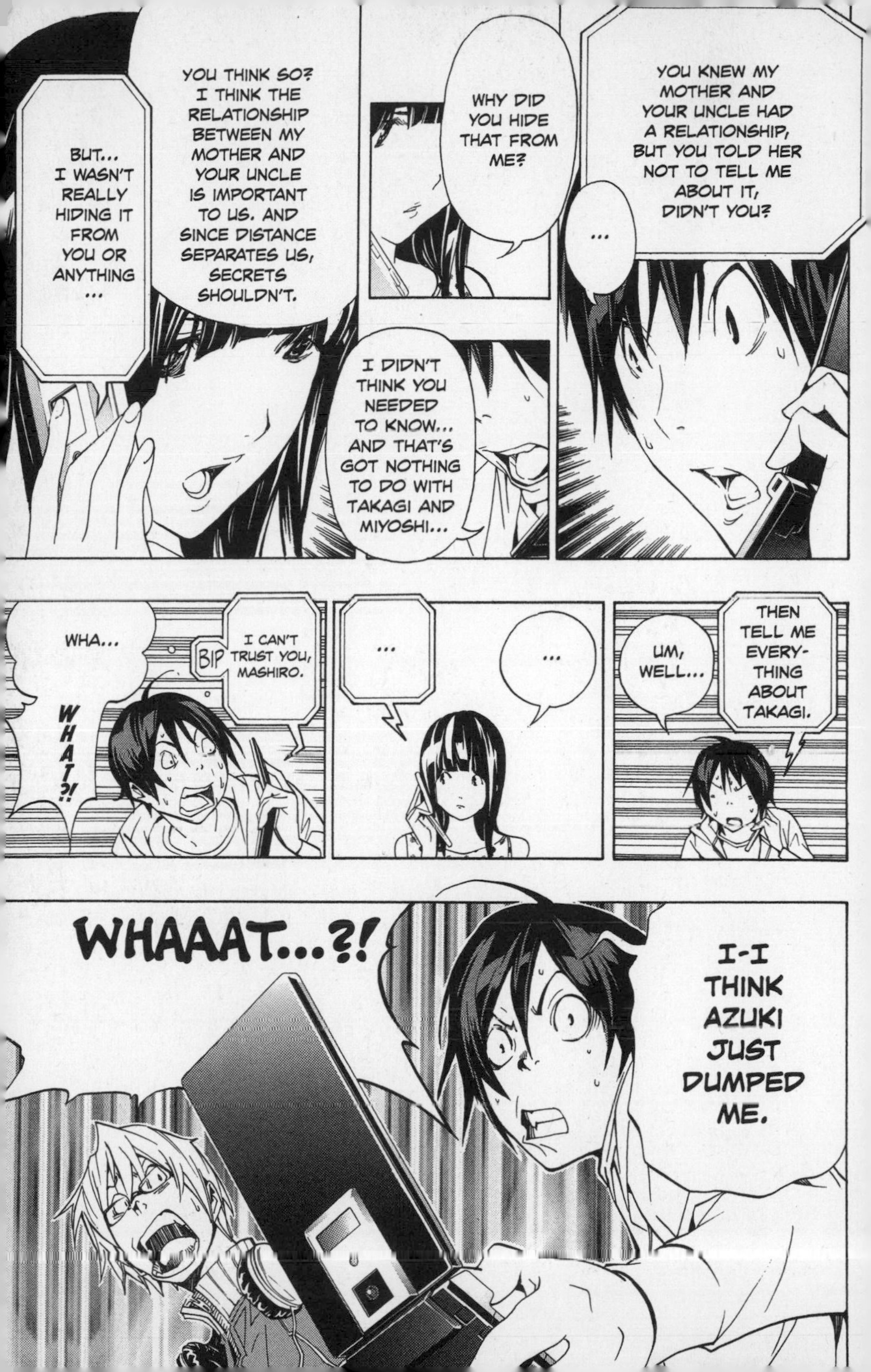
YOU KNEW MY MOTHER AND YOUR UNCLE HAD A RELATIONSHIP, BUT YOU TOLD HER NOT TO TELL ME ABOUT IT, DIDN'T YOU?
...
WHY DID YOU HIDE THAT FROM ME?
I DIDN'T THINK YOU NEEDED TO KNOW... AND THAT'S GOT NOTHING TO DO WITH TAKAGI AND MIYOSHI...
YOU THINK SO? I THINK THE RELATIONSHIP BETWEEN MY MOTHER AND YOUR UNCLE IS IMPORTANT TO US. AND SINCE DISTANCE SEPARATES US, SECRETS SHOULDN'T.
BUT... I WASN'T REALLY HIDING IT FROM YOU OR ANYTHING...
THEN TELL ME EVERY-THING ABOUT TAKAGI.
UM, WELL...
...
...
I CAN'T TRUST YOU, MASHIRO.
BIP
WHA...
WHAT?!
I-I THINK AZUKI JUST DUMPED ME.
WHAAAT...?!

OHBA'S STORYBOARD

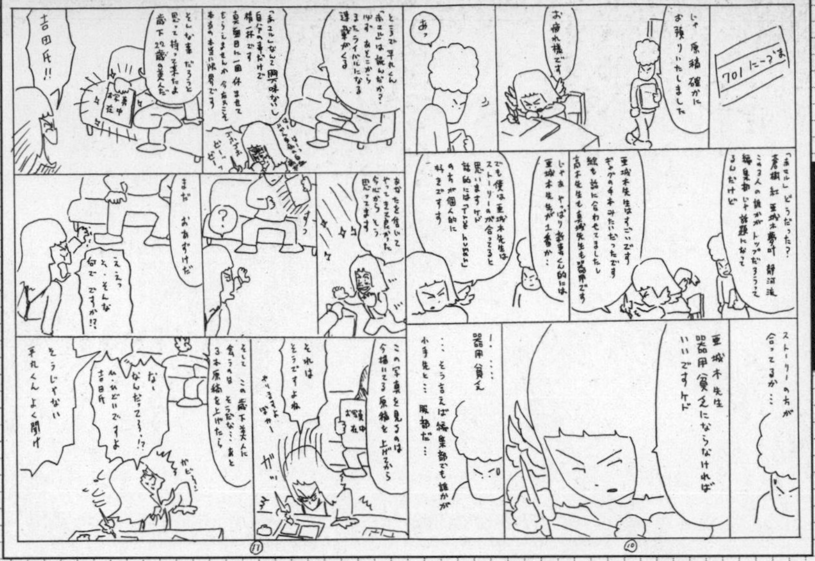
701 にーづま
じゃ 原稿確かにお預りいたしました
お疲れ様です
あっ
「あセル」どうだった？ 蒼樹紅 亜城木夢叶 静河流 この3人の誰かがトップだろうって編集部じゃ話題になってるんだけど
亜城木先生はすごいです ギャグの手本みたいだったです 絵も話に合わせてましたし 高木先生も真城先生も器用です
じゃあ やっぱり新妻くん的には亜城木先生が1番か…
でも僕は亜城木先生はストーリーの方が合ってると思いますケド
ストーリーの方が合ってるか…
亜城木先生 器用貧乏にならなければいいですケド
!…… 器用貧乏
…そう言えば編集部でも誰かが小手先と… 服部だ…
10
またライバルになる連載がくる
「あセル」なんて興味ないし 自分の事だけで精一杯です 真面目に一回休ませてもらえませんか 今度こそ本当の本当に限界です
そんな事だろうと思って持って来たよ 歳下22歳の美人だ
吉田氏!!
あなたを信じてやって来て良かった 今心からそう思ってます
ずっ
?
まだ おあずけだ
ええっ え、そんな 何で ですか!?
この写真を見るのは今描いてる原稿を上げてから
それはそうですよね
ガッ
そして この歳下美人に会うのは そうだな…あと3本原稿を上げたら
な… なんだって…!? ひ・ひどいですよ 吉田氏
そうじゃない 平丸くん よく聞け
11

OBATA'S STORYBOARD

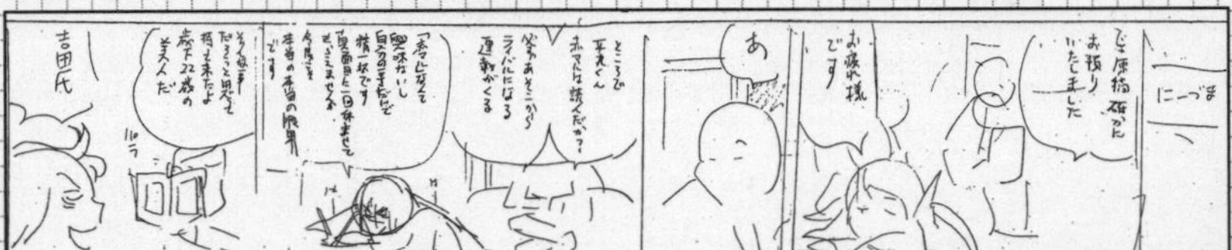
にーづま
お疲れ様です
あ
吉田氏

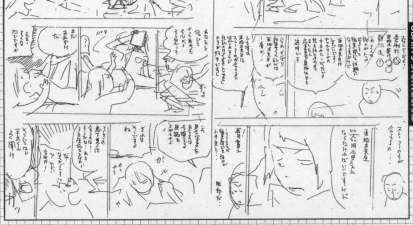

COMPLETE!

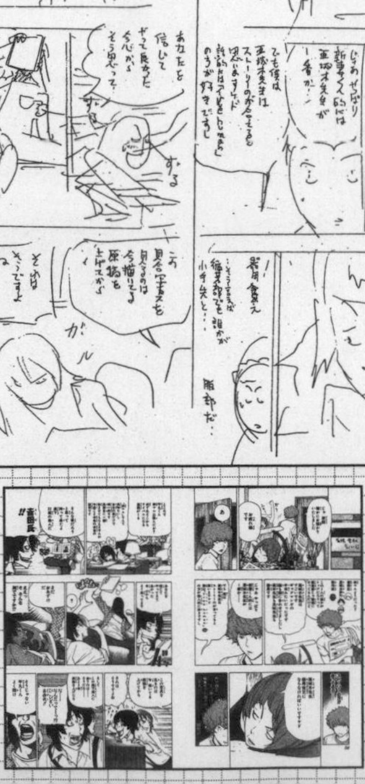

*CREATOR STORYBOARDS AND FINISHED PAGES IN JAPANESE

BAKUMAN。 vol.8

"Until the Final Draft Is Complete"

Chapter 64, pp. 56-57

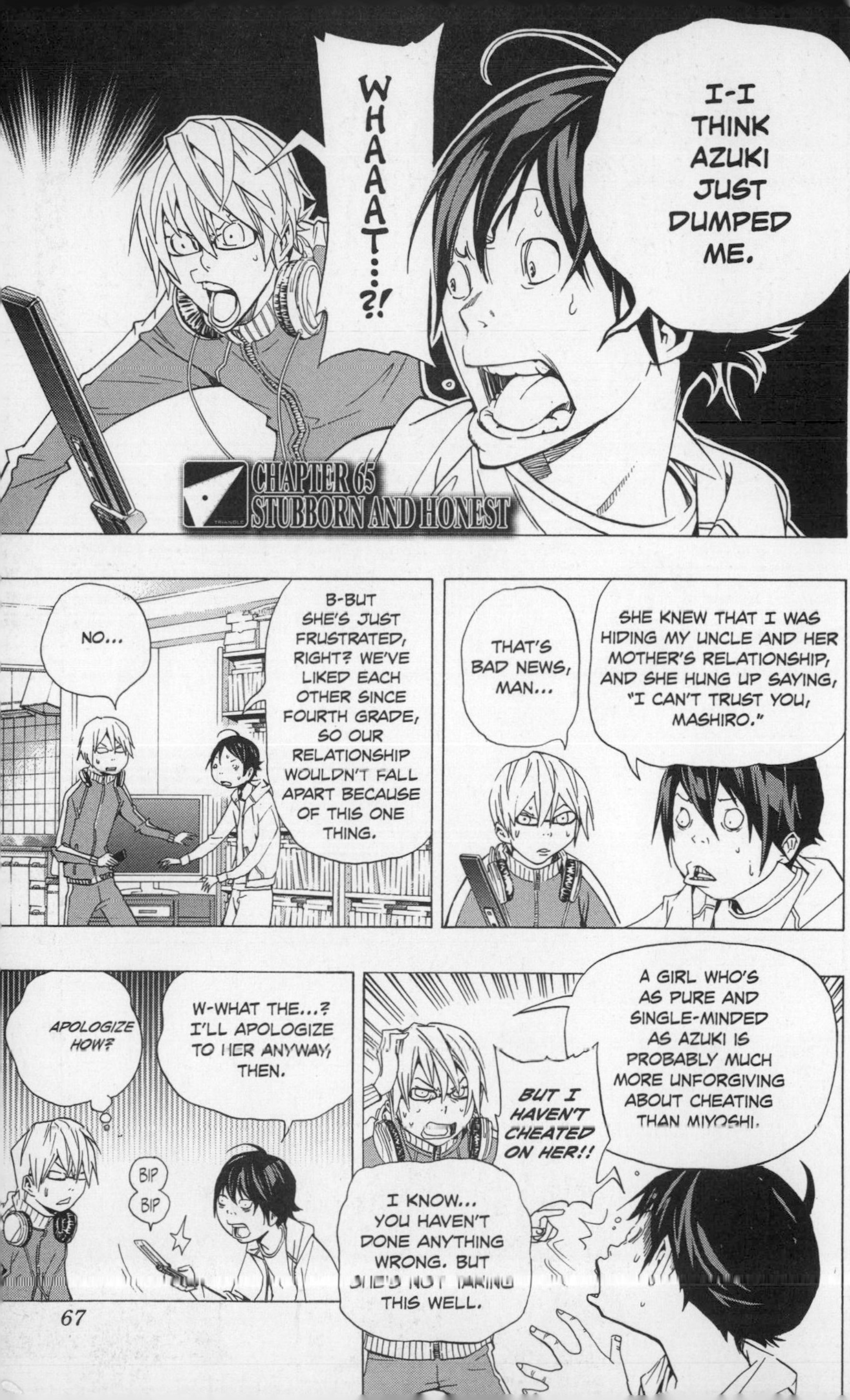
I-I THINK AZUKI JUST DUMPED ME.
WHAAAT...?!
CHAPTER 65 STUBBORN AND HONEST
SHE KNEW THAT I WAS HIDING MY UNCLE AND HER MOTHER'S RELATIONSHIP, AND SHE HUNG UP SAYING, "I CAN'T TRUST YOU, MASHIRO."
THAT'S BAD NEWS, MAN...
B-BUT SHE'S JUST FRUSTRATED, RIGHT? WE'VE LIKED EACH OTHER SINCE FOURTH GRADE, SO OUR RELATIONSHIP WOULDN'T FALL APART BECAUSE OF THIS ONE THING.
NO...
A GIRL WHO'S AS PURE AND SINGLE-MINDED AS AZUKI IS PROBABLY MUCH MORE UNFORGIVING ABOUT CHEATING THAN MIYOSHI.
BUT I HAVEN'T CHEATED ON HER!!
I KNOW... YOU HAVEN'T DONE ANYTHING WRONG. BUT SHE'S NOT TAKING THIS WELL.
W-WHAT THE...? I'LL APOLOGIZE TO HER ANYWAY, THEN.
APOLOGIZE HOW?
BIP
BIP

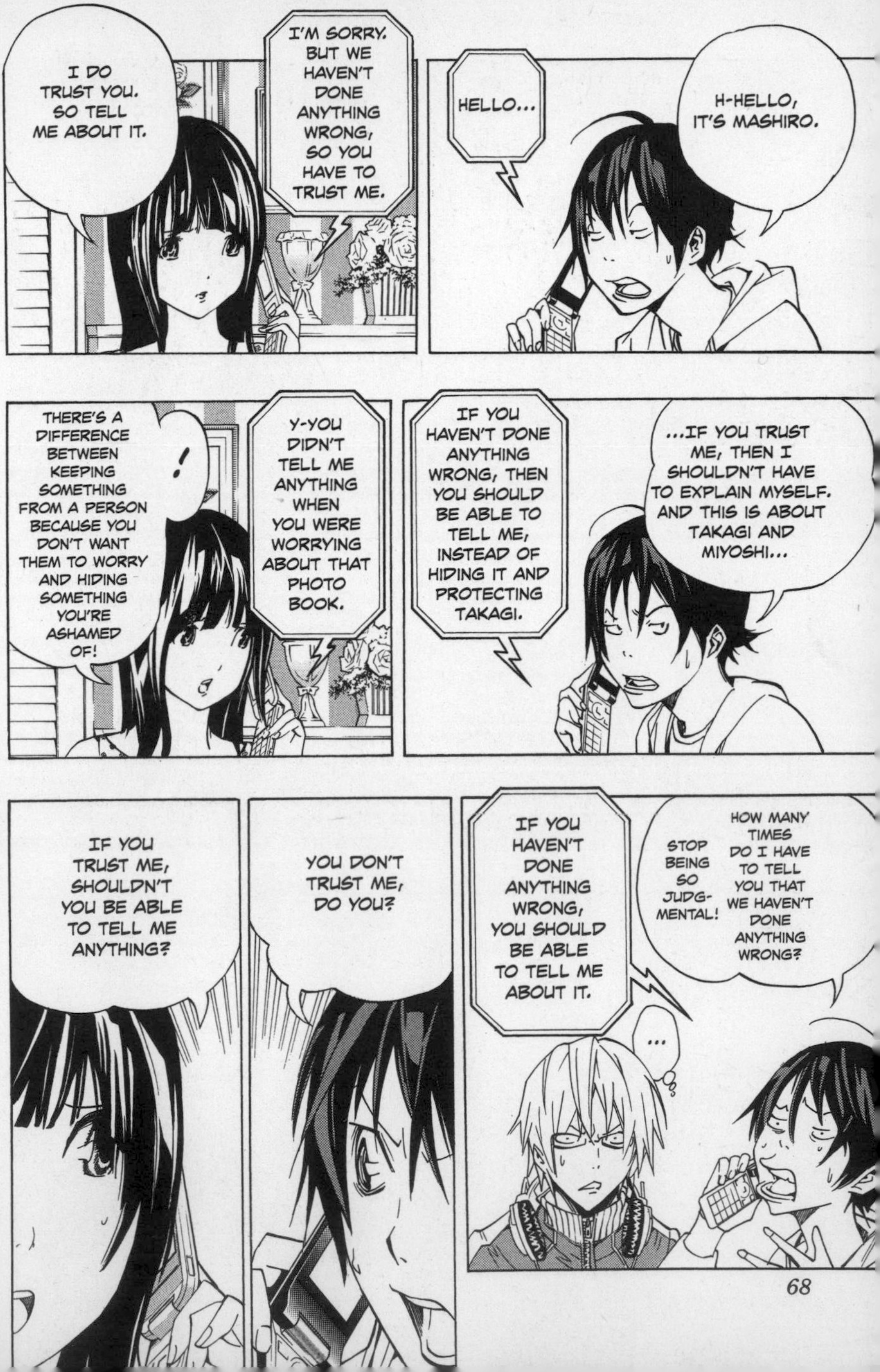
H-HELLO, IT'S MASHIRO.
HELLO...
I'M SORRY. BUT WE HAVEN'T DONE ANYTHING WRONG, SO YOU HAVE TO TRUST ME.
I DO TRUST YOU. SO TELL ME ABOUT IT.
...IF YOU TRUST ME, THEN I SHOULDN'T HAVE TO EXPLAIN MYSELF. AND THIS IS ABOUT TAKAGI AND MIYOSHI...
IF YOU HAVEN'T DONE ANYTHING WRONG, THEN YOU SHOULD BE ABLE TO TELL ME, INSTEAD OF HIDING IT AND PROTECTING TAKAGI.
Y-YOU DIDN'T TELL ME ANYTHING WHEN YOU WERE WORRYING ABOUT THAT PHOTO BOOK.
!
THERE'S A DIFFERENCE BETWEEN KEEPING SOMETHING FROM A PERSON BECAUSE YOU DON'T WANT THEM TO WORRY AND HIDING SOMETHING YOU'RE ASHAMED OF!
HOW MANY TIMES DO I HAVE TO TELL YOU THAT WE HAVEN'T DONE ANYTHING WRONG?
STOP BEING SO JUDG-MENTAL!
IF YOU HAVEN'T DONE ANYTHING WRONG, YOU SHOULD BE ABLE TO TELL ME ABOUT IT.
...
YOU DON'T TRUST ME, DO YOU?
IF YOU TRUST ME, SHOULDN'T YOU BE ABLE TO TELL ME ANYTHING?

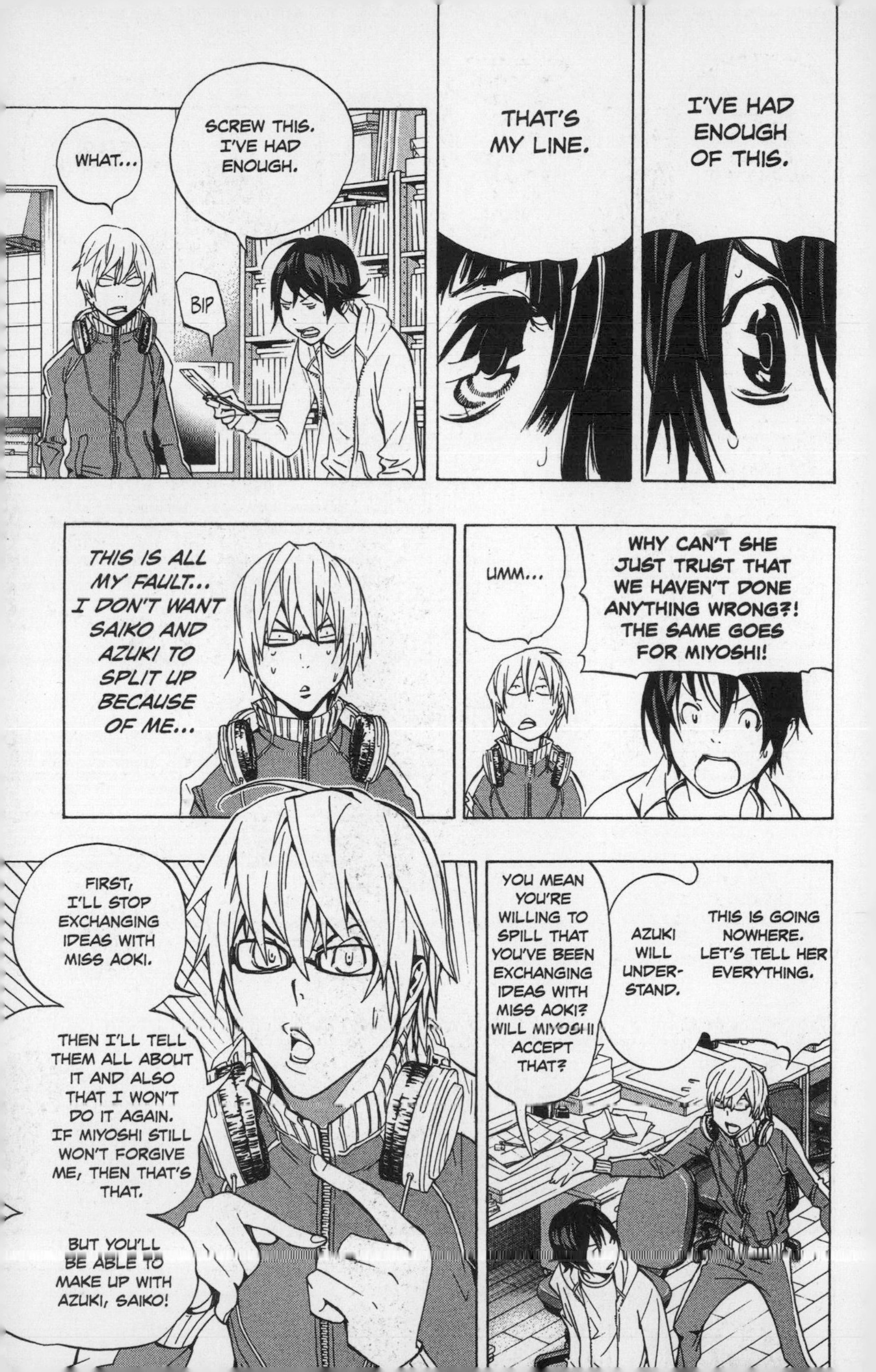
I'VE HAD ENOUGH OF THIS.
THAT'S MY LINE.
SCREW THIS. I'VE HAD ENOUGH.
WHAT...
BIP
WHY CAN'T SHE JUST TRUST THAT WE HAVEN'T DONE ANYTHING WRONG?! THE SAME GOES FOR MIYOSHI!
UMM...
THIS IS ALL MY FAULT... I DON'T WANT SAIKO AND AZUKI TO SPLIT UP BECAUSE OF ME...
THIS IS GOING NOWHERE. LET'S TELL HER EVERYTHING.
AZUKI WILL UNDER-STAND.
YOU MEAN YOU'RE WILLING TO SPILL THAT YOU'VE BEEN EXCHANGING IDEAS WITH MISS AOKI? WILL MIYOSHI ACCEPT THAT?
FIRST, I'LL STOP EXCHANGING IDEAS WITH MISS AOKI.
THEN I'LL TELL THEM ALL ABOUT IT AND ALSO THAT I WON'T DO IT AGAIN. IF MIYOSHI STILL WON'T FORGIVE ME, THEN THAT'S THAT.
BUT YOU'LL BE ABLE TO MAKE UP WITH AZUKI, SAIKO!

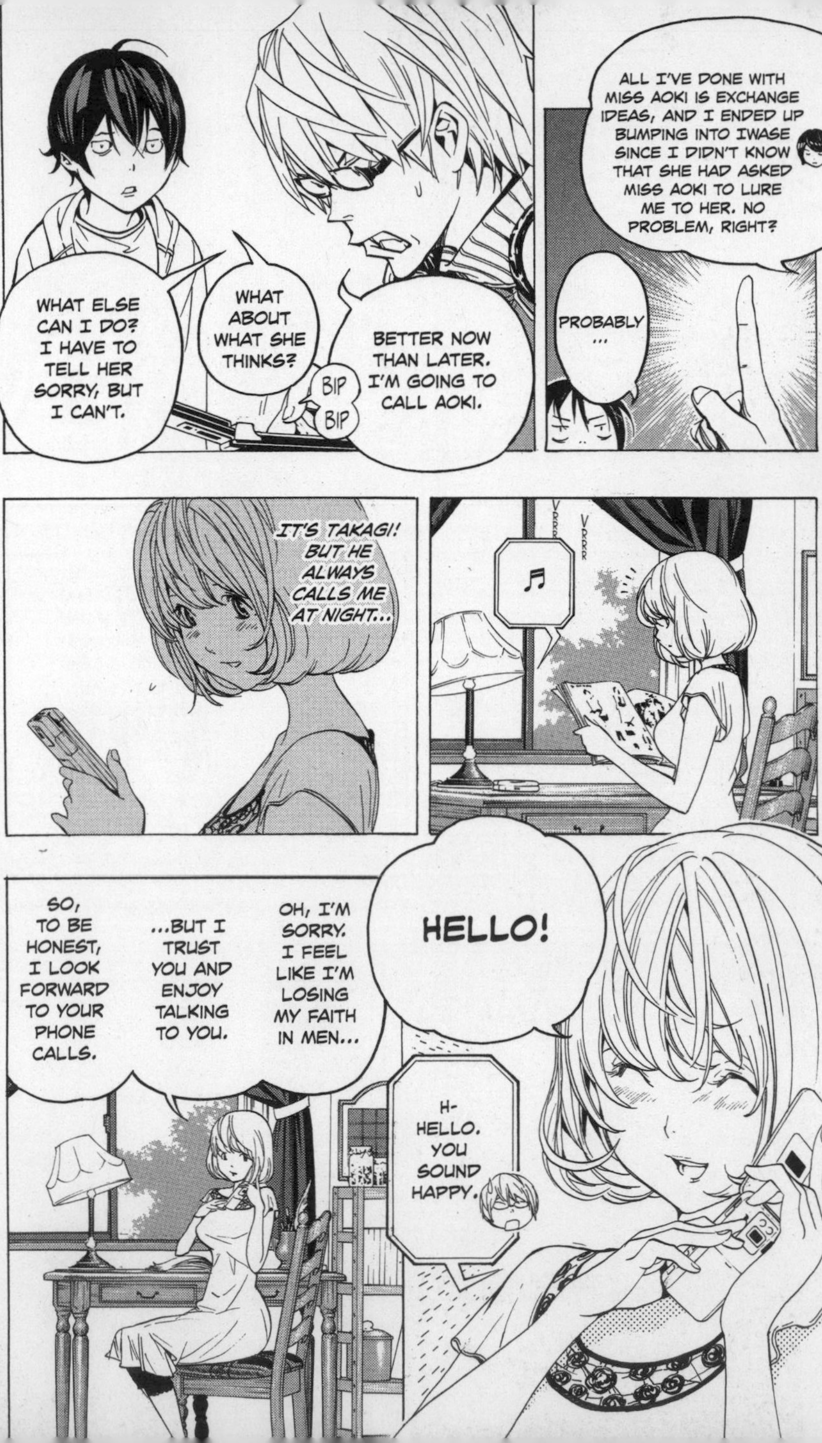
ALL I'VE DONE WITH MISS AOKI IS EXCHANGE IDEAS, AND I ENDED UP BUMPING INTO IWASE SINCE I DIDN'T KNOW THAT SHE HAD ASKED MISS AOKI TO LURE ME TO HER. NO PROBLEM, RIGHT?
PROBABLY...
BETTER NOW THAN LATER. I'M GOING TO CALL AOKI.
BIP
BIP
WHAT ABOUT WHAT SHE THINKS?
WHAT ELSE CAN I DO? I HAVE TO TELL HER SORRY, BUT I CAN'T.
VRRR
VRRR
♪
IT'S TAKAGI! BUT HE ALWAYS CALLS ME AT NIGHT...
HELLO!
H-HELLO. YOU SOUND HAPPY.
OH, I'M SORRY. I FEEL LIKE I'M LOSING MY FAITH IN MEN...
...BUT I TRUST YOU AND ENJOY TALKING TO YOU.
SO, TO BE HONEST, I LOOK FORWARD TO YOUR PHONE CALLS.

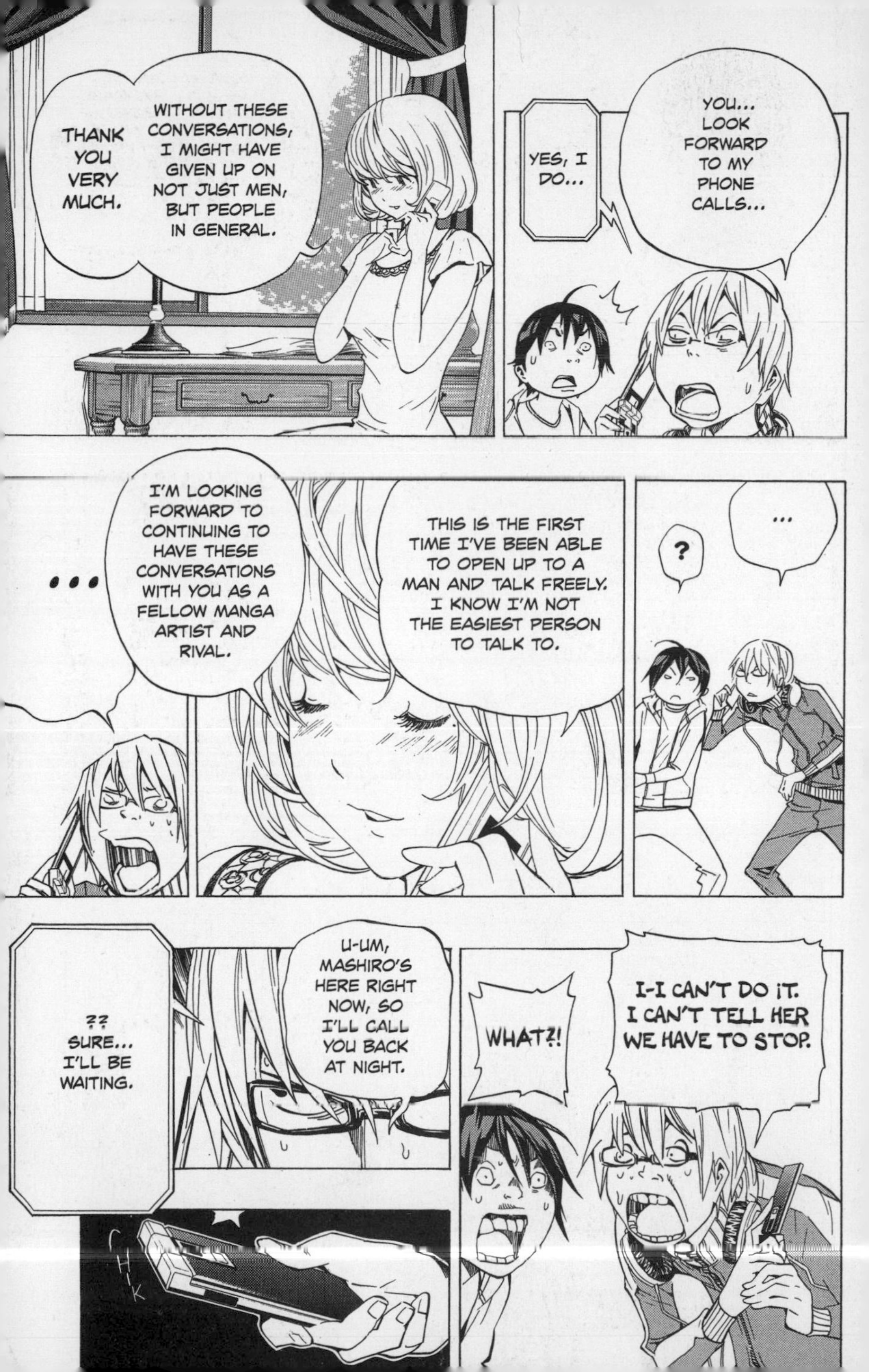
YOU... LOOK FORWARD TO MY PHONE CALLS...
YES, I DO...
WITHOUT THESE CONVERSATIONS, I MIGHT HAVE GIVEN UP ON NOT JUST MEN, BUT PEOPLE IN GENERAL.
THANK YOU VERY MUCH.
...
?
THIS IS THE FIRST TIME I'VE BEEN ABLE TO OPEN UP TO A MAN AND TALK FREELY. I KNOW I'M NOT THE EASIEST PERSON TO TALK TO.
I'M LOOKING FORWARD TO CONTINUING TO HAVE THESE CONVERSATIONS WITH YOU AS A FELLOW MANGA ARTIST AND RIVAL.
• • •
I-I CAN'T DO IT. I CAN'T TELL HER WE HAVE TO STOP.
WHAT?!
U-UM, MASHIRO'S HERE RIGHT NOW, SO I'LL CALL YOU BACK AT NIGHT.
?? SURE... I'LL BE WAITING.
CHK

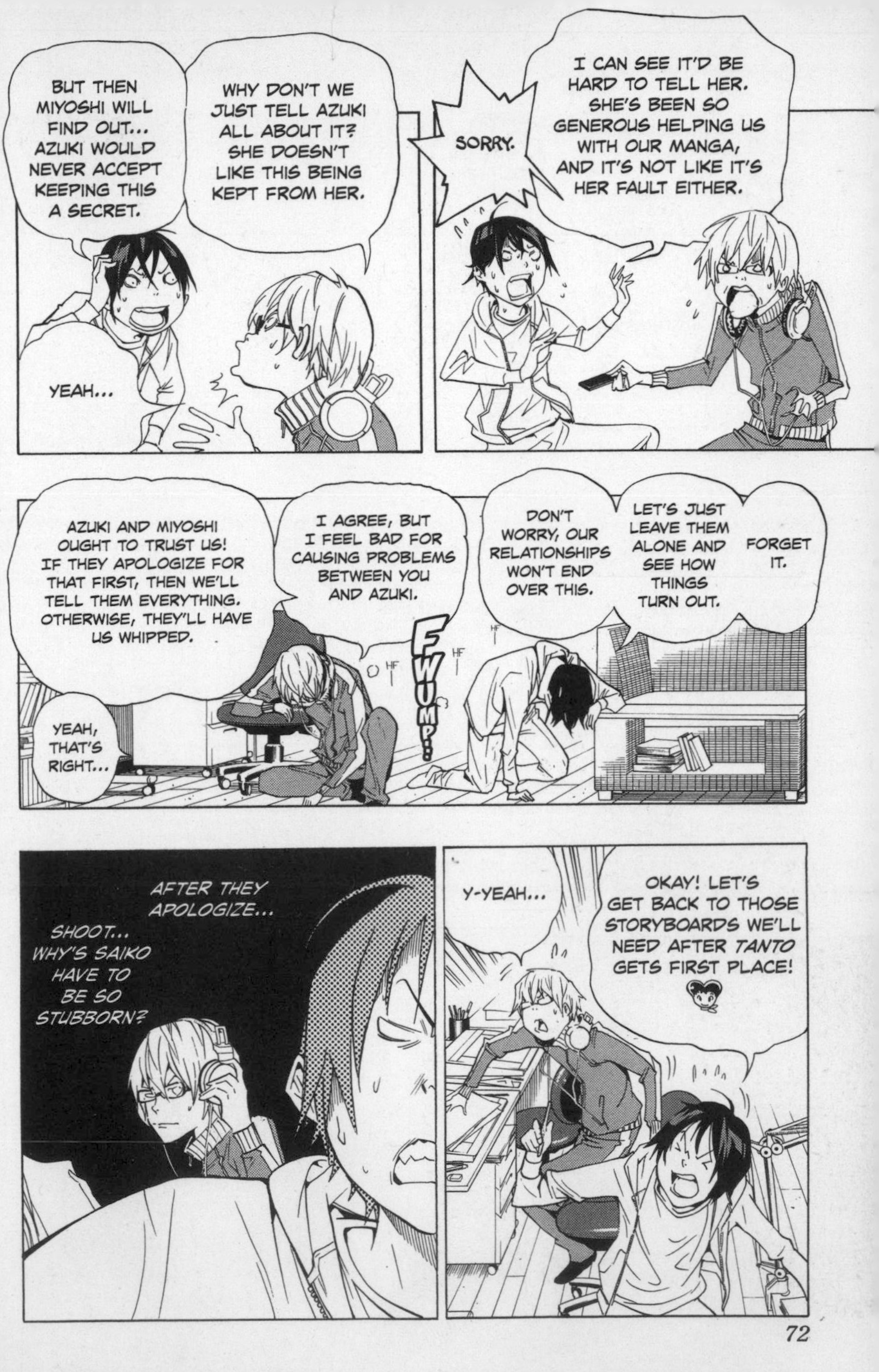
I CAN SEE IT'D BE HARD TO TELL HER. SHE'S BEEN SO GENEROUS HELPING US WITH OUR MANGA, AND IT'S NOT LIKE IT'S HER FAULT EITHER.
SORRY.
WHY DON'T WE JUST TELL AZUKI ALL ABOUT IT? SHE DOESN'T LIKE THIS BEING KEPT FROM HER.
BUT THEN MIYOSHI WILL FIND OUT... AZUKI WOULD NEVER ACCEPT KEEPING THIS A SECRET.
YEAH...
FORGET IT.
LET'S JUST LEAVE THEM ALONE AND SEE HOW THINGS TURN OUT.
DON'T WORRY, OUR RELATIONSHIPS WON'T END OVER THIS.
HF
HF
FWUMP!!
HF
I AGREE, BUT I FEEL BAD FOR CAUSING PROBLEMS BETWEEN YOU AND AZUKI.
AZUKI AND MIYOSHI OUGHT TO TRUST US! IF THEY APOLOGIZE FOR THAT FIRST, THEN WE'LL TELL THEM EVERYTHING. OTHERWISE, THEY'LL HAVE US WHIPPED.
YEAH, THAT'S RIGHT...
OKAY! LET'S GET BACK TO THOSE STORYBOARDS WE'LL NEED AFTER *TANTO* GETS FIRST PLACE!
Y-YEAH...
AFTER THEY APOLOGIZE...
SHOOT... WHY'S SAIKO HAVE TO BE SO STUBBORN?

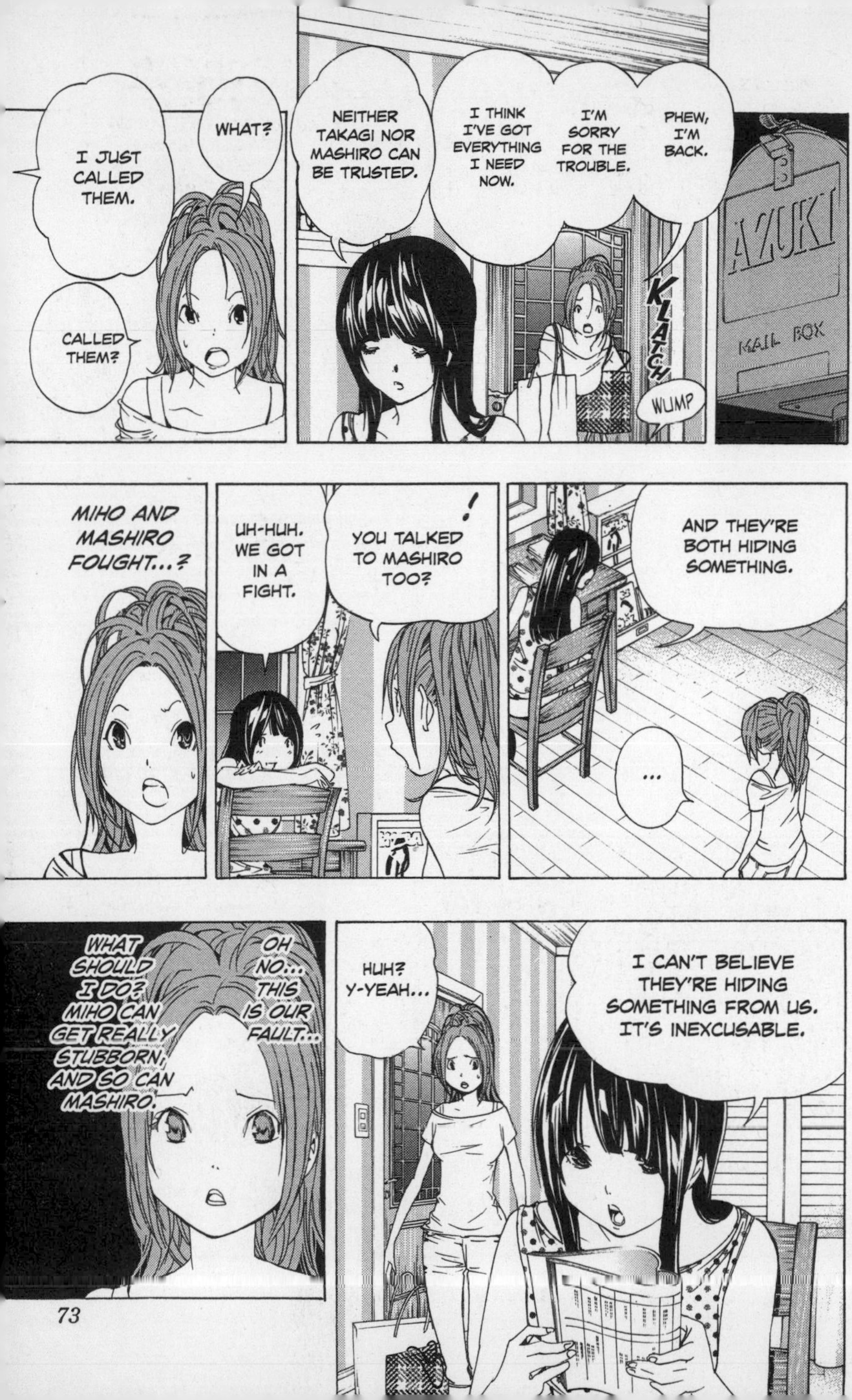
KLATCH
WUMP
PHEW, I'M BACK.
I'M SORRY FOR THE TROUBLE.
I THINK I'VE GOT EVERYTHING I NEED NOW.
NEITHER TAKAGI NOR MASHIRO CAN BE TRUSTED.
AZUKI
MAIL BOX
WHAT?
I JUST CALLED THEM.
CALLED THEM?
AND THEY'RE BOTH HIDING SOMETHING.
...
!
YOU TALKED TO MASHIRO TOO?
UH-HUH. WE GOT IN A FIGHT.
MIHO AND MASHIRO FOUGHT...?
I CAN'T BELIEVE THEY'RE HIDING SOMETHING FROM US. IT'S INEXCUSABLE.
HUH? Y-YEAH...
OH NO... THIS IS OUR FAULT...
WHAT SHOULD I DO? MIHO CAN GET REALLY STUBBORN, AND SO CAN MASHIRO.

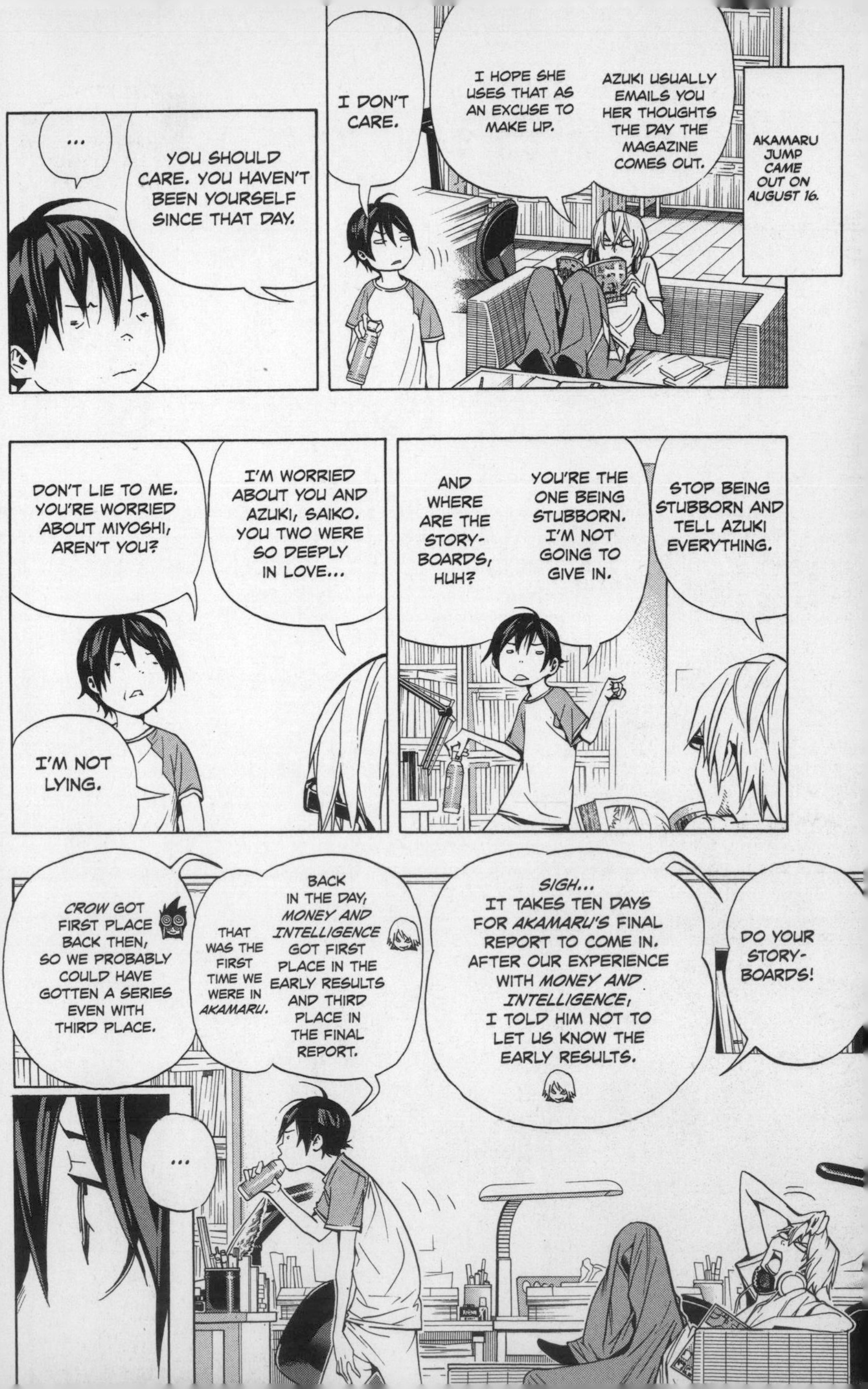
AKAMARU JUMP CAME OUT ON AUGUST 16.
AZUKI USUALLY EMAILS YOU HER THOUGHTS THE DAY THE MAGAZINE COMES OUT.
I HOPE SHE USES THAT AS AN EXCUSE TO MAKE UP.
I DON'T CARE.
YOU SHOULD CARE. YOU HAVEN'T BEEN YOURSELF SINCE THAT DAY.
...
STOP BEING STUBBORN AND TELL AZUKI EVERYTHING.
YOU'RE THE ONE BEING STUBBORN. I'M NOT GOING TO GIVE IN.
AND WHERE ARE THE STORY-BOARDS, HUH?
I'M WORRIED ABOUT YOU AND AZUKI, SAIKO. YOU TWO WERE SO DEEPLY IN LOVE...
DON'T LIE TO ME. YOU'RE WORRIED ABOUT MIYOSHI, AREN'T YOU?
I'M NOT LYING.
DO YOUR STORY-BOARDS!
SIGH... IT TAKES TEN DAYS FOR *AKAMARU'S* FINAL REPORT TO COME IN. AFTER OUR EXPERIENCE WITH *MONEY AND INTELLIGENCE*, I TOLD HIM NOT TO LET US KNOW THE EARLY RESULTS.
BACK IN THE DAY, *MONEY AND INTELLIGENCE* GOT FIRST PLACE IN THE EARLY RESULTS AND THIRD PLACE IN THE FINAL REPORT.
THAT WAS THE FIRST TIME WE WERE IN *AKAMARU*.
CROW GOT FIRST PLACE BACK THEN, SO WE PROBABLY COULD HAVE GOTTEN A SERIES EVEN WITH THIRD PLACE.
...

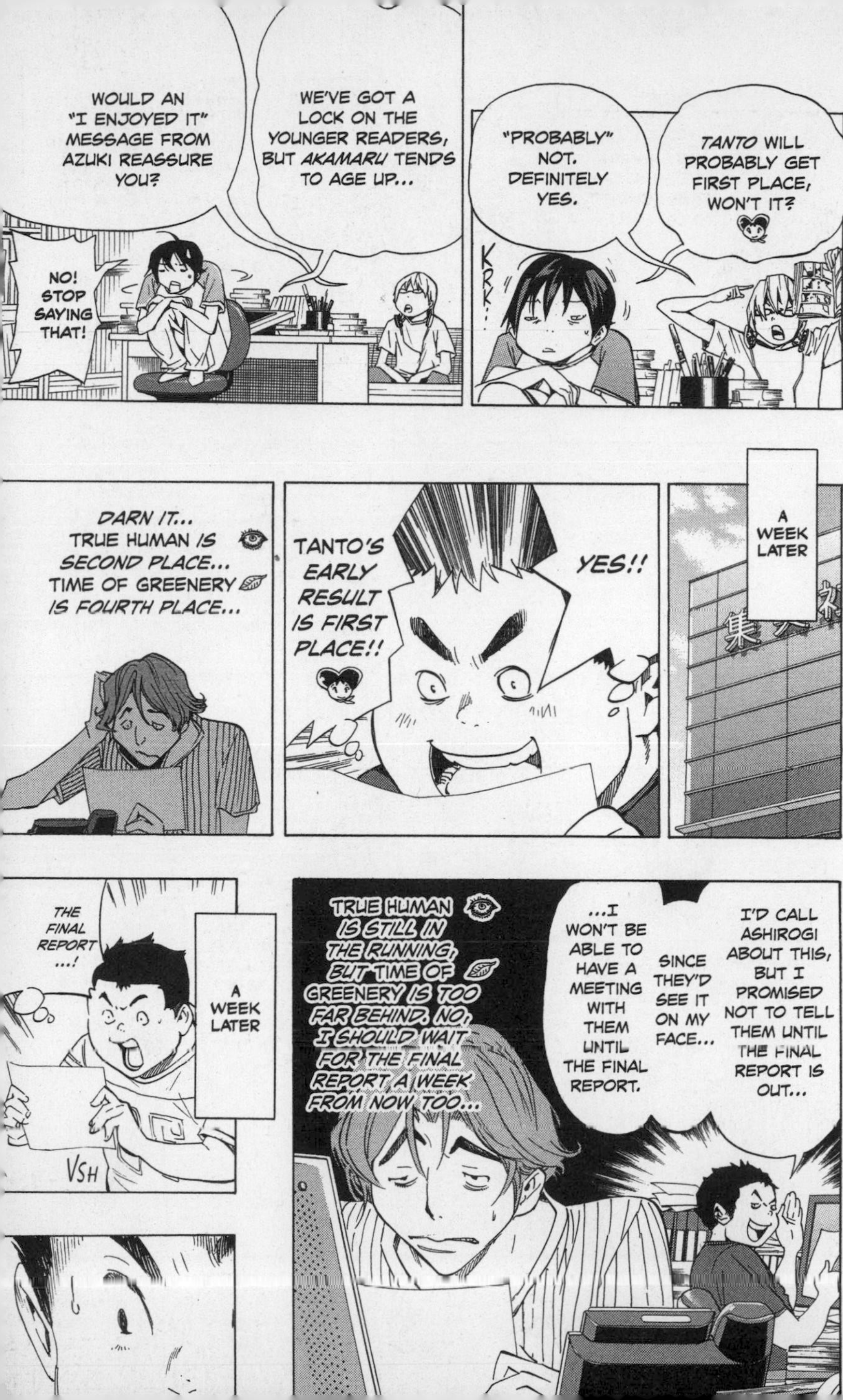
TANTO WILL PROBABLY GET FIRST PLACE, WON'T IT?
"PROBABLY" NOT. DEFINITELY YES.
KRK
WE'VE GOT A LOCK ON THE YOUNGER READERS, BUT AKAMARU TENDS TO AGE UP...
WOULD AN "I ENJOYED IT" MESSAGE FROM AZUKI REASSURE YOU?
NO! STOP SAYING THAT!
A WEEK LATER
YES!!
TANTO'S EARLY RESULT IS FIRST PLACE!!
DARN IT... TRUE HUMAN IS SECOND PLACE... TIME OF GREENERY IS FOURTH PLACE...
I'D CALL ASHIROGI ABOUT THIS, BUT I PROMISED NOT TO TELL THEM UNTIL THE FINAL REPORT IS OUT...
SINCE THEY'D SEE IT ON MY FACE...
...I WON'T BE ABLE TO HAVE A MEETING WITH THEM UNTIL THE FINAL REPORT.
TRUE HUMAN IS STILL IN THE RUNNING, BUT TIME OF GREENERY IS TOO FAR BEHIND. NO, I SHOULD WAIT FOR THE FINAL REPORT A WEEK FROM NOW TOO...
A WEEK LATER
THE FINAL REPORT ...!
VSH

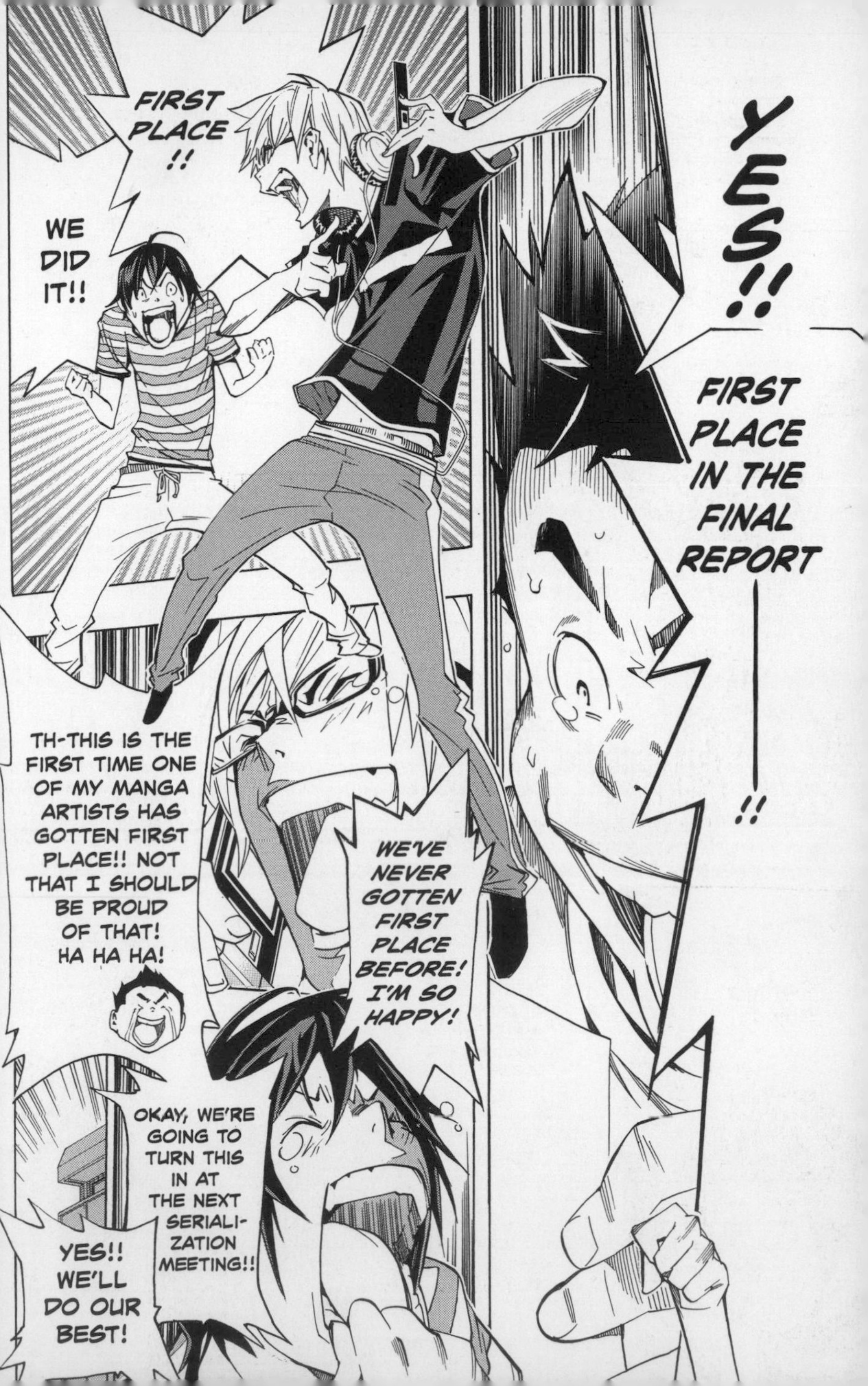
YES!!
FIRST PLACE IN THE FINAL REPORT —!!
FIRST PLACE!!
WE DID IT!!
WE'VE NEVER GOTTEN FIRST PLACE BEFORE! I'M SO HAPPY!
TH-THIS IS THE FIRST TIME ONE OF MY MANGA ARTISTS HAS GOTTEN FIRST PLACE!! NOT THAT I SHOULD BE PROUD OF THAT! HA HA HA!
OKAY, WE'RE GOING TO TURN THIS IN AT THE NEXT SERIALI-ZATION MEETING!!
YES!! WE'LL DO OUR BEST!

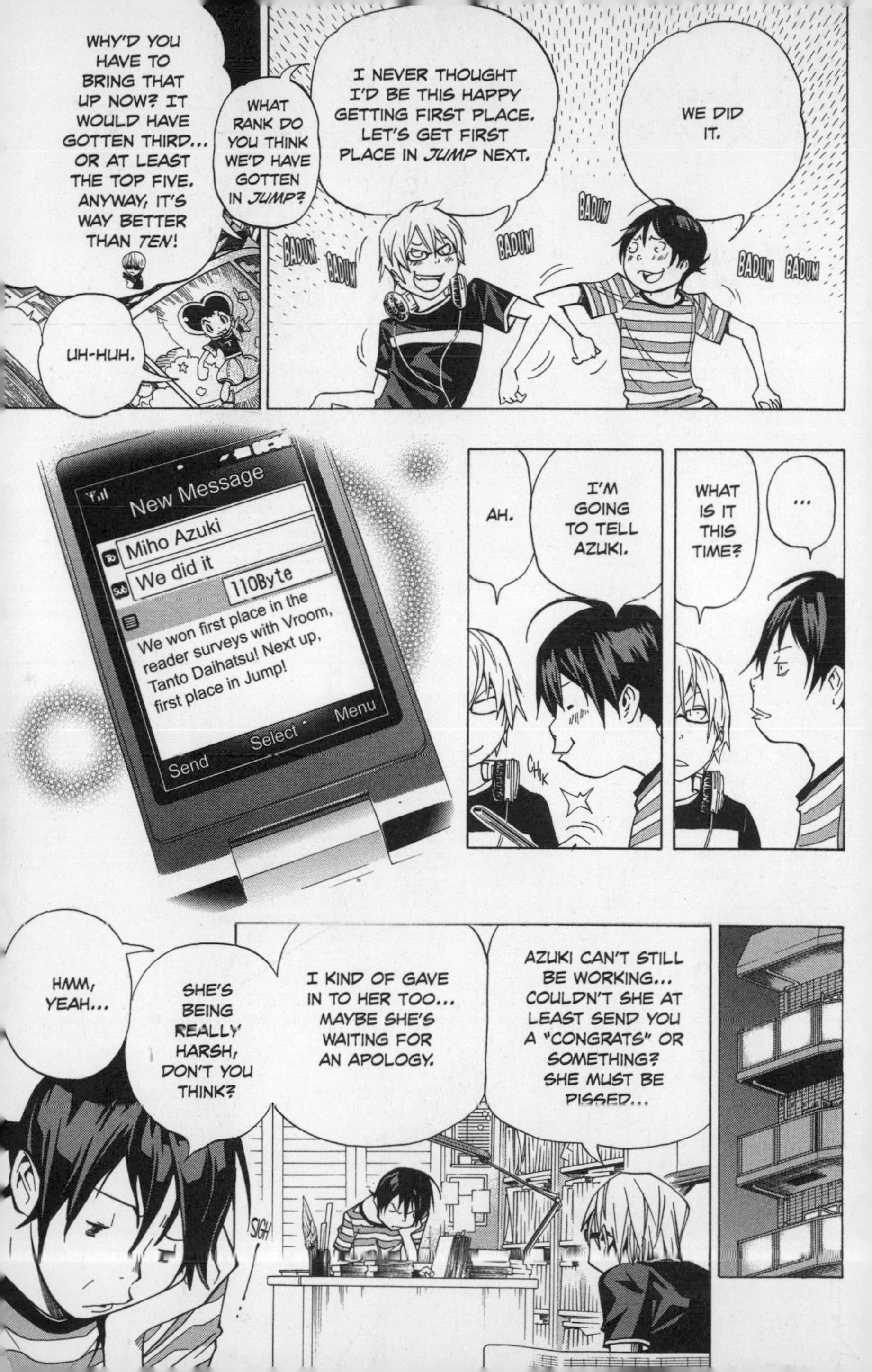
WE DID IT.
I NEVER THOUGHT I'D BE THIS HAPPY GETTING FIRST PLACE. LET'S GET FIRST PLACE IN *JUMP* NEXT.
BADUM BADUM
BADUM
BADUM BADUM
WHAT RANK DO YOU THINK WE'D HAVE GOTTEN IN *JUMP*?
WHY'D YOU HAVE TO BRING THAT UP NOW? IT WOULD HAVE GOTTEN THIRD... OR AT LEAST THE TOP FIVE. ANYWAY, IT'S WAY BETTER THAN *TEN*!
UH-HUH.
...
WHAT IS IT THIS TIME?
I'M GOING TO TELL AZUKI.
AH.
CHIK
New Message
Miho Azuki
We did it
110Byte
We won first place in the reader surveys with Vroom, Tanto Daihatsu! Next up, first place in Jump!
Send
Select
Menu
AZUKI CAN'T STILL BE WORKING... COULDN'T SHE AT LEAST SEND YOU A "CONGRATS" OR SOMETHING? SHE MUST BE PISSED...
I KIND OF GAVE IN TO HER TOO... MAYBE SHE'S WAITING FOR AN APOLOGY.
SHE'S BEING REALLY HARSH, DON'T YOU THINK?
HMM, YEAH...
SIGH

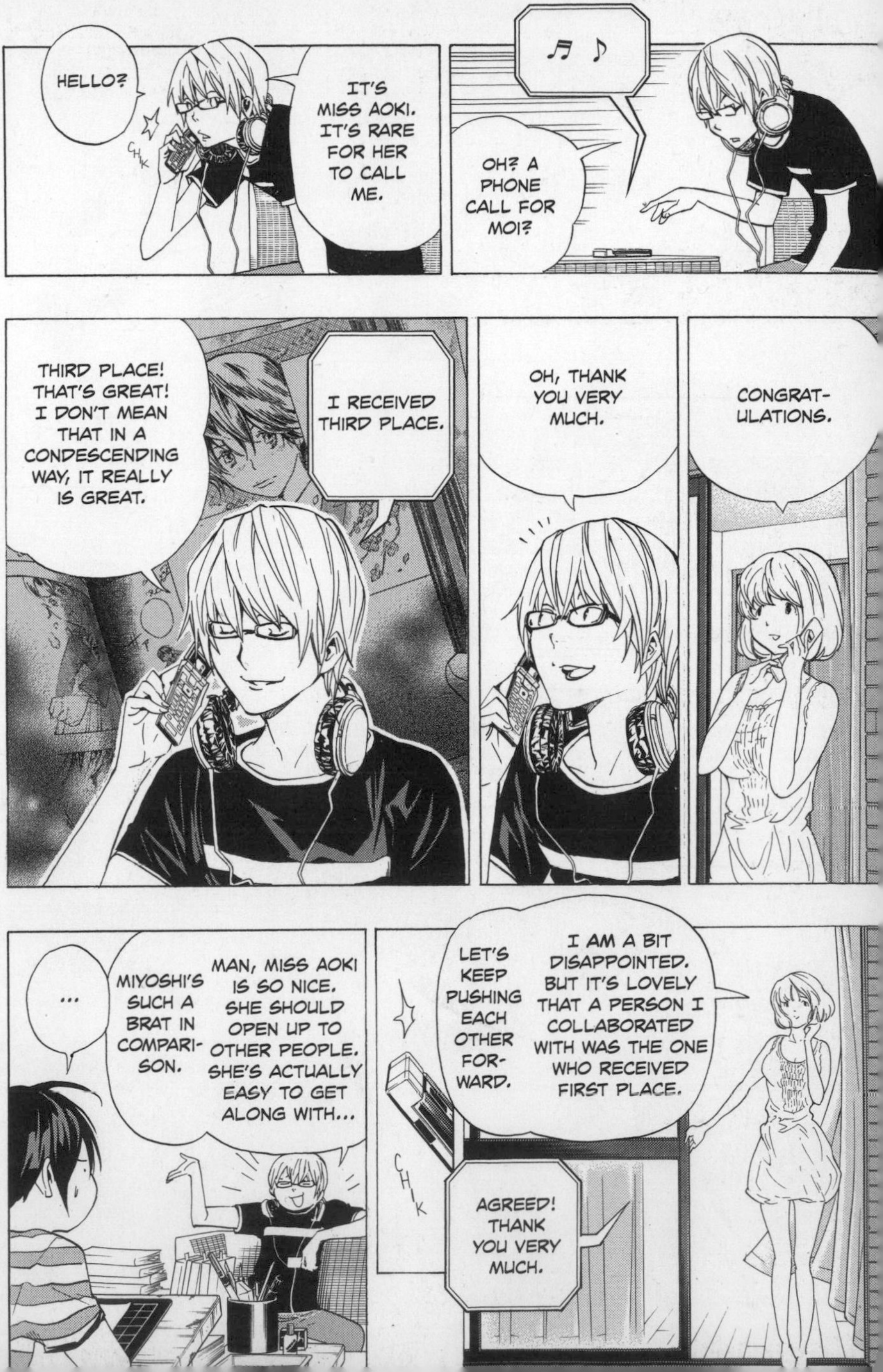
♬ ♪
OH? A PHONE CALL FOR MOI?
IT'S MISS AOKI. IT'S RARE FOR HER TO CALL ME.
HELLO?
CHIK
CONGRAT-ULATIONS.
OH, THANK YOU VERY MUCH.
I RECEIVED THIRD PLACE.
THIRD PLACE! THAT'S GREAT! I DON'T MEAN THAT IN A CONDESCENDING WAY, IT REALLY IS GREAT.
I AM A BIT DISAPPOINTED. BUT IT'S LOVELY THAT A PERSON I COLLABORATED WITH WAS THE ONE WHO RECEIVED FIRST PLACE.
LET'S KEEP PUSHING EACH OTHER FOR-WARD.
AGREED! THANK YOU VERY MUCH.
CHIK
MAN, MISS AOKI IS SO NICE. SHE SHOULD OPEN UP TO OTHER PEOPLE. SHE'S ACTUALLY EASY TO GET ALONG WITH...
MIYOSHI'S SUCH A BRAT IN COMPARI-SON.
...

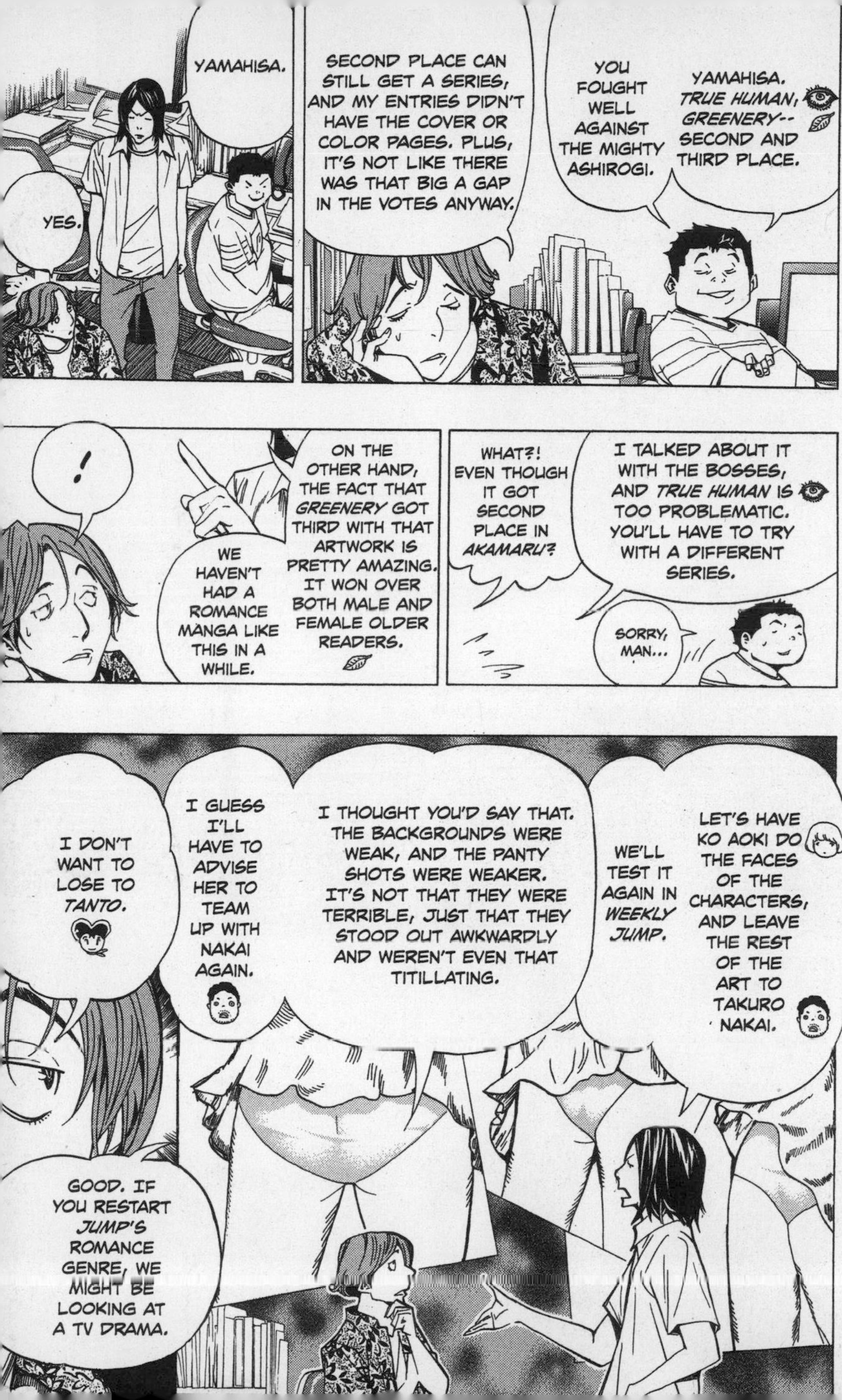
YAMAHISA. *TRUE HUMAN*, *GREENERY*-- SECOND AND THIRD PLACE.
YOU FOUGHT WELL AGAINST THE MIGHTY ASHIROGI.
SECOND PLACE CAN STILL GET A SERIES, AND MY ENTRIES DIDN'T HAVE THE COVER OR COLOR PAGES. PLUS, IT'S NOT LIKE THERE WAS THAT BIG A GAP IN THE VOTES ANYWAY.
YAMAHISA.
YES.
I TALKED ABOUT IT WITH THE BOSSES, AND *TRUE HUMAN* IS TOO PROBLEMATIC. YOU'LL HAVE TO TRY WITH A DIFFERENT SERIES.
WHAT?! EVEN THOUGH IT GOT SECOND PLACE IN *AKAMARU*?
SORRY, MAN...
ON THE OTHER HAND, THE FACT THAT *GREENERY* GOT THIRD WITH THAT ARTWORK IS PRETTY AMAZING. IT WON OVER BOTH MALE AND FEMALE OLDER READERS.
WE HAVEN'T HAD A ROMANCE MANGA LIKE THIS IN A WHILE.
!
LET'S HAVE KO AOKI DO THE FACES OF THE CHARACTERS, AND LEAVE THE REST OF THE ART TO TAKURO NAKAI.
WE'LL TEST IT AGAIN IN *WEEKLY JUMP*.
I THOUGHT YOU'D SAY THAT. THE BACKGROUNDS WERE WEAK, AND THE PANTY SHOTS WERE WEAKER. IT'S NOT THAT THEY WERE TERRIBLE, JUST THAT THEY STOOD OUT AWKWARDLY AND WEREN'T EVEN THAT TITILLATING.
I GUESS I'LL HAVE TO ADVISE HER TO TEAM UP WITH NAKAI AGAIN.
I DON'T WANT TO LOSE TO *TANTO*.
GOOD. IF YOU RESTART *JUMP'S* ROMANCE GENRE, WE MIGHT BE LOOKING AT A TV DRAMA.

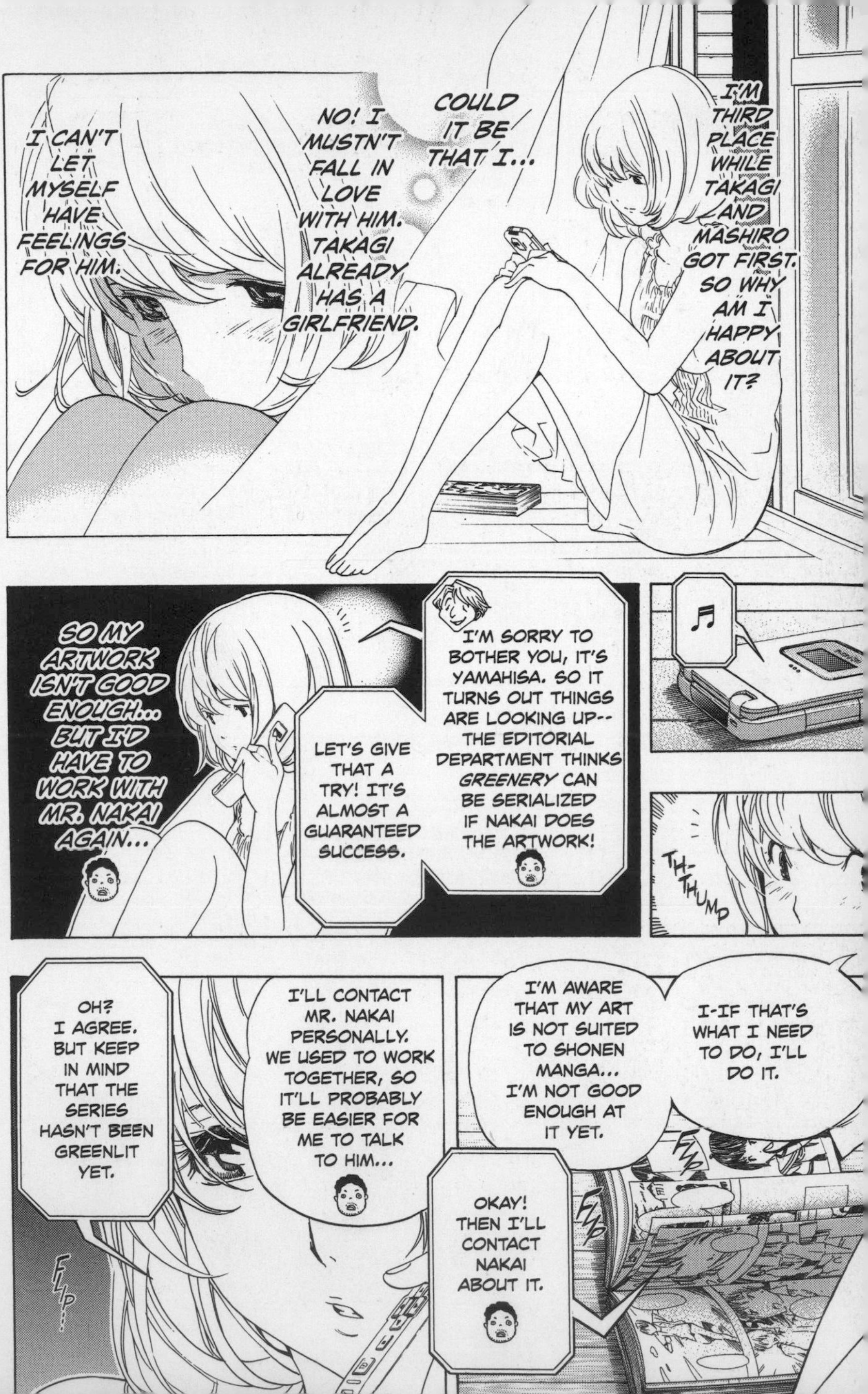
I'M THIRD PLACE WHILE TAKAGI AND MASHIRO GOT FIRST. SO WHY AM I HAPPY ABOUT IT?
COULD IT BE THAT I...
NO! I MUSTN'T FALL IN LOVE WITH HIM. TAKAGI ALREADY HAS A GIRLFRIEND.
I CAN'T LET MYSELF HAVE FEELINGS FOR HIM.
♫
TH-THUMP
I'M SORRY TO BOTHER YOU, IT'S YAMAHISA. SO IT TURNS OUT THINGS ARE LOOKING UP-- THE EDITORIAL DEPARTMENT THINKS GREENERY CAN BE SERIALIZED IF NAKAI DOES THE ARTWORK!
LET'S GIVE THAT A TRY! IT'S ALMOST A GUARANTEED SUCCESS.
SO MY ARTWORK ISN'T GOOD ENOUGH... BUT I'D HAVE TO WORK WITH MR. NAKAI AGAIN...
I-IF THAT'S WHAT I NEED TO DO, I'LL DO IT.
I'M AWARE THAT MY ART IS NOT SUITED TO SHONEN MANGA... I'M NOT GOOD ENOUGH AT IT YET.
FWP
FWP
OKAY! THEN I'LL CONTACT NAKAI ABOUT IT.
I'LL CONTACT MR. NAKAI PERSONALLY. WE USED TO WORK TOGETHER, SO IT'LL PROBABLY BE EASIER FOR ME TO TALK TO HIM...
OH? I AGREE. BUT KEEP IN MIND THAT THE SERIES HASN'T BEEN GREENLIT YET.
FLIP...

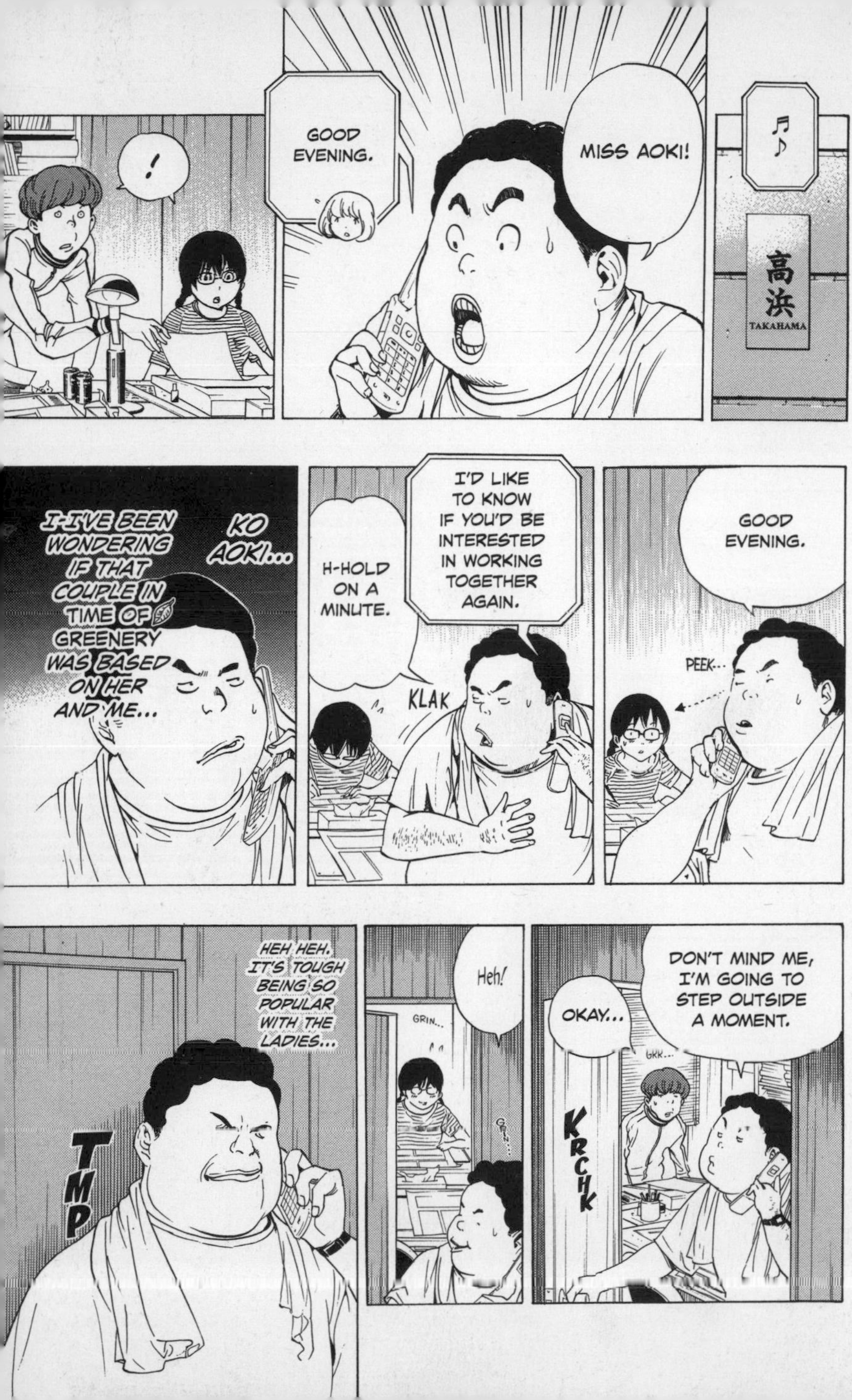

高浜
TAKAHAMA
MISS AOKI!
GOOD EVENING.
!
PEEK...
GOOD EVENING.
I'D LIKE TO KNOW IF YOU'D BE INTERESTED IN WORKING TOGETHER AGAIN.
H-HOLD ON A MINUTE.
KLAK
KO AOKI...
I-I'VE BEEN WONDERING IF THAT COUPLE IN TIME OF GREENERY WAS BASED ON HER AND ME...
DON'T MIND ME, I'M GOING TO STEP OUTSIDE A MOMENT.
OKAY...
GRR...
KRCHK
Heh!
GRIN...
GRIN...
HEH HEH. IT'S TOUGH BEING SO POPULAR WITH THE LADIES...
TMP

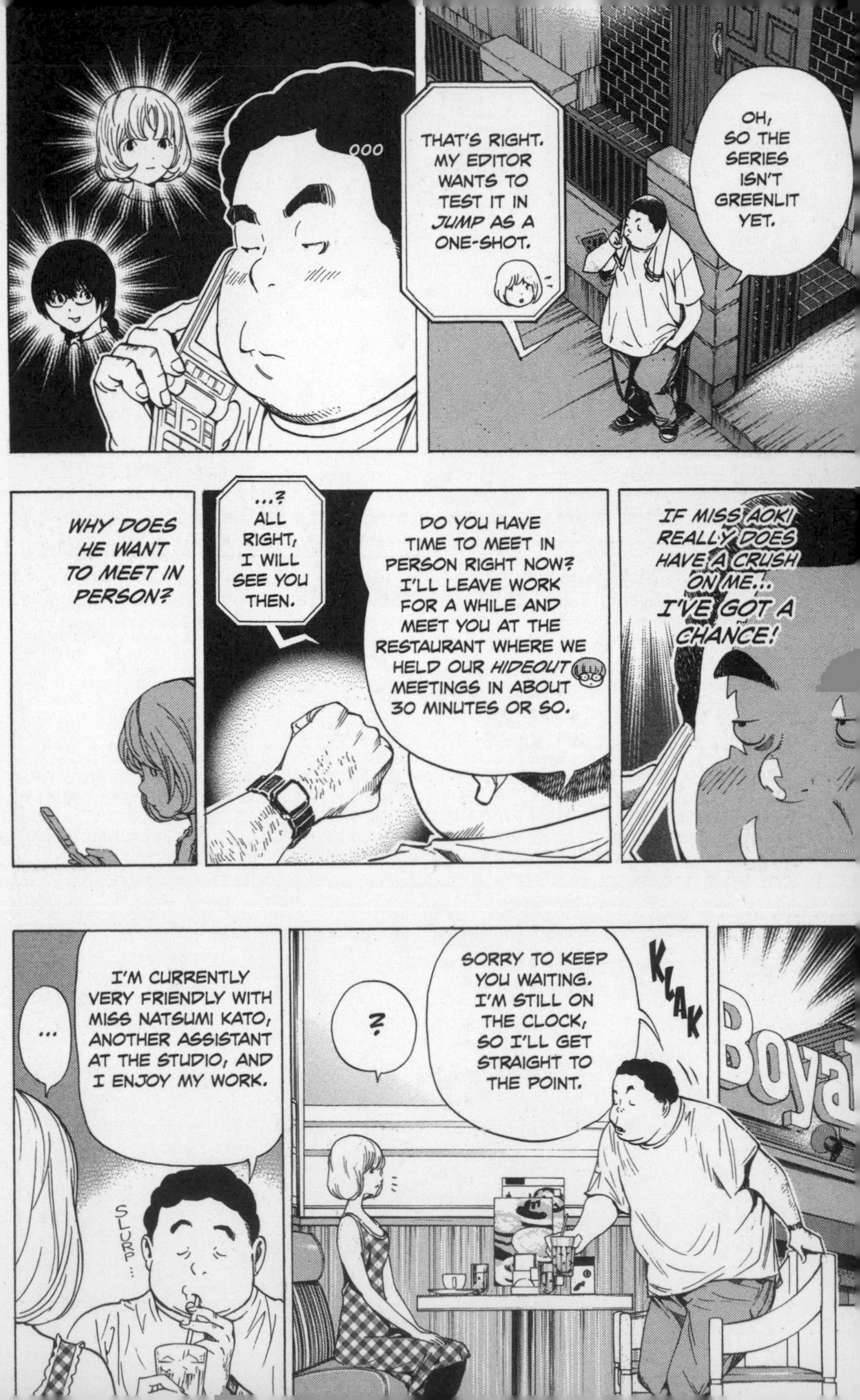
OH, SO THE SERIES ISN'T GREENLIT YET.
THAT'S RIGHT. MY EDITOR WANTS TO TEST IT IN *JUMP* AS A ONE-SHOT.
IF MISS AOKI REALLY DOES HAVE A CRUSH ON ME... I'VE GOT A CHANCE!
DO YOU HAVE TIME TO MEET IN PERSON RIGHT NOW? I'LL LEAVE WORK FOR A WHILE AND MEET YOU AT THE RESTAURANT WHERE WE HELD OUR *HIDEOUT* MEETINGS IN ABOUT 30 MINUTES OR SO.
...? ALL RIGHT, I WILL SEE YOU THEN.
WHY DOES HE WANT TO MEET IN PERSON?
KLAK
SORRY TO KEEP YOU WAITING. I'M STILL ON THE CLOCK, SO I'LL GET STRAIGHT TO THE POINT.
?
I'M CURRENTLY VERY FRIENDLY WITH MISS NATSUMI KATO, ANOTHER ASSISTANT AT THE STUDIO, AND I ENJOY MY WORK.
...
SLURP...

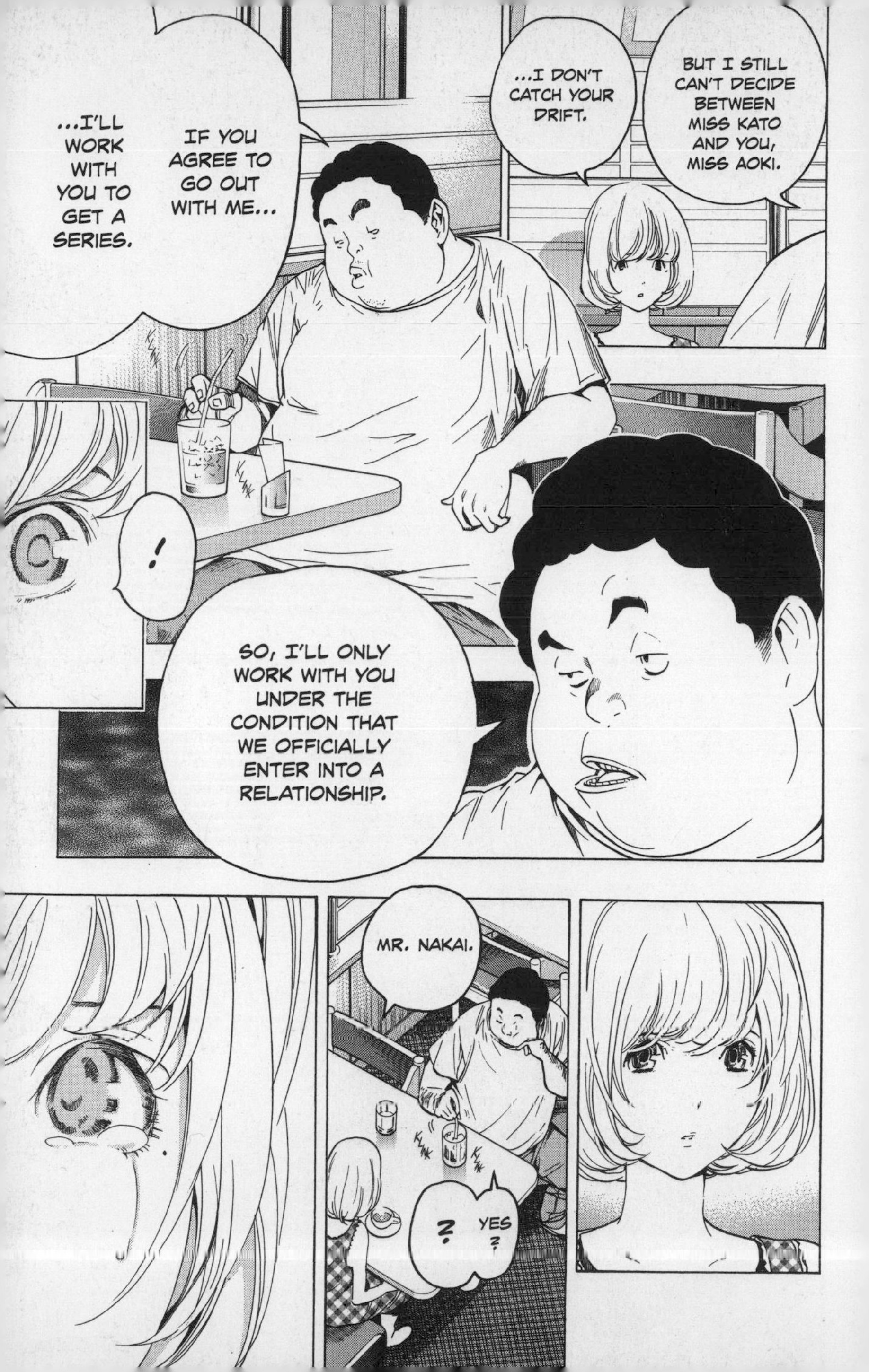
BUT I STILL CAN'T DECIDE BETWEEN MISS KATO AND YOU, MISS AOKI.
...I DON'T CATCH YOUR DRIFT.
IF YOU AGREE TO GO OUT WITH ME...
...I'LL WORK WITH YOU TO GET A SERIES.
KLINK
KLINK
SO, I'LL ONLY WORK WITH YOU UNDER THE CONDITION THAT WE OFFICIALLY ENTER INTO A RELATIONSHIP.
!
MR. NAKAI.
KLINK
KLINK
? YES ?

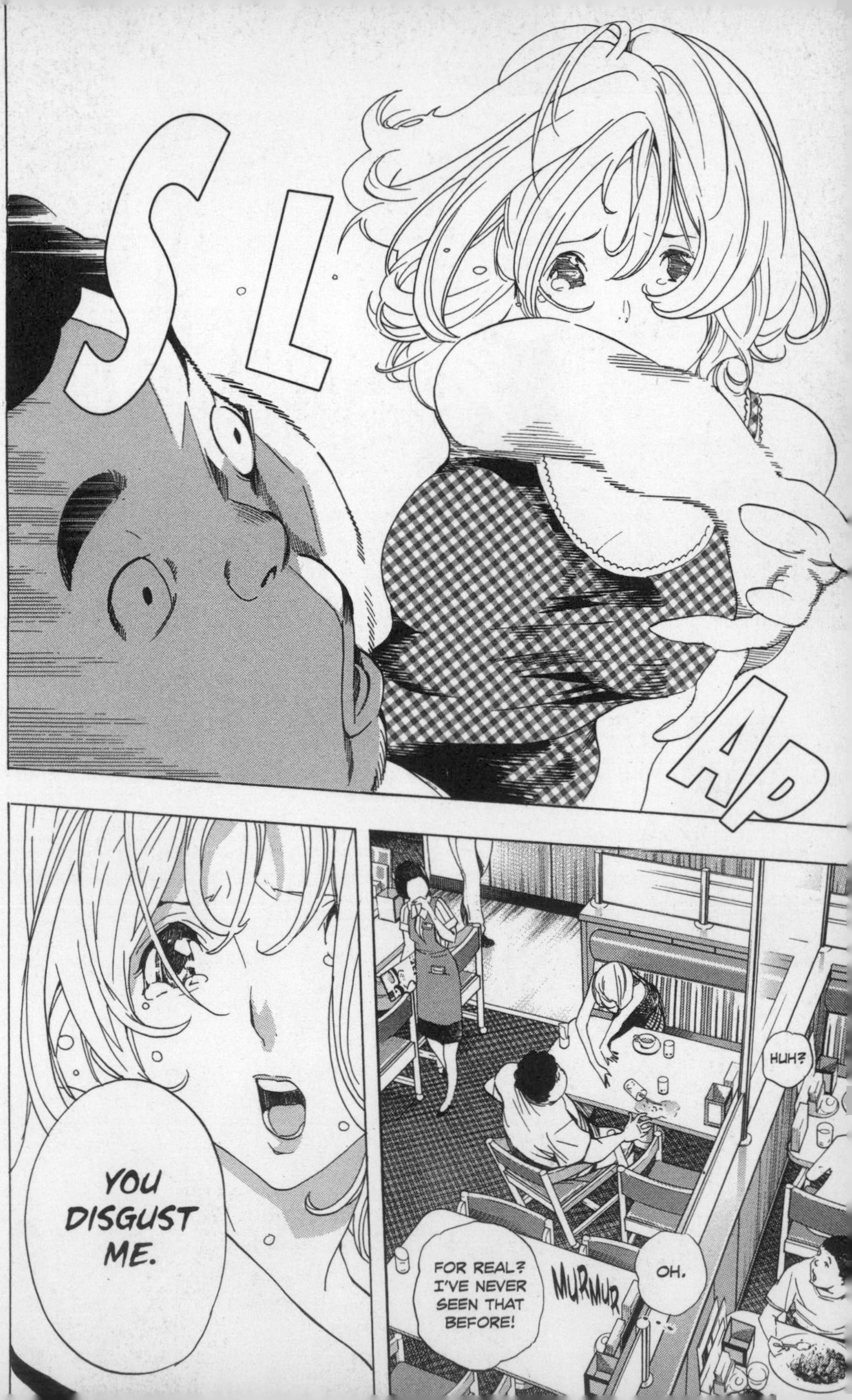
SLAP
HUH?
OH.
MURMUR
FOR REAL? I'VE NEVER SEEN THAT BEFORE!
YOU DISGUST ME.

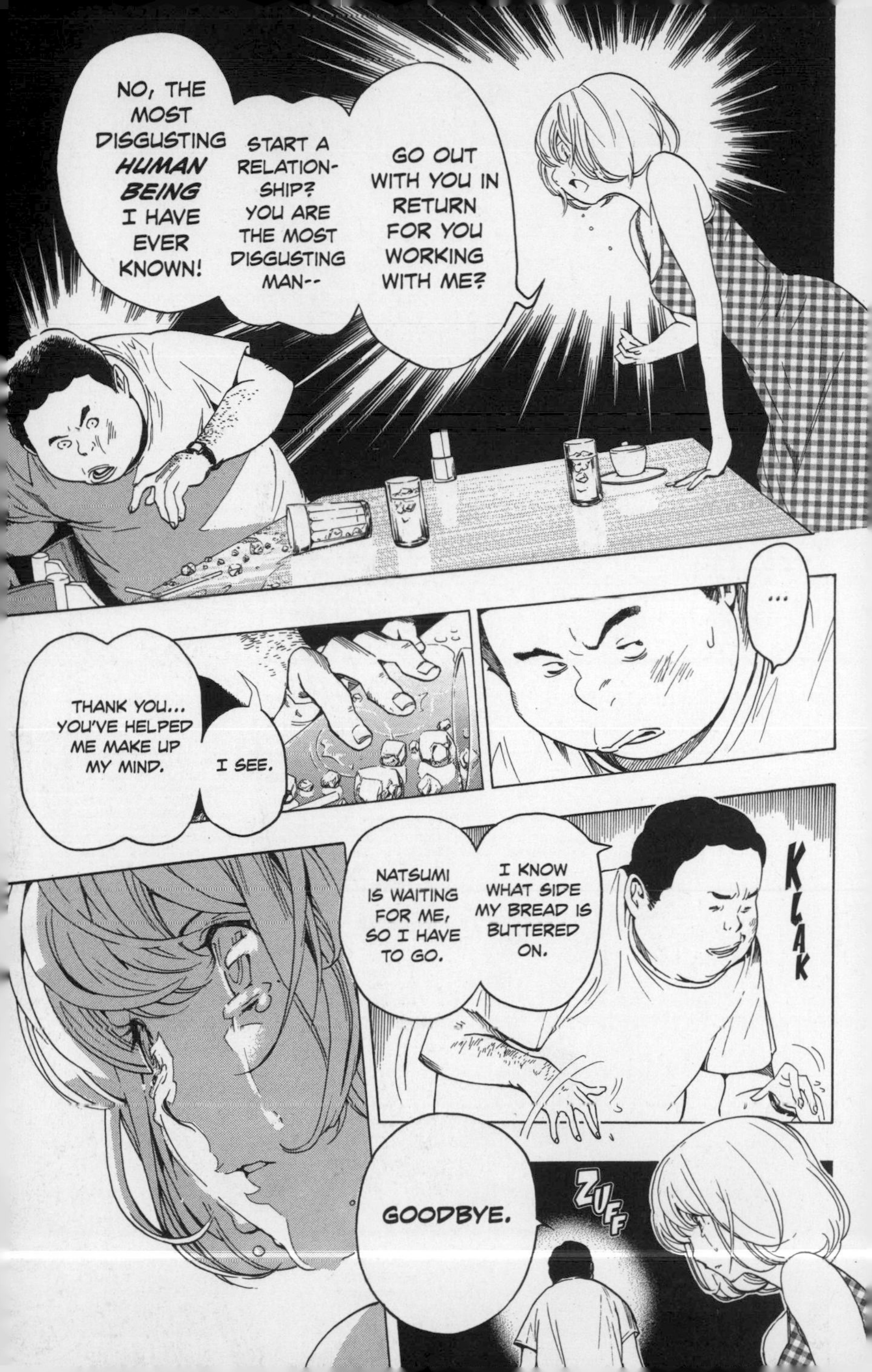
GO OUT WITH YOU IN RETURN FOR YOU WORKING WITH ME?
START A RELATION-SHIP? YOU ARE THE MOST DISGUSTING MAN--
NO, THE MOST DISGUSTING ***HUMAN BEING*** I HAVE EVER KNOWN!
...
I SEE.
THANK YOU... YOU'VE HELPED ME MAKE UP MY MIND.
KLAK
I KNOW WHAT SIDE MY BREAD IS BUTTERED ON.
NATSUMI IS WAITING FOR ME, SO I HAVE TO GO.
ZUFF
GOODBYE.

OHBA'S STORYBOARD

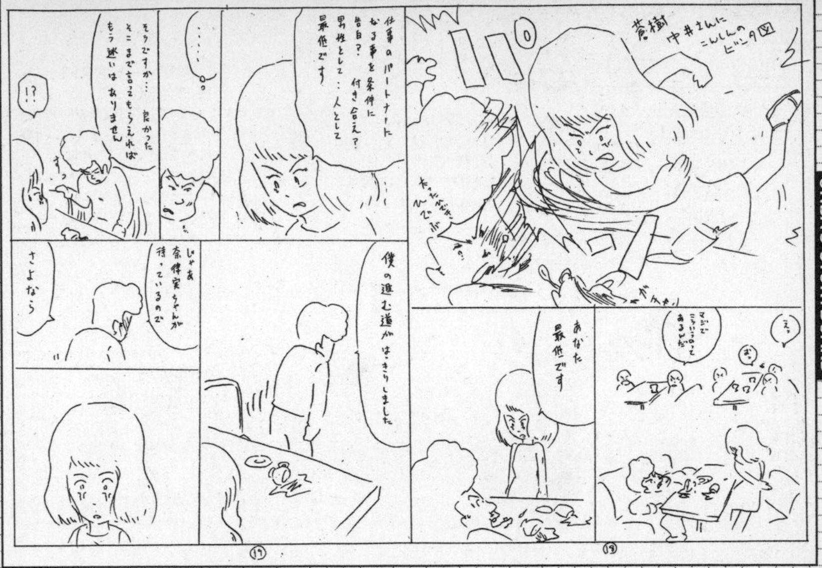
蒼樹 中井さんに こんしんの ビンタ図
あなた最低です
マジでこういうのってあるんだ
仕事のパートナーになる事を条件に告白? 付き合え? 男性として…人として最低です
……
そうですか… 良かった そこまで言ってもらえれば もう迷いはありません
!?
僕の進む道がはっきりしました
じゃあ 奈律実ちゃんが待っているので
さよなら

OBATA'S STORYBOARD

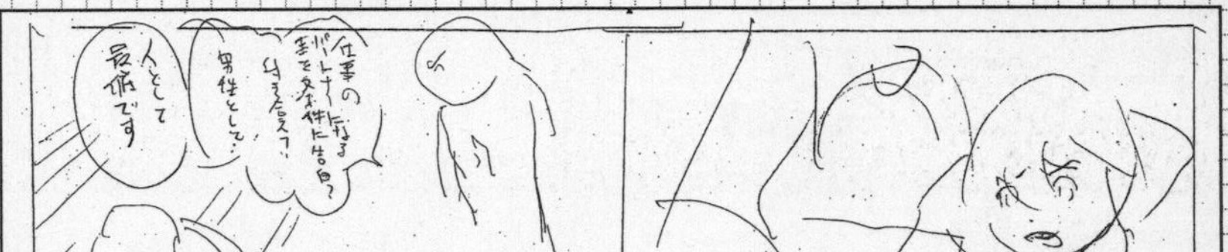
あなた最低です
仕事のパートナーになる事を条件に告白?
人として最低です
さよなら

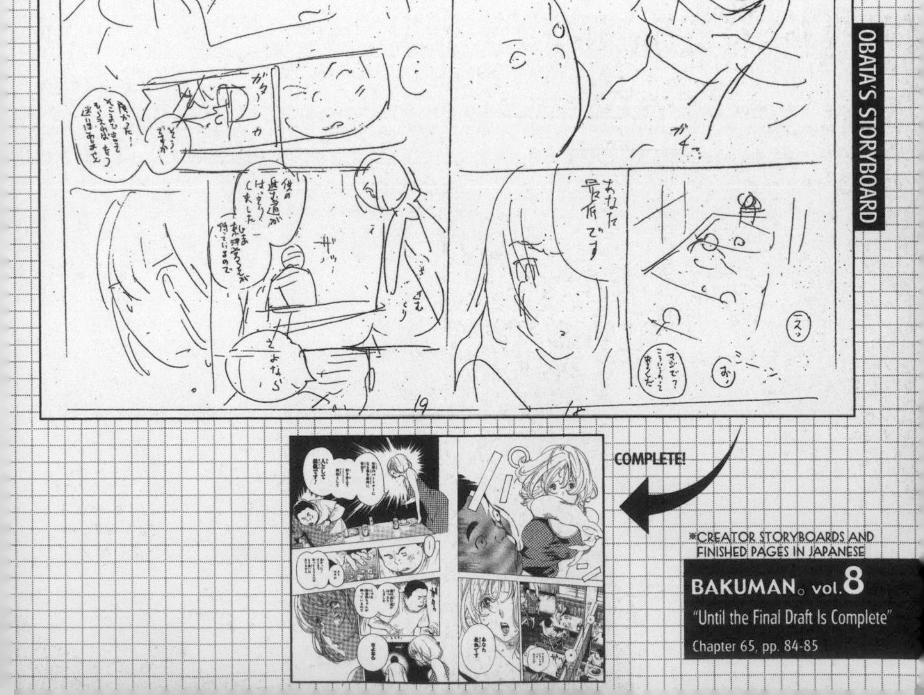

COMPLETE!

*CREATOR STORYBOARDS AND FINISHED PAGES IN JAPANESE

BAKUMAN。 vol.8

"Until the Final Draft Is Complete"

Chapter 65, pp. 84-85

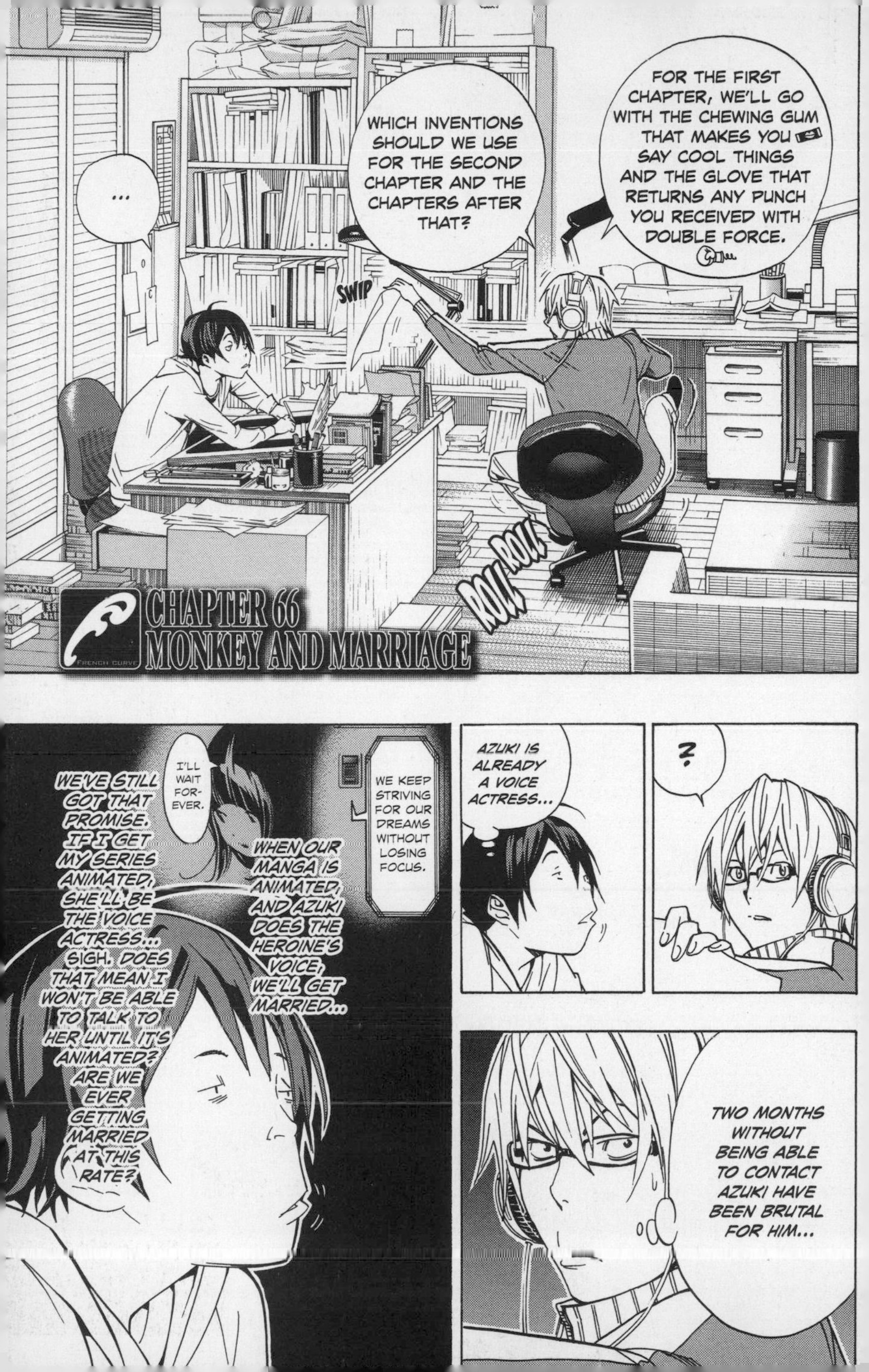
FOR THE FIRST CHAPTER, WE'LL GO WITH THE CHEWING GUM THAT MAKES YOU SAY COOL THINGS AND THE GLOVE THAT RETURNS ANY PUNCH YOU RECEIVED WITH DOUBLE FORCE.
WHICH INVENTIONS SHOULD WE USE FOR THE SECOND CHAPTER AND THE CHAPTERS AFTER THAT?
...
SWIP
ROLL ROLL
CHAPTER 66
MONKEY AND MARRIAGE
FRENCH CURVE
?
AZUKI IS ALREADY A VOICE ACTRESS...
TWO MONTHS WITHOUT BEING ABLE TO CONTACT AZUKI HAVE BEEN BRUTAL FOR HIM...
WE KEEP STRIVING FOR OUR DREAMS WITHOUT LOSING FOCUS.
I'LL WAIT FOR-EVER.
WHEN OUR MANGA IS ANIMATED, AND AZUKI DOES THE HEROINE'S VOICE, WE'LL GET MARRIED...
WE'VE STILL GOT THAT PROMISE. IF I GET MY SERIES ANIMATED, SHE'LL BE THE VOICE ACTRESS... SIGH. DOES THAT MEAN I WON'T BE ABLE TO TALK TO HER UNTIL IT'S ANIMATED? ARE WE EVER GETTING MARRIED AT THIS RATE?

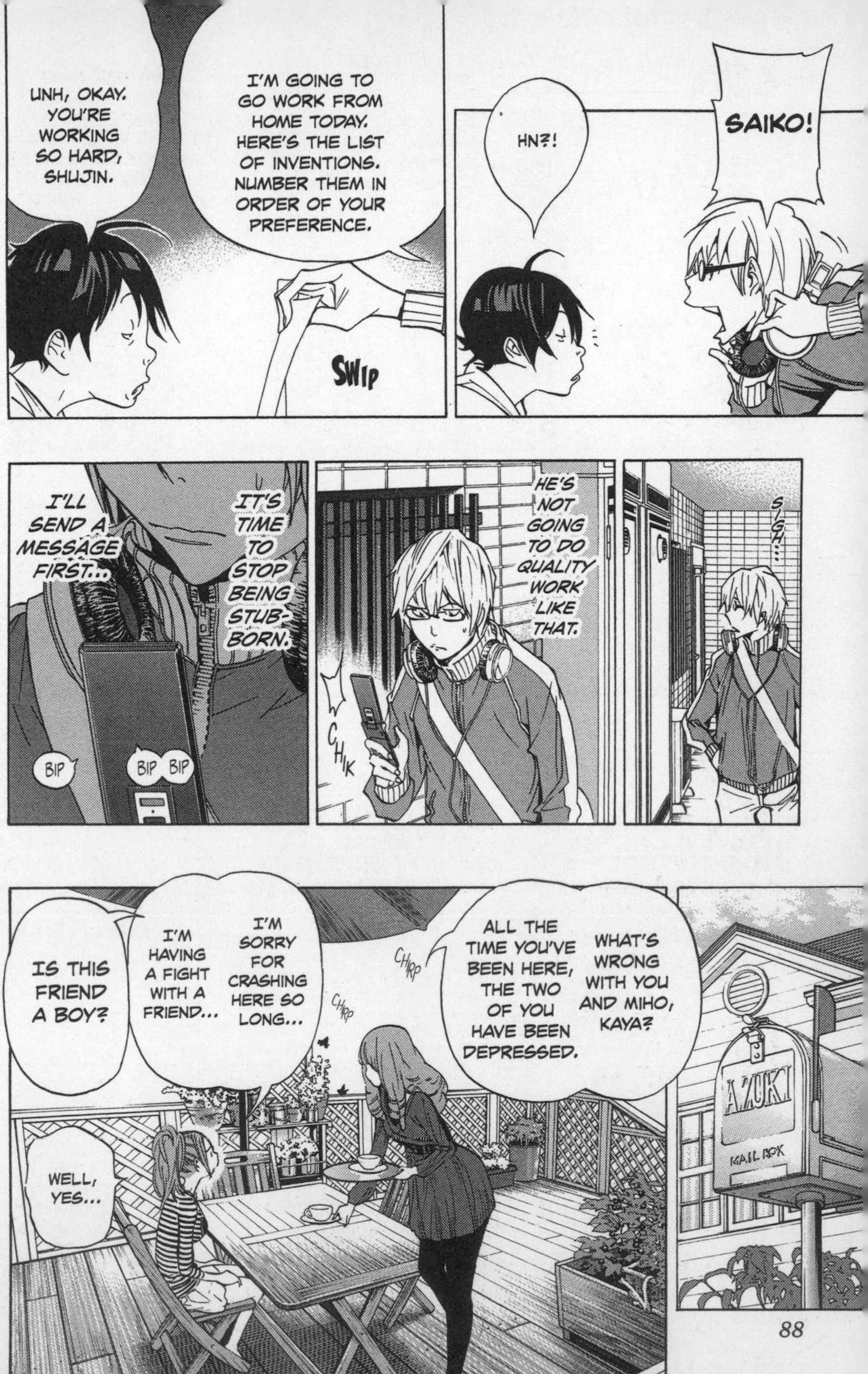
SAIKO!
HN?!
I'M GOING TO GO WORK FROM HOME TODAY. HERE'S THE LIST OF INVENTIONS. NUMBER THEM IN ORDER OF YOUR PREFERENCE.
UNH, OKAY. YOU'RE WORKING SO HARD, SHUJIN.
SWIP
SIGH...
HE'S NOT GOING TO DO QUALITY WORK LIKE THAT.
CHIK
IT'S TIME TO STOP BEING STUB-BORN.
I'LL SEND A MESSAGE FIRST...
BIP
BIP BIP
BIP
AZUKI
MAIL BOX
WHAT'S WRONG WITH YOU AND MIHO, KAYA?
ALL THE TIME YOU'VE BEEN HERE, THE TWO OF YOU HAVE BEEN DEPRESSED.
CHIRP
CHIRP
I'M SORRY FOR CRASHING HERE SO LONG...
I'M HAVING A FIGHT WITH A FRIEND...
IS THIS FRIEND A BOY?
WELL, YES...

READ THIS WAY

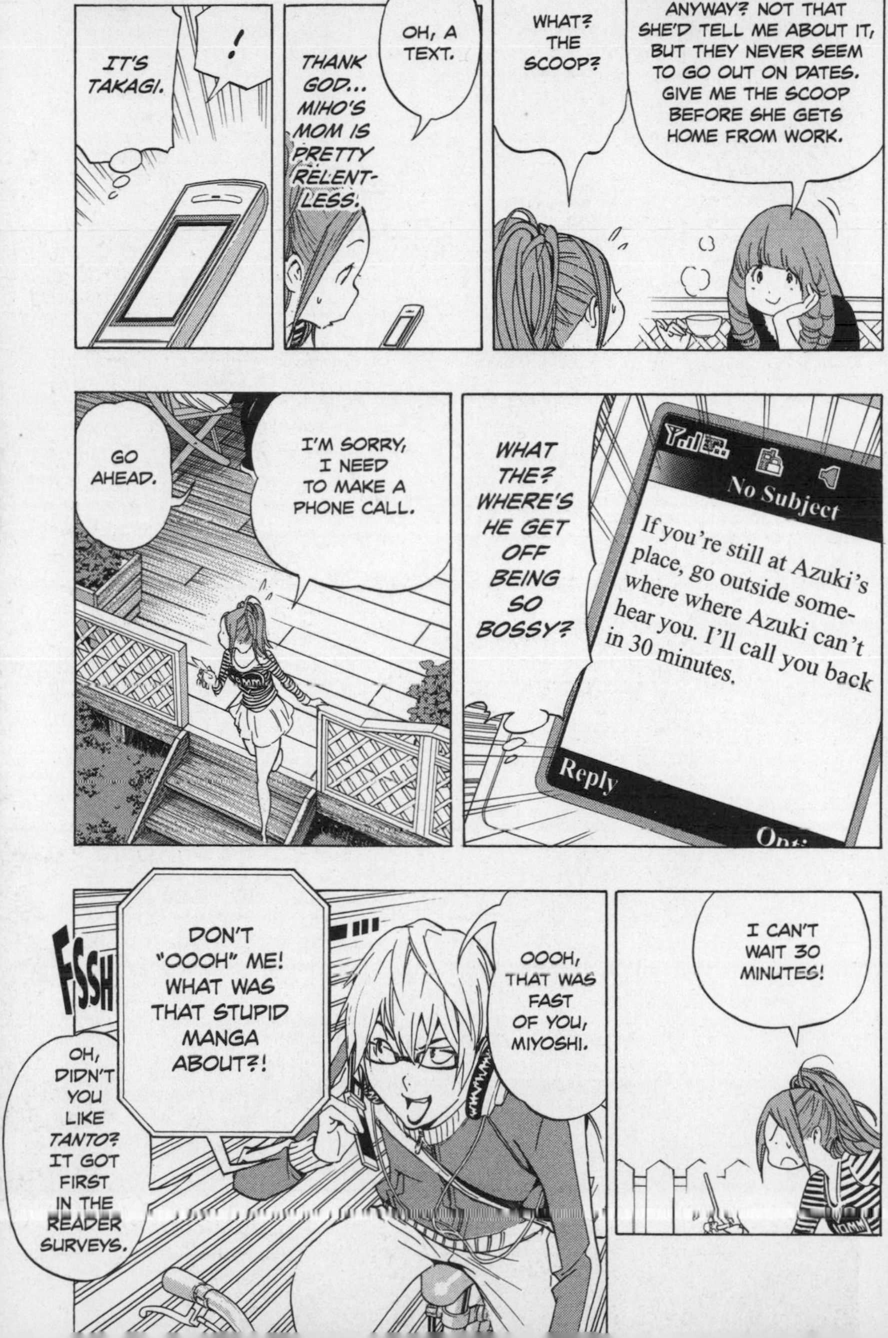
HOW ARE MIHO AND MASHIRO DOING, ANYWAY? NOT THAT SHE'D TELL ME ABOUT IT, BUT THEY NEVER SEEM TO GO OUT ON DATES. GIVE ME THE SCOOP BEFORE SHE GETS HOME FROM WORK.
WHAT? THE SCOOP?
OH, A TEXT.
THANK GOD... MIHO'S MOM IS PRETTY RELENT-LESS.
!
IT'S TAKAGI.
No Subject
If you're still at Azuki's place, go outside some-where where Azuki can't hear you. I'll call you back in 30 minutes.
Reply
WHAT THE? WHERE'S HE GET OFF BEING SO BOSSY?
I'M SORRY, I NEED TO MAKE A PHONE CALL.
GO AHEAD.
I CAN'T WAIT 30 MINUTES!
OOOH, THAT WAS FAST OF YOU, MIYOSHI.
DON'T "OOOH" ME! WHAT WAS THAT STUPID MANGA ABOUT?!
FSSH
OH, DIDN'T YOU LIKE *TANTO*? IT GOT FIRST IN THE READER SURVEYS.

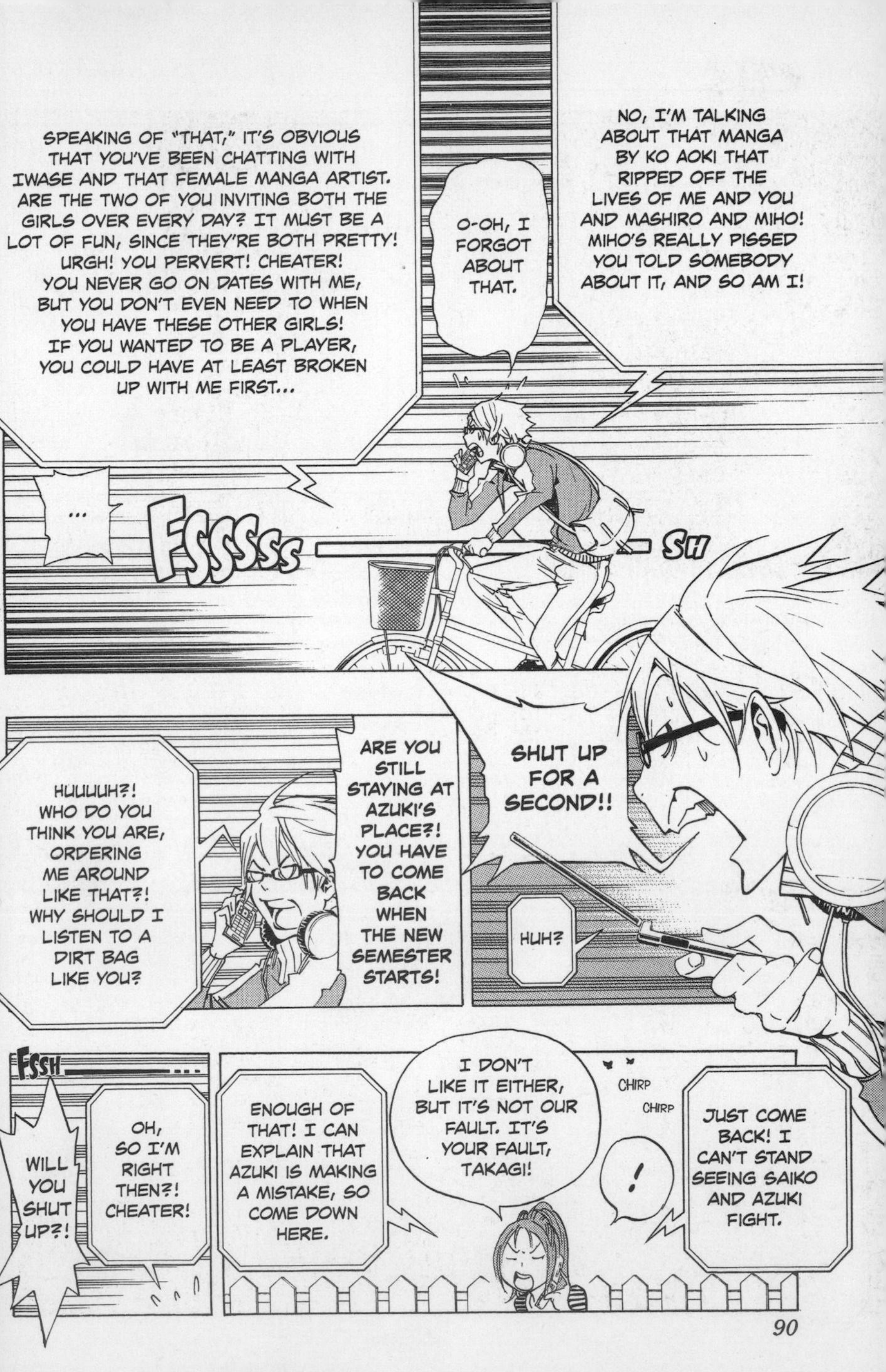
NO, I'M TALKING ABOUT THAT MANGA BY KO AOKI THAT RIPPED OFF THE LIVES OF ME AND YOU AND MASHIRO AND MIHO! MIHO'S REALLY PISSED YOU TOLD SOMEBODY ABOUT IT, AND SO AM I!
O-OH, I FORGOT ABOUT THAT.
SPEAKING OF "THAT," IT'S OBVIOUS THAT YOU'VE BEEN CHATTING WITH IWASE AND THAT FEMALE MANGA ARTIST. ARE THE TWO OF YOU INVITING BOTH THE GIRLS OVER EVERY DAY? IT MUST BE A LOT OF FUN, SINCE THEY'RE BOTH PRETTY! URGH! YOU PERVERT! CHEATER! YOU NEVER GO ON DATES WITH ME, BUT YOU DON'T EVEN NEED TO WHEN YOU HAVE THESE OTHER GIRLS! IF YOU WANTED TO BE A PLAYER, YOU COULD HAVE AT LEAST BROKEN UP WITH ME FIRST...
SH
FSSSSS
...
SHUT UP FOR A SECOND!!
HUH?
ARE YOU STILL STAYING AT AZUKI'S PLACE?! YOU HAVE TO COME BACK WHEN THE NEW SEMESTER STARTS!
HUUUUH?! WHO DO YOU THINK YOU ARE, ORDERING ME AROUND LIKE THAT?! WHY SHOULD I LISTEN TO A DIRT BAG LIKE YOU?
JUST COME BACK! I CAN'T STAND SEEING SAIKO AND AZUKI FIGHT.
CHIRP
CHIRP
!
I DON'T LIKE IT EITHER, BUT IT'S NOT OUR FAULT. IT'S YOUR FAULT, TAKAGI!
ENOUGH OF THAT! I CAN EXPLAIN THAT AZUKI IS MAKING A MISTAKE, SO COME DOWN HERE.
FSSH
OH, SO I'M RIGHT THEN?! CHEATER!
WILL YOU SHUT UP?!

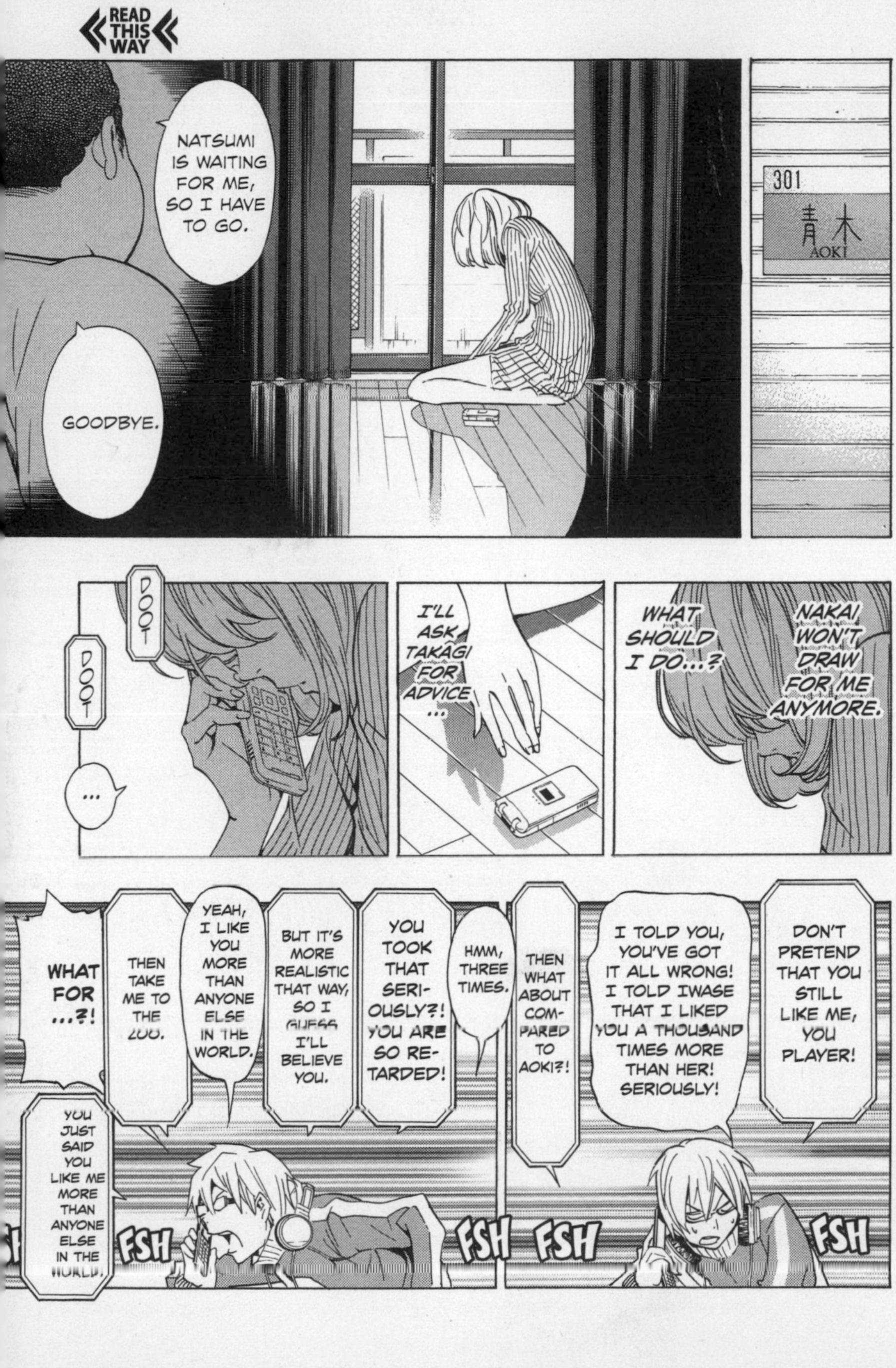
READ THIS WAY
301
青木
AOKI
NATSUMI IS WAITING FOR ME, SO I HAVE TO GO.
GOODBYE.
NAKAI WON'T DRAW FOR ME ANYMORE.
WHAT SHOULD I DO...?
I'LL ASK TAKAGI FOR ADVICE...
DOOT
DOOT
...
DON'T PRETEND THAT YOU STILL LIKE ME, YOU PLAYER!
I TOLD YOU, YOU'VE GOT IT ALL WRONG! I TOLD IWASE THAT I LIKED YOU A THOUSAND TIMES MORE THAN HER! SERIOUSLY!
THEN WHAT ABOUT COMPARED TO AOKI?!
FSH
FSH
HMM, THREE TIMES.
YOU TOOK THAT SERIOUSLY?! YOU ARE SO RETARDED!
BUT IT'S MORE REALISTIC THAT WAY, SO I GUESS I'LL BELIEVE YOU.
YEAH, I LIKE YOU MORE THAN ANYONE ELSE IN THE WORLD.
THEN TAKE ME TO THE ZOO.
WHAT FOR...?!
YOU JUST SAID YOU LIKE ME MORE THAN ANYONE ELSE IN THE WORLD.
FSH

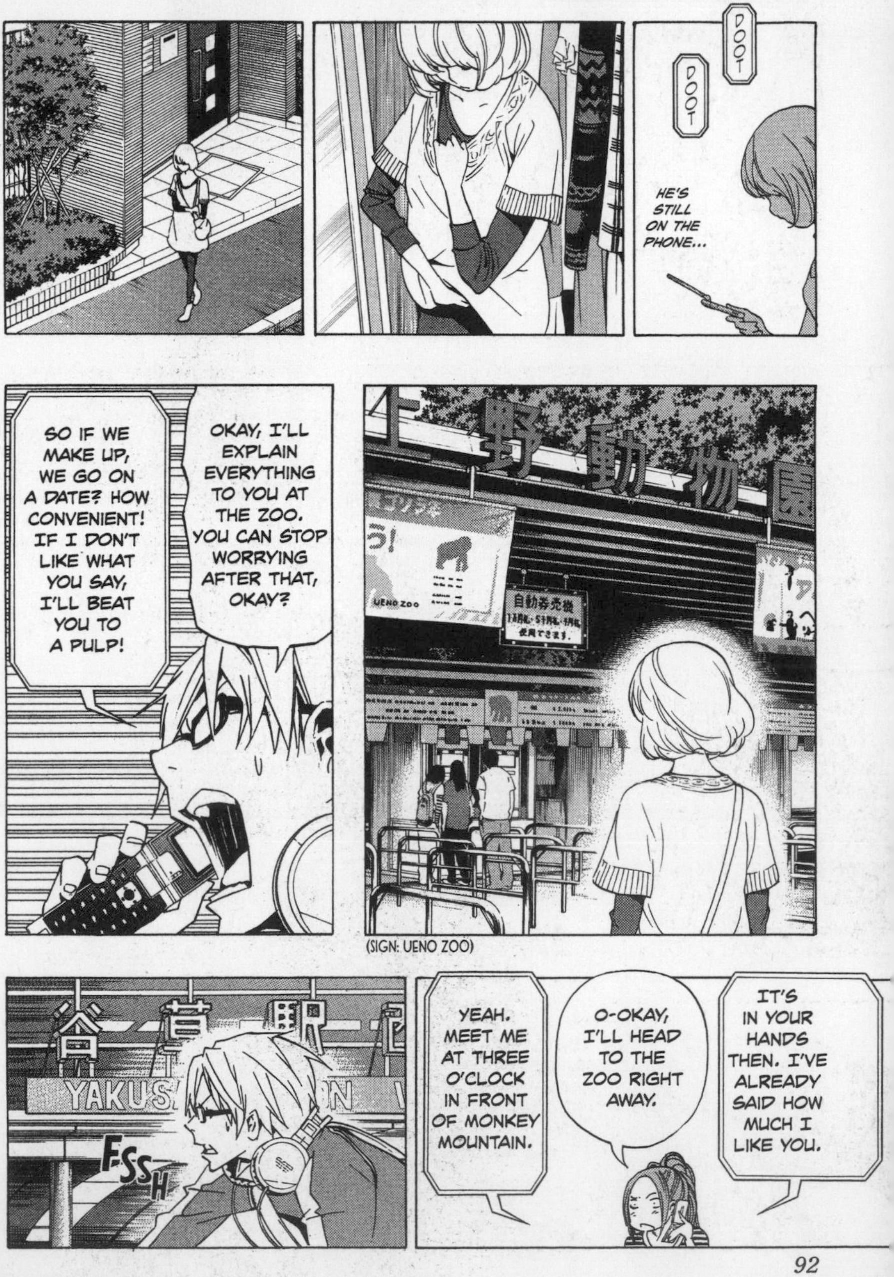
DOOT DOOT
DOOT DOOT
HE'S STILL ON THE PHONE...
上野動物園
UENO ZOO
自動券売機
OKAY, I'LL EXPLAIN EVERYTHING TO YOU AT THE ZOO. YOU CAN STOP WORRYING AFTER THAT, OKAY?
SO IF WE MAKE UP, WE GO ON A DATE? HOW CONVENIENT! IF I DON'T LIKE WHAT YOU SAY, I'LL BEAT YOU TO A PULP!
IT'S IN YOUR HANDS THEN. I'VE ALREADY SAID HOW MUCH I LIKE YOU.
O-OKAY, I'LL HEAD TO THE ZOO RIGHT AWAY.
YEAH. MEET ME AT THREE O'CLOCK IN FRONT OF MONKEY MOUNTAIN.
YAKUS ON
F-S-S-H
(SIGN: UENO ZOO)

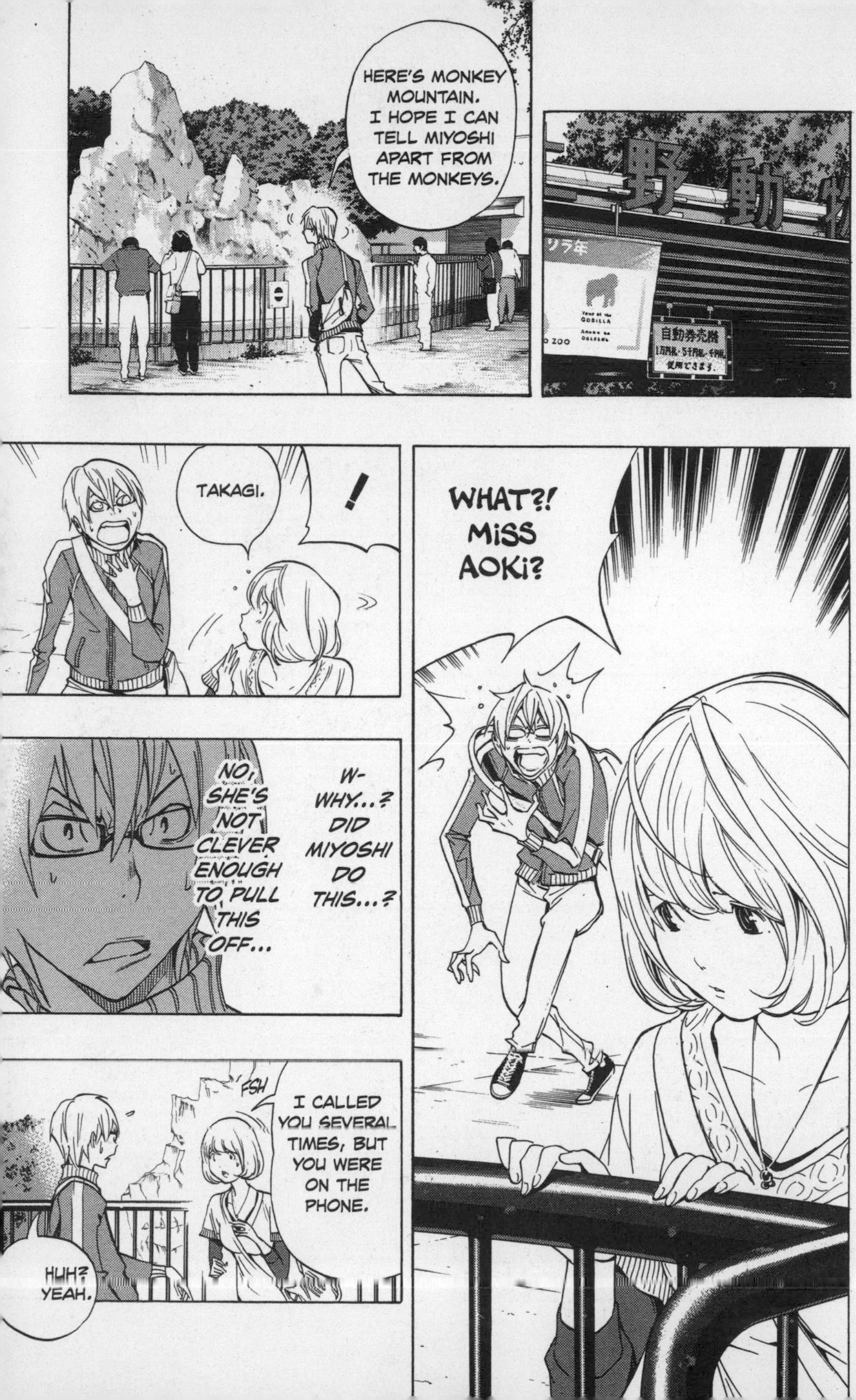
自動券売機
使用できます。
HERE'S MONKEY MOUNTAIN. I HOPE I CAN TELL MIYOSHI APART FROM THE MONKEYS.
WHAT?! MISS AOKI?
TAKAGI.
!
W-WHY...? DID MIYOSHI DO THIS...?
NO, SHE'S NOT CLEVER ENOUGH TO PULL THIS OFF...
FSH
I CALLED YOU SEVERAL TIMES, BUT YOU WERE ON THE PHONE.
HUH? YEAH.

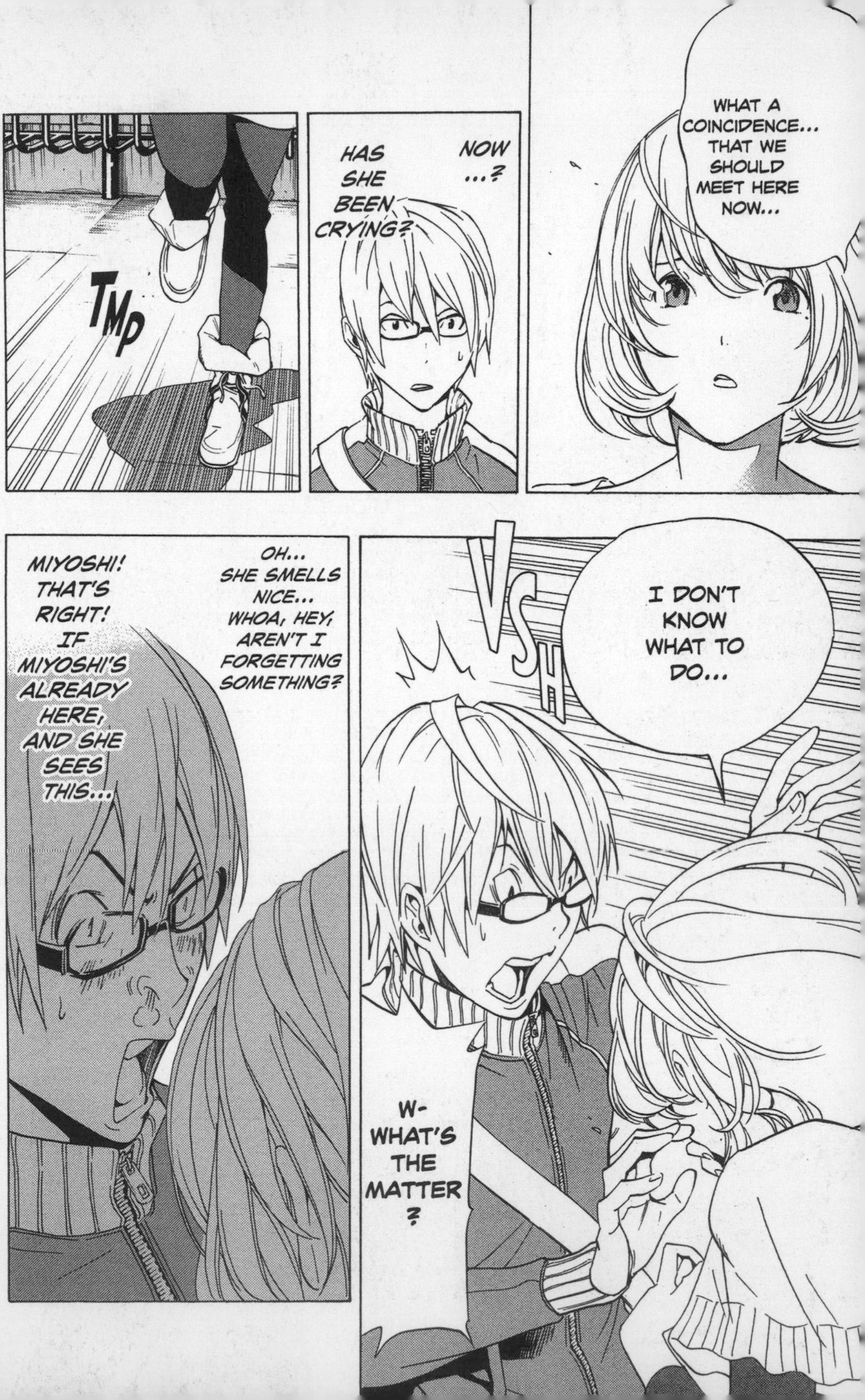
WHAT A COINCIDENCE... THAT WE SHOULD MEET HERE NOW...
NOW ...?
HAS SHE BEEN CRYING?
TMP
VSH
I DON'T KNOW WHAT TO DO...
W- WHAT'S THE MATTER?
OH... SHE SMELLS NICE... WHOA, HEY, AREN'T I FORGETTING SOMETHING?
MIYOSHI! THAT'S RIGHT! IF MIYOSHI'S ALREADY HERE, AND SHE SEES THIS...

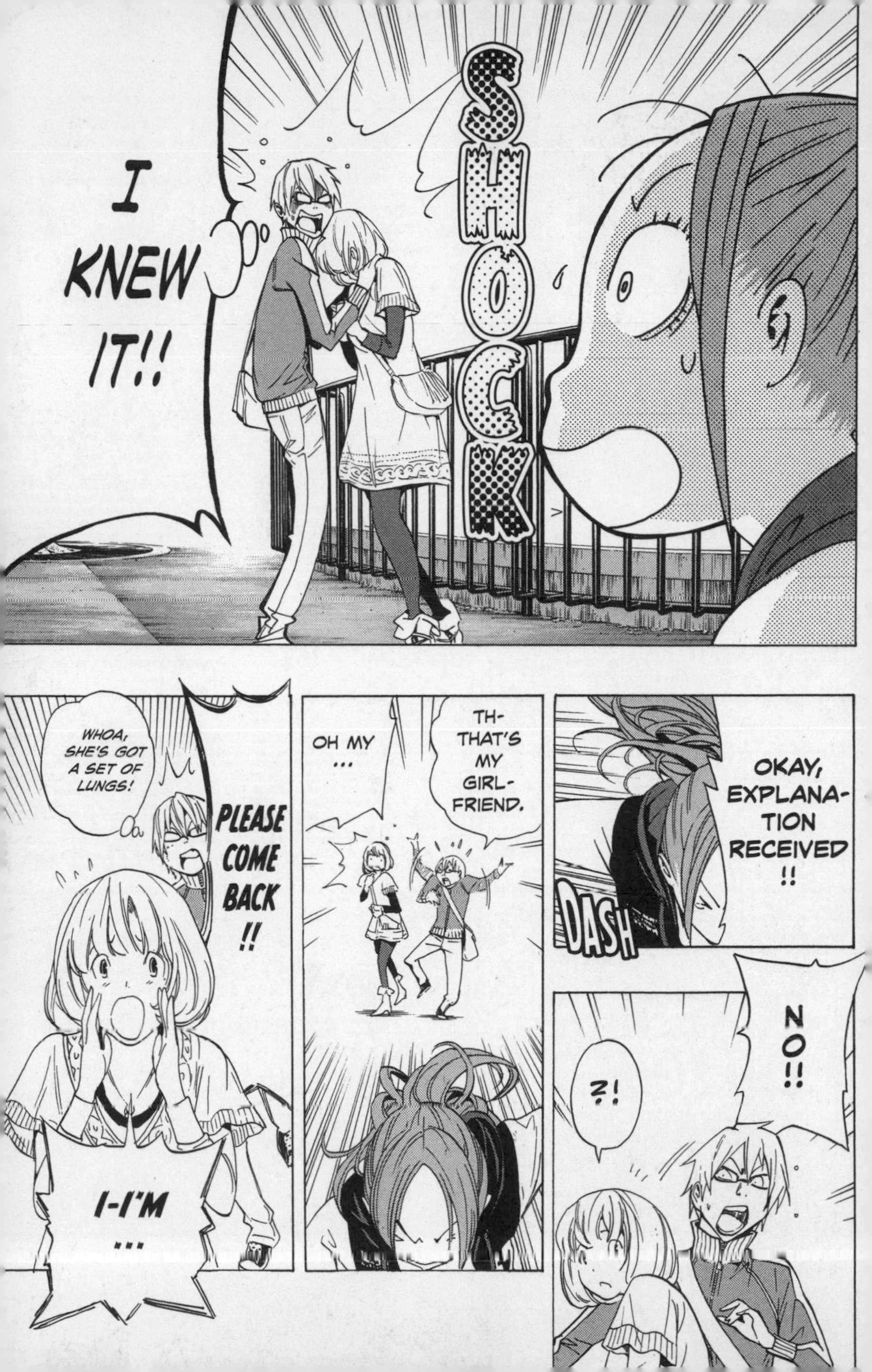
SHOCK
I KNEW IT!!
OKAY, EXPLANATION RECEIVED!!
DASH
NO!!
?!
TH-THAT'S MY GIRLFRIEND.
OH MY ...
PLEASE COME BACK!!
WHOA, SHE'S GOT A SET OF LUNGS!
I-I'M ...

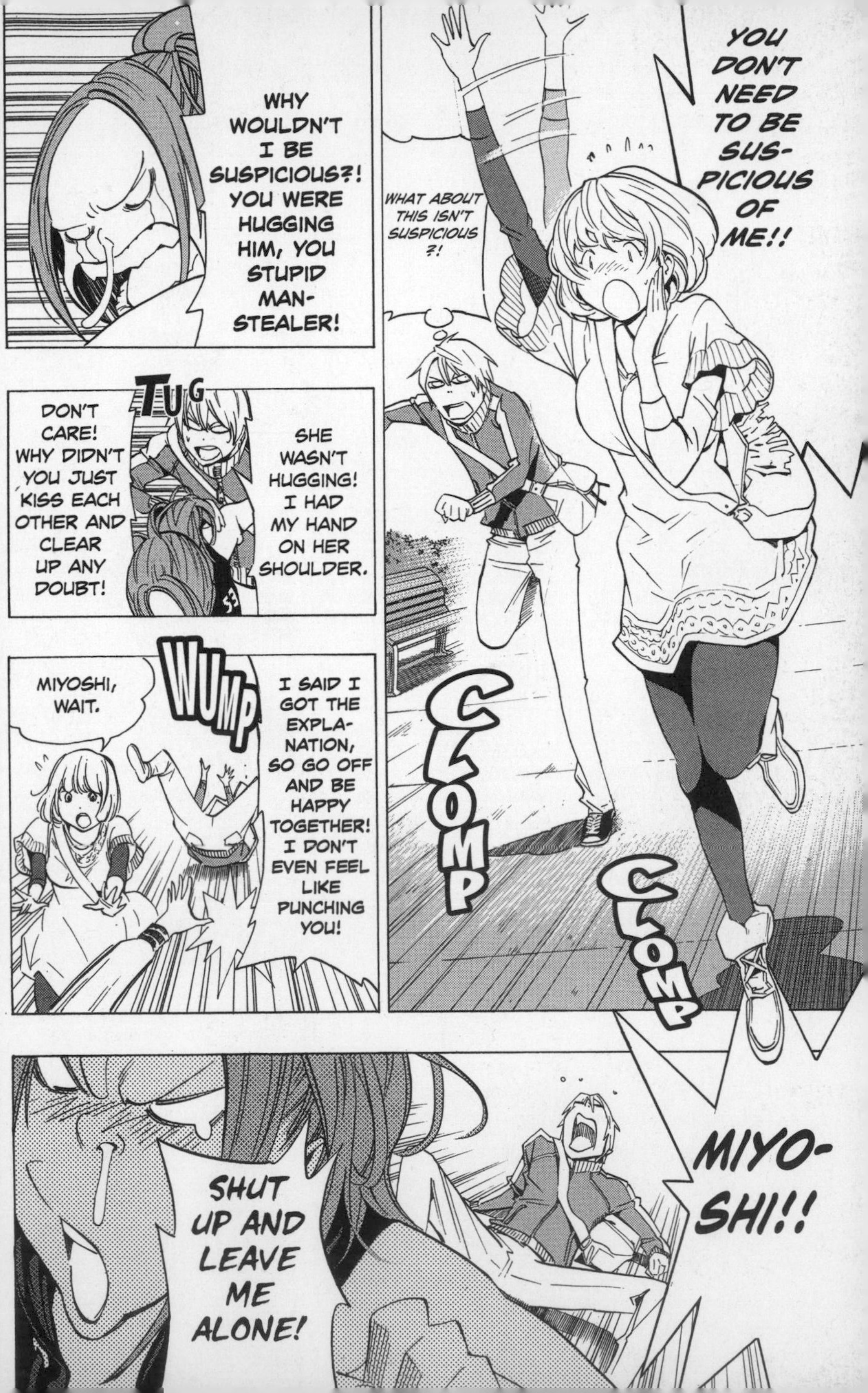
YOU DON'T NEED TO BE SUS-PICIOUS OF ME!!
WHAT ABOUT THIS ISN'T SUSPICIOUS ?!
CLOMP
CLOMP
WHY WOULDN'T I BE SUSPICIOUS?! YOU WERE HUGGING HIM, YOU STUPID MAN-STEALER!
SHE WASN'T HUGGING! I HAD MY HAND ON HER SHOULDER.
TUG
DON'T CARE! WHY DIDN'T YOU JUST KISS EACH OTHER AND CLEAR UP ANY DOUBT!
I SAID I GOT THE EXPLA-NATION, SO GO OFF AND BE HAPPY TOGETHER! I DON'T EVEN FEEL LIKE PUNCHING YOU!
WUMP
MIYOSHI, WAIT.
MIYO-SHI!!
SHUT UP AND LEAVE ME ALONE!

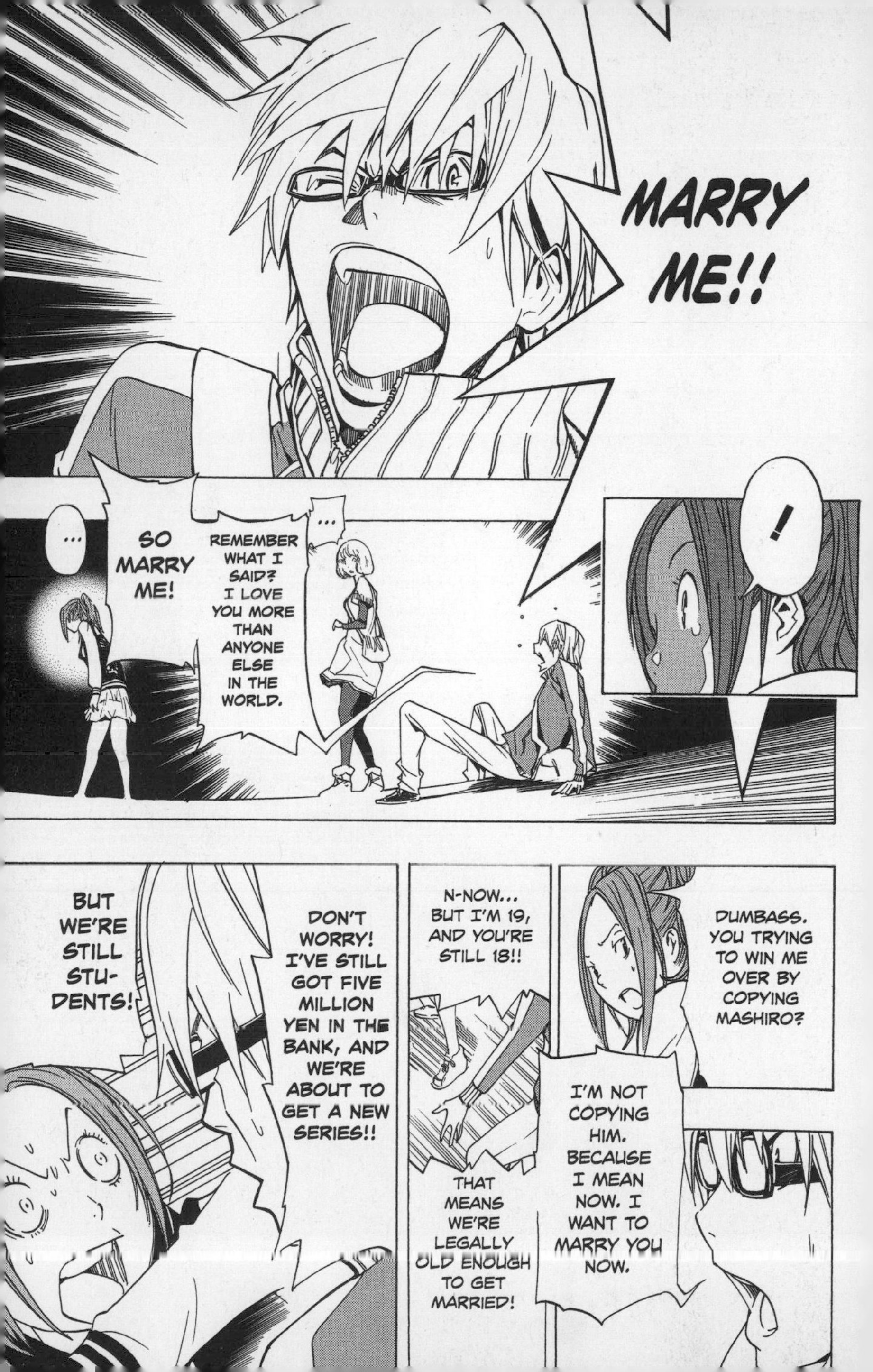
MARRY ME!!
!
...
REMEMBER WHAT I SAID? I LOVE YOU MORE THAN ANYONE ELSE IN THE WORLD.
SO MARRY ME!
...
DUMBASS. YOU TRYING TO WIN ME OVER BY COPYING MASHIRO?
I'M NOT COPYING HIM. BECAUSE I MEAN NOW. I WANT TO MARRY YOU NOW.
N-NOW... BUT I'M 19, AND YOU'RE STILL 18!!
THAT MEANS WE'RE LEGALLY OLD ENOUGH TO GET MARRIED!
BUT WE'RE STILL STU-DENTS!
DON'T WORRY! I'VE STILL GOT FIVE MILLION YEN IN THE BANK, AND WE'RE ABOUT TO GET A NEW SERIES!!

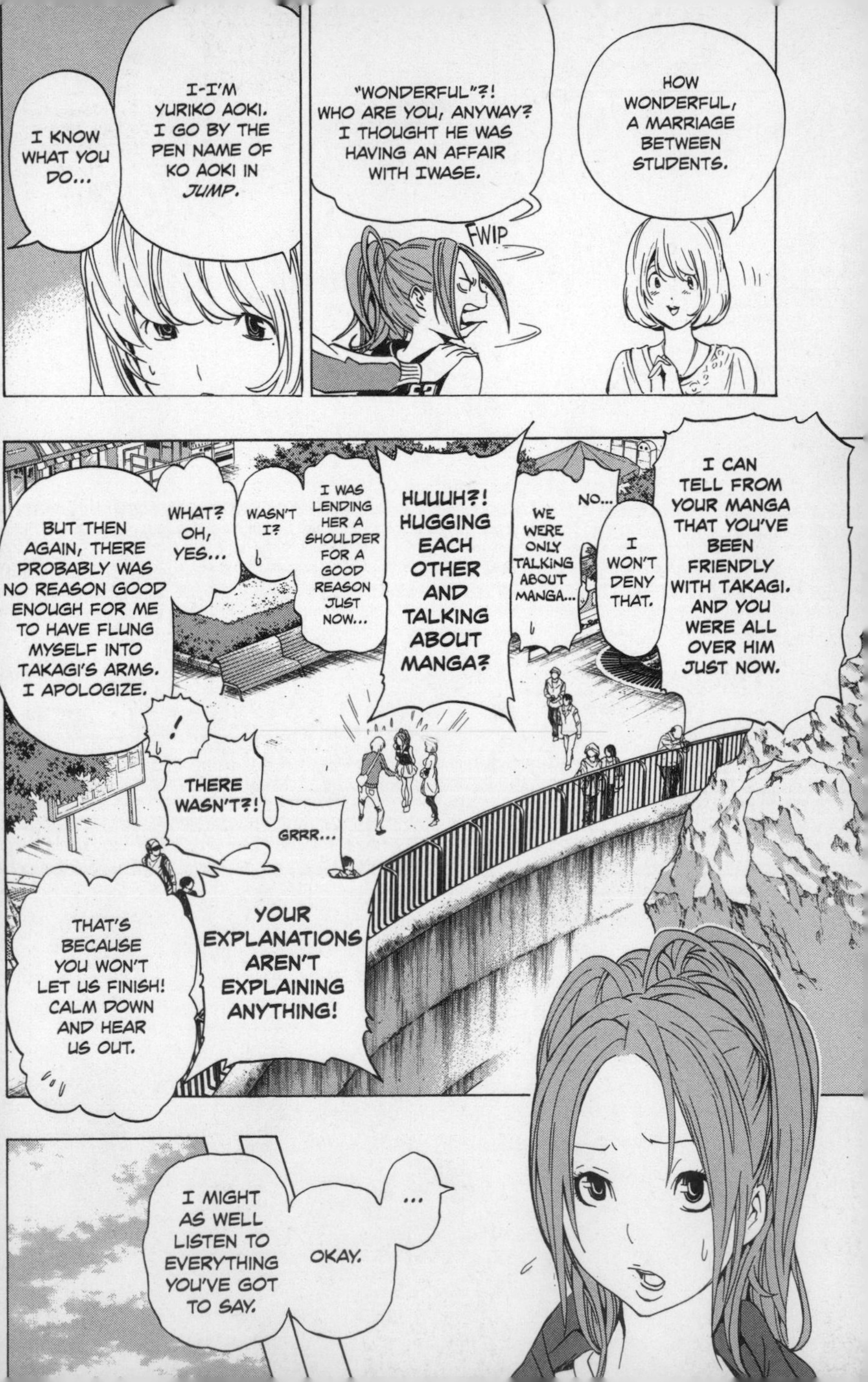
HOW WONDERFUL, A MARRIAGE BETWEEN STUDENTS.
"WONDERFUL"?! WHO ARE YOU, ANYWAY? I THOUGHT HE WAS HAVING AN AFFAIR WITH IWASE.
FWIP
I-I'M YURIKO AOKI. I GO BY THE PEN NAME OF KO AOKI IN *JUMP*.
I KNOW WHAT YOU DO...
I CAN TELL FROM YOUR MANGA THAT YOU'VE BEEN FRIENDLY WITH TAKAGI. AND YOU WERE ALL OVER HIM JUST NOW.
I WON'T DENY THAT.
NO...
WE WERE ONLY TALKING ABOUT MANGA...
HUUUH?! HUGGING EACH OTHER AND TALKING ABOUT MANGA?
I WAS LENDING HER A SHOULDER FOR A GOOD REASON JUST NOW...
WASN'T I?
WHAT? OH, YES...
BUT THEN AGAIN, THERE PROBABLY WAS NO REASON GOOD ENOUGH FOR ME TO HAVE FLUNG MYSELF INTO TAKAGI'S ARMS. I APOLOGIZE.
!
THERE WASN'T?!
GRRR...
YOUR EXPLANATIONS AREN'T EXPLAINING ANYTHING!
THAT'S BECAUSE YOU WON'T LET US FINISH! CALM DOWN AND HEAR US OUT.
...
OKAY.
I MIGHT AS WELL LISTEN TO EVERYTHING YOU'VE GOT TO SAY.

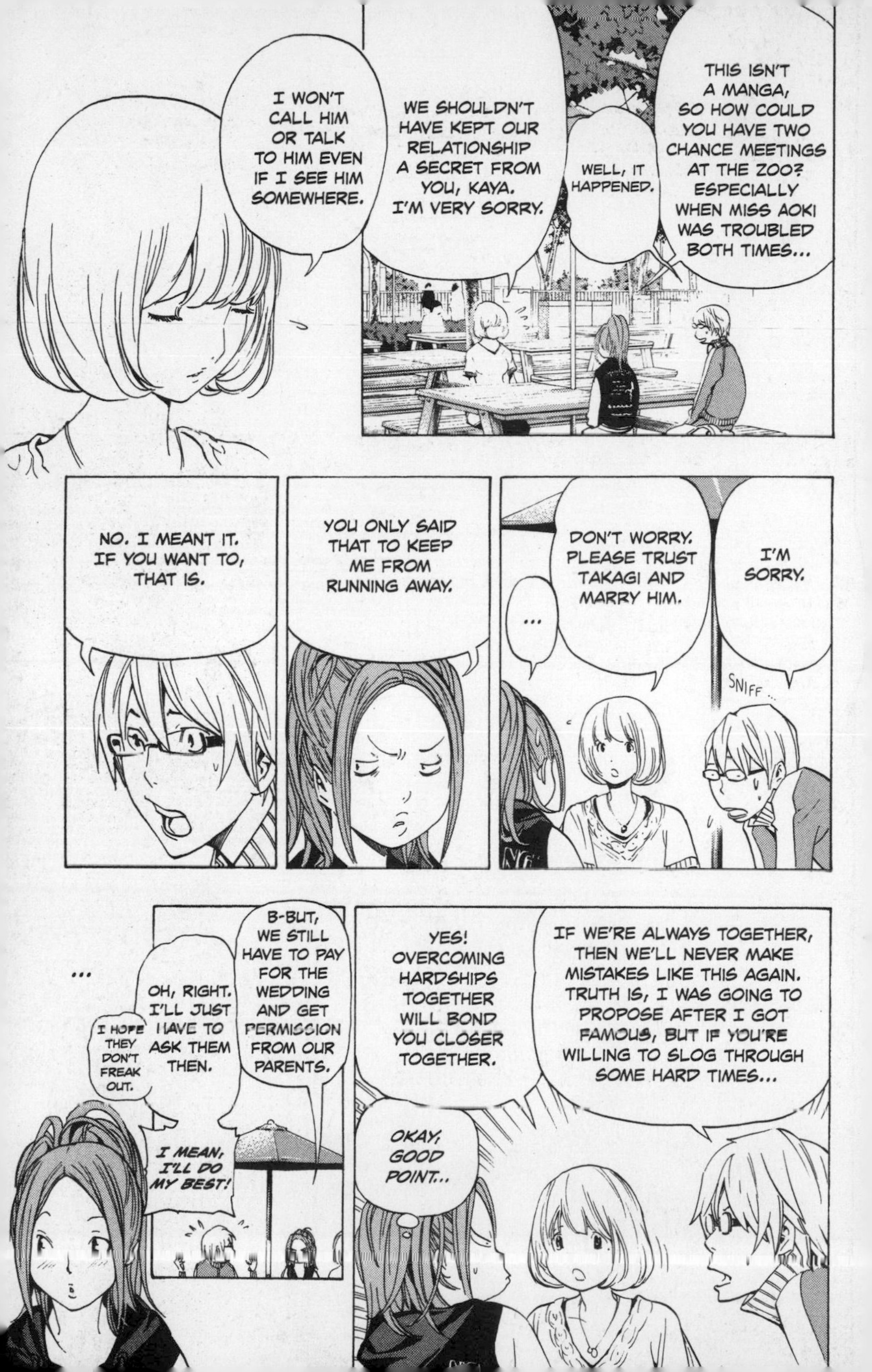
THIS ISN'T A MANGA, SO HOW COULD YOU HAVE TWO CHANCE MEETINGS AT THE ZOO? ESPECIALLY WHEN MISS AOKI WAS TROUBLED BOTH TIMES...
WELL, IT HAPPENED.
WE SHOULDN'T HAVE KEPT OUR RELATIONSHIP A SECRET FROM YOU, KAYA. I'M VERY SORRY.
I WON'T CALL HIM OR TALK TO HIM EVEN IF I SEE HIM SOMEWHERE.
I'M SORRY.
SNIFF...
DON'T WORRY. PLEASE TRUST TAKAGI AND MARRY HIM.
...
YOU ONLY SAID THAT TO KEEP ME FROM RUNNING AWAY.
NO. I MEANT IT. IF YOU WANT TO, THAT IS.
IF WE'RE ALWAYS TOGETHER, THEN WE'LL NEVER MAKE MISTAKES LIKE THIS AGAIN. TRUTH IS, I WAS GOING TO PROPOSE AFTER I GOT FAMOUS, BUT IF YOU'RE WILLING TO SLOG THROUGH SOME HARD TIMES...
YES! OVERCOMING HARDSHIPS TOGETHER WILL BOND YOU CLOSER TOGETHER.
OKAY, GOOD POINT...
B-BUT, WE STILL HAVE TO PAY FOR THE WEDDING AND GET PERMISSION FROM OUR PARENTS.
OH, RIGHT. I'LL JUST HAVE TO ASK THEM THEN.
I HOPE THEY DON'T FREAK OUT.
...
I MEAN, I'LL DO MY BEST!

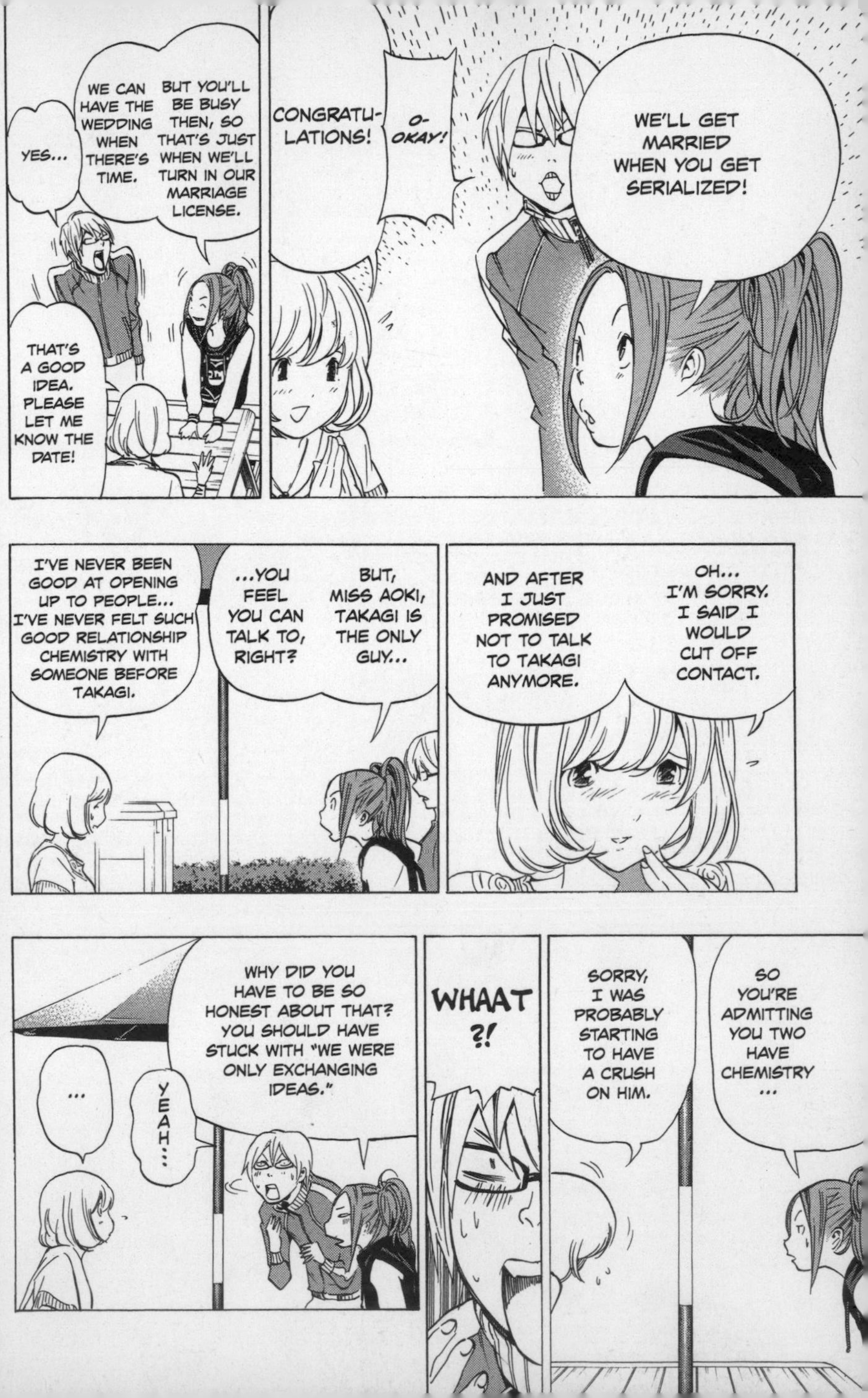
WE'LL GET MARRIED WHEN YOU GET SERIALIZED!
O-OKAY!
CONGRATULATIONS!
BUT YOU'LL BE BUSY THEN, SO THAT'S JUST WHEN WE'LL TURN IN OUR MARRIAGE LICENSE.
WE CAN HAVE THE WEDDING WHEN THERE'S TIME.
YES...
THAT'S A GOOD IDEA. PLEASE LET ME KNOW THE DATE!
OH... I'M SORRY. I SAID I WOULD CUT OFF CONTACT.
AND AFTER I JUST PROMISED NOT TO TALK TO TAKAGI ANYMORE.
BUT, MISS AOKI, TAKAGI IS THE ONLY GUY...
...YOU FEEL YOU CAN TALK TO, RIGHT?
I'VE NEVER BEEN GOOD AT OPENING UP TO PEOPLE... I'VE NEVER FELT SUCH GOOD RELATIONSHIP CHEMISTRY WITH SOMEONE BEFORE TAKAGI.
SO YOU'RE ADMITTING YOU TWO HAVE CHEMISTRY...
SORRY, I WAS PROBABLY STARTING TO HAVE A CRUSH ON HIM.
WHAAT ?!
WHY DID YOU HAVE TO BE SO HONEST ABOUT THAT? YOU SHOULD HAVE STUCK WITH "WE WERE ONLY EXCHANGING IDEAS."
YEAH...
...

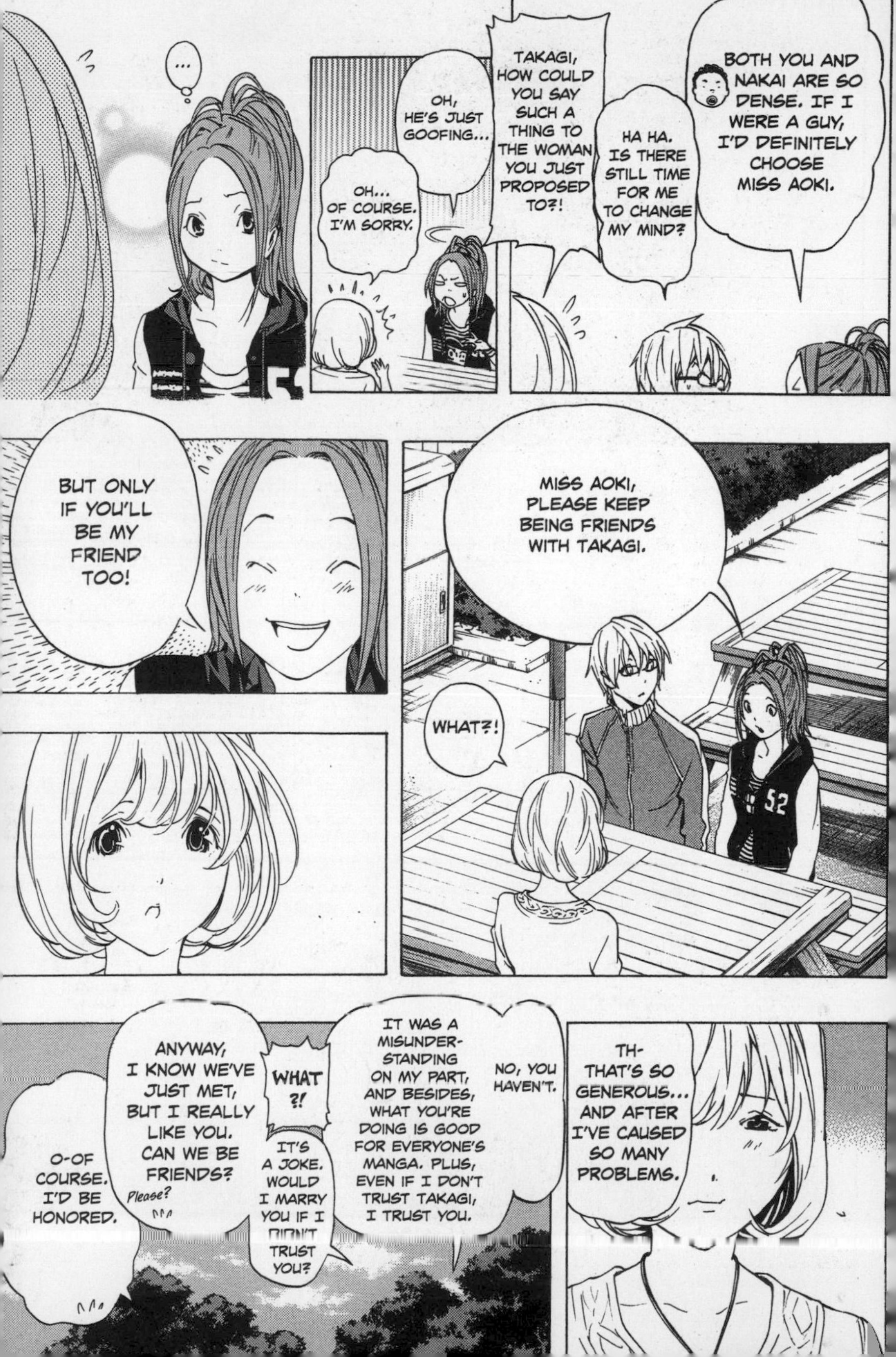
BOTH YOU AND NAKAI ARE SO DENSE. IF I WERE A GUY, I'D DEFINITELY CHOOSE MISS AOKI.
HA HA. IS THERE STILL TIME FOR ME TO CHANGE MY MIND?
TAKAGI, HOW COULD YOU SAY SUCH A THING TO THE WOMAN YOU JUST PROPOSED TO?!
OH, HE'S JUST GOOFING...
OH... OF COURSE. I'M SORRY.
...
MISS AOKI, PLEASE KEEP BEING FRIENDS WITH TAKAGI.
WHAT?!
BUT ONLY IF YOU'LL BE MY FRIEND TOO!
TH- THAT'S SO GENEROUS... AND AFTER I'VE CAUSED SO MANY PROBLEMS.
NO, YOU HAVEN'T.
IT WAS A MISUNDERSTANDING ON MY PART, AND BESIDES, WHAT YOU'RE DOING IS GOOD FOR EVERYONE'S MANGA. PLUS, EVEN IF I DON'T TRUST TAKAGI, I TRUST YOU.
IT'S A JOKE. WOULD I MARRY YOU IF I DIDN'T TRUST YOU?
WHAT ?!
ANYWAY, I KNOW WE'VE JUST MET, BUT I REALLY LIKE YOU. CAN WE BE FRIENDS?
Please?
O-OF COURSE. I'D BE HONORED.

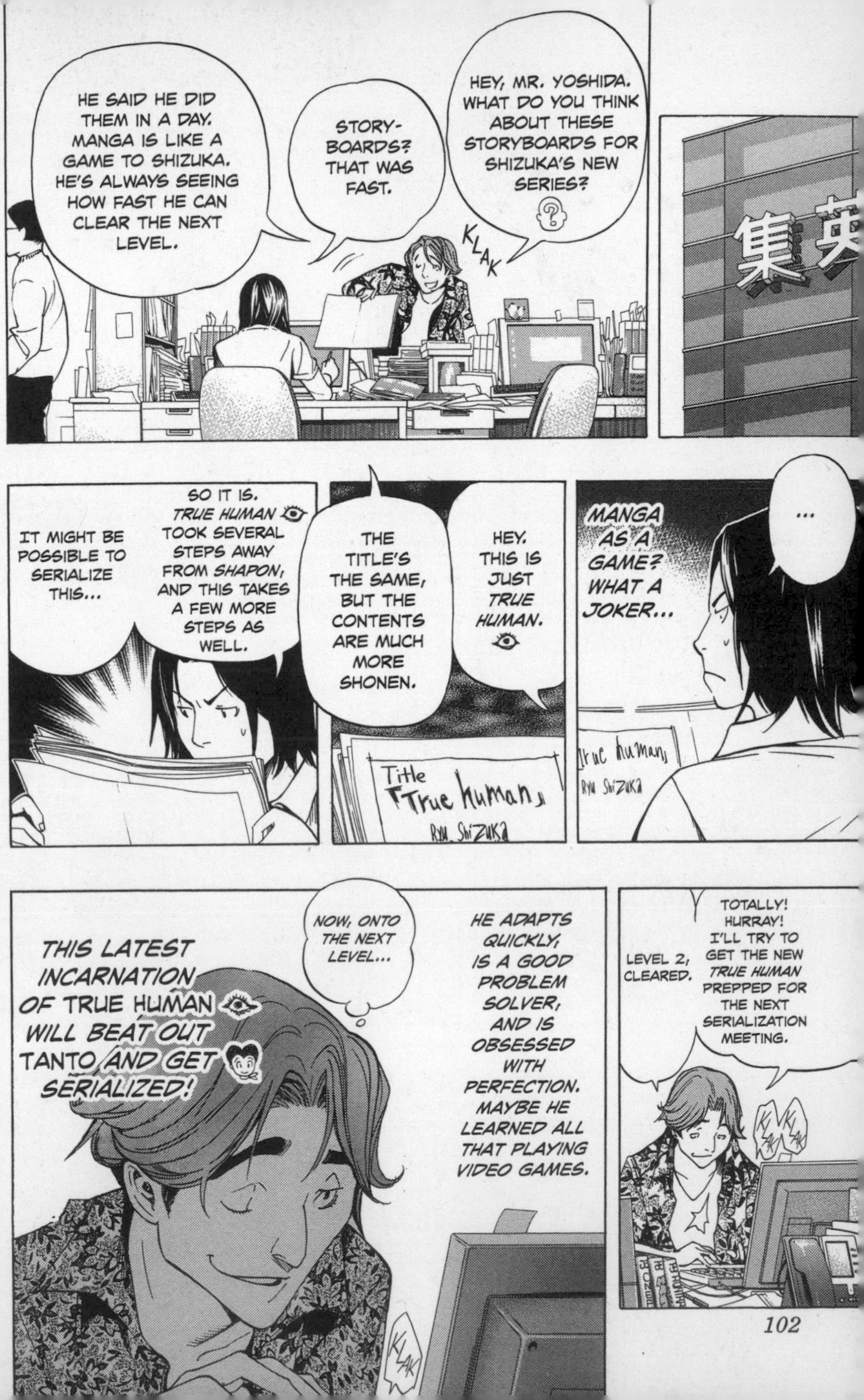
集英
HEY, MR. YOSHIDA. WHAT DO YOU THINK ABOUT THESE STORYBOARDS FOR SHIZUKA'S NEW SERIES?
KLAK
STORY-BOARDS? THAT WAS FAST.
HE SAID HE DID THEM IN A DAY. MANGA IS LIKE A GAME TO SHIZUKA. HE'S ALWAYS SEEING HOW FAST HE CAN CLEAR THE NEXT LEVEL.
...
MANGA AS A GAME? WHAT A JOKER...
True human, Ryu Shizuka
HEY. THIS IS JUST TRUE HUMAN.
THE TITLE'S THE SAME, BUT THE CONTENTS ARE MUCH MORE SHONEN.
Title True human, Ryu Shizuka
SO IT IS. TRUE HUMAN TOOK SEVERAL STEPS AWAY FROM SHAPON, AND THIS TAKES A FEW MORE STEPS AS WELL.
IT MIGHT BE POSSIBLE TO SERIALIZE THIS...
TOTALLY! HURRAY! I'LL TRY TO GET THE NEW TRUE HUMAN PREPPED FOR THE NEXT SERIALIZATION MEETING.
LEVEL 2, CLEARED.
KLAK KLAK
HE ADAPTS QUICKLY, IS A GOOD PROBLEM SOLVER, AND IS OBSESSED WITH PERFECTION. MAYBE HE LEARNED ALL THAT PLAYING VIDEO GAMES.
NOW, ONTO THE NEXT LEVEL...
THIS LATEST INCARNATION OF TRUE HUMAN WILL BEAT OUT TANTO AND GET SERIALIZED!
KLAK

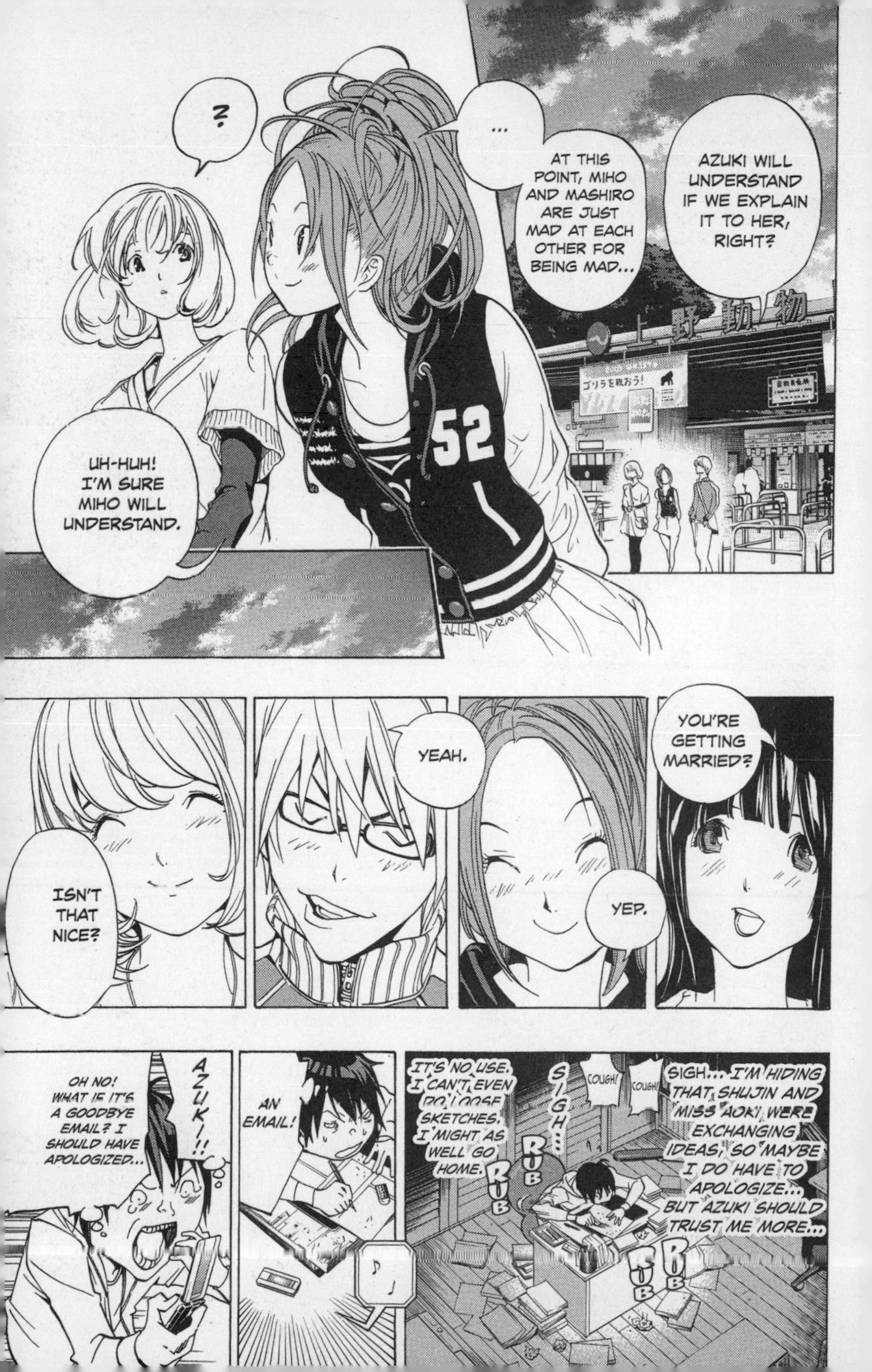
AZUKI WILL UNDERSTAND IF WE EXPLAIN IT TO HER, RIGHT?
...
AT THIS POINT, MIHO AND MASHIRO ARE JUST MAD AT EACH OTHER FOR BEING MAD...
?
UH-HUH! I'M SURE MIHO WILL UNDERSTAND.
YOU'RE GETTING MARRIED?
YEP.
YEAH.
ISN'T THAT NICE?
SIGH... I'M HIDING THAT SHUJIN AND MISS AOKI WERE EXCHANGING IDEAS, SO MAYBE I DO HAVE TO APOLOGIZE... BUT AZUKI SHOULD TRUST ME MORE...
COUGH!
COUGH!
RUB
RUB
SIGH...
RUB
RUB
IT'S NO USE. I CAN'T EVEN DO LOOSE SKETCHES. I MIGHT AS WELL GO HOME.
AN EMAIL!
AZUKI!!
OH NO! WHAT IF IT'S A GOODBYE EMAIL? I SHOULD HAVE APOLOGIZED...

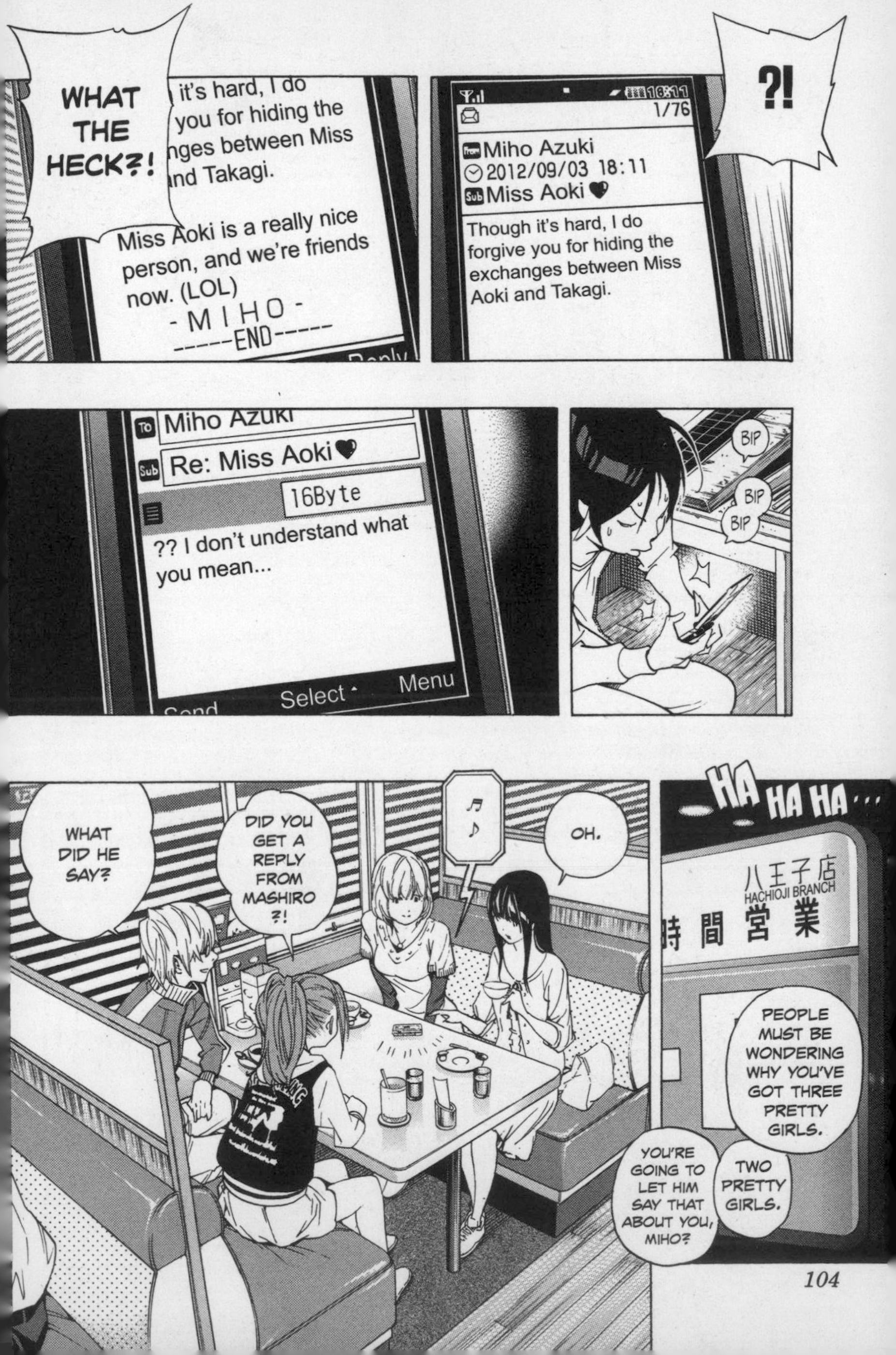
?!
1/76
Miho Azuki
2012/09/03 18:11
Miss Aoki ♥
Though it's hard, I do forgive you for hiding the exchanges between Miss Aoki and Takagi.
WHAT THE HECK?!
it's hard, I do you for hiding the nges between Miss nd Takagi.
Miss Aoki is a really nice person, and we're friends now. (LOL)
-MIHO-
-----END-----
BIP
BIP
BIP
To Miho Azuki
Sub Re: Miss Aoki ♥
16Byte
?? I don't understand what you mean...
Select
Menu
HA HA HA...
八王子店
HACHIOJI BRANCH
時間営業
PEOPLE MUST BE WONDERING WHY YOU'VE GOT THREE PRETTY GIRLS.
TWO PRETTY GIRLS.
YOU'RE GOING TO LET HIM SAY THAT ABOUT YOU, MIHO?
OH.
♪ ♪
DID YOU GET A REPLY FROM MASHIRO?!
WHAT DID HE SAY?

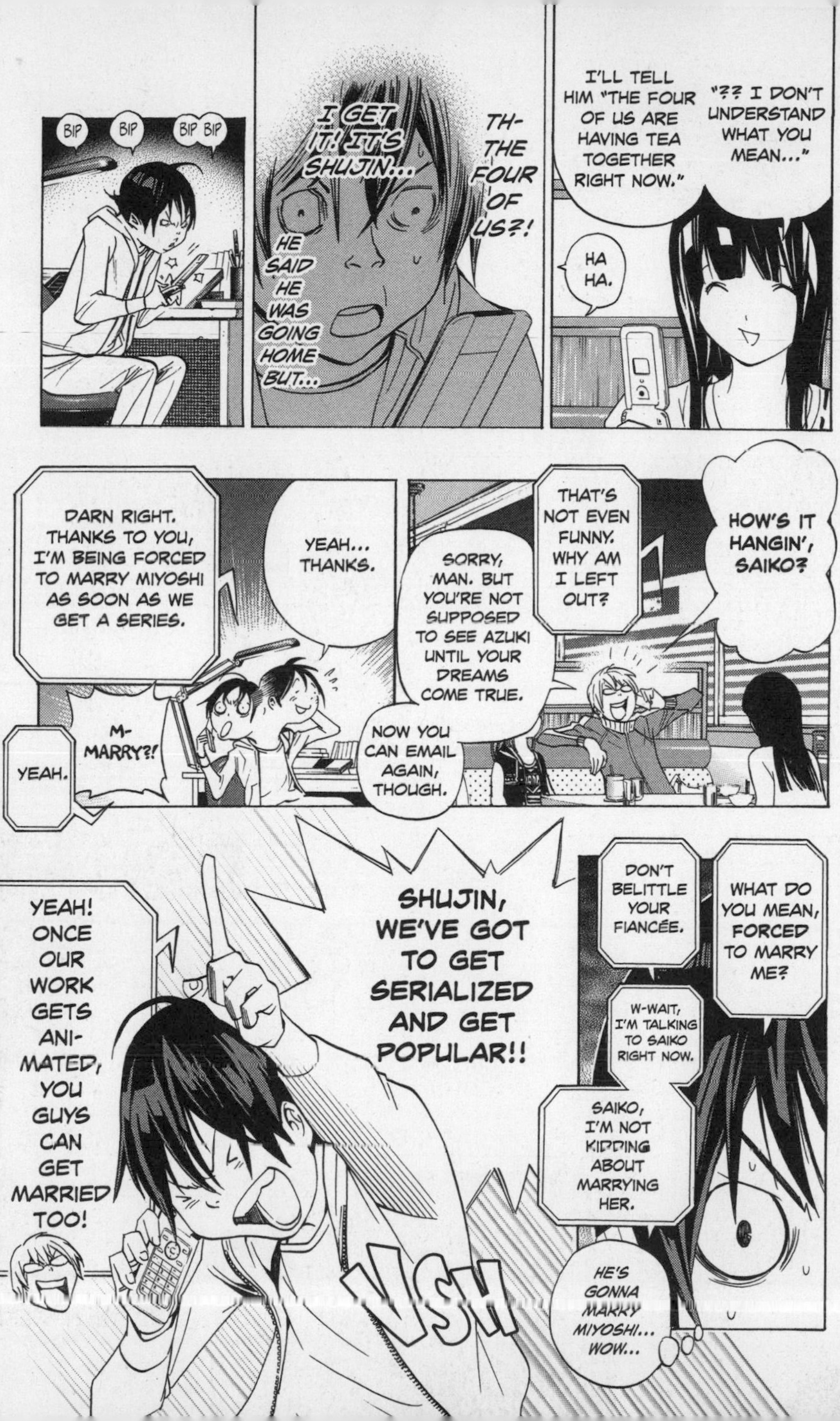
"?? I DON'T UNDERSTAND WHAT YOU MEAN..."
I'LL TELL HIM "THE FOUR OF US ARE HAVING TEA TOGETHER RIGHT NOW."
HA HA.
TH-THE FOUR OF US?!
I GET IT! IT'S SHUJIN...
HE SAID HE WAS GOING HOME BUT...
BIP
BIP
BIP BIP
HOW'S IT HANGIN', SAIKO?
THAT'S NOT EVEN FUNNY. WHY AM I LEFT OUT?
SORRY, MAN. BUT YOU'RE NOT SUPPOSED TO SEE AZUKI UNTIL YOUR DREAMS COME TRUE.
NOW YOU CAN EMAIL AGAIN, THOUGH.
YEAH... THANKS.
DARN RIGHT. THANKS TO YOU, I'M BEING FORCED TO MARRY MIYOSHI AS SOON AS WE GET A SERIES.
M-MARRY?!
YEAH.
WHAT DO YOU MEAN, FORCED TO MARRY ME?
DON'T BELITTLE YOUR FIANCÉE.
W-WAIT, I'M TALKING TO SAIKO RIGHT NOW.
SAIKO, I'M NOT KIDDING ABOUT MARRYING HER.
HE'S GONNA MARRY MIYOSHI... WOW...
SHUJIN, WE'VE GOT TO GET SERIALIZED AND GET POPULAR!!
YEAH! ONCE OUR WORK GETS ANI-MATED, YOU GUYS CAN GET MARRIED TOO!
VSH

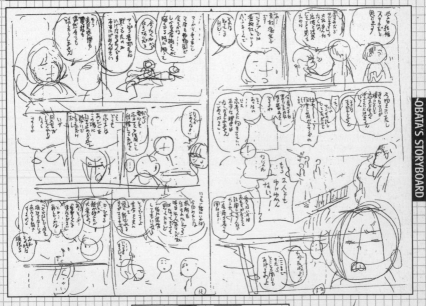

OHBA'S STORYBOARD

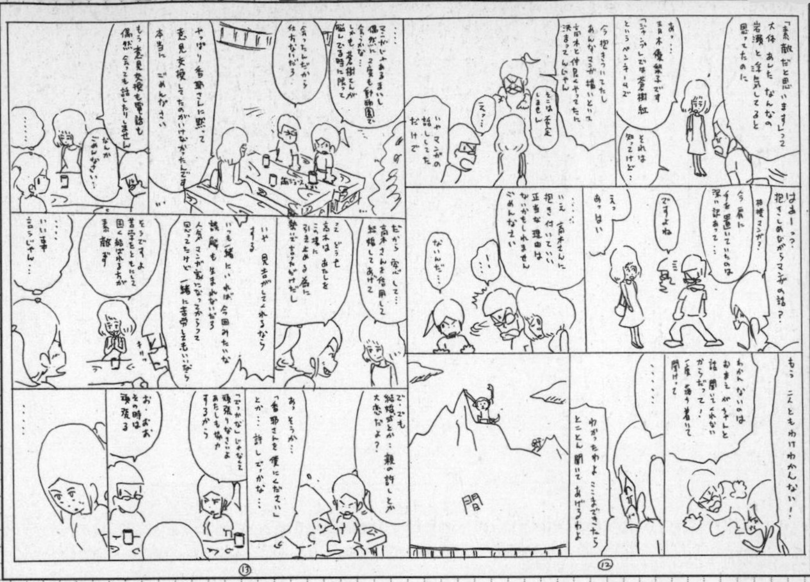
「素敵だと思います」って 大体あしたなんなの 岩瀬と浮気してると思ってたのに
あ…青木優梨子です 「ジャンプ」では蒼樹紅というペンネームで
それは知ってるけど…
今抱きついてたし あんなマンガ描いといて 高木と仲良くやってたし 決まってんじゃん
そこは否定しません
え…
いやマンガの話してただけで
はぁー…っ? 抱きしめながらマンガの話?
今肩に手を置いていたのは深い訳あって…
ですよね
えっ あっはい
…… いえ 高木さんに抱き付いていい正当な理由はないかもしれません ごめんなさい
…!
ないんだ…
もう二人ともわけわかんない!
わかんないのはおまえがちゃんと話聞いてくれないからだって! 一度落ち着いて聞けって
……
わかったわよ ここまできたら とことん聞いてあげるわよ
間
……マンガじゃあるまいし 偶然に2度も動物園で会うかな… しかも蒼樹さんが悩んでる時に限って
会ったんだから仕方ないだろ
やっぱり香耶さんに黙って意見交換してたのがいけなかったんです 本当にごめんなさい
もう意見交換も電話も偶然会っても話したりしません
なんか ごめんなさい…
……
だから安心して… 高木さんを信用して結婚してあげて
そ どうせ 高木は あたしを この場に引きとめる為に 勢いで言っただけだし
いつも一緒にいれば今回みたいな誤解も生まれないだろ 人気マンガ家になってからって思ってたけど 一緒に苦労しても いいなら
そうですよ 苦労をともにして 固く結ばれる方が 素敵です
…… いい事言うじゃん…
でも 結婚式とか… 親の許しとか 大変だよ?
あっそうか… 「香耶さんを僕にください」とか… 許してくれるかな…
「くれるかな」じゃなくて 頑張りなさいよ あたしも協力するから
お、おお その時は頑張る
……

OBATA'S STORYBOARD

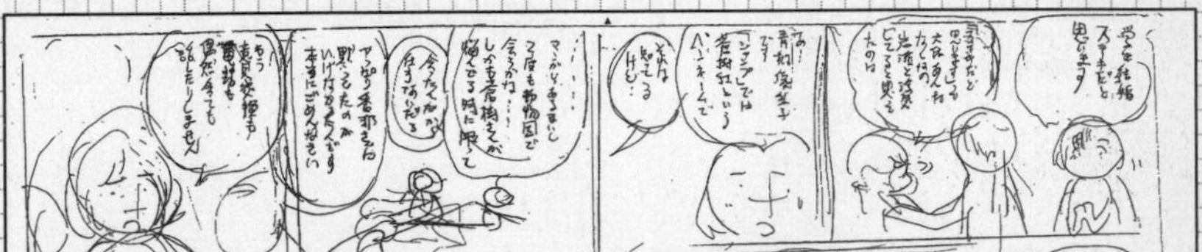

COMPLETE!

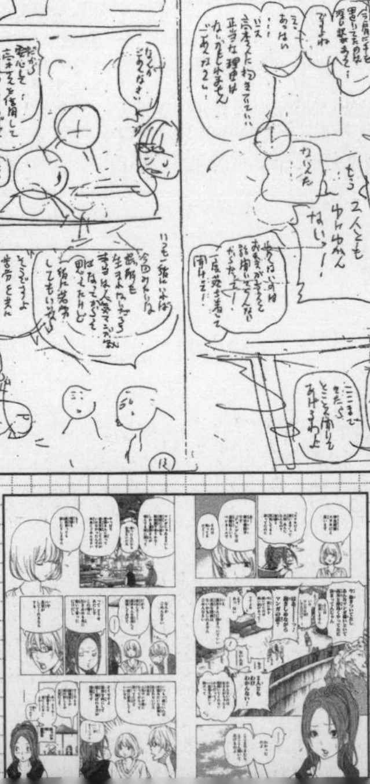

*CREATOR STORYBOARDS AND FINISHED PAGES IN JAPANESE

BAKUMAN。 vol.8

"Until the Final Draft Is Complete"

Chapter 66, pp. 98-99

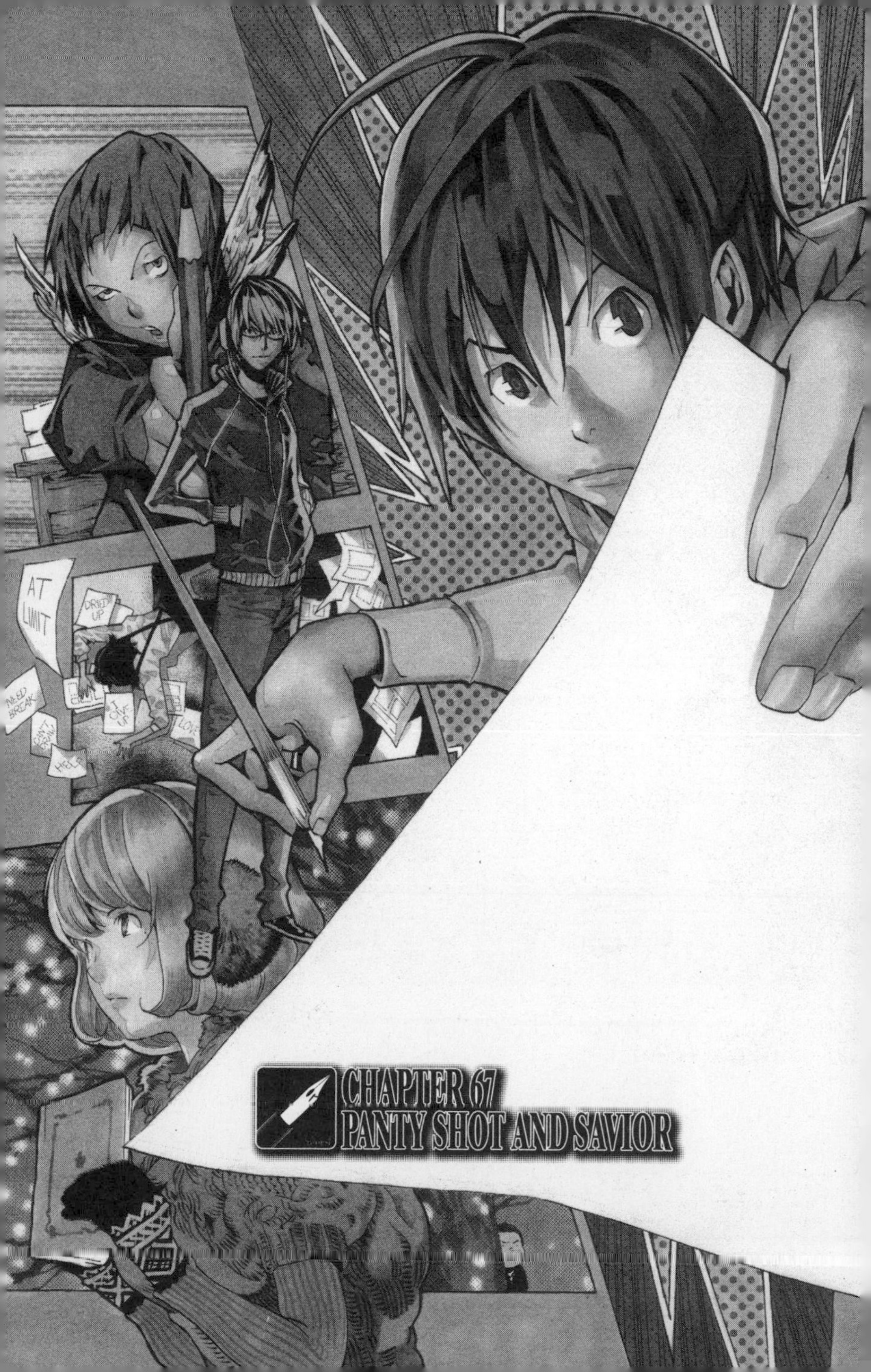
AT LIMIT
DRIED UP
NEED BREAK
I GIVE UP
CAN'T DRAW
HELP
LOVE
CHAPTER 67
PANTY SHOT AND SAVIOR

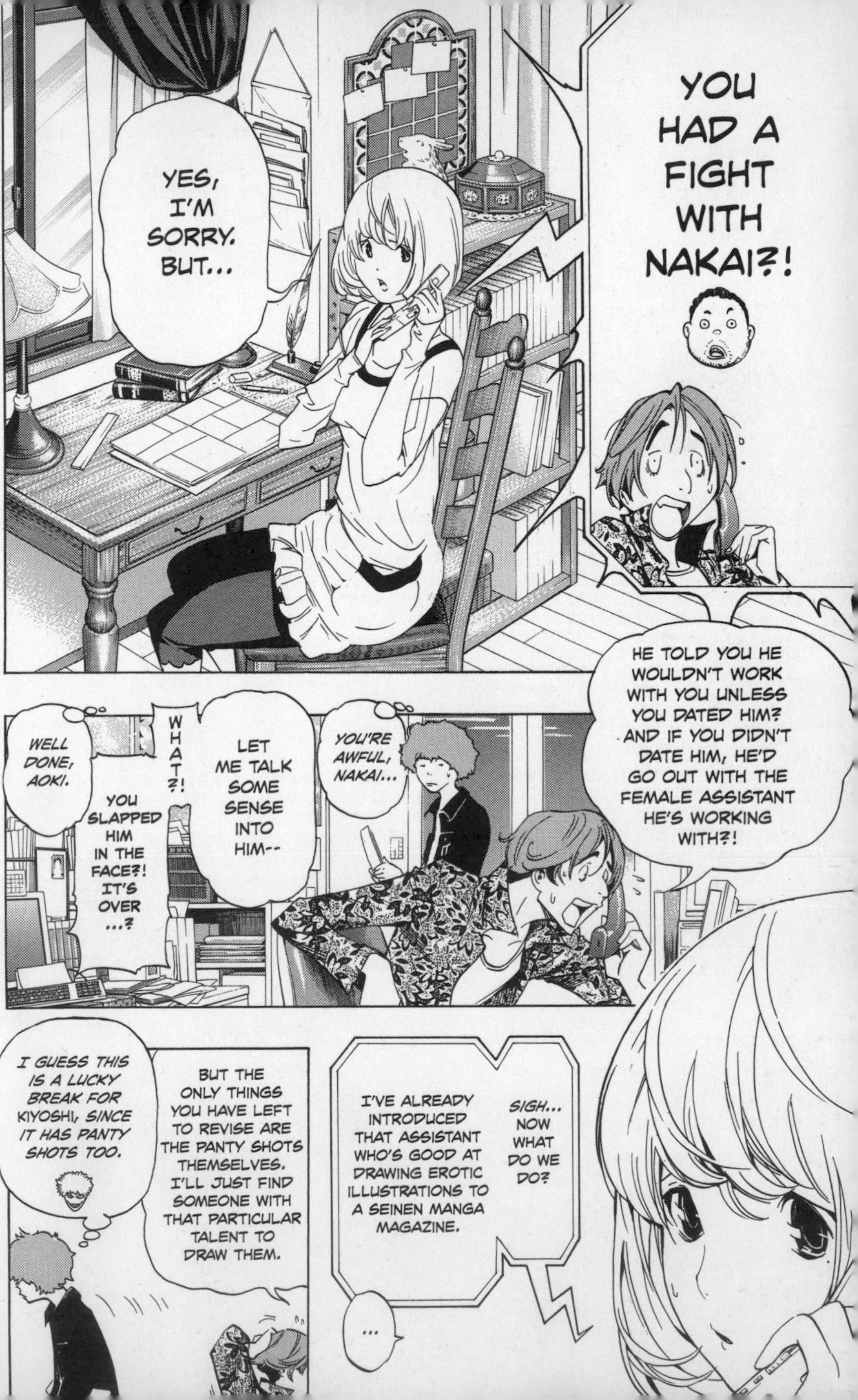
YOU HAD A FIGHT WITH NAKAI?!
YES, I'M SORRY. BUT...
HE TOLD YOU HE WOULDN'T WORK WITH YOU UNLESS YOU DATED HIM? AND IF YOU DIDN'T DATE HIM, HE'D GO OUT WITH THE FEMALE ASSISTANT HE'S WORKING WITH?!
YOU'RE AWFUL, NAKAI...
LET ME TALK SOME SENSE INTO HIM--
WHAT?!
WELL DONE, AOKI.
YOU SLAPPED HIM IN THE FACE?! IT'S OVER...?
SIGH... NOW WHAT DO WE DO?
I'VE ALREADY INTRODUCED THAT ASSISTANT WHO'S GOOD AT DRAWING EROTIC ILLUSTRATIONS TO A SEINEN MANGA MAGAZINE.
...
BUT THE ONLY THINGS YOU HAVE LEFT TO REVISE ARE THE PANTY SHOTS THEMSELVES. I'LL JUST FIND SOMEONE WITH THAT PARTICULAR TALENT TO DRAW THEM.
I GUESS THIS IS A LUCKY BREAK FOR KIYOSHI, SINCE IT HAS PANTY SHOTS TOO.

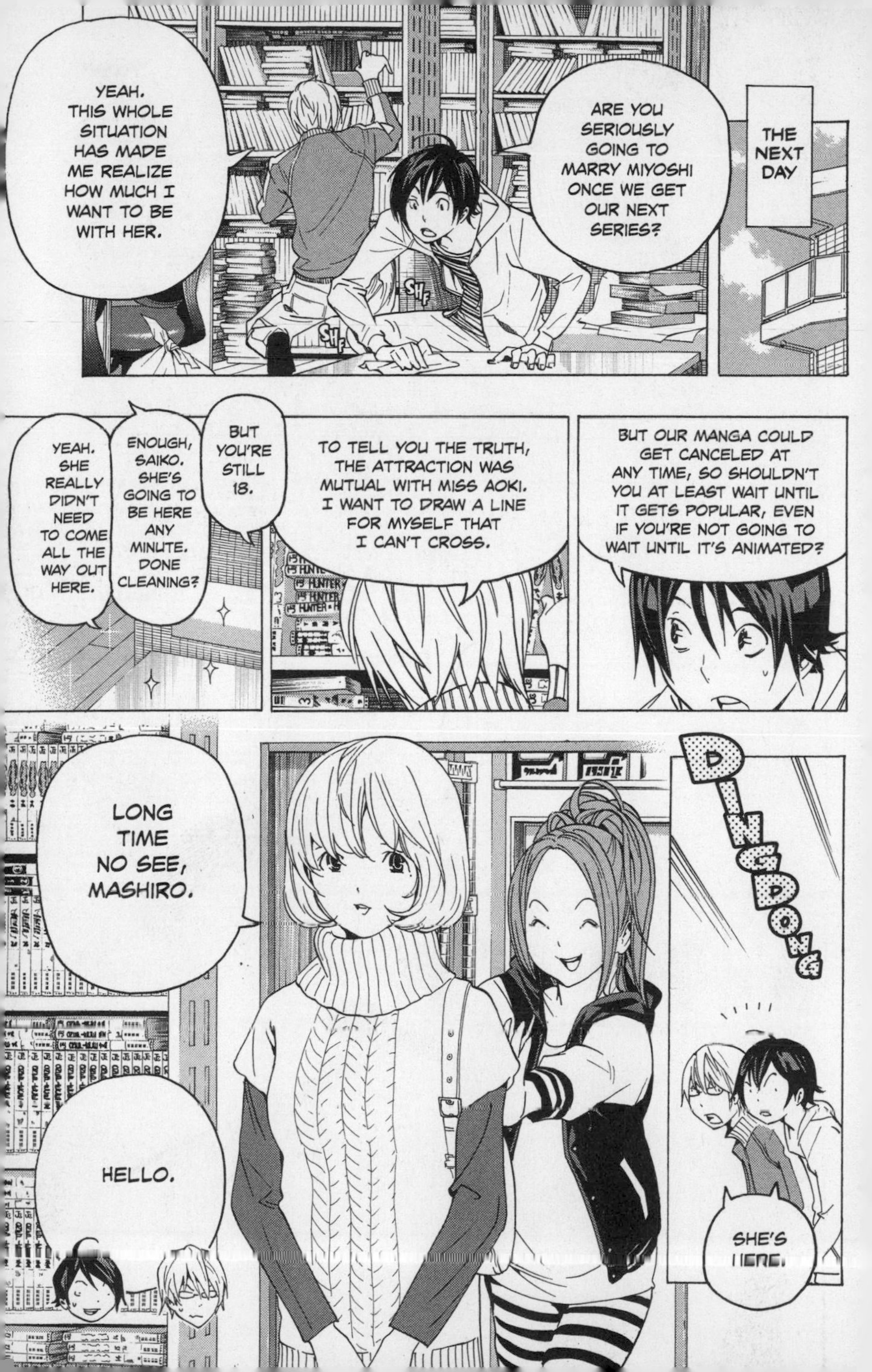
THE NEXT DAY
ARE YOU SERIOUSLY GOING TO MARRY MIYOSHI ONCE WE GET OUR NEXT SERIES?
SHF
SHF
YEAH. THIS WHOLE SITUATION HAS MADE ME REALIZE HOW MUCH I WANT TO BE WITH HER.
BUT OUR MANGA COULD GET CANCELED AT ANY TIME, SO SHOULDN'T YOU AT LEAST WAIT UNTIL IT GETS POPULAR, EVEN IF YOU'RE NOT GOING TO WAIT UNTIL IT'S ANIMATED?
TO TELL YOU THE TRUTH, THE ATTRACTION WAS MUTUAL WITH MISS AOKI. I WANT TO DRAW A LINE FOR MYSELF THAT I CAN'T CROSS.
BUT YOU'RE STILL 18.
ENOUGH, SAIKO. SHE'S GOING TO BE HERE ANY MINUTE. DONE CLEANING?
YEAH. SHE REALLY DIDN'T NEED TO COME ALL THE WAY OUT HERE.
DINGDONG
SHE'S HERE.
LONG TIME NO SEE, MASHIRO.
HELLO.

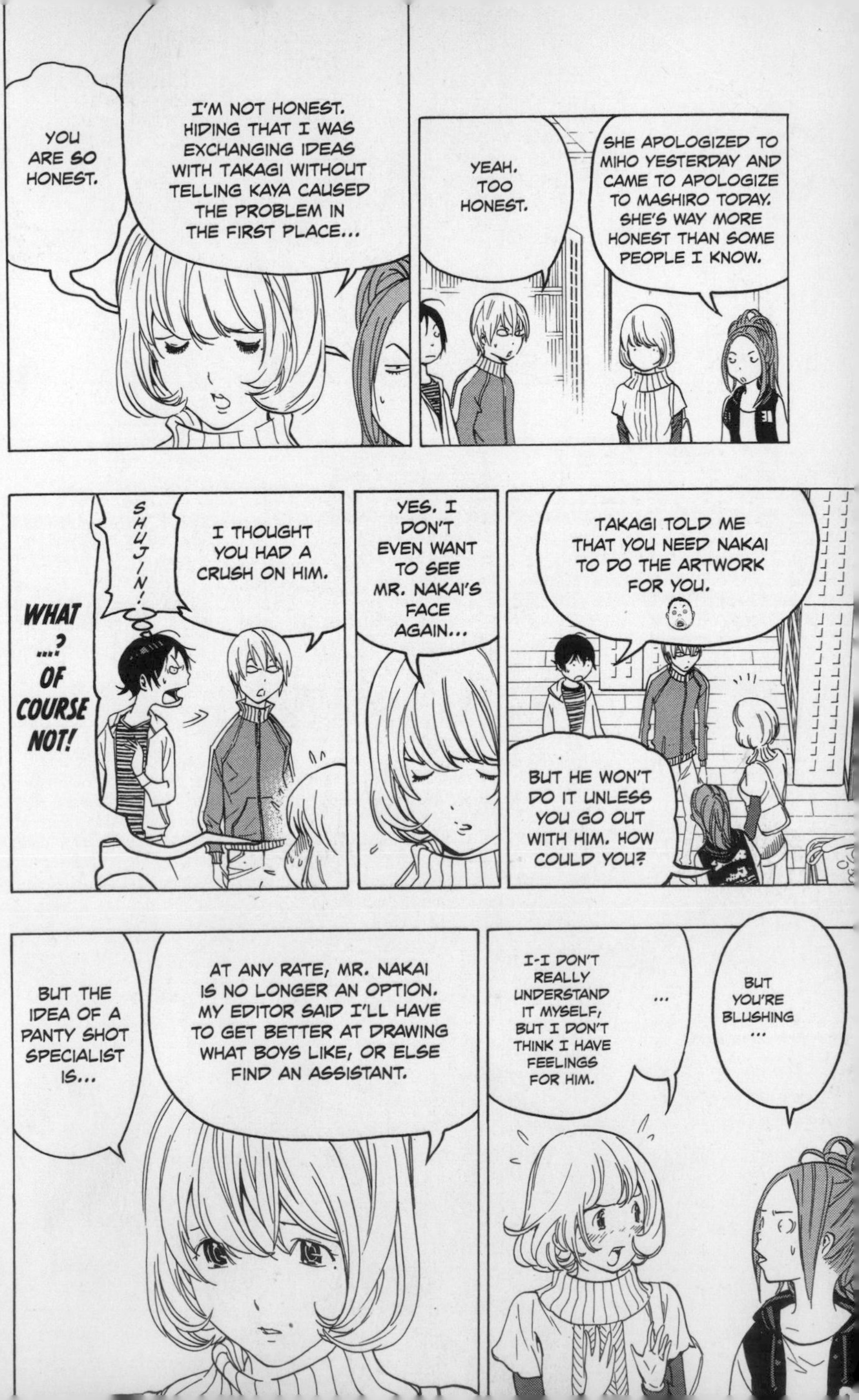
SHE APOLOGIZED TO MIHO YESTERDAY AND CAME TO APOLOGIZE TO MASHIRO TODAY. SHE'S WAY MORE HONEST THAN SOME PEOPLE I KNOW.
YEAH. TOO HONEST.
I'M NOT HONEST. HIDING THAT I WAS EXCHANGING IDEAS WITH TAKAGI WITHOUT TELLING KAYA CAUSED THE PROBLEM IN THE FIRST PLACE...
YOU ARE SO HONEST.
TAKAGI TOLD ME THAT YOU NEED NAKAI TO DO THE ARTWORK FOR YOU.
BUT HE WON'T DO IT UNLESS YOU GO OUT WITH HIM. HOW COULD YOU?
YES. I DON'T EVEN WANT TO SEE MR. NAKAI'S FACE AGAIN...
I THOUGHT YOU HAD A CRUSH ON HIM.
SHUJIN!
WHAT ...? OF COURSE NOT!
BUT YOU'RE BLUSHING ...
...
I-I DON'T REALLY UNDERSTAND IT MYSELF, BUT I DON'T THINK I HAVE FEELINGS FOR HIM.
AT ANY RATE, MR. NAKAI IS NO LONGER AN OPTION. MY EDITOR SAID I'LL HAVE TO GET BETTER AT DRAWING WHAT BOYS LIKE, OR ELSE FIND AN ASSISTANT.
BUT THE IDEA OF A PANTY SHOT SPECIALIST IS...

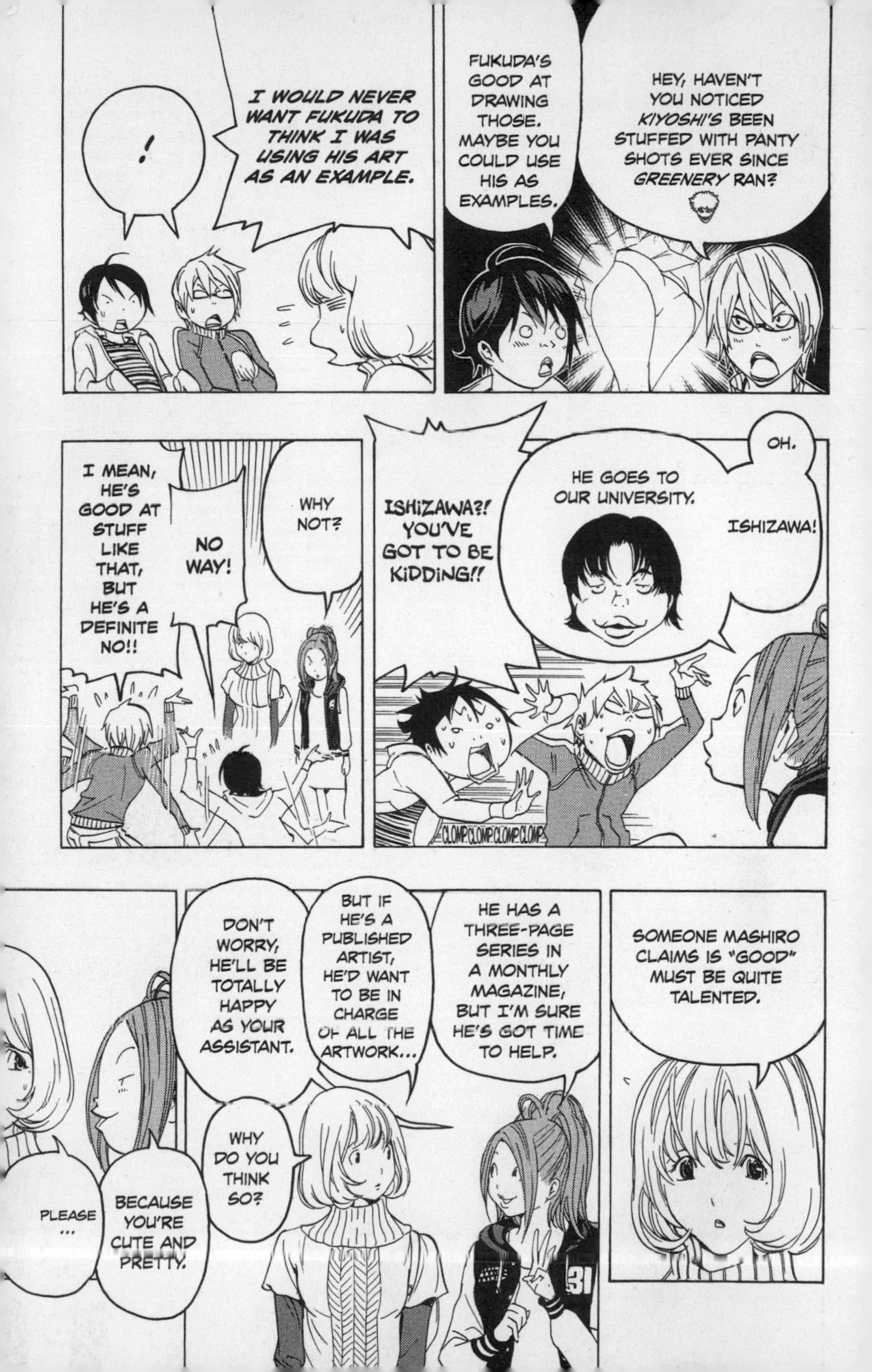
HEY, HAVEN'T YOU NOTICED KIYOSHI'S BEEN STUFFED WITH PANTY SHOTS EVER SINCE GREENERY RAN?
FUKUDA'S GOOD AT DRAWING THOSE. MAYBE YOU COULD USE HIS AS EXAMPLES.
I WOULD NEVER WANT FUKUDA TO THINK I WAS USING HIS ART AS AN EXAMPLE.
!
OH.
ISHIZAWA!
HE GOES TO OUR UNIVERSITY.
ISHIZAWA?! YOU'VE GOT TO BE KIDDING!!
CLOMP CLOMP CLOMP CLOMP
WHY NOT?
NO WAY!
I MEAN, HE'S GOOD AT STUFF LIKE THAT, BUT HE'S A DEFINITE NO!!
SOMEONE MASHIRO CLAIMS IS "GOOD" MUST BE QUITE TALENTED.
HE HAS A THREE-PAGE SERIES IN A MONTHLY MAGAZINE, BUT I'M SURE HE'S GOT TIME TO HELP.
BUT IF HE'S A PUBLISHED ARTIST, HE'D WANT TO BE IN CHARGE OF ALL THE ARTWORK...
DON'T WORRY, HE'LL BE TOTALLY HAPPY AS YOUR ASSISTANT.
WHY DO YOU THINK SO?
BECAUSE YOU'RE CUTE AND PRETTY.
PLEASE...

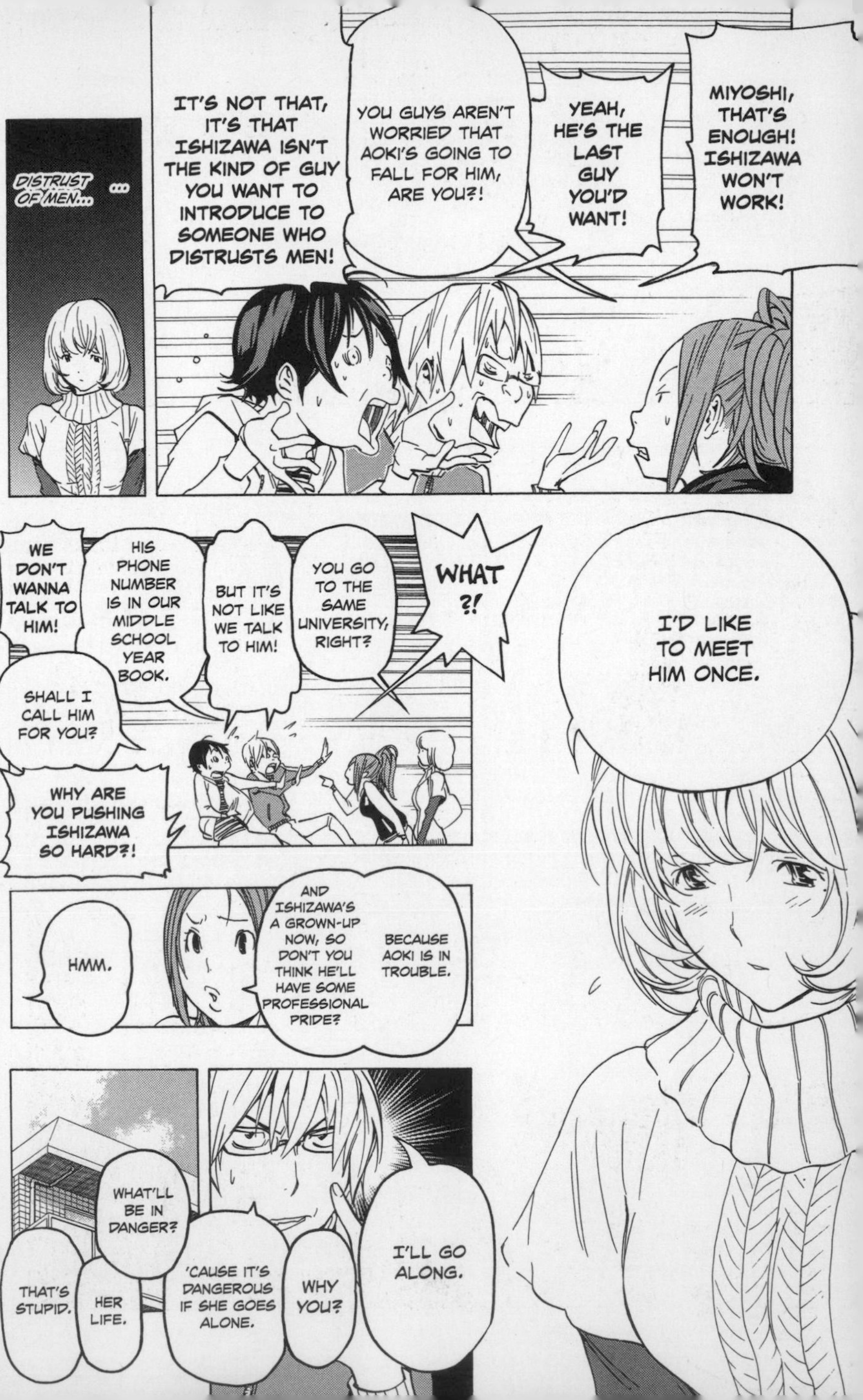
MIYOSHI, THAT'S ENOUGH! ISHIZAWA WON'T WORK!
YEAH, HE'S THE LAST GUY YOU'D WANT!
YOU GUYS AREN'T WORRIED THAT AOKI'S GOING TO FALL FOR HIM, ARE YOU?!
IT'S NOT THAT, IT'S THAT ISHIZAWA ISN'T THE KIND OF GUY YOU WANT TO INTRODUCE TO SOMEONE WHO DISTRUSTS MEN!
...
DISTRUST OF MEN...
I'D LIKE TO MEET HIM ONCE.
WHAT?!
YOU GO TO THE SAME UNIVERSITY, RIGHT?
BUT IT'S NOT LIKE WE TALK TO HIM!
HIS PHONE NUMBER IS IN OUR MIDDLE SCHOOL YEAR BOOK.
WE DON'T WANNA TALK TO HIM!
SHALL I CALL HIM FOR YOU?
WHY ARE YOU PUSHING ISHIZAWA SO HARD?!
BECAUSE AOKI IS IN TROUBLE.
AND ISHIZAWA'S A GROWN-UP NOW, SO DON'T YOU THINK HE'LL HAVE SOME PROFESSIONAL PRIDE?
HMM.
I'LL GO ALONG.
WHY YOU?
'CAUSE IT'S DANGEROUS IF SHE GOES ALONE.
WHAT'LL BE IN DANGER?
HER LIFE.
THAT'S STUPID.

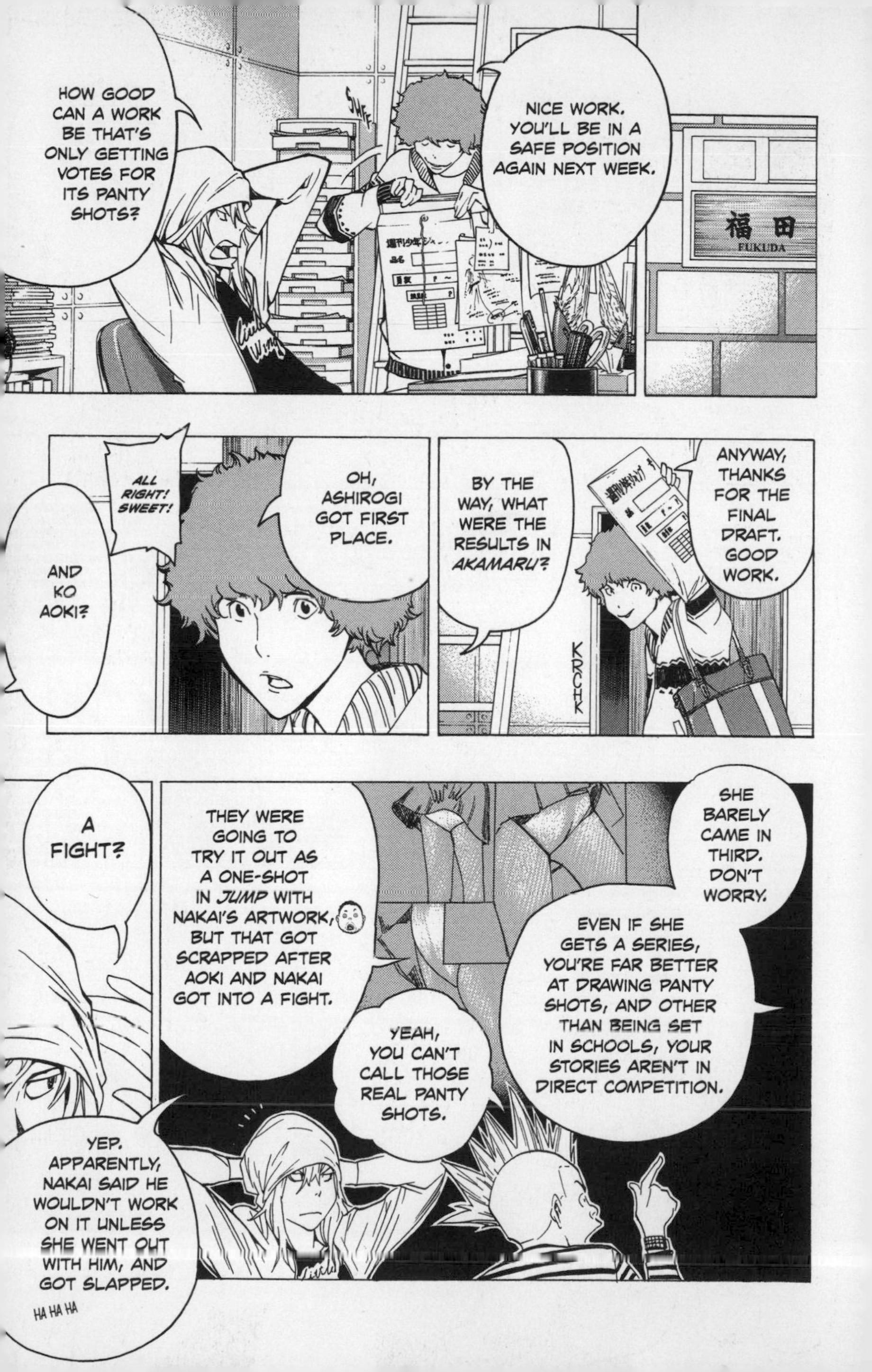
NICE WORK. YOU'LL BE IN A SAFE POSITION AGAIN NEXT WEEK.
福田
FUKUDA
HOW GOOD CAN A WORK BE THAT'S ONLY GETTING VOTES FOR ITS PANTY SHOTS?
ANYWAY, THANKS FOR THE FINAL DRAFT. GOOD WORK.
BY THE WAY, WHAT WERE THE RESULTS IN *AKAMARU*?
KRCHK
OH, ASHIROGI GOT FIRST PLACE.
ALL RIGHT! SWEET!
AND KO AOKI?
SHE BARELY CAME IN THIRD. DON'T WORRY.
EVEN IF SHE GETS A SERIES, YOU'RE FAR BETTER AT DRAWING PANTY SHOTS, AND OTHER THAN BEING SET IN SCHOOLS, YOUR STORIES AREN'T IN DIRECT COMPETITION.
YEAH, YOU CAN'T CALL THOSE REAL PANTY SHOTS.
THEY WERE GOING TO TRY IT OUT AS A ONE-SHOT IN *JUMP* WITH NAKAI'S ARTWORK, BUT THAT GOT SCRAPPED AFTER AOKI AND NAKAI GOT INTO A FIGHT.
A FIGHT?
YEP. APPARENTLY, NAKAI SAID HE WOULDN'T WORK ON IT UNLESS SHE WENT OUT WITH HIM, AND GOT SLAPPED.
HA HA HA

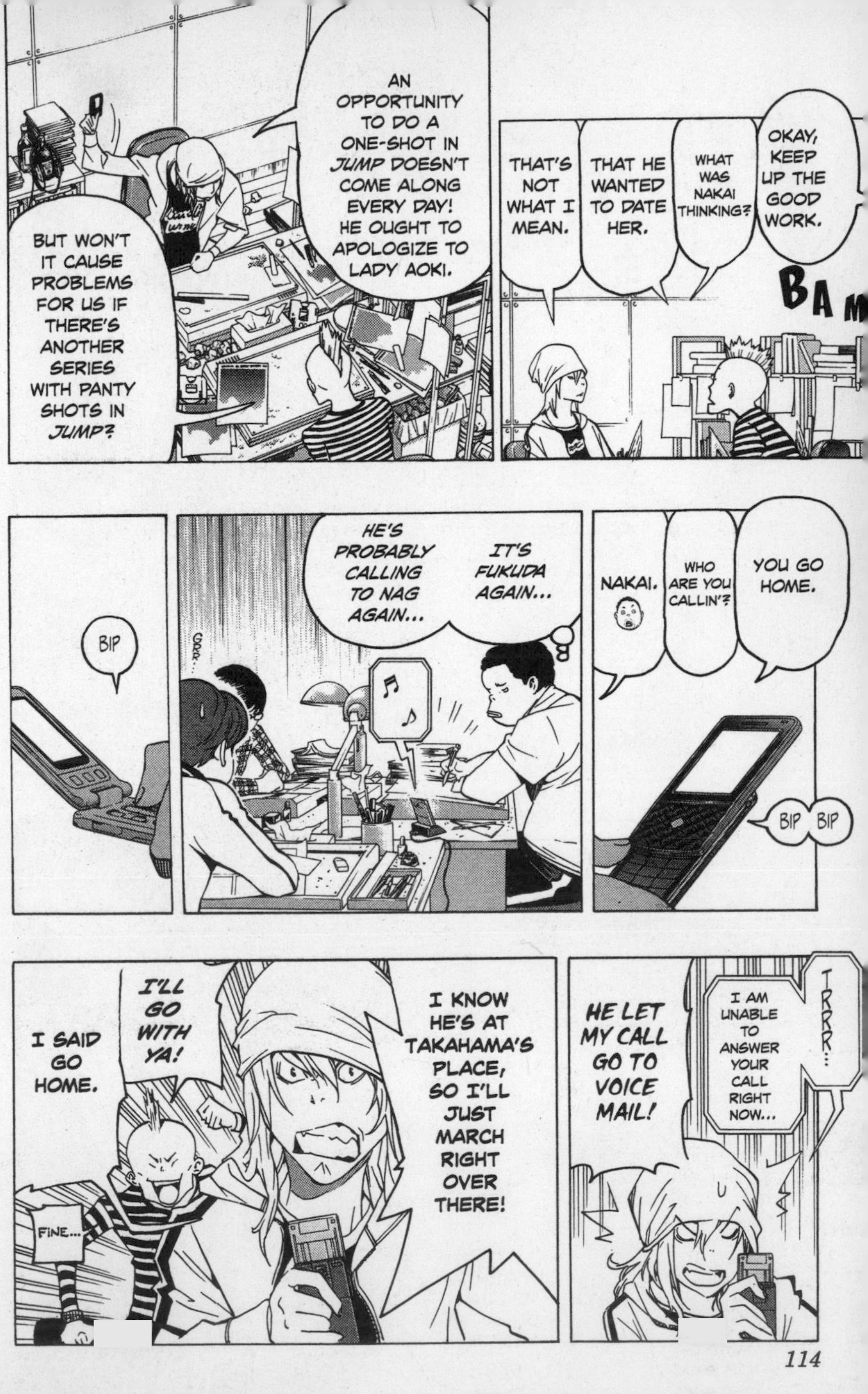
OKAY, KEEP UP THE GOOD WORK.
BAM
WHAT WAS NAKAI THINKING?
THAT HE WANTED TO DATE HER.
THAT'S NOT WHAT I MEAN.
AN OPPORTUNITY TO DO A ONE-SHOT IN *JUMP* DOESN'T COME ALONG EVERY DAY! HE OUGHT TO APOLOGIZE TO LADY AOKI.
BUT WON'T IT CAUSE PROBLEMS FOR US IF THERE'S ANOTHER SERIES WITH PANTY SHOTS IN *JUMP*?
YOU GO HOME.
WHO ARE YOU CALLIN'?
NAKAI.
BIP BIP
IT'S FUKUDA AGAIN...
HE'S PROBABLY CALLING TO NAG AGAIN...
GRR...
BIP
TRRR...
I AM UNABLE TO ANSWER YOUR CALL RIGHT NOW...
HE LET MY CALL GO TO VOICE MAIL!
I KNOW HE'S AT TAKAHAMA'S PLACE, SO I'LL JUST MARCH RIGHT OVER THERE!
I'LL GO WITH YA!
I SAID GO HOME.
FINE...

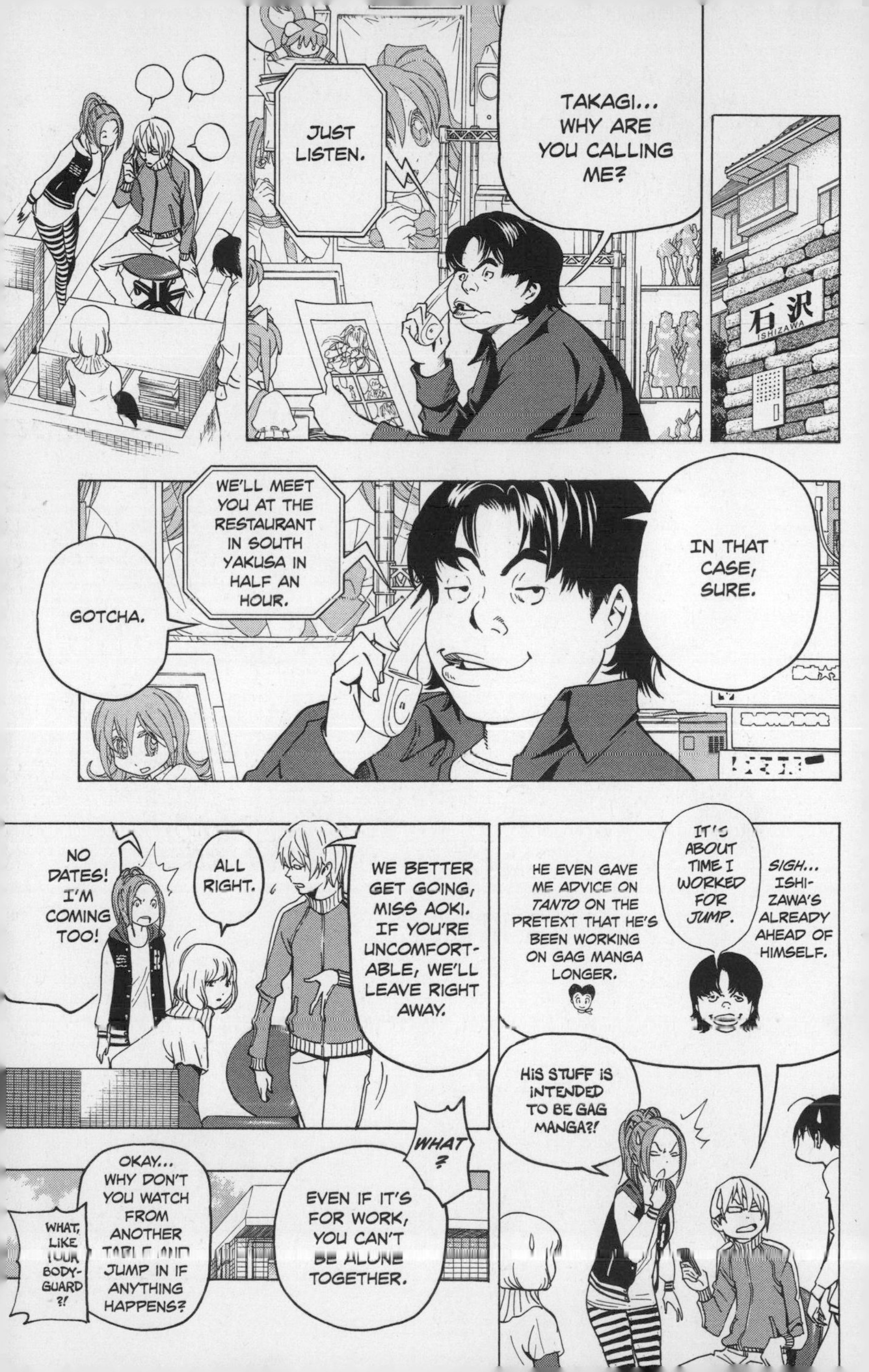
石沢
ISHIZAWA
TAKAGI... WHY ARE YOU CALLING ME?
JUST LISTEN.
IN THAT CASE, SURE.
WE'LL MEET YOU AT THE RESTAURANT IN SOUTH YAKUSA IN HALF AN HOUR.
GOTCHA.
SIGH... ISHIZAWA'S ALREADY AHEAD OF HIMSELF.
IT'S ABOUT TIME I WORKED FOR *JUMP*.
HE EVEN GAVE ME ADVICE ON *TANTO* ON THE PRETEXT THAT HE'S BEEN WORKING ON GAG MANGA LONGER.
HIS STUFF IS INTENDED TO BE GAG MANGA?!
WE BETTER GET GOING, MISS AOKI. IF YOU'RE UNCOMFORTABLE, WE'LL LEAVE RIGHT AWAY.
ALL RIGHT.
NO DATES! I'M COMING TOO!
WHAT?
EVEN IF IT'S FOR WORK, YOU CAN'T BE ALONE TOGETHER.
OKAY... WHY DON'T YOU WATCH FROM ANOTHER TABLE AND JUMP IN IF ANYTHING HAPPENS?
WHAT, LIKE YOUR BODYGUARD?!

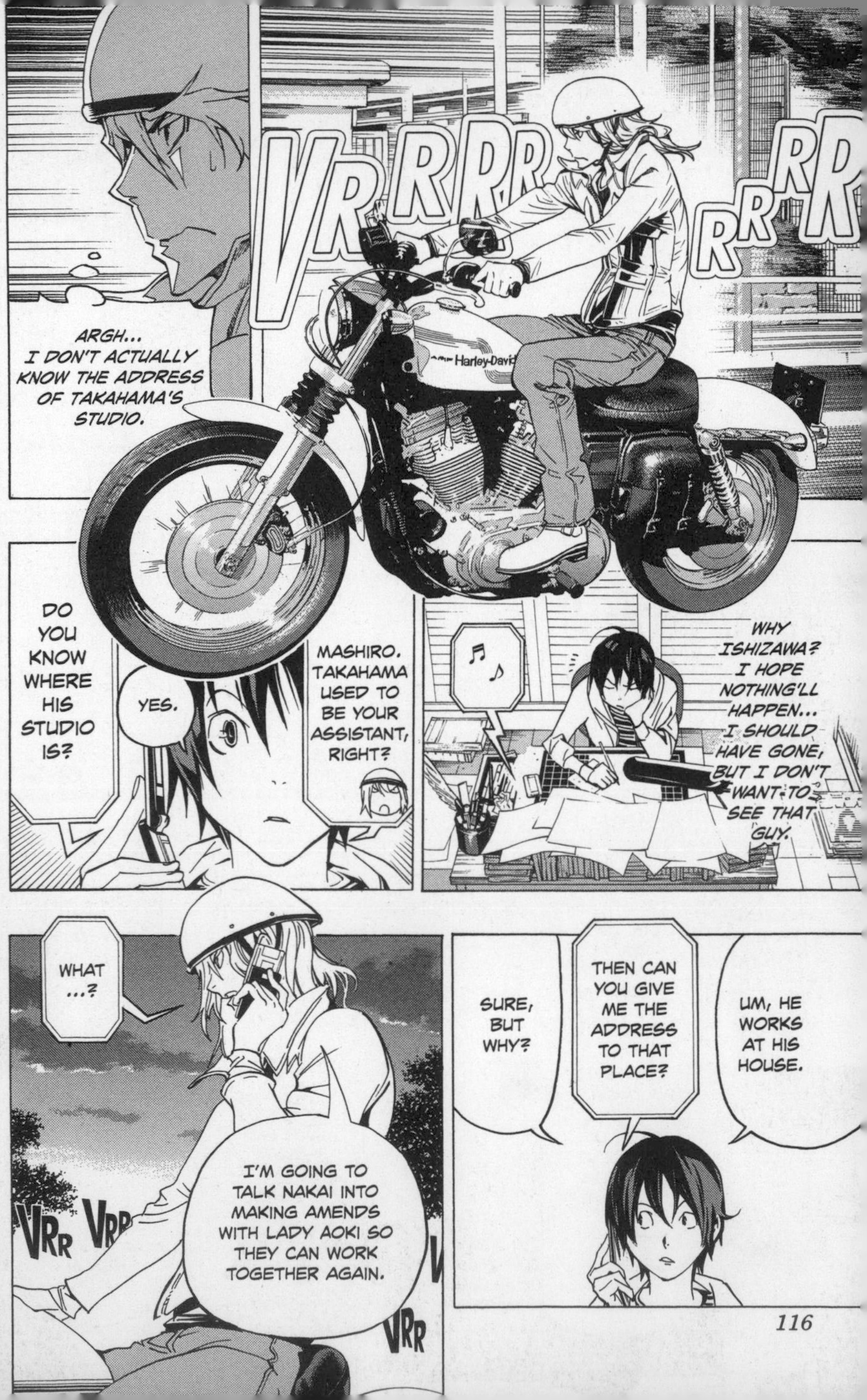
VRRRRR
RRRR
Harley-David
ARGH... I DON'T ACTUALLY KNOW THE ADDRESS OF TAKAHAMA'S STUDIO.
WHY ISHIZAWA? I HOPE NOTHING'LL HAPPEN... I SHOULD HAVE GONE, BUT I DON'T WANT TO SEE THAT GUY.
MASHIRO. TAKAHAMA USED TO BE YOUR ASSISTANT, RIGHT?
YES.
DO YOU KNOW WHERE HIS STUDIO IS?
UM, HE WORKS AT HIS HOUSE.
THEN CAN YOU GIVE ME THE ADDRESS TO THAT PLACE?
SURE, BUT WHY?
WHAT ...?
I'M GOING TO TALK NAKAI INTO MAKING AMENDS WITH LADY AOKI SO THEY CAN WORK TOGETHER AGAIN.
VRR
VRR
VRR

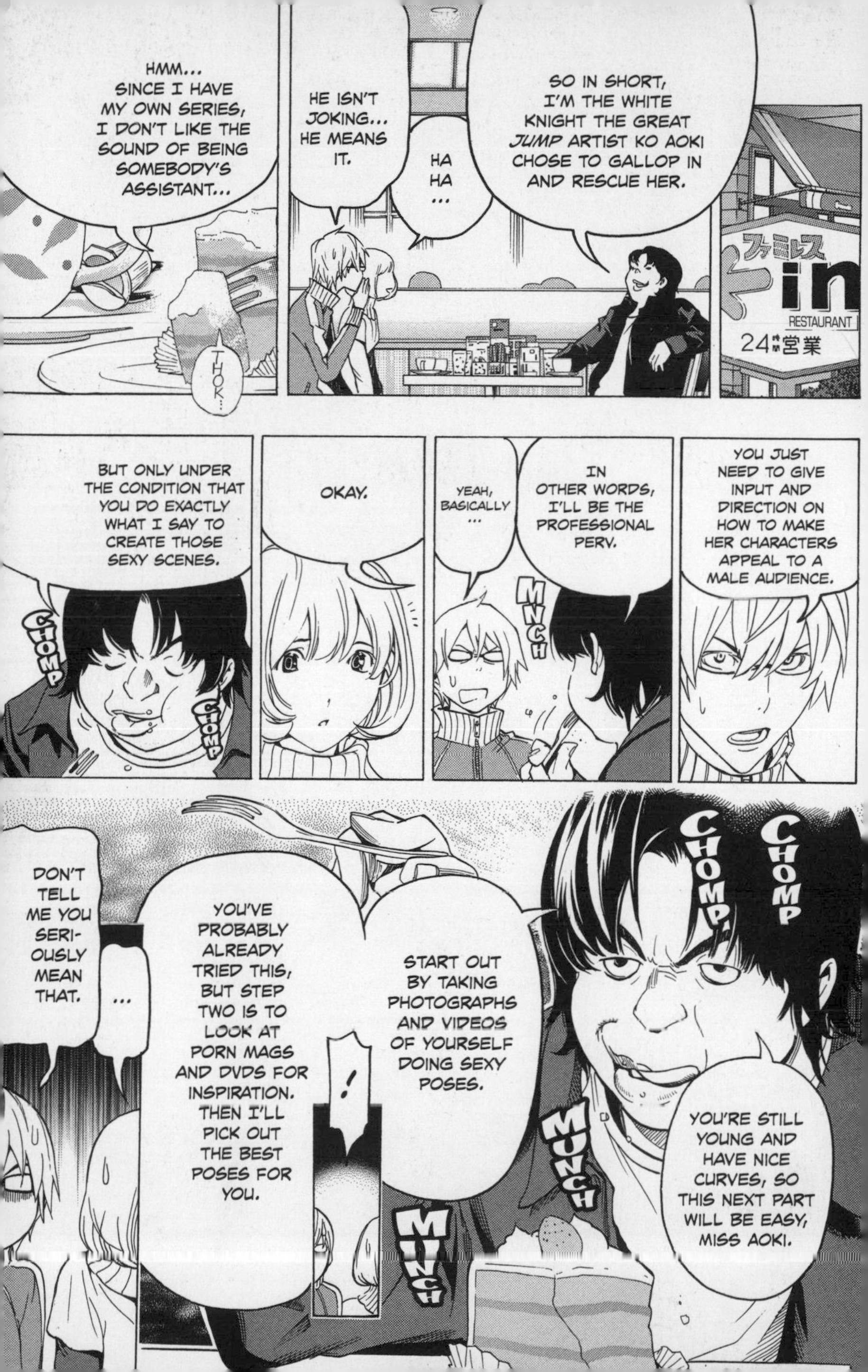

ファミレス
in
RESTAURANT
24時間営業
SO IN SHORT, I'M THE WHITE KNIGHT THE GREAT *JUMP* ARTIST KO AOKI CHOSE TO GALLOP IN AND RESCUE HER.
HA HA ...
HE ISN'T JOKING... HE MEANS IT.
HMM... SINCE I HAVE MY OWN SERIES, I DON'T LIKE THE SOUND OF BEING SOMEBODY'S ASSISTANT...
THOK...
YOU JUST NEED TO GIVE INPUT AND DIRECTION ON HOW TO MAKE HER CHARACTERS APPEAL TO A MALE AUDIENCE.
IN OTHER WORDS, I'LL BE THE PROFESSIONAL PERV.
MNCH
YEAH, BASICALLY ...
OKAY.
BUT ONLY UNDER THE CONDITION THAT YOU DO EXACTLY WHAT I SAY TO CREATE THOSE SEXY SCENES.
CHOMP
CHOMP
CHOMP
CHOMP
YOU'RE STILL YOUNG AND HAVE NICE CURVES, SO THIS NEXT PART WILL BE EASY, MISS AOKI.
START OUT BY TAKING PHOTOGRAPHS AND VIDEOS OF YOURSELF DOING SEXY POSES.
MUNCH
YOU'VE PROBABLY ALREADY TRIED THIS, BUT STEP TWO IS TO LOOK AT PORN MAGS AND DVDS FOR INSPIRATION. THEN I'LL PICK OUT THE BEST POSES FOR YOU.
MUNCH
!
...
DON'T TELL ME YOU SERI-OUSLY MEAN THAT.

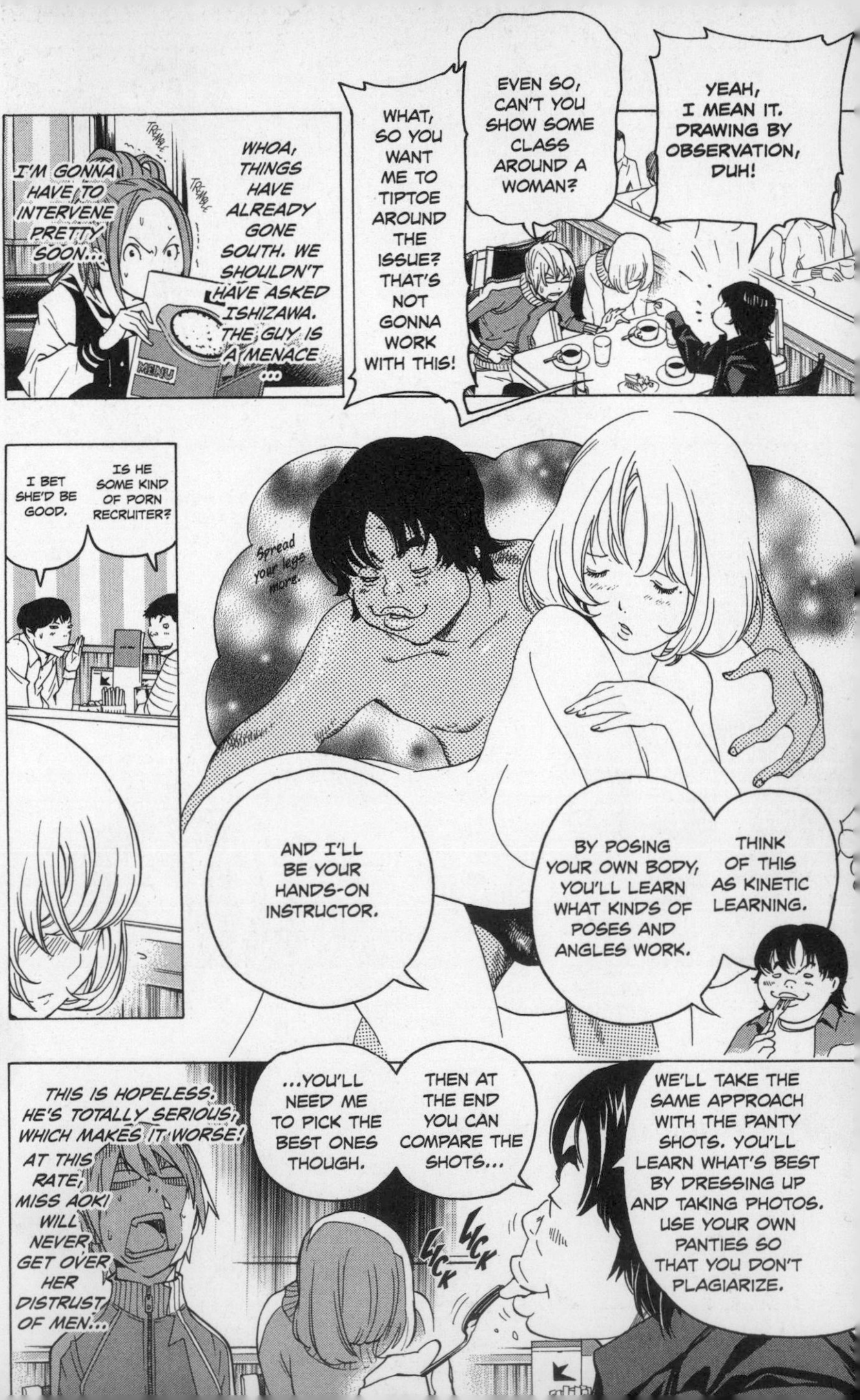
YEAH, I MEAN IT. DRAWING BY OBSERVATION, DUH!
EVEN SO, CAN'T YOU SHOW SOME CLASS AROUND A WOMAN?
WHAT, SO YOU WANT ME TO TIPTOE AROUND THE ISSUE? THAT'S NOT GONNA WORK WITH THIS!
WHOA, THINGS HAVE ALREADY GONE SOUTH. WE SHOULDN'T HAVE ASKED ISHIZAWA. THE GUY IS A MENACE...
TREMBLE
TREMBLE
MENU
I'M GONNA HAVE TO INTERVENE PRETTY SOON...
THINK OF THIS AS KINETIC LEARNING.
BY POSING YOUR OWN BODY, YOU'LL LEARN WHAT KINDS OF POSES AND ANGLES WORK.
AND I'LL BE YOUR HANDS-ON INSTRUCTOR.
Spread your legs more.
IS HE SOME KIND OF PORN RECRUITER?
I BET SHE'D BE GOOD.
WE'LL TAKE THE SAME APPROACH WITH THE PANTY SHOTS. YOU'LL LEARN WHAT'S BEST BY DRESSING UP AND TAKING PHOTOS. USE YOUR OWN PANTIES SO THAT YOU DON'T PLAGIARIZE.
THEN AT THE END YOU CAN COMPARE THE SHOTS...
...YOU'LL NEED ME TO PICK THE BEST ONES THOUGH.
LICK
LICK
THIS IS HOPELESS. HE'S TOTALLY SERIOUS, WHICH MAKES IT WORSE!
AT THIS RATE, MISS AOKI WILL NEVER GET OVER HER DISTRUST OF MEN...

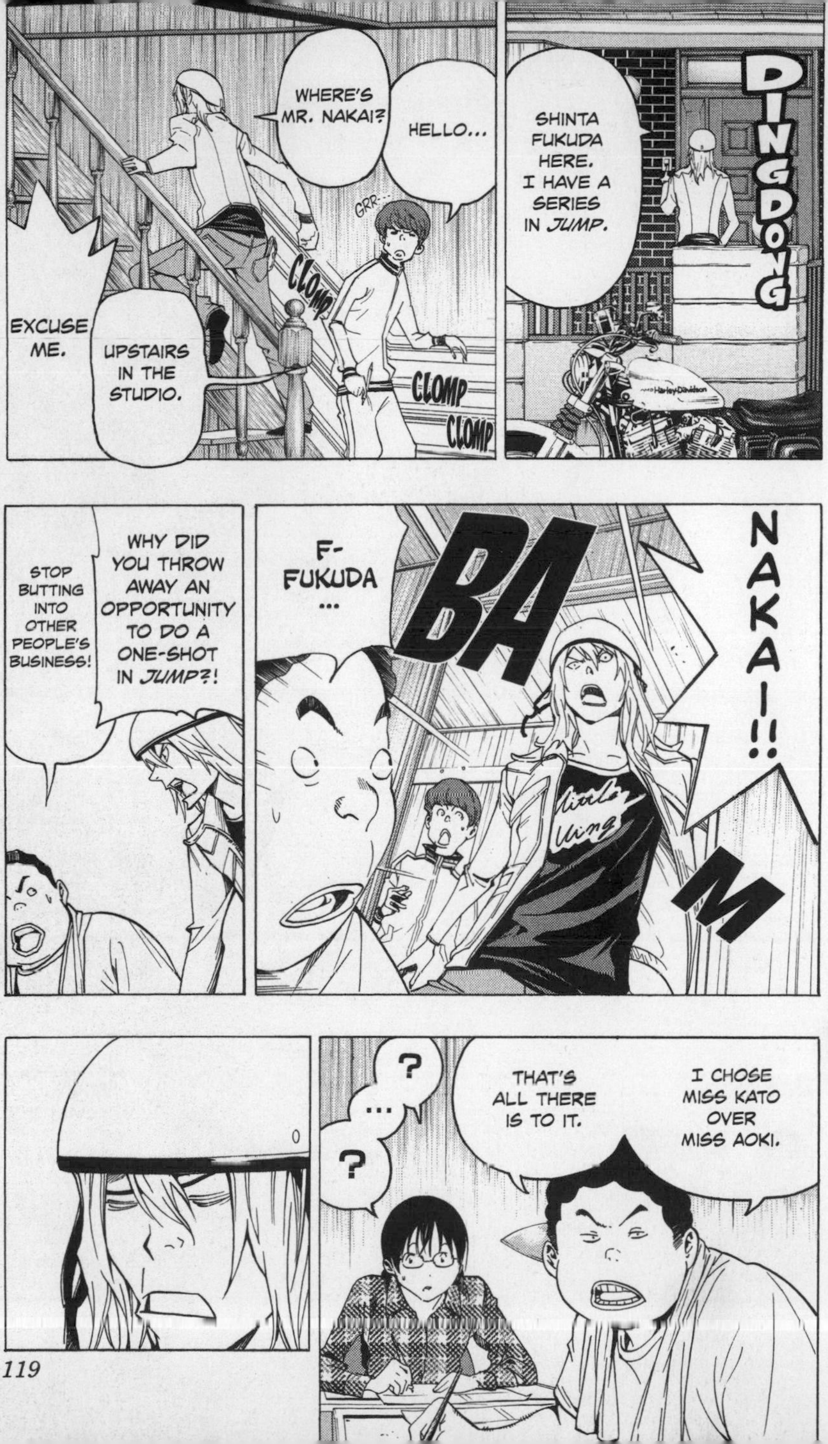
DINGDONG
SHINTA FUKUDA HERE. I HAVE A SERIES IN JUMP.
HELLO...
WHERE'S MR. NAKAI?
GRR...
CLOMP
UPSTAIRS IN THE STUDIO.
EXCUSE ME.
CLOMP
CLOMP
NAKAI!!
BAM
F-FUKUDA...
WHY DID YOU THROW AWAY AN OPPORTUNITY TO DO A ONE-SHOT IN JUMP?!
STOP BUTTING INTO OTHER PEOPLE'S BUSINESS!
I CHOSE MISS KATO OVER MISS AOKI.
THAT'S ALL THERE IS TO IT.
?
...
?

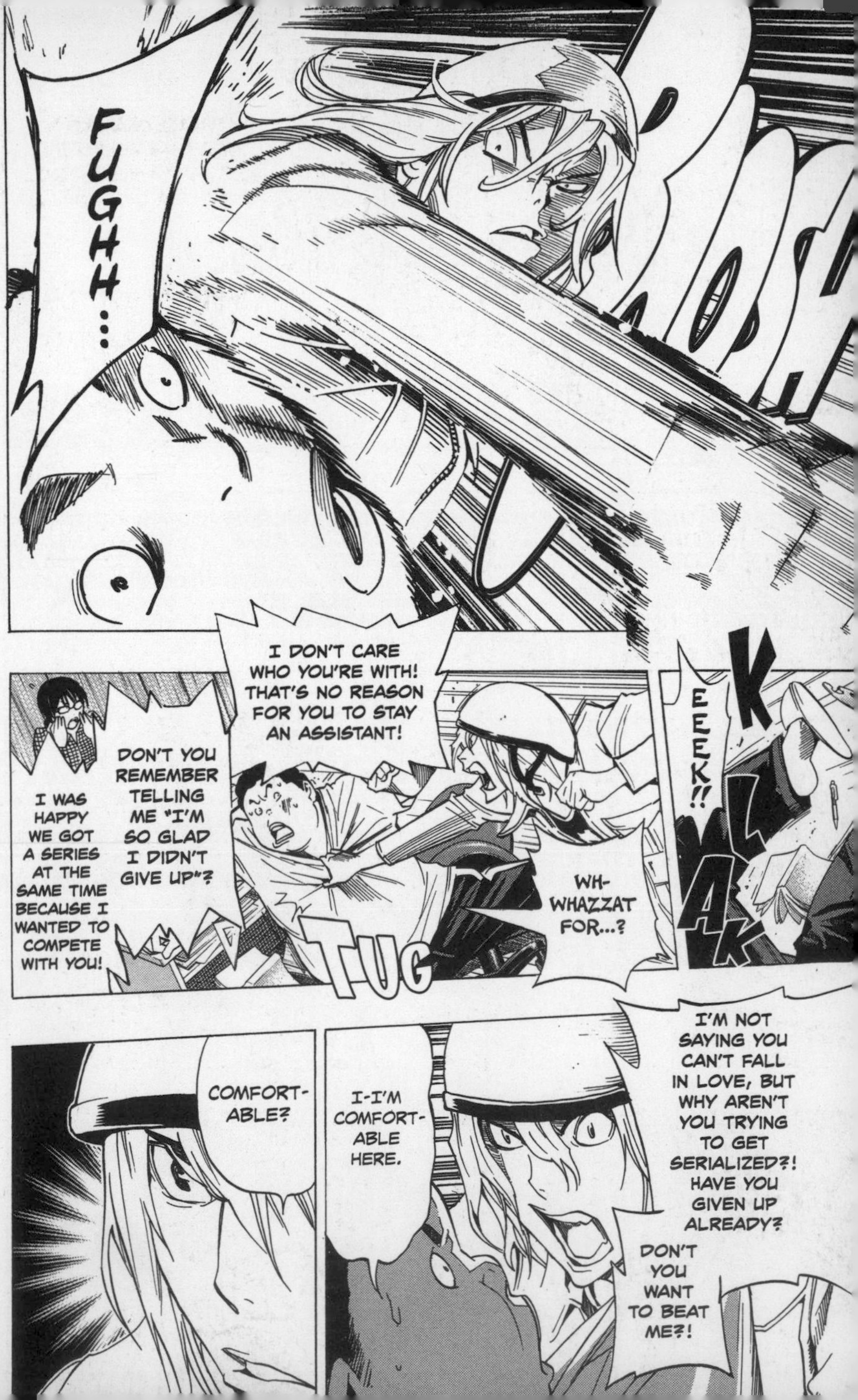
FUGHH...
KLAK
EEEEK!!
WH-WHAZZAT FOR...?
I DON'T CARE WHO YOU'RE WITH! THAT'S NO REASON FOR YOU TO STAY AN ASSISTANT!
TUG
DON'T YOU REMEMBER TELLING ME "I'M SO GLAD I DIDN'T GIVE UP"?
I WAS HAPPY WE GOT A SERIES AT THE SAME TIME BECAUSE I WANTED TO COMPETE WITH YOU!
I'M NOT SAYING YOU CAN'T FALL IN LOVE, BUT WHY AREN'T YOU TRYING TO GET SERIALIZED?! HAVE YOU GIVEN UP ALREADY?
DON'T YOU WANT TO BEAT ME?!
I-I'M COMFORT-ABLE HERE.
COMFORT-ABLE?

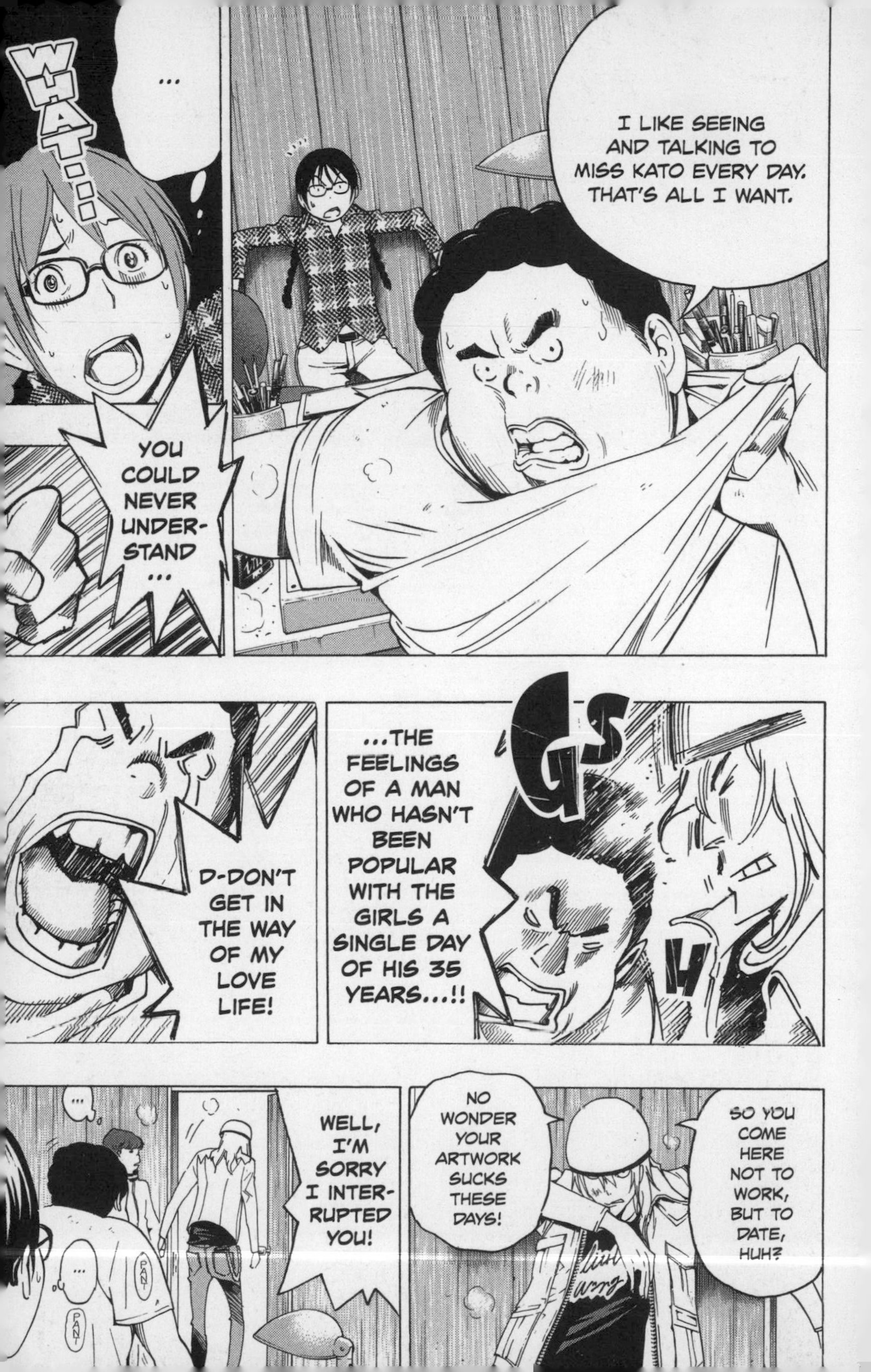
I LIKE SEEING AND TALKING TO MISS KATO EVERY DAY. THAT'S ALL I WANT.
...
WHAT...
YOU COULD NEVER UNDER-STAND ...
...THE FEELINGS OF A MAN WHO HASN'T BEEN POPULAR WITH THE GIRLS A SINGLE DAY OF HIS 35 YEARS...!!
D-DON'T GET IN THE WAY OF MY LOVE LIFE!
SO YOU COME HERE NOT TO WORK, BUT TO DATE, HUH?
NO WONDER YOUR ARTWORK SUCKS THESE DAYS!
WELL, I'M SORRY I INTER-RUPTED YOU!
...
...
PANT
PANT

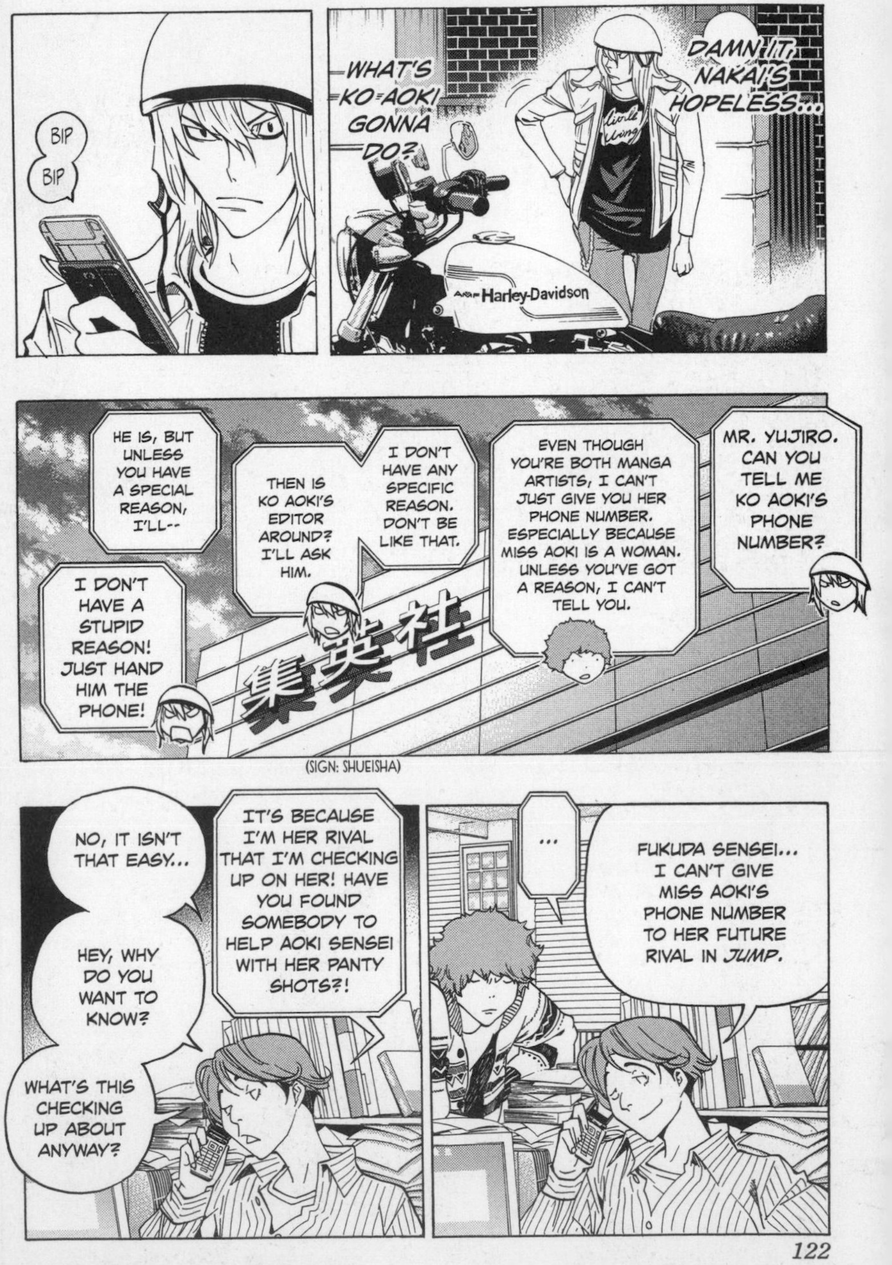
DAMN IT, NAKAI'S HOPELESS...
WHAT'S KO AOKI GONNA DO?
BIP BIP
MR. YUJIRO. CAN YOU TELL ME KO AOKI'S PHONE NUMBER?
EVEN THOUGH YOU'RE BOTH MANGA ARTISTS, I CAN'T JUST GIVE YOU HER PHONE NUMBER. ESPECIALLY BECAUSE MISS AOKI IS A WOMAN. UNLESS YOU'VE GOT A REASON, I CAN'T TELL YOU.
I DON'T HAVE ANY SPECIFIC REASON. DON'T BE LIKE THAT.
THEN IS KO AOKI'S EDITOR AROUND? I'LL ASK HIM.
HE IS, BUT UNLESS YOU HAVE A SPECIAL REASON, I'LL--
I DON'T HAVE A STUPID REASON! JUST HAND HIM THE PHONE!
集英社
(SIGN: SHUEISHA)
...
FUKUDA SENSEI... I CAN'T GIVE MISS AOKI'S PHONE NUMBER TO HER FUTURE RIVAL IN JUMP.
IT'S BECAUSE I'M HER RIVAL THAT I'M CHECKING UP ON HER! HAVE YOU FOUND SOMEBODY TO HELP AOKI SENSEI WITH HER PANTY SHOTS?!
NO, IT ISN'T THAT EASY...
HEY, WHY DO YOU WANT TO KNOW?
WHAT'S THIS CHECKING UP ABOUT ANYWAY?

READ THIS WAY

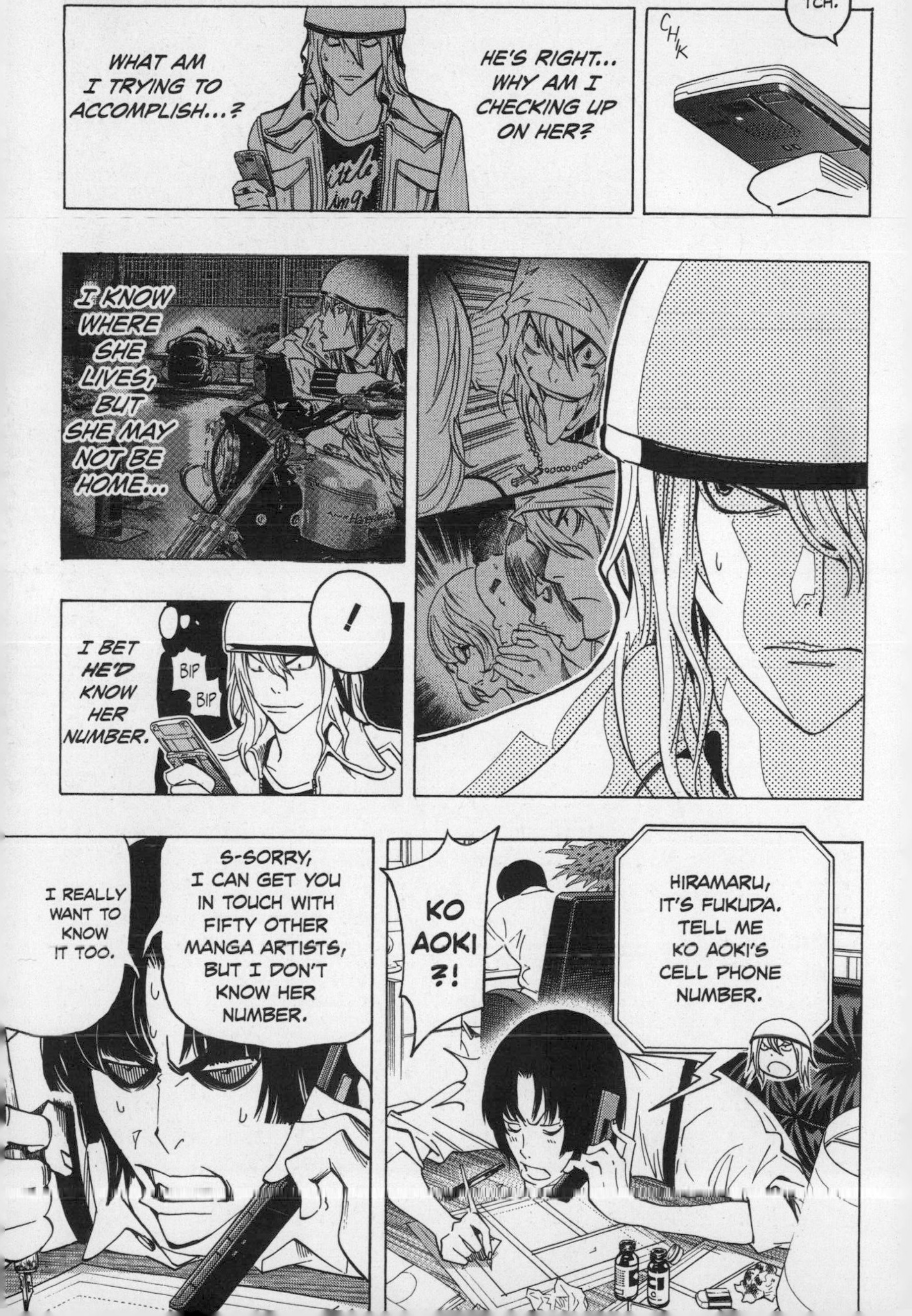
TCH.
CHIK
HE'S RIGHT... WHY AM I CHECKING UP ON HER?
WHAT AM I TRYING TO ACCOMPLISH...?
I KNOW WHERE SHE LIVES, BUT SHE MAY NOT BE HOME...
!
BIP BIP
I BET HE'D KNOW HER NUMBER.
HIRAMARU, IT'S FUKUDA. TELL ME KO AOKI'S CELL PHONE NUMBER.
KO AOKI?!
S-SORRY, I CAN GET YOU IN TOUCH WITH FIFTY OTHER MANGA ARTISTS, BUT I DON'T KNOW HER NUMBER.
I REALLY WANT TO KNOW IT TOO.

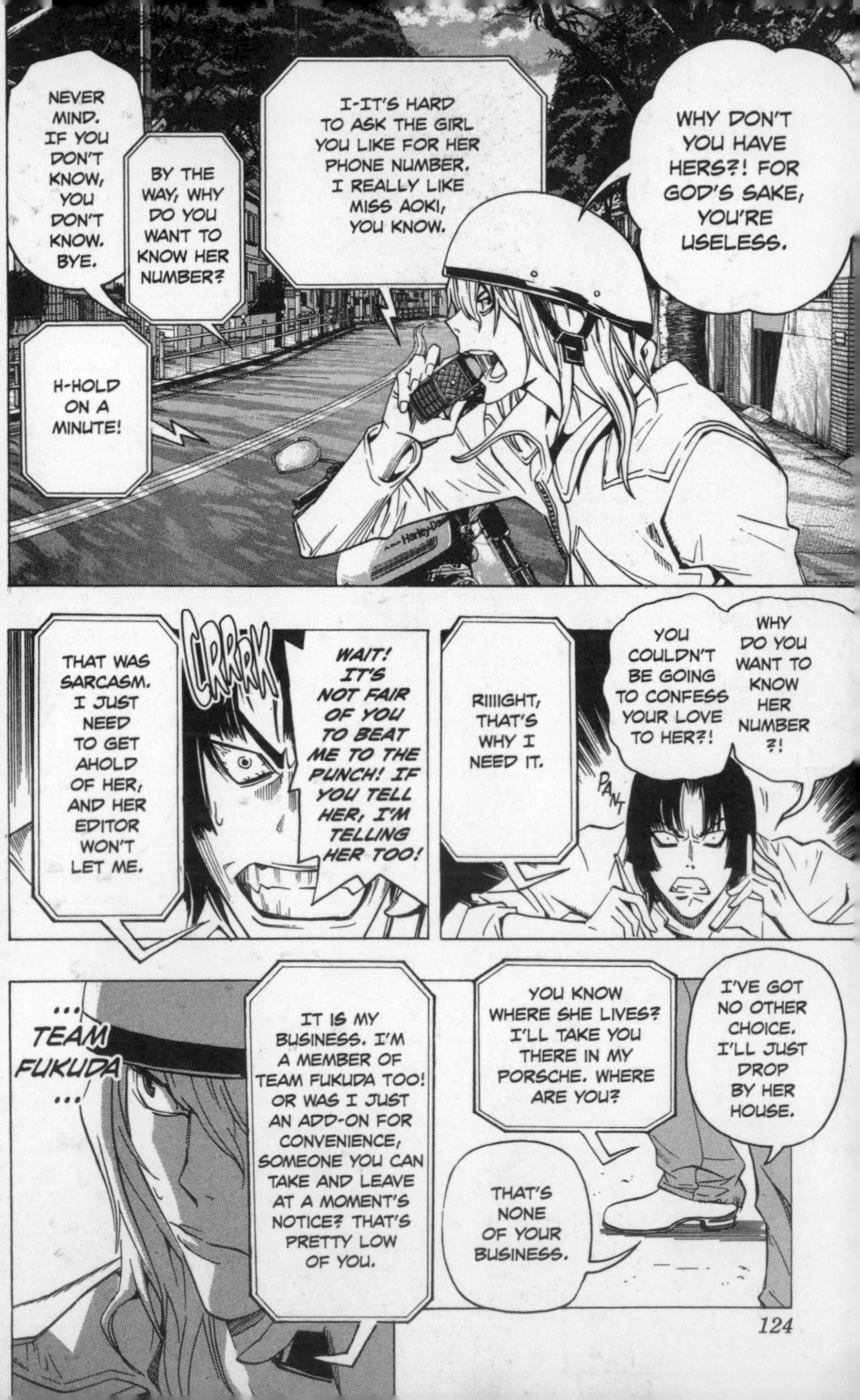
WHY DON'T YOU HAVE HERS?! FOR GOD'S SAKE, YOU'RE USELESS.
I-IT'S HARD TO ASK THE GIRL YOU LIKE FOR HER PHONE NUMBER. I REALLY LIKE MISS AOKI, YOU KNOW.
BY THE WAY, WHY DO YOU WANT TO KNOW HER NUMBER?
NEVER MIND. IF YOU DON'T KNOW, YOU DON'T KNOW. BYE.
H-HOLD ON A MINUTE!
WHY DO YOU WANT TO KNOW HER NUMBER ?!
YOU COULDN'T BE GOING TO CONFESS YOUR LOVE TO HER?!
PANT
RIIIIGHT, THAT'S WHY I NEED IT.
WAIT! IT'S NOT FAIR OF YOU TO BEAT ME TO THE PUNCH! IF YOU TELL HER, I'M TELLING HER TOO!
CRRRK
THAT WAS SARCASM. I JUST NEED TO GET AHOLD OF HER, AND HER EDITOR WON'T LET ME.
I'VE GOT NO OTHER CHOICE. I'LL JUST DROP BY HER HOUSE.
YOU KNOW WHERE SHE LIVES? I'LL TAKE YOU THERE IN MY PORSCHE. WHERE ARE YOU?
THAT'S NONE OF YOUR BUSINESS.
IT IS MY BUSINESS. I'M A MEMBER OF TEAM FUKUDA TOO! OR WAS I JUST AN ADD-ON FOR CONVENIENCE, SOMEONE YOU CAN TAKE AND LEAVE AT A MOMENT'S NOTICE? THAT'S PRETTY LOW OF YOU.
...TEAM FUKUDA...

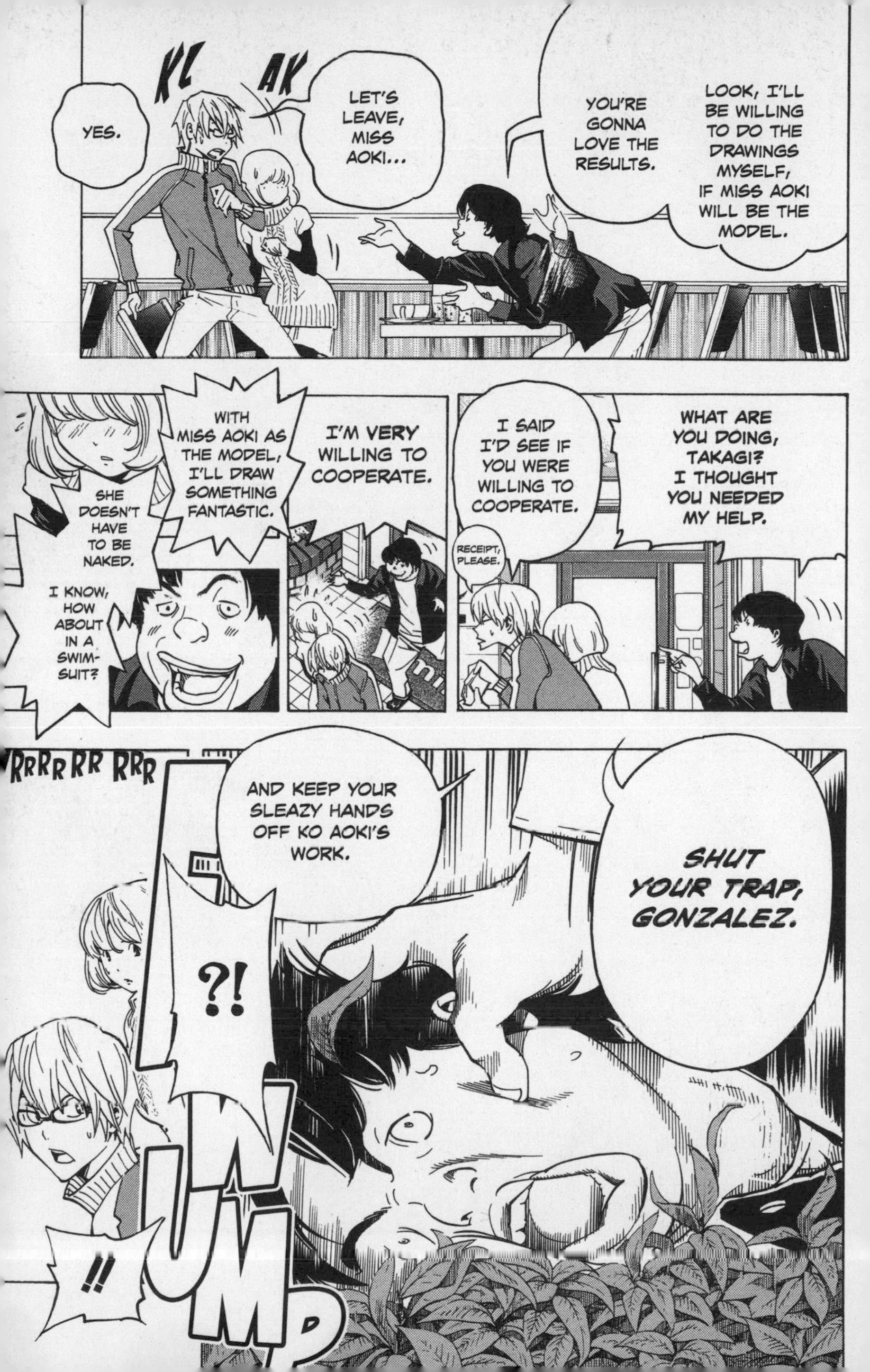
LOOK, I'LL BE WILLING TO DO THE DRAWINGS MYSELF, IF MISS AOKI WILL BE THE MODEL.
YOU'RE GONNA LOVE THE RESULTS.
KL AK
LET'S LEAVE, MISS AOKI...
YES.
WHAT ARE YOU DOING, TAKAGI? I THOUGHT YOU NEEDED MY HELP.
I SAID I'D SEE IF YOU WERE WILLING TO COOPERATE.
RECEIPT, PLEASE.
I'M VERY WILLING TO COOPERATE.
WITH MISS AOKI AS THE MODEL, I'LL DRAW SOMETHING FANTASTIC.
SHE DOESN'T HAVE TO BE NAKED.
I KNOW, HOW ABOUT IN A SWIMSUIT?
SHUT YOUR TRAP, GONZALEZ.
AND KEEP YOUR SLEAZY HANDS OFF KO AOKI'S WORK.
RRRRRR RRR
?!
WUMP
!!

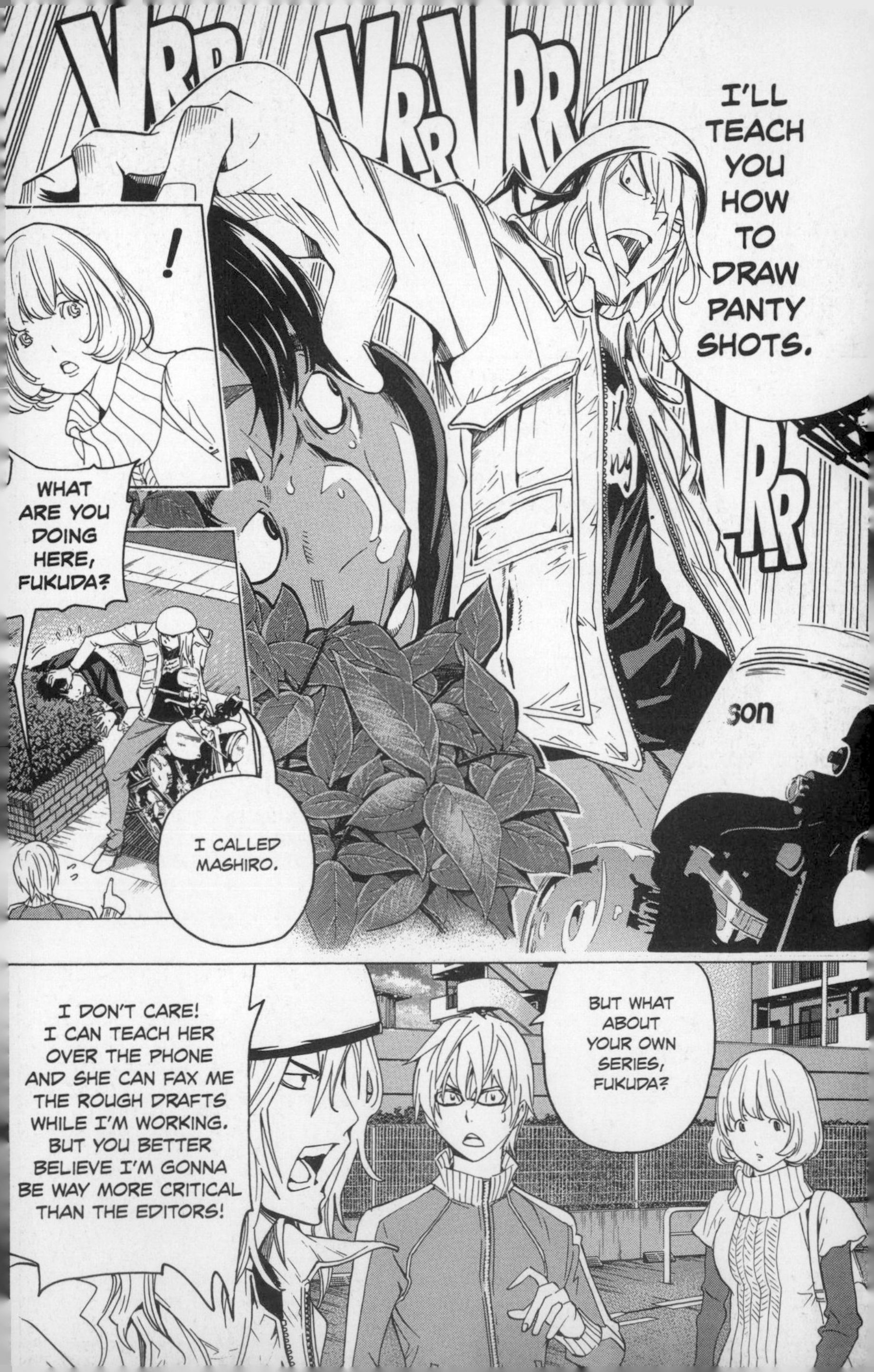
VRR VRR VRR
I'LL TEACH YOU HOW TO DRAW PANTY SHOTS.
VRR
!
WHAT ARE YOU DOING HERE, FUKUDA?
I CALLED MASHIRO.
son
BUT WHAT ABOUT YOUR OWN SERIES, FUKUDA?
I DON'T CARE! I CAN TEACH HER OVER THE PHONE AND SHE CAN FAX ME THE ROUGH DRAFTS WHILE I'M WORKING. BUT YOU BETTER BELIEVE I'M GONNA BE WAY MORE CRITICAL THAN THE EDITORS!

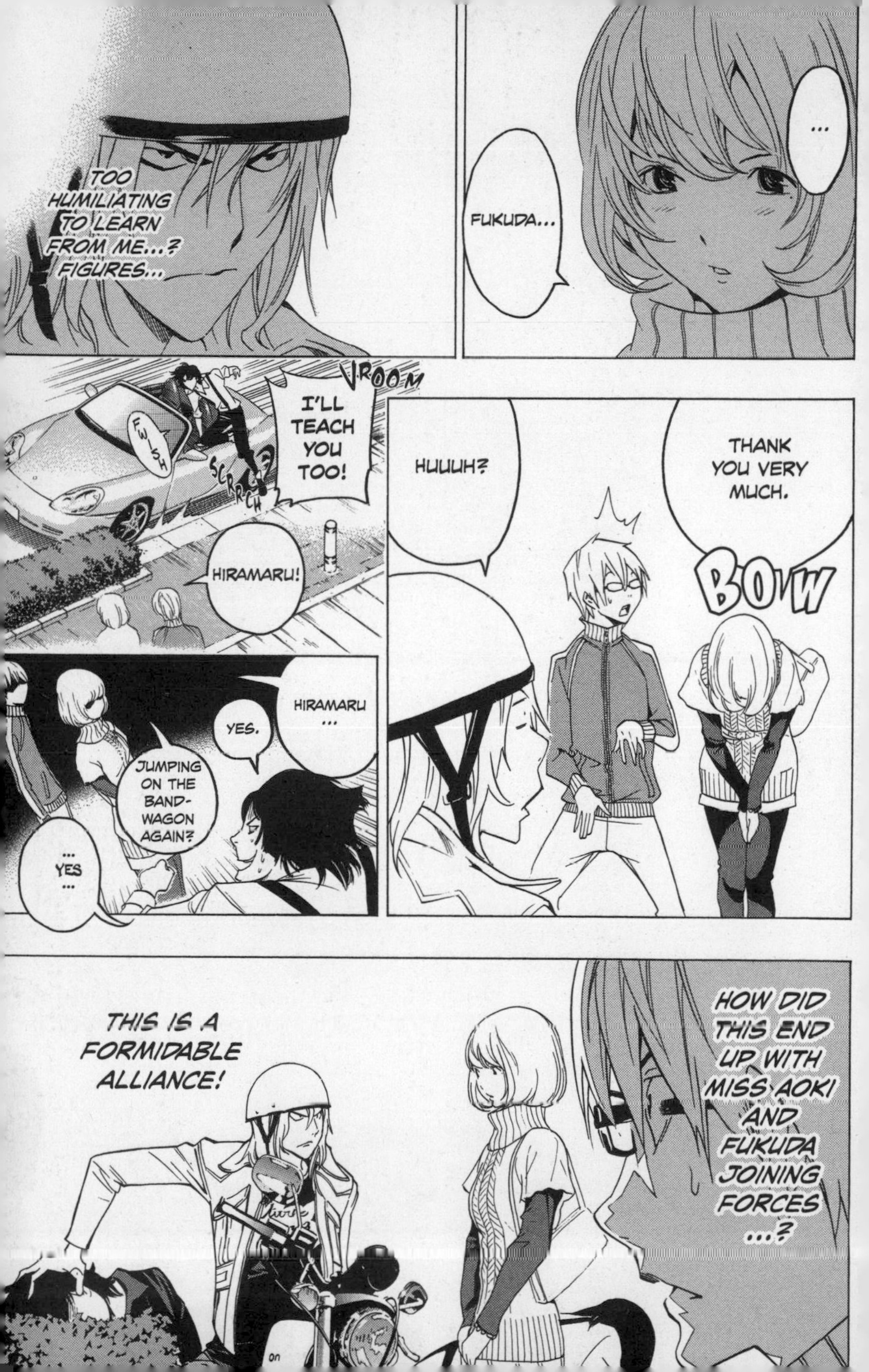
...
FUKUDA...
TOO HUMILIATING TO LEARN FROM ME...? FIGURES...
THANK YOU VERY MUCH.
BOW
HUUUH?
VROOM
I'LL TEACH YOU TOO!
FWISH
SCRRCH
HIRAMARU!
HIRAMARU ...
YES.
JUMPING ON THE BAND-WAGON AGAIN?
... YES ...
HOW DID THIS END UP WITH MISS AOKI AND FUKUDA JOINING FORCES ...?
THIS IS A FORMIDABLE ALLIANCE!

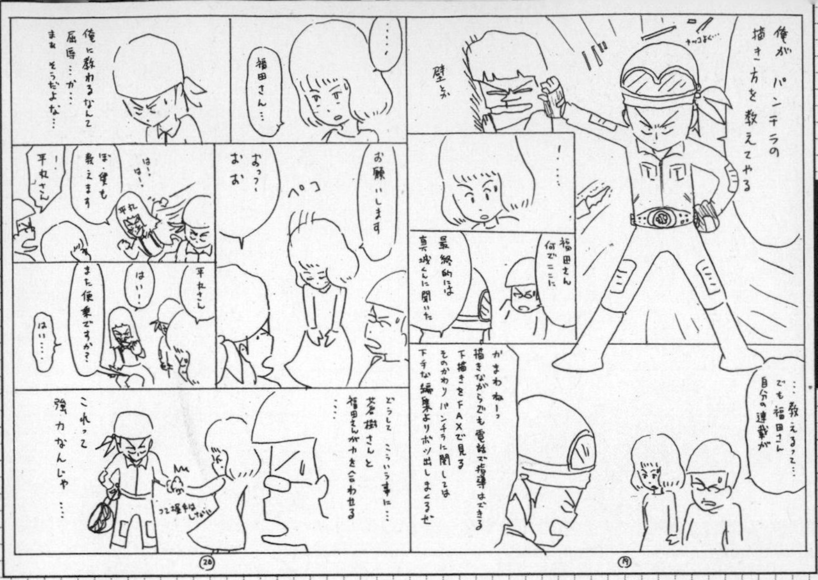

俺がパンテラの描き方を教えてやる
カッコよく…
壁とか
!…
福田さん何でここに
最終的には真城くんに聞いた
…教えるって…でも福田さん自分の連載が
かまわねーっ描きながらでも電話で指導はできる
下描きをFAXで見る
そのかわりパンチラに関しては下手な編集よりボツ出しまくるぜ
…!
福田さん…
俺に教わるなんて屈辱…か… まぁそうだよな…
お願いします
ペコ
おっ!おお
ぼ・僕も教えます
は…は…
平丸さん!
平丸さん
はい!
また便乗ですか?
はい……
どうして…こういう事に…
蒼樹さんと福田さんがかき合わせる
これって強力なんじゃ…

OHBA'S STORYBOARD

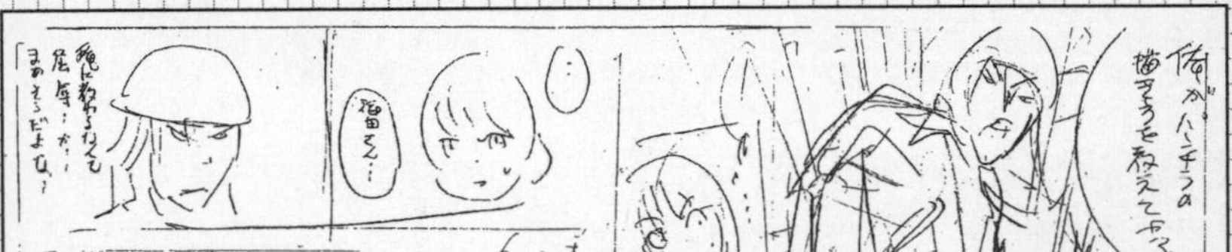

OBATA'S STORYBOARD

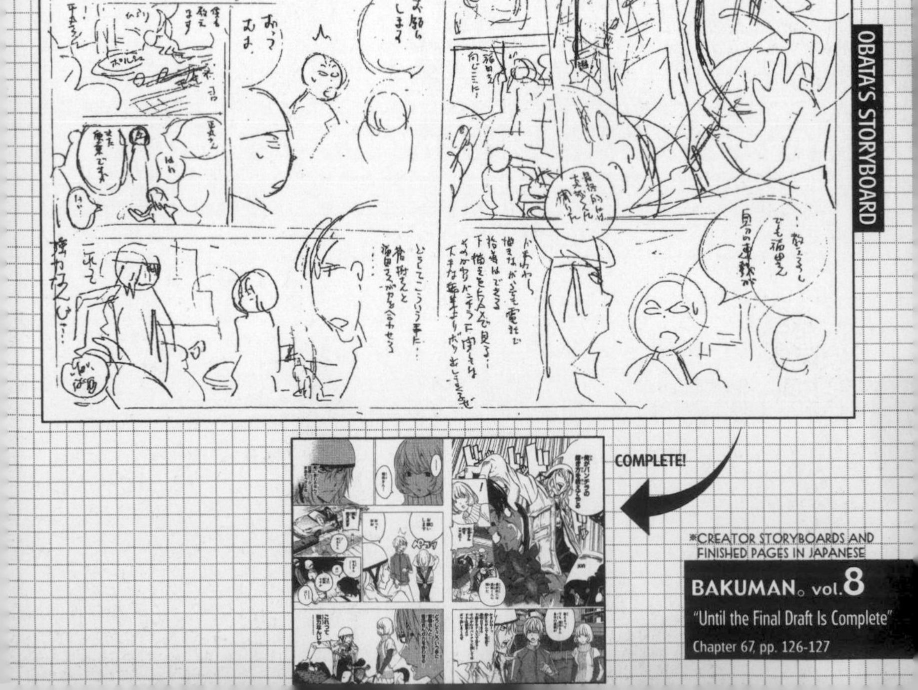

COMPLETE!

※CREATOR STORYBOARDS AND FINISHED PAGES IN JAPANESE

BAKUMAN。 vol.8

"Until the Final Draft Is Complete"

Chapter 67, pp. 126-127

CHAPTER 68
TOILET AND BATH

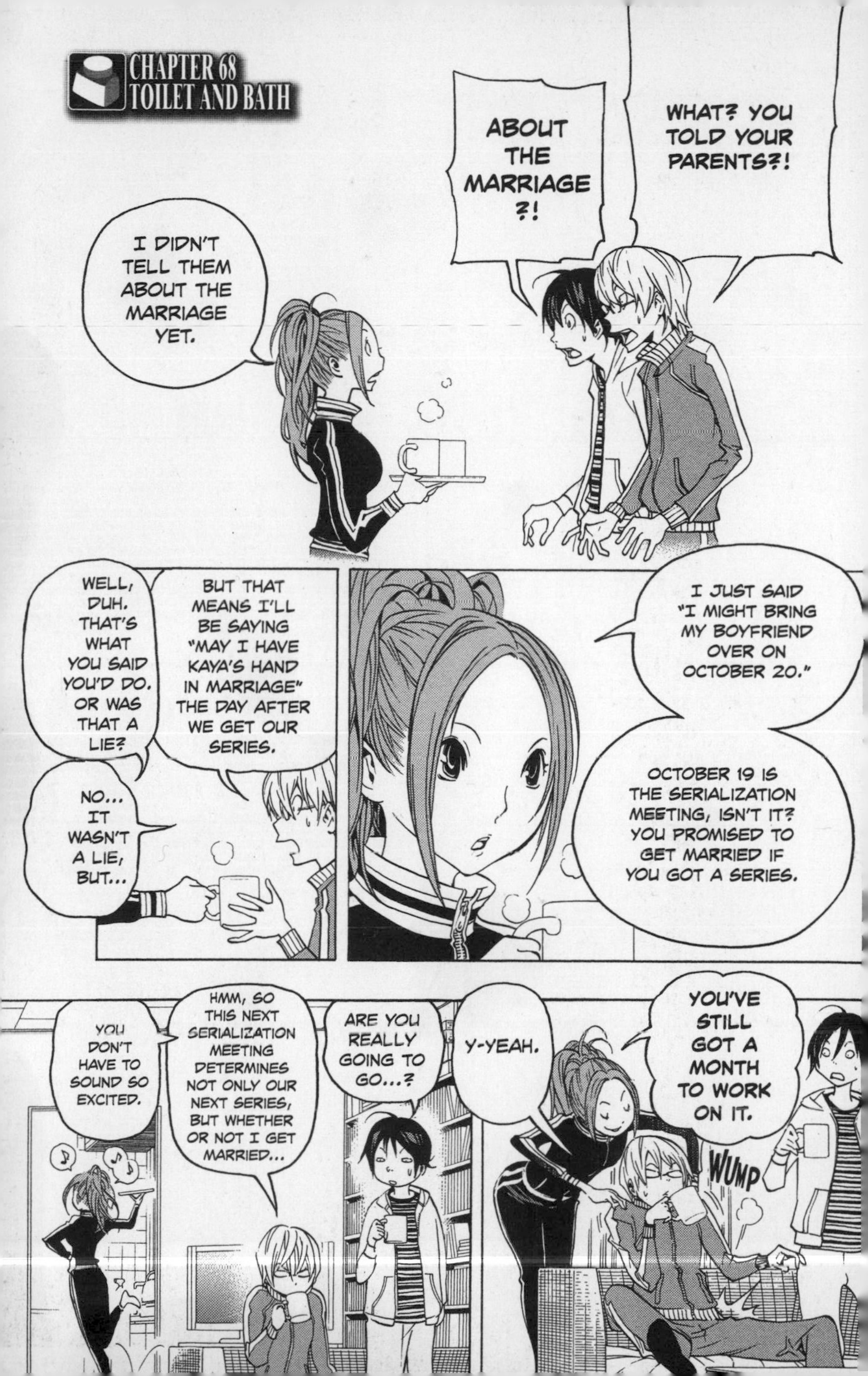

WHAT? YOU TOLD YOUR PARENTS?!
ABOUT THE MARRIAGE ?!
I DIDN'T TELL THEM ABOUT THE MARRIAGE YET.
I JUST SAID "I MIGHT BRING MY BOYFRIEND OVER ON OCTOBER 20."
OCTOBER 19 IS THE SERIALIZATION MEETING, ISN'T IT? YOU PROMISED TO GET MARRIED IF YOU GOT A SERIES.
BUT THAT MEANS I'LL BE SAYING "MAY I HAVE KAYA'S HAND IN MARRIAGE" THE DAY AFTER WE GET OUR SERIES.
WELL, DUH. THAT'S WHAT YOU SAID YOU'D DO. OR WAS THAT A LIE?
NO... IT WASN'T A LIE, BUT...
YOU'VE STILL GOT A MONTH TO WORK ON IT.
WUMP
Y-YEAH.
ARE YOU REALLY GOING TO GO...?
HMM, SO THIS NEXT SERIALIZATION MEETING DETERMINES NOT ONLY OUR NEXT SERIES, BUT WHETHER OR NOT I GET MARRIED...
YOU DON'T HAVE TO SOUND SO EXCITED.

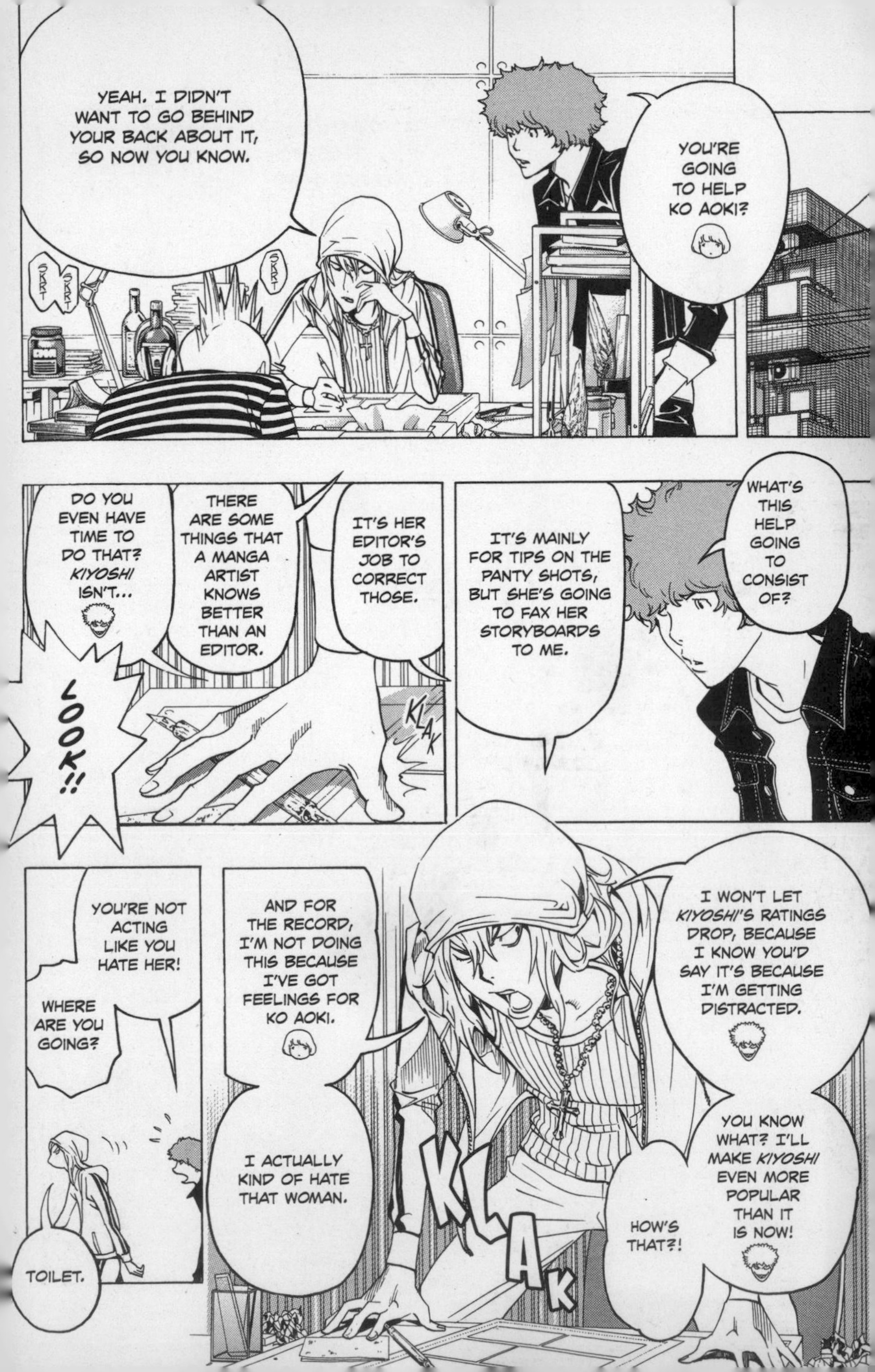
YOU'RE GOING TO HELP KO AOKI?
YEAH. I DIDN'T WANT TO GO BEHIND YOUR BACK ABOUT IT, SO NOW YOU KNOW.
SKRT
SKRT SKRT
WHAT'S THIS HELP GOING TO CONSIST OF?
IT'S MAINLY FOR TIPS ON THE PANTY SHOTS, BUT SHE'S GOING TO FAX HER STORYBOARDS TO ME.
IT'S HER EDITOR'S JOB TO CORRECT THOSE.
KLAK
THERE ARE SOME THINGS THAT A MANGA ARTIST KNOWS BETTER THAN AN EDITOR.
DO YOU EVEN HAVE TIME TO DO THAT? *KIYOSHI* ISN'T...
LOOK!!
I WON'T LET *KIYOSHI*'S RATINGS DROP, BECAUSE I KNOW YOU'D SAY IT'S BECAUSE I'M GETTING DISTRACTED.
YOU KNOW WHAT? I'LL MAKE *KIYOSHI* EVEN MORE POPULAR THAN IT IS NOW!
HOW'S THAT?!
AND FOR THE RECORD, I'M NOT DOING THIS BECAUSE I'VE GOT FEELINGS FOR KO AOKI.
I ACTUALLY KIND OF HATE THAT WOMAN.
KLAK
YOU'RE NOT ACTING LIKE YOU HATE HER!
WHERE ARE YOU GOING?
TOILET.

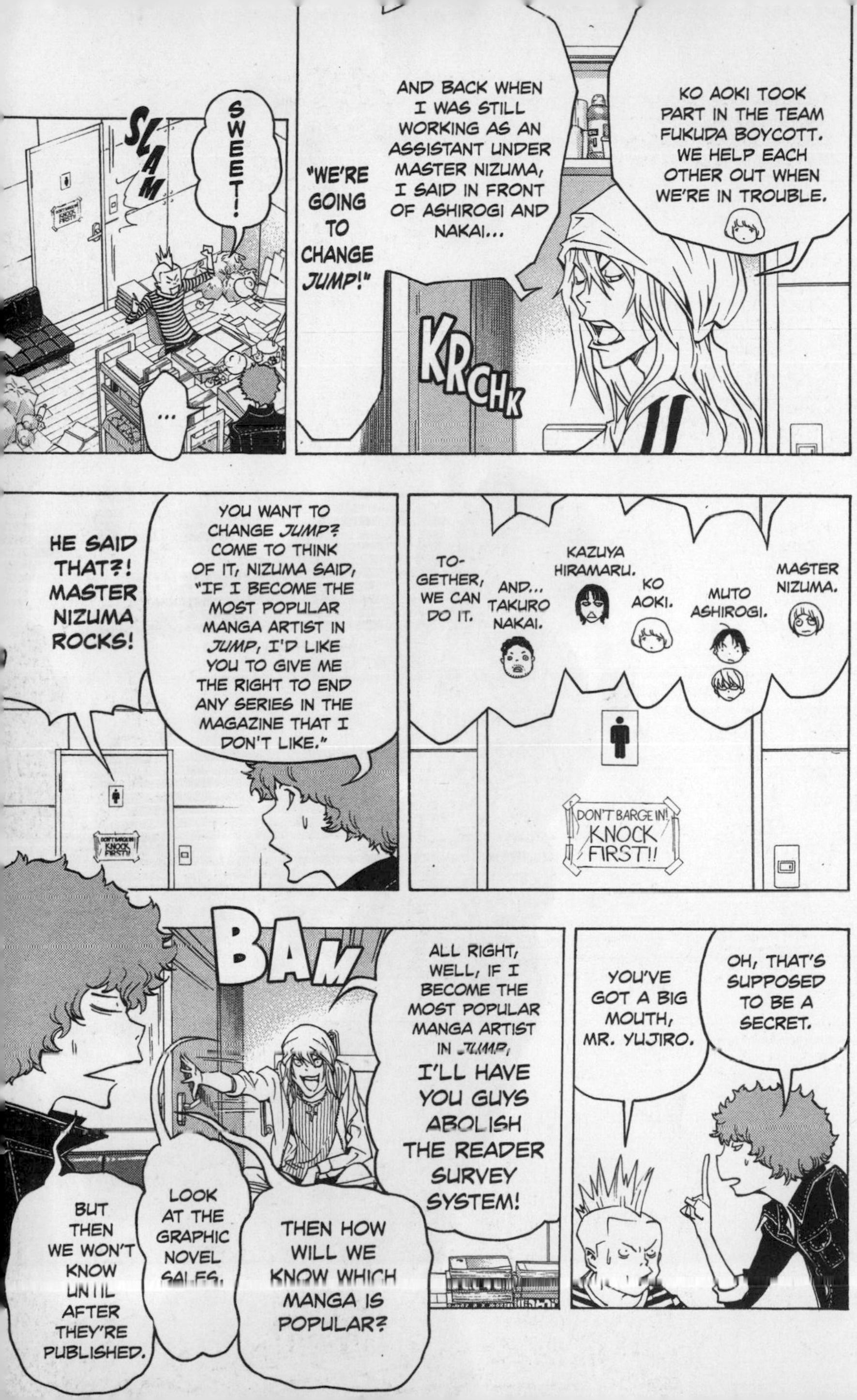
KO AOKI TOOK PART IN THE TEAM FUKUDA BOYCOTT. WE HELP EACH OTHER OUT WHEN WE'RE IN TROUBLE.
AND BACK WHEN I WAS STILL WORKING AS AN ASSISTANT UNDER MASTER NIZUMA, I SAID IN FRONT OF ASHIROGI AND NAKAI...
"WE'RE GOING TO CHANGE *JUMP!*"
KRCHK
SLAM
SWEET!
...
MASTER NIZUMA.
MUTO ASHIROGI.
KO AOKI.
KAZUYA HIRAMARU.
AND... TAKURO NAKAI.
TO-GETHER, WE CAN DO IT.
DON'T BARGE IN! KNOCK FIRST!!
YOU WANT TO CHANGE *JUMP?* COME TO THINK OF IT, NIZUMA SAID, "IF I BECOME THE MOST POPULAR MANGA ARTIST IN *JUMP*, I'D LIKE YOU TO GIVE ME THE RIGHT TO END ANY SERIES IN THE MAGAZINE THAT I DON'T LIKE."
HE SAID THAT?! MASTER NIZUMA ROCKS!
OH, THAT'S SUPPOSED TO BE A SECRET.
YOU'VE GOT A BIG MOUTH, MR. YUJIRO.
BAM
ALL RIGHT, WELL, IF I BECOME THE MOST POPULAR MANGA ARTIST IN *JUMP*, I'LL HAVE YOU GUYS ABOLISH THE READER SURVEY SYSTEM!
THEN HOW WILL WE KNOW WHICH MANGA IS POPULAR?
LOOK AT THE GRAPHIC NOVEL SALES.
BUT THEN WE WON'T KNOW UNTIL AFTER THEY'RE PUBLISHED.

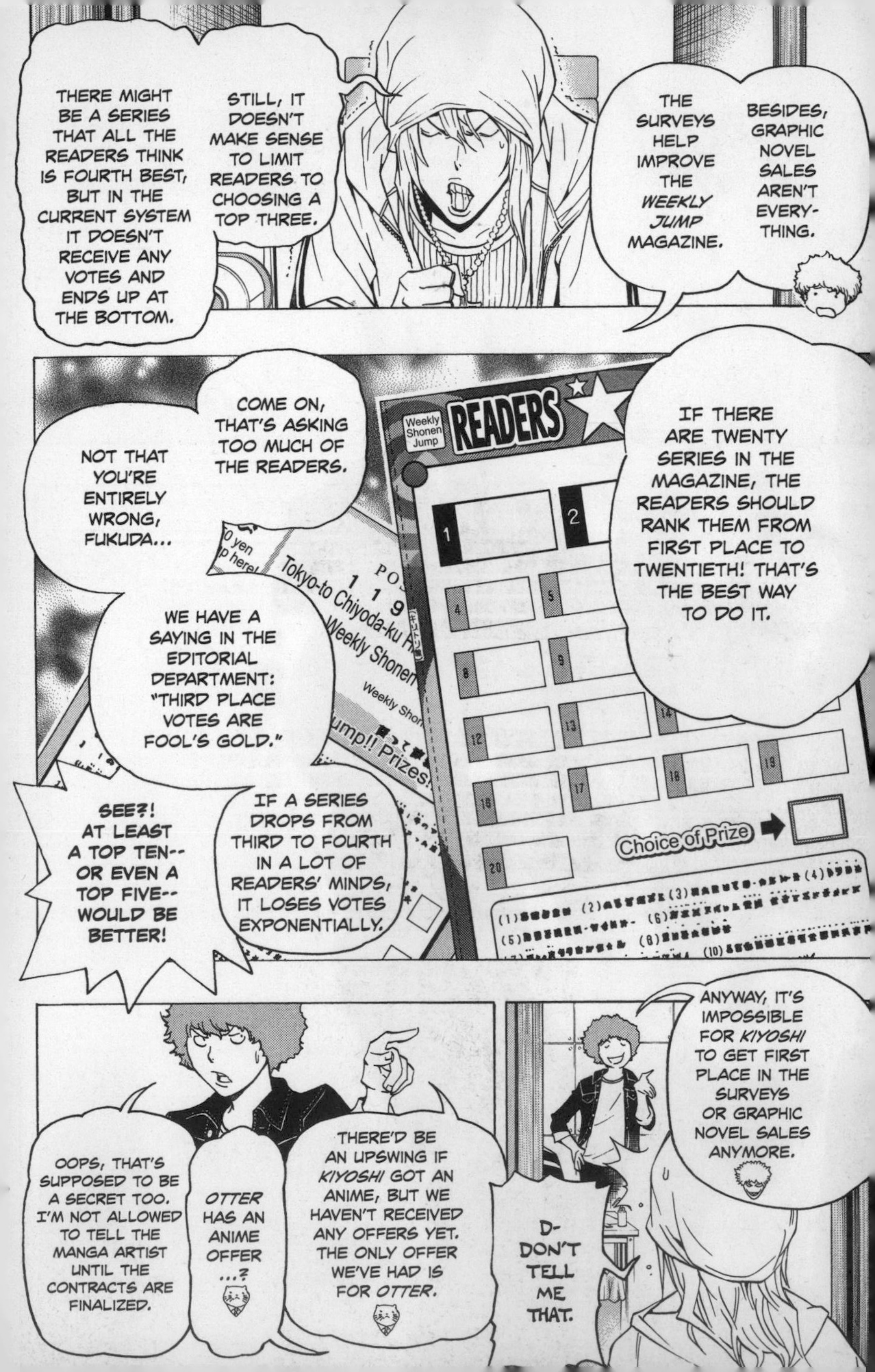
BESIDES, GRAPHIC NOVEL SALES AREN'T EVERYTHING.
THE SURVEYS HELP IMPROVE THE *WEEKLY JUMP* MAGAZINE.
STILL, IT DOESN'T MAKE SENSE TO LIMIT READERS TO CHOOSING A TOP THREE.
THERE MIGHT BE A SERIES THAT ALL THE READERS THINK IS FOURTH BEST, BUT IN THE CURRENT SYSTEM IT DOESN'T RECEIVE ANY VOTES AND ENDS UP AT THE BOTTOM.
IF THERE ARE TWENTY SERIES IN THE MAGAZINE, THE READERS SHOULD RANK THEM FROM FIRST PLACE TO TWENTIETH! THAT'S THE BEST WAY TO DO IT.
Weekly Shonen Jump
READERS
Tokyo-to Chiyoda-ku
Weekly Shonen
Jump!! Prizes!
Choice of Prize
COME ON, THAT'S ASKING TOO MUCH OF THE READERS.
NOT THAT YOU'RE ENTIRELY WRONG, FUKUDA...
WE HAVE A SAYING IN THE EDITORIAL DEPARTMENT: "THIRD PLACE VOTES ARE FOOL'S GOLD."
IF A SERIES DROPS FROM THIRD TO FOURTH IN A LOT OF READERS' MINDS, IT LOSES VOTES EXPONENTIALLY.
SEE?! AT LEAST A TOP TEN--OR EVEN A TOP FIVE--WOULD BE BETTER!
ANYWAY, IT'S IMPOSSIBLE FOR *KIYOSHI* TO GET FIRST PLACE IN THE SURVEYS OR GRAPHIC NOVEL SALES ANYMORE.
D-DON'T TELL ME THAT.
THERE'D BE AN UPSWING IF *KIYOSHI* GOT AN ANIME, BUT WE HAVEN'T RECEIVED ANY OFFERS YET. THE ONLY OFFER WE'VE HAD IS FOR *OTTER*.
OTTER HAS AN ANIME OFFER ...?
OOPS, THAT'S SUPPOSED TO BE A SECRET TOO. I'M NOT ALLOWED TO TELL THE MANGA ARTIST UNTIL THE CONTRACTS ARE FINALIZED.

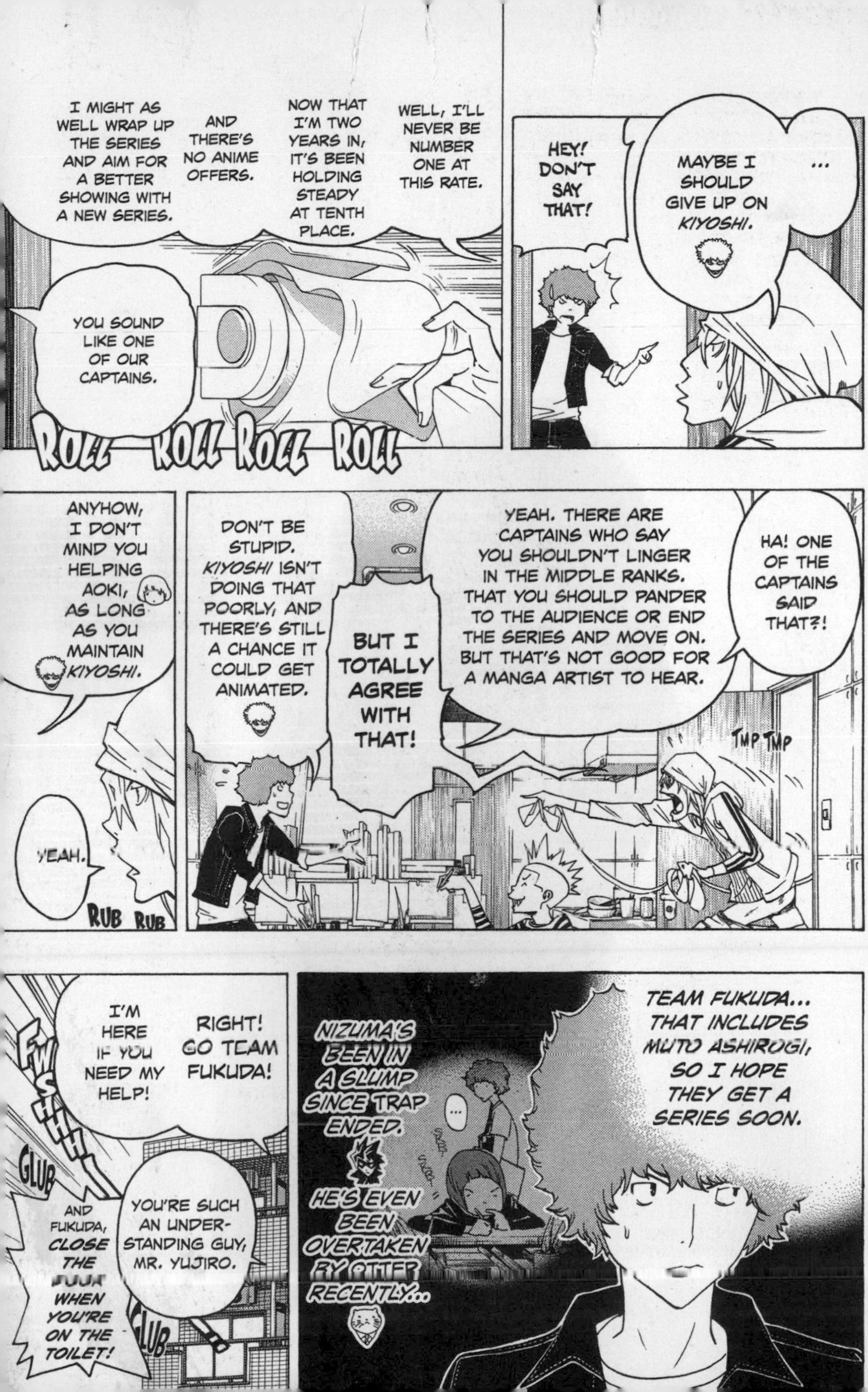
...
MAYBE I SHOULD GIVE UP ON KIYOSHI.
HEY! DON'T SAY THAT!
WELL, I'LL NEVER BE NUMBER ONE AT THIS RATE.
NOW THAT I'M TWO YEARS IN, IT'S BEEN HOLDING STEADY AT TENTH PLACE.
AND THERE'S NO ANIME OFFERS.
I MIGHT AS WELL WRAP UP THE SERIES AND AIM FOR A BETTER SHOWING WITH A NEW SERIES.
YOU SOUND LIKE ONE OF OUR CAPTAINS.
ROLL ROLL ROLL ROLL
HA! ONE OF THE CAPTAINS SAID THAT?!
YEAH. THERE ARE CAPTAINS WHO SAY YOU SHOULDN'T LINGER IN THE MIDDLE RANKS. THAT YOU SHOULD PANDER TO THE AUDIENCE OR END THE SERIES AND MOVE ON. BUT THAT'S NOT GOOD FOR A MANGA ARTIST TO HEAR.
BUT I TOTALLY AGREE WITH THAT!
DON'T BE STUPID. KIYOSHI ISN'T DOING THAT POORLY, AND THERE'S STILL A CHANCE IT COULD GET ANIMATED.
TMP TMP
ANYHOW, I DON'T MIND YOU HELPING AOKI, AS LONG AS YOU MAINTAIN KIYOSHI.
YEAH.
RUB RUB
TEAM FUKUDA... THAT INCLUDES MUTO ASHIROGI, SO I HOPE THEY GET A SERIES SOON.
NIZUMA'S BEEN IN A SLUMP SINCE TRAP ENDED.
...
HE'S EVEN BEEN OVERTAKEN BY OTTER RECENTLY...
RIGHT! GO TEAM FUKUDA!
I'M HERE IF YOU NEED MY HELP!
FWSHHH
GLUB
YOU'RE SUCH AN UNDERSTANDING GUY, MR. YUJIRO.
AND FUKUDA, CLOSE THE
WHEN YOU'RE ON THE TOILET!
GLUB

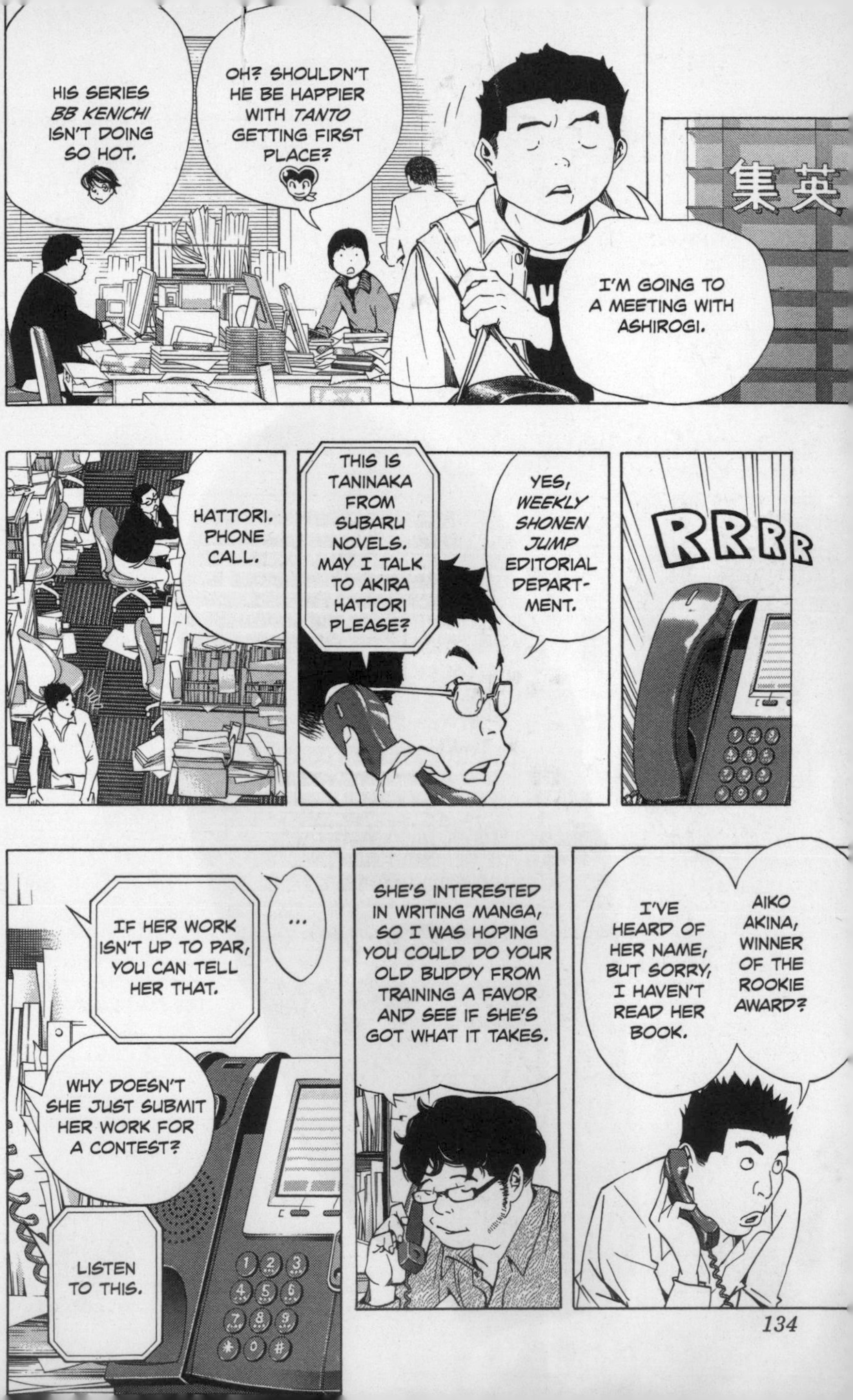
I'M GOING TO A MEETING WITH ASHIROGI.
集英
OH? SHOULDN'T HE BE HAPPIER WITH *TANTO* GETTING FIRST PLACE?
HIS SERIES *BB KENICHI* ISN'T DOING SO HOT.
RRRR
YES, *WEEKLY SHONEN JUMP* EDITORIAL DEPARTMENT.
THIS IS TANINAKA FROM SUBARU NOVELS. MAY I TALK TO AKIRA HATTORI PLEASE?
HATTORI. PHONE CALL.
AIKO AKINA, WINNER OF THE ROOKIE AWARD?
I'VE HEARD OF HER NAME, BUT SORRY, I HAVEN'T READ HER BOOK.
SHE'S INTERESTED IN WRITING MANGA, SO I WAS HOPING YOU COULD DO YOUR OLD BUDDY FROM TRAINING A FAVOR AND SEE IF SHE'S GOT WHAT IT TAKES.
...
IF HER WORK ISN'T UP TO PAR, YOU CAN TELL HER THAT.
WHY DOESN'T SHE JUST SUBMIT HER WORK FOR A CONTEST?
LISTEN TO THIS.

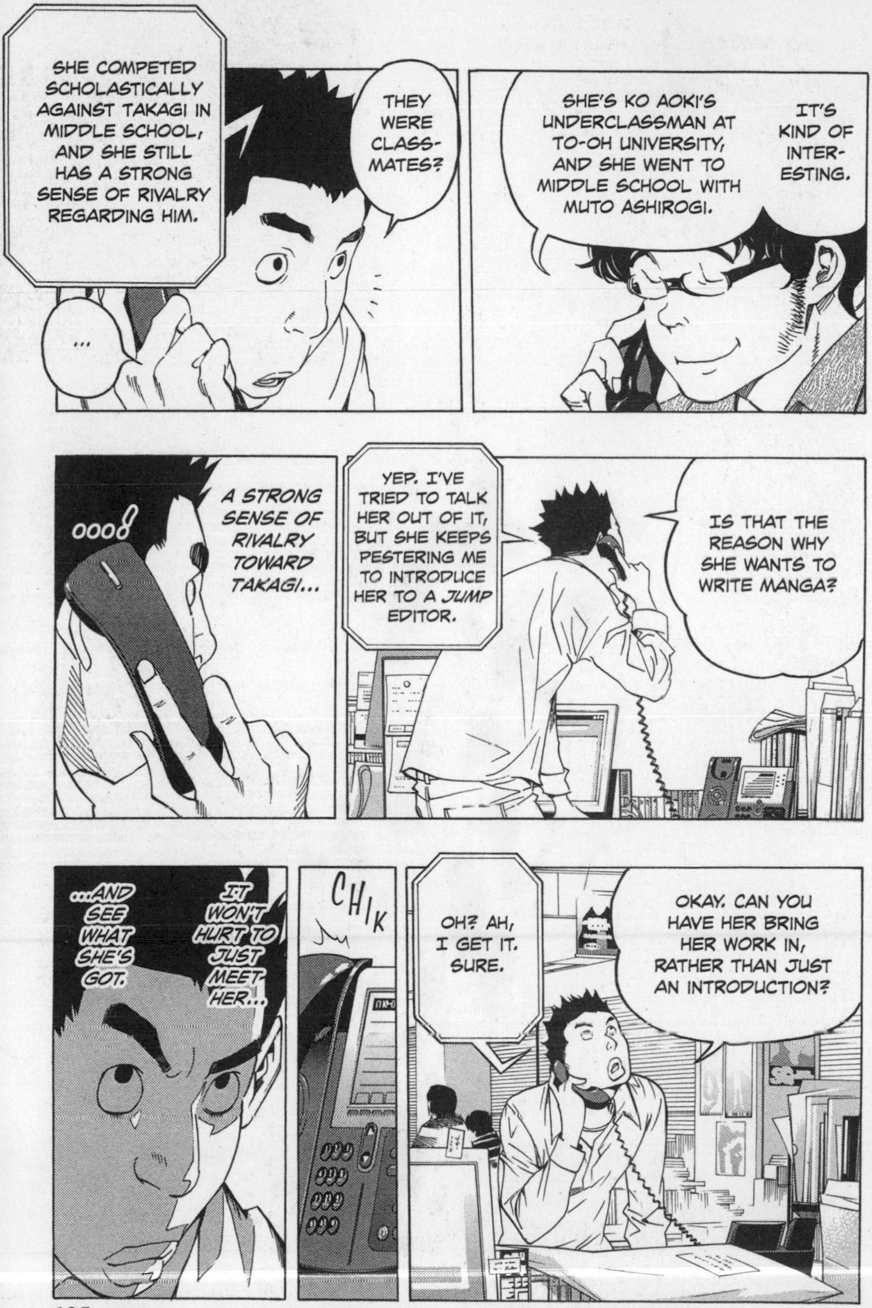
IT'S KIND OF INTERESTING.
SHE'S KO AOKI'S UNDERCLASSMAN AT TO-OH UNIVERSITY, AND SHE WENT TO MIDDLE SCHOOL WITH MUTO ASHIROGI.
THEY WERE CLASSMATES?
SHE COMPETED SCHOLASTICALLY AGAINST TAKAGI IN MIDDLE SCHOOL, AND SHE STILL HAS A STRONG SENSE OF RIVALRY REGARDING HIM.
...
IS THAT THE REASON WHY SHE WANTS TO WRITE MANGA?
YEP. I'VE TRIED TO TALK HER OUT OF IT, BUT SHE KEEPS PESTERING ME TO INTRODUCE HER TO A JUMP EDITOR.
A STRONG SENSE OF RIVALRY TOWARD TAKAGI...
OOO!
OKAY. CAN YOU HAVE HER BRING HER WORK IN, RATHER THAN JUST AN INTRODUCTION?
OH? AH, I GET IT. SURE.
CHIK
IT WON'T HURT TO JUST MEET HER...
...AND SEE WHAT SHE'S GOT.

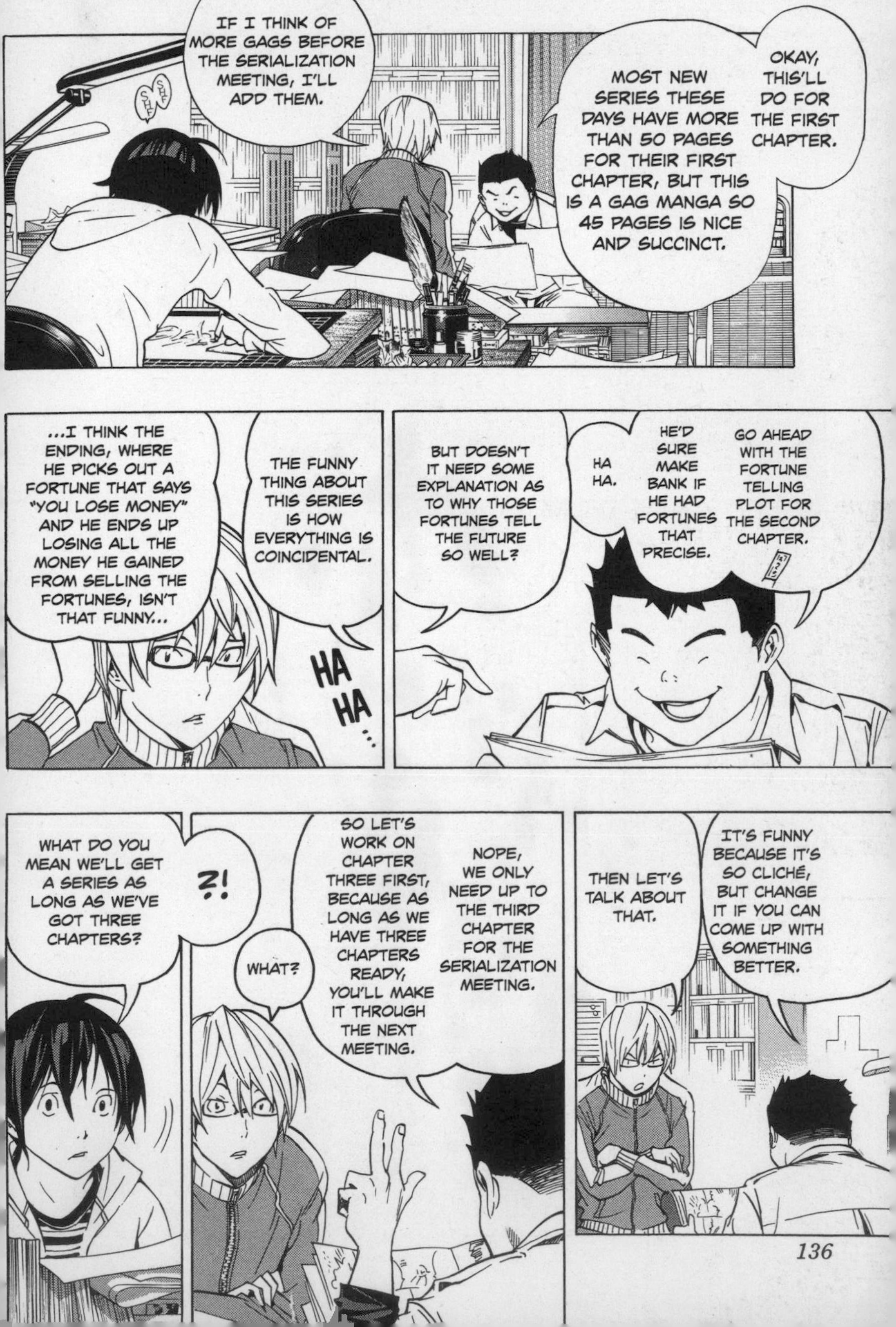
OKAY, THIS'LL DO FOR THE FIRST CHAPTER.
MOST NEW SERIES THESE DAYS HAVE MORE THAN 50 PAGES FOR THEIR FIRST CHAPTER, BUT THIS IS A GAG MANGA SO 45 PAGES IS NICE AND SUCCINCT.
IF I THINK OF MORE GAGS BEFORE THE SERIALIZATION MEETING, I'LL ADD THEM.
SHF SHF
GO AHEAD WITH THE FORTUNE TELLING PLOT FOR THE SECOND CHAPTER.
HE'D SURE MAKE BANK IF HE HAD FORTUNES THAT PRECISE.
HA HA.
BUT DOESN'T IT NEED SOME EXPLANATION AS TO WHY THOSE FORTUNES TELL THE FUTURE SO WELL?
THE FUNNY THING ABOUT THIS SERIES IS HOW EVERYTHING IS COINCIDENTAL.
...I THINK THE ENDING, WHERE HE PICKS OUT A FORTUNE THAT SAYS "YOU LOSE MONEY" AND HE ENDS UP LOSING ALL THE MONEY HE GAINED FROM SELLING THE FORTUNES, ISN'T THAT FUNNY...
HA HA...
IT'S FUNNY BECAUSE IT'S SO CLICHÉ, BUT CHANGE IT IF YOU CAN COME UP WITH SOMETHING BETTER.
THEN LET'S TALK ABOUT THAT.
NOPE, WE ONLY NEED UP TO THE THIRD CHAPTER FOR THE SERIALIZATION MEETING.
SO LET'S WORK ON CHAPTER THREE FIRST, BECAUSE AS LONG AS WE HAVE THREE CHAPTERS READY, YOU'LL MAKE IT THROUGH THE NEXT MEETING.
WHAT?
?!
WHAT DO YOU MEAN WE'LL GET A SERIES AS LONG AS WE'VE GOT THREE CHAPTERS?

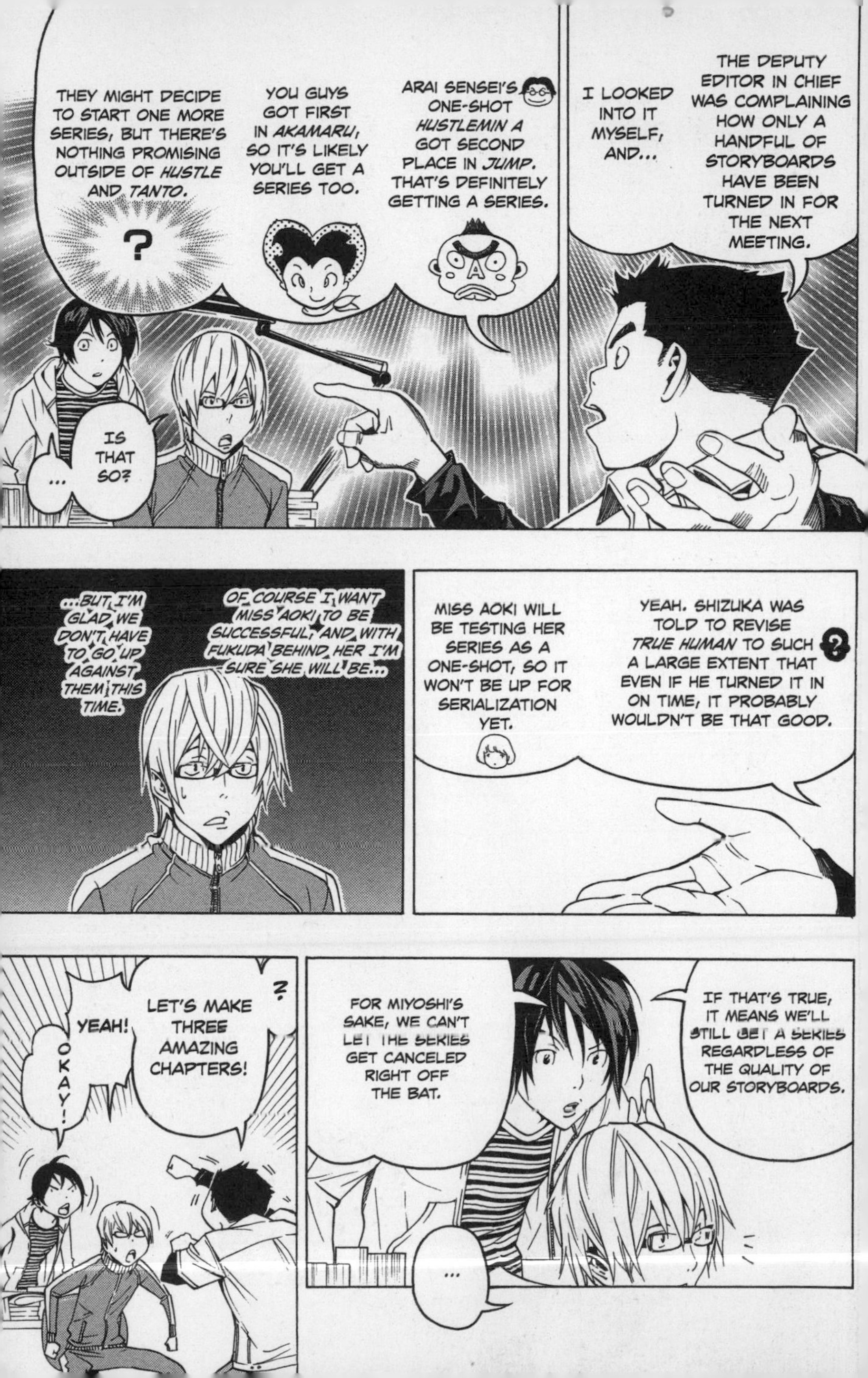
THE DEPUTY EDITOR IN CHIEF WAS COMPLAINING HOW ONLY A HANDFUL OF STORYBOARDS HAVE BEEN TURNED IN FOR THE NEXT MEETING.
I LOOKED INTO IT MYSELF, AND...
ARAI SENSEI'S ONE-SHOT *HUSTLEMIN A* GOT SECOND PLACE IN *JUMP*. THAT'S DEFINITELY GETTING A SERIES.
YOU GUYS GOT FIRST IN *AKAMARU*, SO IT'S LIKELY YOU'LL GET A SERIES TOO.
THEY MIGHT DECIDE TO START ONE MORE SERIES, BUT THERE'S NOTHING PROMISING OUTSIDE OF *HUSTLE* AND *TANTO*.
?
IS THAT SO?
...
YEAH. SHIZUKA WAS TOLD TO REVISE *TRUE HUMAN* TO SUCH A LARGE EXTENT THAT EVEN IF HE TURNED IT IN ON TIME, IT PROBABLY WOULDN'T BE THAT GOOD.
?
MISS AOKI WILL BE TESTING HER SERIES AS A ONE-SHOT, SO IT WON'T BE UP FOR SERIALIZATION YET.
OF COURSE I WANT MISS AOKI TO BE SUCCESSFUL, AND WITH FUKUDA BEHIND HER I'M SURE SHE WILL BE...
...BUT I'M GLAD WE DON'T HAVE TO GO UP AGAINST THEM THIS TIME.
IF THAT'S TRUE, IT MEANS WE'LL STILL GET A SERIES REGARDLESS OF THE QUALITY OF OUR STORYBOARDS.
FOR MIYOSHI'S SAKE, WE CAN'T LET THE SERIES GET CANCELED RIGHT OFF THE BAT.
...
?
LET'S MAKE THREE AMAZING CHAPTERS!
YEAH!
OKAY!

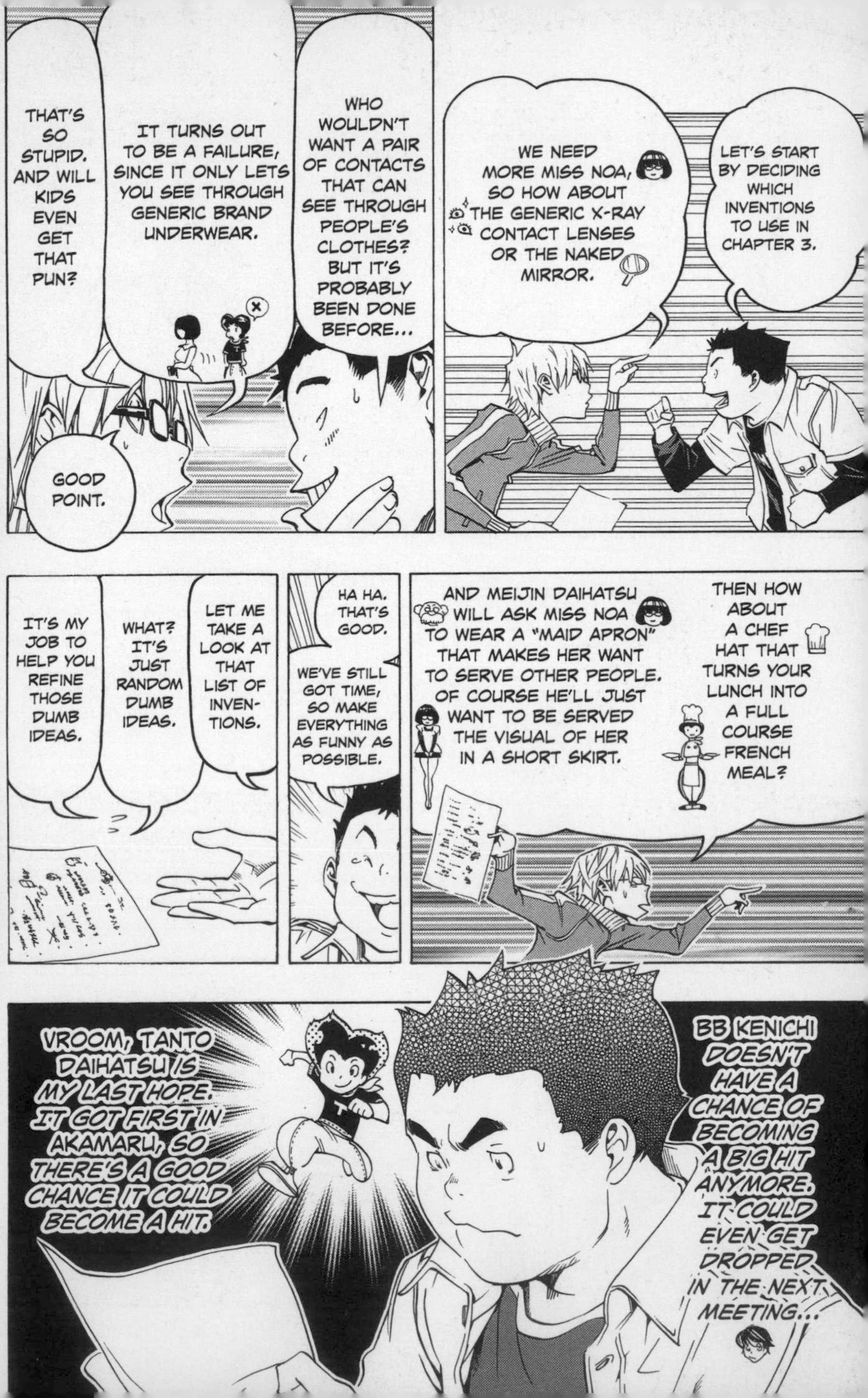
LET'S START BY DECIDING WHICH INVENTIONS TO USE IN CHAPTER 3.
WE NEED MORE MISS NOA, SO HOW ABOUT THE GENERIC X-RAY CONTACT LENSES OR THE NAKED MIRROR.
WHO WOULDN'T WANT A PAIR OF CONTACTS THAT CAN SEE THROUGH PEOPLE'S CLOTHES? BUT IT'S PROBABLY BEEN DONE BEFORE...
IT TURNS OUT TO BE A FAILURE, SINCE IT ONLY LETS YOU SEE THROUGH GENERIC BRAND UNDERWEAR.
THAT'S SO STUPID. AND WILL KIDS EVEN GET THAT PUN?
GOOD POINT.
THEN HOW ABOUT A CHEF HAT THAT TURNS YOUR LUNCH INTO A FULL COURSE FRENCH MEAL?
AND MEIJIN DAIHATSU WILL ASK MISS NOA TO WEAR A "MAID APRON" THAT MAKES HER WANT TO SERVE OTHER PEOPLE. OF COURSE HE'LL JUST WANT TO BE SERVED THE VISUAL OF HER IN A SHORT SKIRT.
HA HA. THAT'S GOOD.
WE'VE STILL GOT TIME, SO MAKE EVERYTHING AS FUNNY AS POSSIBLE.
LET ME TAKE A LOOK AT THAT LIST OF INVEN-TIONS.
WHAT? IT'S JUST RANDOM DUMB IDEAS.
IT'S MY JOB TO HELP YOU REFINE THOSE DUMB IDEAS.
BB KENICHI DOESN'T HAVE A CHANCE OF BECOMING A BIG HIT ANYMORE. IT COULD EVEN GET DROPPED IN THE NEXT MEETING...
VROOM, TANTO DAIHATSU IS MY LAST HOPE. IT GOT FIRST IN AKAMARU, SO THERE'S A GOOD CHANCE IT COULD BECOME A HIT.

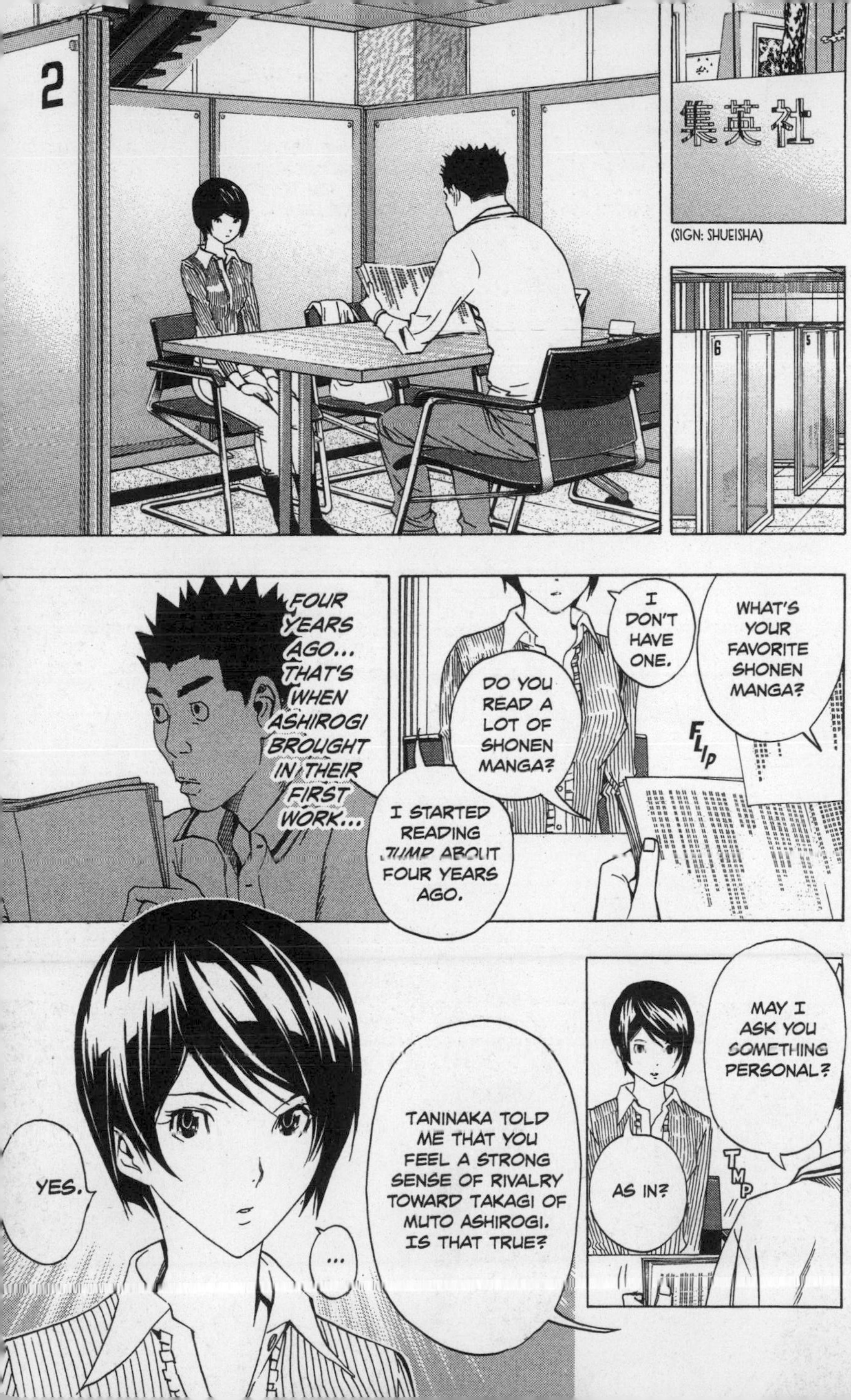

集英社
(SIGN: SHUEISHA)
2
WHAT'S YOUR FAVORITE SHONEN MANGA?
I DON'T HAVE ONE.
FLIP
DO YOU READ A LOT OF SHONEN MANGA?
I STARTED READING JUMP ABOUT FOUR YEARS AGO.
FOUR YEARS AGO... THAT'S WHEN ASHIROGI BROUGHT IN THEIR FIRST WORK...
MAY I ASK YOU SOMETHING PERSONAL?
TMP
AS IN?
TANINAKA TOLD ME THAT YOU FEEL A STRONG SENSE OF RIVALRY TOWARD TAKAGI OF MUTO ASHIROGI. IS THAT TRUE?
...
YES.

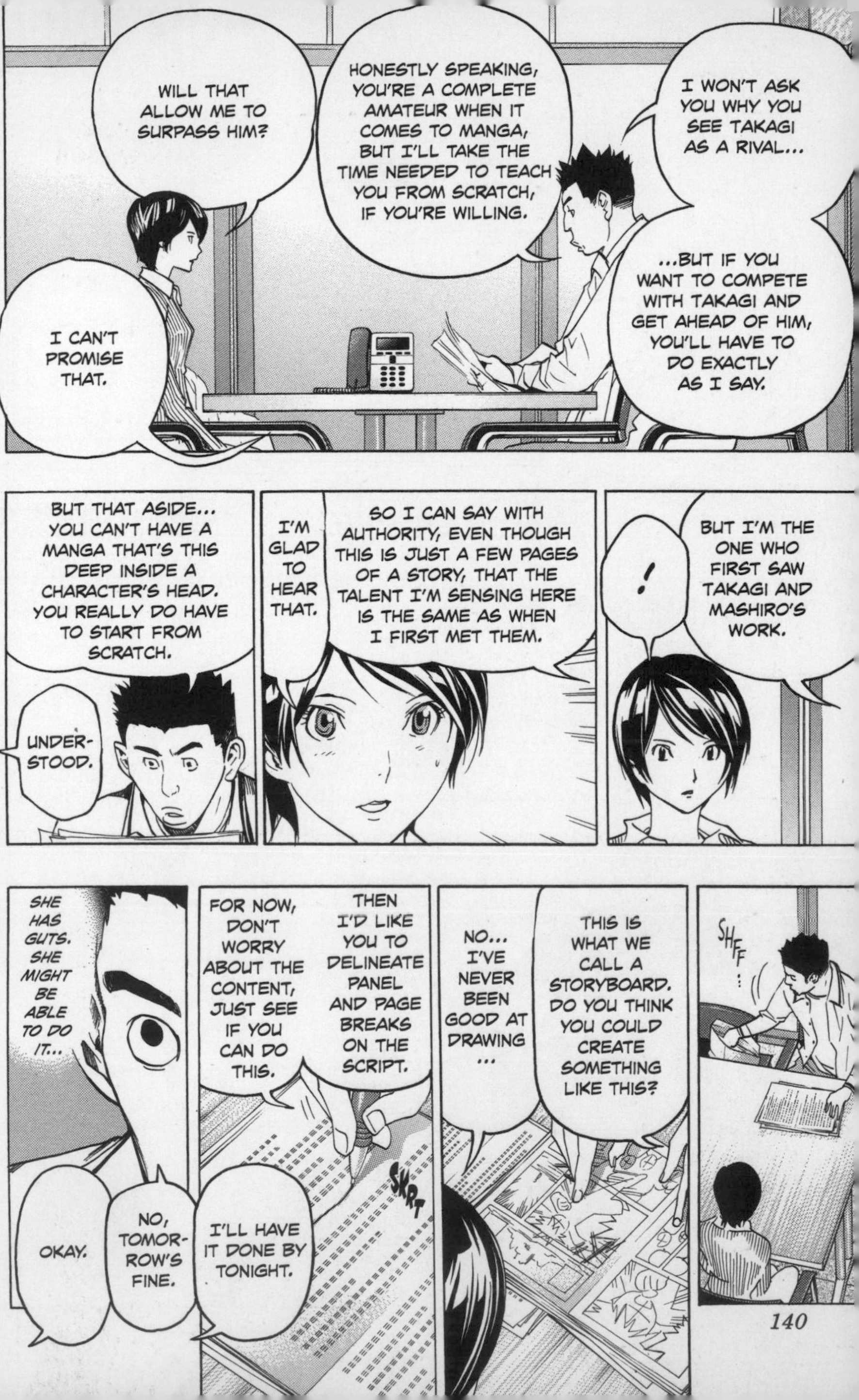
I WON'T ASK YOU WHY YOU SEE TAKAGI AS A RIVAL...
...BUT IF YOU WANT TO COMPETE WITH TAKAGI AND GET AHEAD OF HIM, YOU'LL HAVE TO DO EXACTLY AS I SAY.
HONESTLY SPEAKING, YOU'RE A COMPLETE AMATEUR WHEN IT COMES TO MANGA, BUT I'LL TAKE THE TIME NEEDED TO TEACH YOU FROM SCRATCH, IF YOU'RE WILLING.
WILL THAT ALLOW ME TO SURPASS HIM?
I CAN'T PROMISE THAT.
!
BUT I'M THE ONE WHO FIRST SAW TAKAGI AND MASHIRO'S WORK.
SO I CAN SAY WITH AUTHORITY, EVEN THOUGH THIS IS JUST A FEW PAGES OF A STORY, THAT THE TALENT I'M SENSING HERE IS THE SAME AS WHEN I FIRST MET THEM.
I'M GLAD TO HEAR THAT.
BUT THAT ASIDE... YOU CAN'T HAVE A MANGA THAT'S THIS DEEP INSIDE A CHARACTER'S HEAD. YOU REALLY DO HAVE TO START FROM SCRATCH.
UNDER-STOOD.
SHFF...
THIS IS WHAT WE CALL A STORYBOARD. DO YOU THINK YOU COULD CREATE SOMETHING LIKE THIS?
NO... I'VE NEVER BEEN GOOD AT DRAWING...
THEN I'D LIKE YOU TO DELINEATE PANEL AND PAGE BREAKS ON THE SCRIPT.
FOR NOW, DON'T WORRY ABOUT THE CONTENT, JUST SEE IF YOU CAN DO THIS.
SKRT
I'LL HAVE IT DONE BY TONIGHT.
SHE HAS GUTS. SHE MIGHT BE ABLE TO DO IT...
NO, TOMORROW'S FINE.
OKAY.

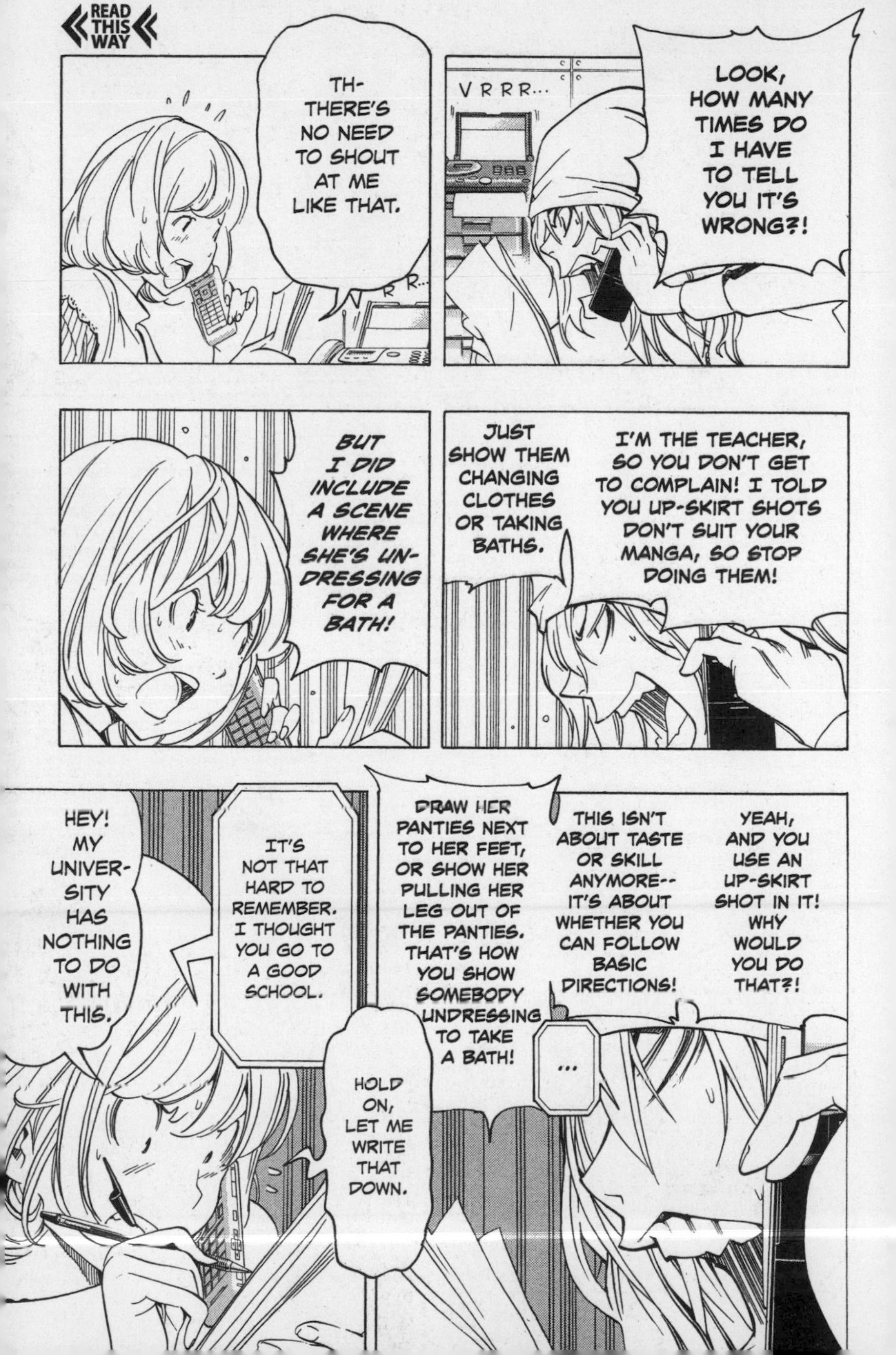
READ THIS WAY
LOOK, HOW MANY TIMES DO I HAVE TO TELL YOU IT'S WRONG?!
VRRR...
TH- THERE'S NO NEED TO SHOUT AT ME LIKE THAT.
RR...
I'M THE TEACHER, SO YOU DON'T GET TO COMPLAIN! I TOLD YOU UP-SKIRT SHOTS DON'T SUIT YOUR MANGA, SO STOP DOING THEM!
JUST SHOW THEM CHANGING CLOTHES OR TAKING BATHS.
BUT I DID INCLUDE A SCENE WHERE SHE'S UNDRESSING FOR A BATH!
YEAH, AND YOU USE AN UP-SKIRT SHOT IN IT! WHY WOULD YOU DO THAT?!
THIS ISN'T ABOUT TASTE OR SKILL ANYMORE--IT'S ABOUT WHETHER YOU CAN FOLLOW BASIC DIRECTIONS!
DRAW HER PANTIES NEXT TO HER FEET, OR SHOW HER PULLING HER LEG OUT OF THE PANTIES. THAT'S HOW YOU SHOW SOMEBODY UNDRESSING TO TAKE A BATH!
...
HOLD ON, LET ME WRITE THAT DOWN.
IT'S NOT THAT HARD TO REMEMBER. I THOUGHT YOU GO TO A GOOD SCHOOL.
HEY! MY UNIVERSITY HAS NOTHING TO DO WITH THIS.

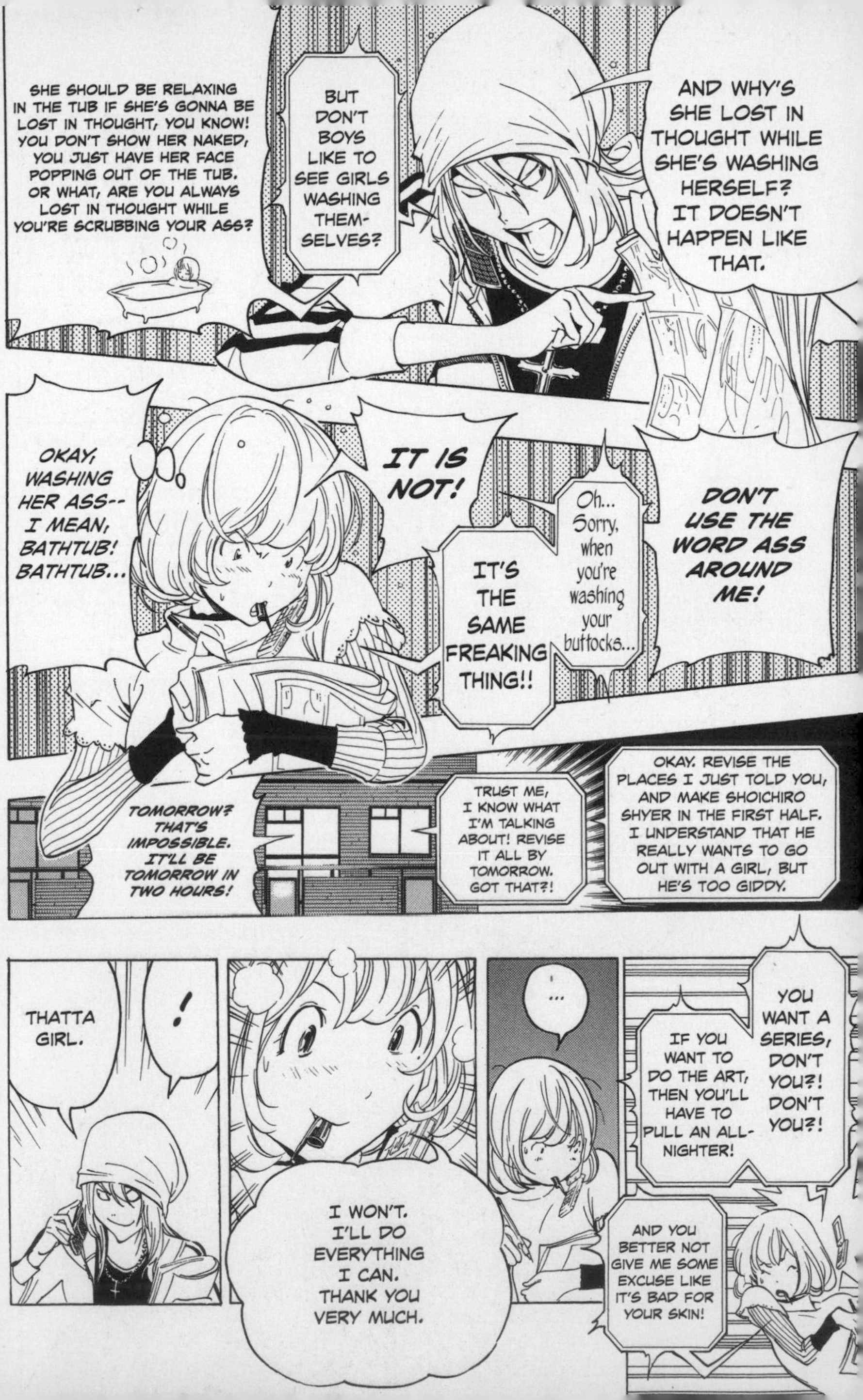
AND WHY'S SHE LOST IN THOUGHT WHILE SHE'S WASHING HERSELF? IT DOESN'T HAPPEN LIKE THAT.
BUT DON'T BOYS LIKE TO SEE GIRLS WASHING THEM-SELVES?
SHE SHOULD BE RELAXING IN THE TUB IF SHE'S GONNA BE LOST IN THOUGHT, YOU KNOW! YOU DON'T SHOW HER NAKED, YOU JUST HAVE HER FACE POPPING OUT OF THE TUB. OR WHAT, ARE YOU ALWAYS LOST IN THOUGHT WHILE YOU'RE SCRUBBING YOUR ASS?
DON'T USE THE WORD ASS AROUND ME!
Oh... Sorry, when you're washing your buttocks...
IT IS NOT!
IT'S THE SAME FREAKING THING!!
OKAY, WASHING HER ASS-- I MEAN, BATHTUB! BATHTUB...
OKAY. REVISE THE PLACES I JUST TOLD YOU, AND MAKE SHOICHIRO SHYER IN THE FIRST HALF. I UNDERSTAND THAT HE REALLY WANTS TO GO OUT WITH A GIRL, BUT HE'S TOO GIDDY.
TRUST ME, I KNOW WHAT I'M TALKING ABOUT! REVISE IT ALL BY TOMORROW. GOT THAT?!
TOMORROW? THAT'S IMPOSSIBLE. IT'LL BE TOMORROW IN TWO HOURS!
YOU WANT A SERIES, DON'T YOU?! DON'T YOU?!
IF YOU WANT TO DO THE ART, THEN YOU'LL HAVE TO PULL AN ALL-NIGHTER!
AND YOU BETTER NOT GIVE ME SOME EXCUSE LIKE IT'S BAD FOR YOUR SKIN!
...
I WON'T. I'LL DO EVERYTHING I CAN. THANK YOU VERY MUCH.
!
THATTA GIRL.

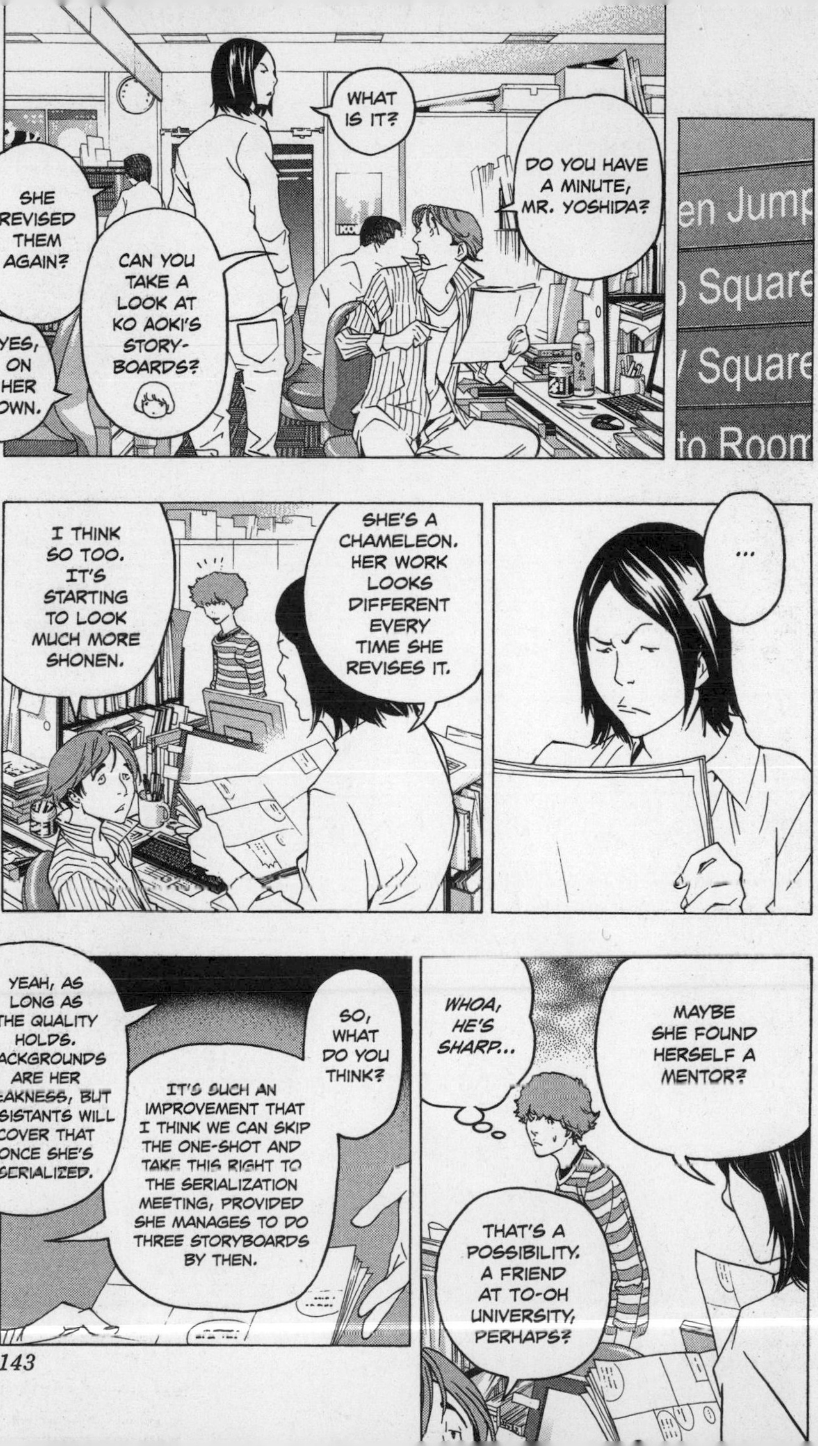
en Jump
Square
Square
to Room
DO YOU HAVE A MINUTE, MR. YOSHIDA?
WHAT IS IT?
CAN YOU TAKE A LOOK AT KO AOKI'S STORYBOARDS?
SHE REVISED THEM AGAIN?
YES, ON HER OWN.
...
SHE'S A CHAMELEON. HER WORK LOOKS DIFFERENT EVERY TIME SHE REVISES IT.
I THINK SO TOO. IT'S STARTING TO LOOK MUCH MORE SHONEN.
MAYBE SHE FOUND HERSELF A MENTOR?
WHOA, HE'S SHARP...
THAT'S A POSSIBILITY. A FRIEND AT TO-OH UNIVERSITY, PERHAPS?
SO, WHAT DO YOU THINK?
IT'S SUCH AN IMPROVEMENT THAT I THINK WE CAN SKIP THE ONE-SHOT AND TAKE THIS RIGHT TO THE SERIALIZATION MEETING, PROVIDED SHE MANAGES TO DO THREE STORYBOARDS BY THEN.
YEAH, AS LONG AS THE QUALITY HOLDS. BACKGROUNDS ARE HER WEAKNESS, BUT ASSISTANTS WILL COVER THAT ONCE SHE'S SERIALIZED.

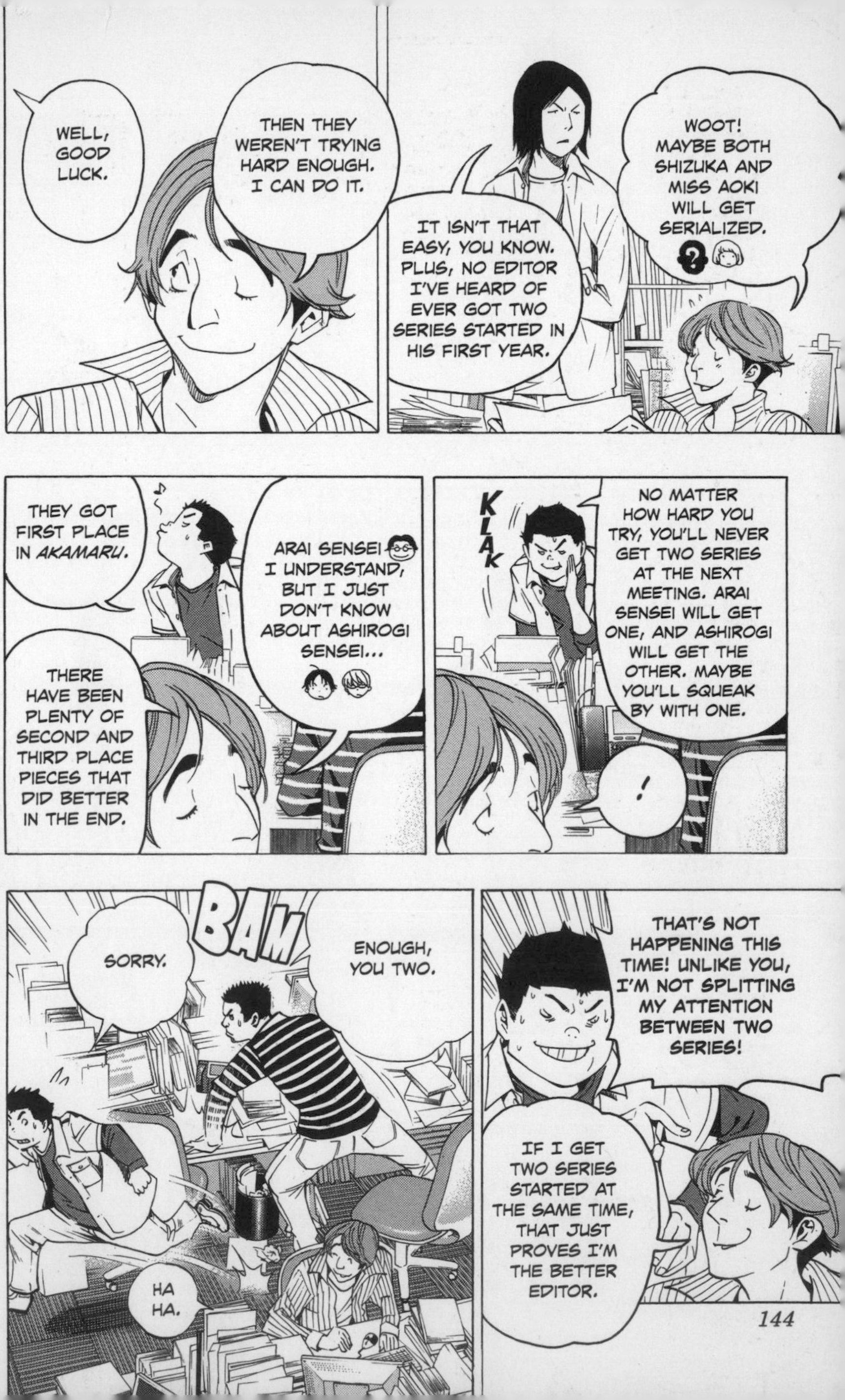
WOOT! MAYBE BOTH SHIZUKA AND MISS AOKI WILL GET SERIALIZED.
IT ISN'T THAT EASY, YOU KNOW. PLUS, NO EDITOR I'VE HEARD OF EVER GOT TWO SERIES STARTED IN HIS FIRST YEAR.
THEN THEY WEREN'T TRYING HARD ENOUGH. I CAN DO IT.
WELL, GOOD LUCK.
KLAK
NO MATTER HOW HARD YOU TRY, YOU'LL NEVER GET TWO SERIES AT THE NEXT MEETING. ARAI SENSEI WILL GET ONE, AND ASHIROGI WILL GET THE OTHER. MAYBE YOU'LL SQUEAK BY WITH ONE.
!
ARAI SENSEI I UNDERSTAND, BUT I JUST DON'T KNOW ABOUT ASHIROGI SENSEI...
THEY GOT FIRST PLACE IN *AKAMARU*.
THERE HAVE BEEN PLENTY OF SECOND AND THIRD PLACE PIECES THAT DID BETTER IN THE END.
THAT'S NOT HAPPENING THIS TIME! UNLIKE YOU, I'M NOT SPLITTING MY ATTENTION BETWEEN TWO SERIES!
IF I GET TWO SERIES STARTED AT THE SAME TIME, THAT JUST PROVES I'M THE BETTER EDITOR.
BAM
ENOUGH, YOU TWO.
SORRY.
HA HA.

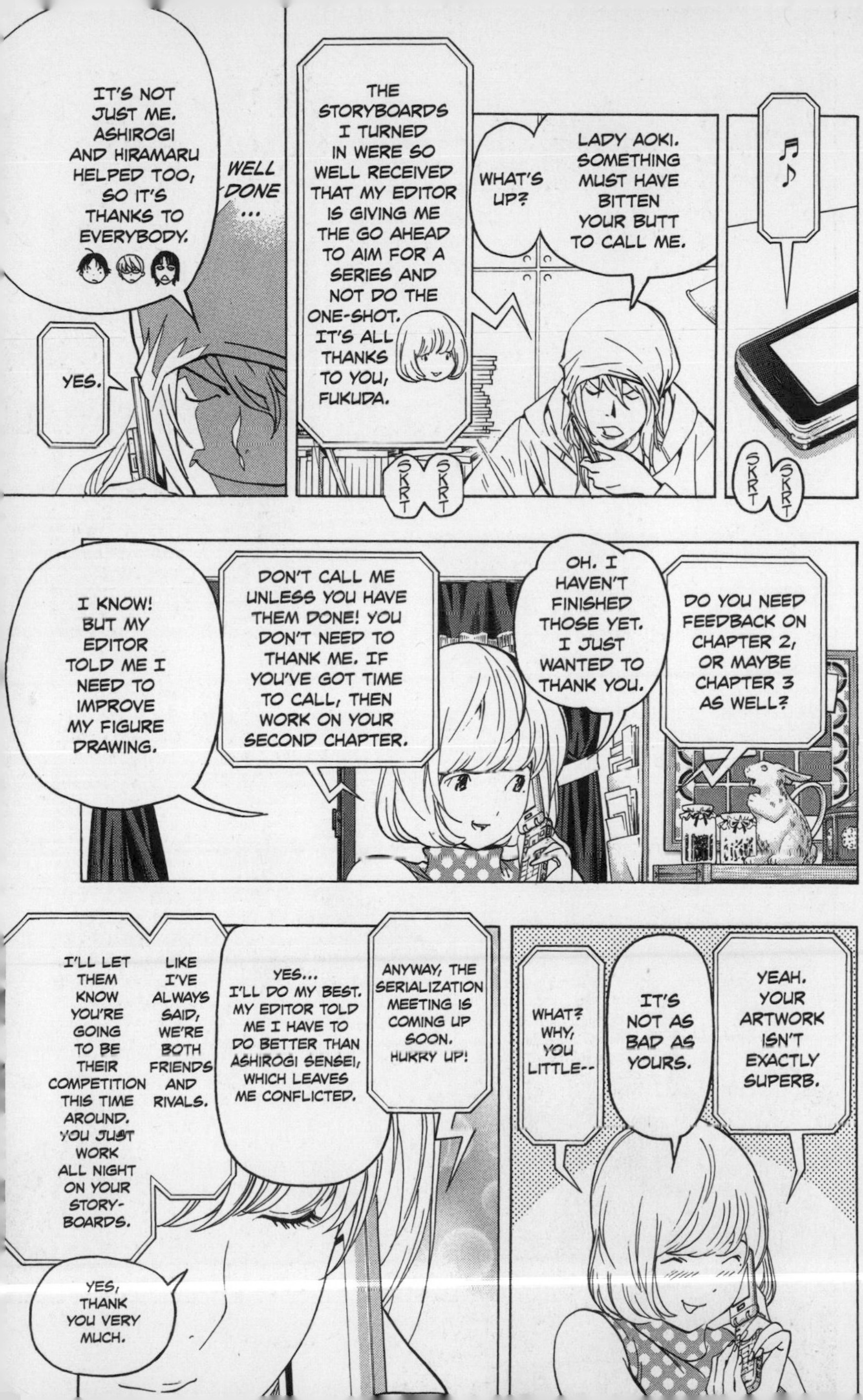
♬ ♪
SKRT SKRT
LADY AOKI. SOMETHING MUST HAVE BITTEN YOUR BUTT TO CALL ME.
WHAT'S UP?
THE STORYBOARDS I TURNED IN WERE SO WELL RECEIVED THAT MY EDITOR IS GIVING ME THE GO AHEAD TO AIM FOR A SERIES AND NOT DO THE ONE-SHOT. IT'S ALL THANKS TO YOU, FUKUDA.
SKRT SKRT
WELL DONE ...
IT'S NOT JUST ME. ASHIROGI AND HIRAMARU HELPED TOO, SO IT'S THANKS TO EVERYBODY.
YES.
DO YOU NEED FEEDBACK ON CHAPTER 2, OR MAYBE CHAPTER 3 AS WELL?
OH. I HAVEN'T FINISHED THOSE YET. I JUST WANTED TO THANK YOU.
DON'T CALL ME UNLESS YOU HAVE THEM DONE! YOU DON'T NEED TO THANK ME. IF YOU'VE GOT TIME TO CALL, THEN WORK ON YOUR SECOND CHAPTER.
I KNOW! BUT MY EDITOR TOLD ME I NEED TO IMPROVE MY FIGURE DRAWING.
YEAH. YOUR ARTWORK ISN'T EXACTLY SUPERB.
IT'S NOT AS BAD AS YOURS.
WHAT? WHY, YOU LITTLE--
ANYWAY, THE SERIALIZATION MEETING IS COMING UP SOON. HURRY UP!
YES... I'LL DO MY BEST. MY EDITOR TOLD ME I HAVE TO DO BETTER THAN ASHIROGI SENSEI, WHICH LEAVES ME CONFLICTED.
LIKE I'VE ALWAYS SAID, WE'RE BOTH FRIENDS AND RIVALS.
I'LL LET THEM KNOW YOU'RE GOING TO BE THEIR COMPETITION THIS TIME AROUND. YOU JUST WORK ALL NIGHT ON YOUR STORYBOARDS.
YES, THANK YOU VERY MUCH.

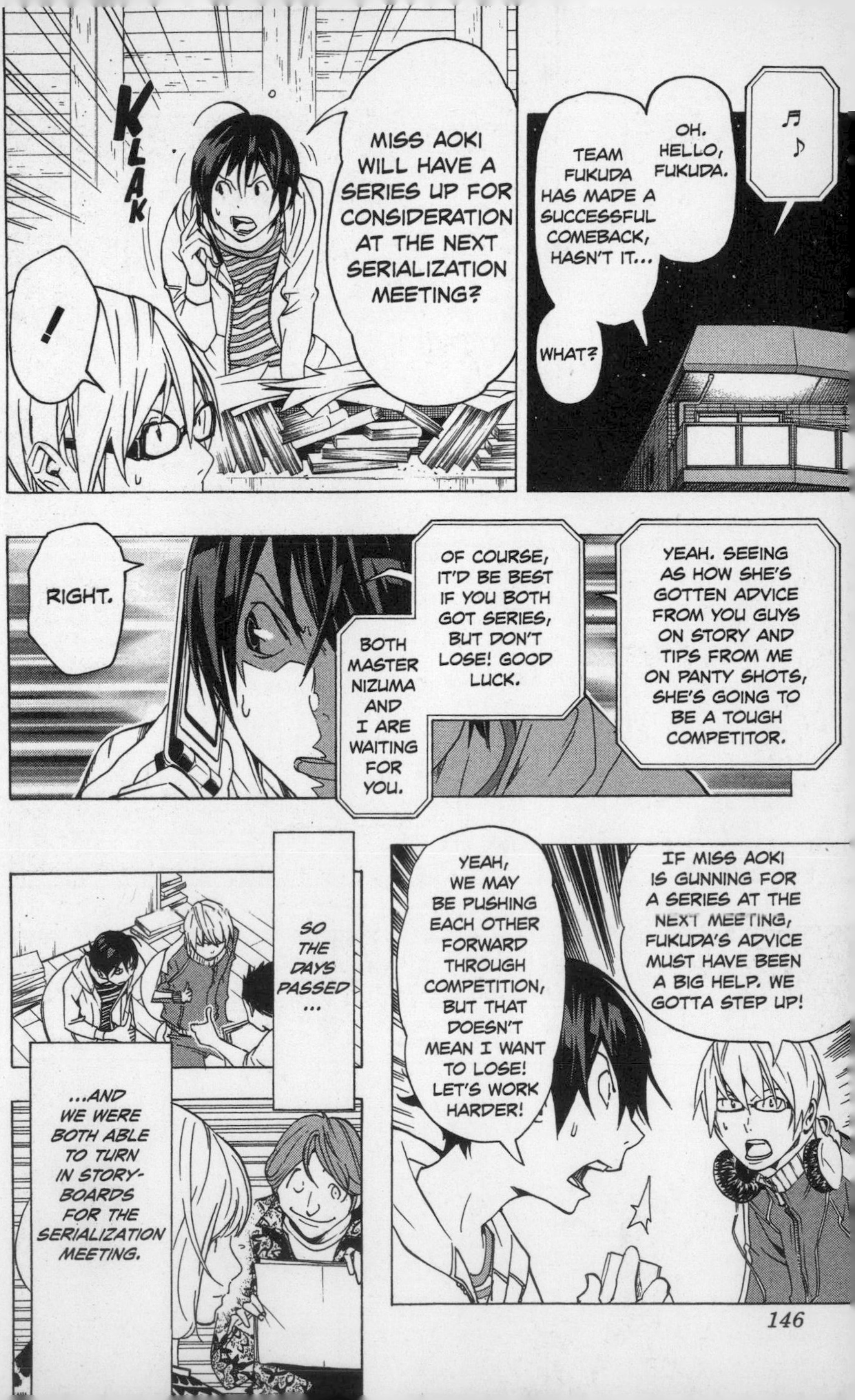
♬ ♪
OH. HELLO, FUKUDA.
TEAM FUKUDA HAS MADE A SUCCESSFUL COMEBACK, HASN'T IT...
WHAT?
KLAK
MISS AOKI WILL HAVE A SERIES UP FOR CONSIDERATION AT THE NEXT SERIALIZATION MEETING?
!
YEAH. SEEING AS HOW SHE'S GOTTEN ADVICE FROM YOU GUYS ON STORY AND TIPS FROM ME ON PANTY SHOTS, SHE'S GOING TO BE A TOUGH COMPETITOR.
OF COURSE, IT'D BE BEST IF YOU BOTH GOT SERIES, BUT DON'T LOSE! GOOD LUCK.
BOTH MASTER NIZUMA AND I ARE WAITING FOR YOU.
RIGHT.
IF MISS AOKI IS GUNNING FOR A SERIES AT THE NEXT MEETING, FUKUDA'S ADVICE MUST HAVE BEEN A BIG HELP. WE GOTTA STEP UP!
YEAH, WE MAY BE PUSHING EACH OTHER FORWARD THROUGH COMPETITION, BUT THAT DOESN'T MEAN I WANT TO LOSE! LET'S WORK HARDER!
SO THE DAYS PASSED...
...AND WE WERE BOTH ABLE TO TURN IN STORYBOARDS FOR THE SERIALIZATION MEETING.

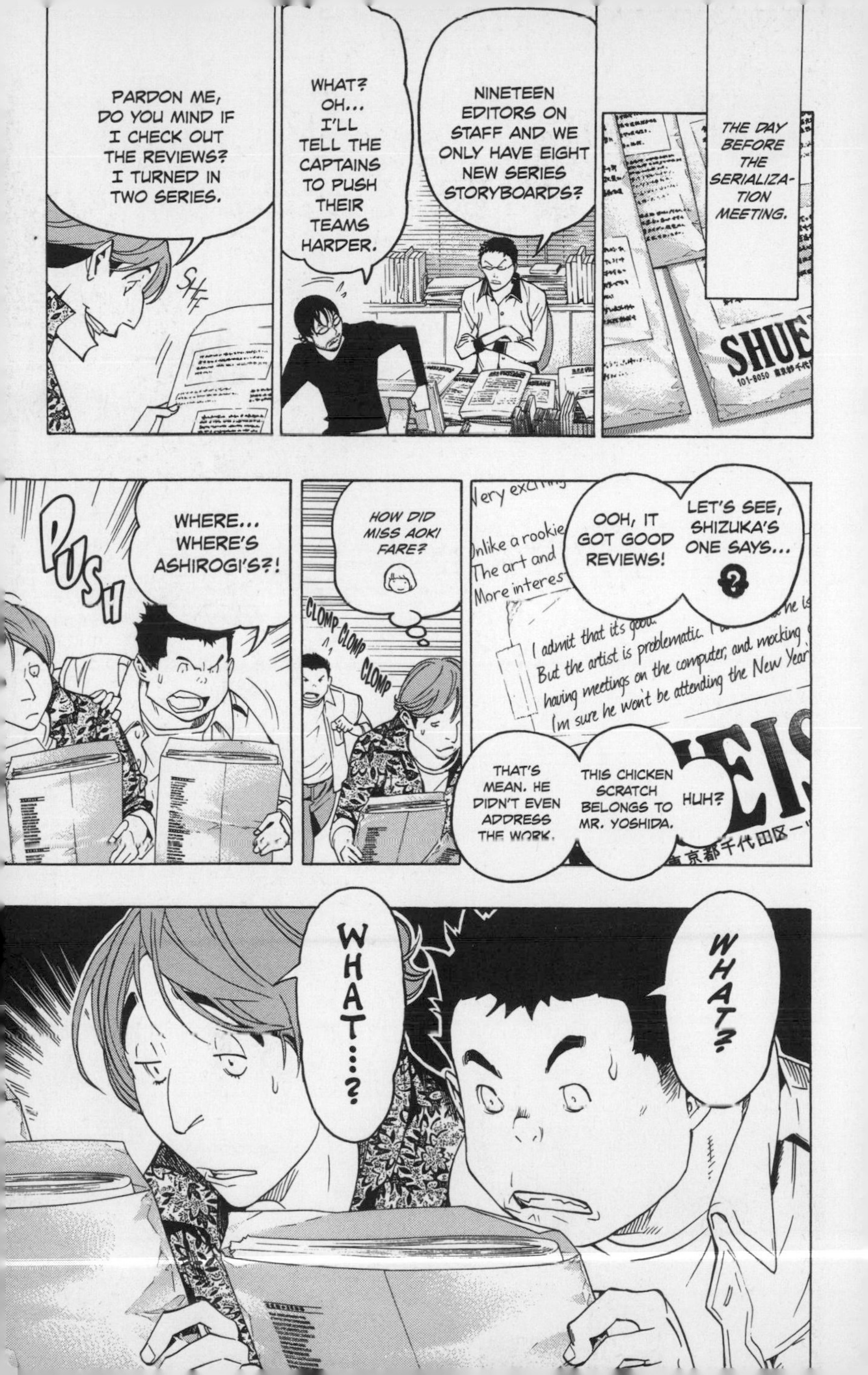
THE DAY BEFORE THE SERIALIZATION MEETING.
SHUE
101-8050
NINETEEN EDITORS ON STAFF AND WE ONLY HAVE EIGHT NEW SERIES STORYBOARDS?
WHAT? OH... I'LL TELL THE CAPTAINS TO PUSH THEIR TEAMS HARDER.
PARDON ME, DO YOU MIND IF I CHECK OUT THE REVIEWS? I TURNED IN TWO SERIES.
SHFF
LET'S SEE, SHIZUKA'S ONE SAYS...
?
OOH, IT GOT GOOD REVIEWS!
HUH?
THIS CHICKEN SCRATCH BELONGS TO MR. YOSHIDA.
THAT'S MEAN. HE DIDN'T EVEN ADDRESS THE WORK.
HOW DID MISS AOKI FARE?
CLOMP CLOMP CLOMP CLOMP
WHERE... WHERE'S ASHIROGI'S?!
PUSH
WHAT?
WHAT...?

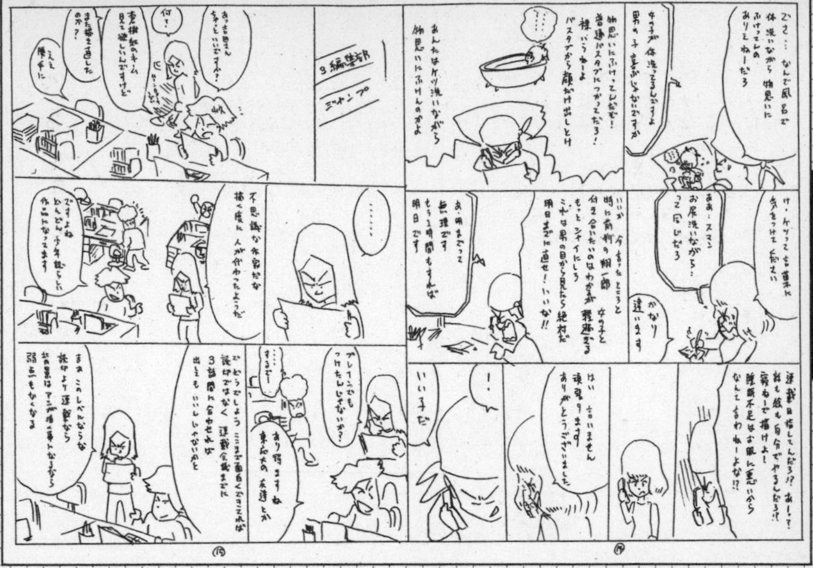
でさ… なんで風呂で体洗いながら物思いにふけってんのありえねーだろ
女の子が体洗ってるんですよ 男の子喜ぶじゃないですか
あんたはケツ洗いながら物思いにふけんのかよ
まあ・スマン お尻洗いながら…って同じだろ
かなり違います
あ・明日までって無理です もう1時間もすれば明日です
はい 言いません 頑張ります ありがとうございました
!
いい子だ
3編集部
ジャンプ
何?
また担当通したのか?
ええ 勝手に
……
不思議な作家だな 描く度に人が代わったようだ
ですよね どんどん少年誌らしい作品になってます
あり得ますね 東応大の友達とか

OHBA'S STORYBOARD

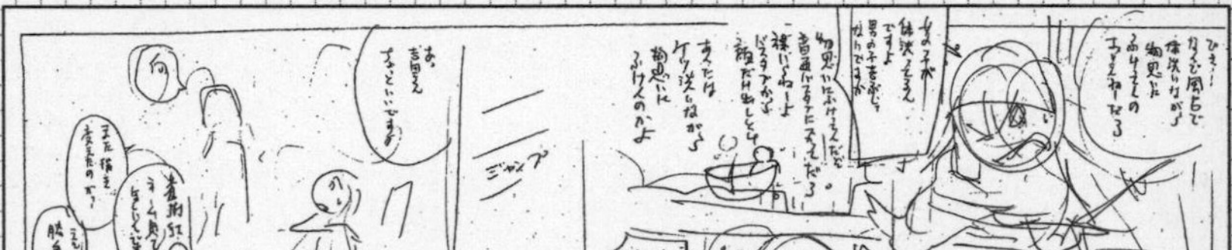

OBATA'S STORYBOARD

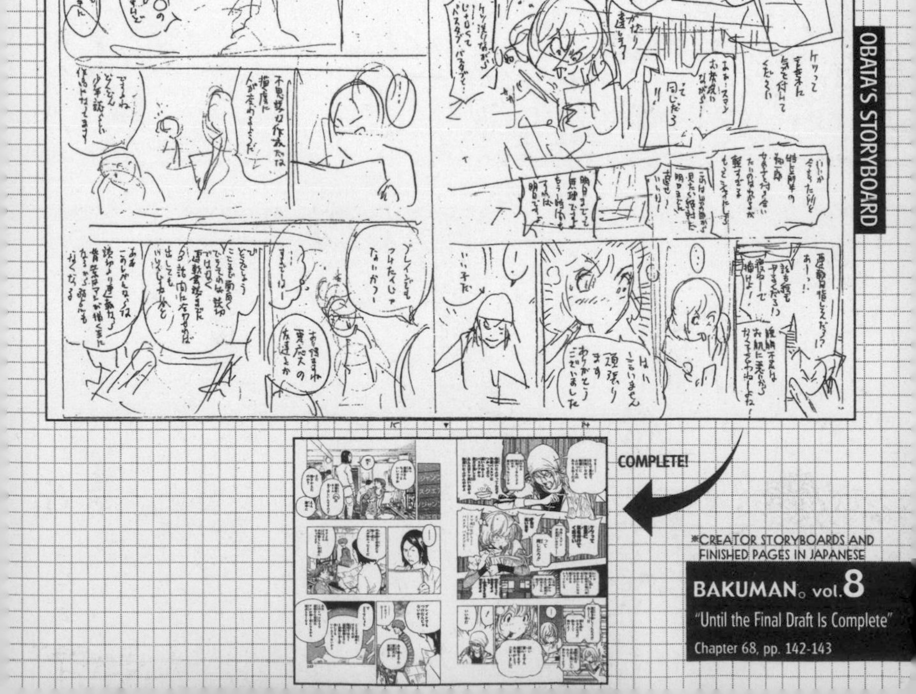

COMPLETE!

*CREATOR STORYBOARDS AND FINISHED PAGES IN JAPANESE

BAKUMAN。 vol.8

"Until the Final Draft Is Complete"

Chapter 68, pp. 142-143

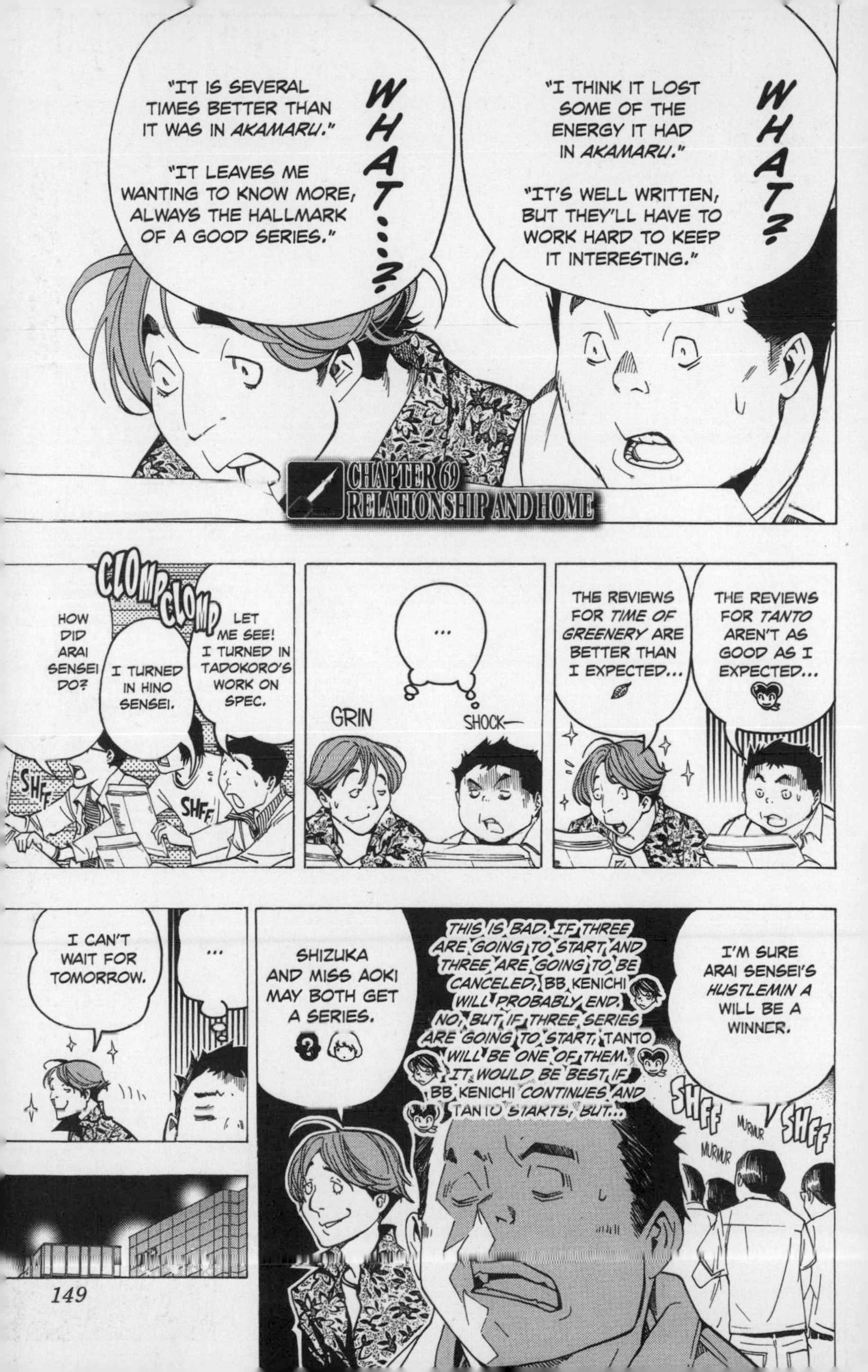
"I THINK IT LOST SOME OF THE ENERGY IT HAD IN AKAMARU."
"IT'S WELL WRITTEN, BUT THEY'LL HAVE TO WORK HARD TO KEEP IT INTERESTING."
WHAT?
"IT IS SEVERAL TIMES BETTER THAN IT WAS IN AKAMARU."
"IT LEAVES ME WANTING TO KNOW MORE, ALWAYS THE HALLMARK OF A GOOD SERIES."
WHAT...?
CHAPTER 69
RELATIONSHIP AND HOME
THE REVIEWS FOR TANTO AREN'T AS GOOD AS I EXPECTED...
THE REVIEWS FOR TIME OF GREENERY ARE BETTER THAN I EXPECTED...
...
GRIN
SHOCK—
CLOMP CLOMP
LET ME SEE! I TURNED IN TADOKORO'S WORK ON SPEC.
HOW DID ARAI SENSEI DO?
I TURNED IN HINO SENSEI.
SHFF
SHFF
I'M SURE ARAI SENSEI'S HUSTLEMIN A WILL BE A WINNER.
THIS IS BAD. IF THREE ARE GOING TO START AND THREE ARE GOING TO BE CANCELED, BB KENICHI WILL PROBABLY END. NO, BUT IF THREE SERIES ARE GOING TO START, TANTO WILL BE ONE OF THEM. IT WOULD BE BEST IF BB KENICHI CONTINUES AND TANTO STARTS, BUT...
SHIZUKA AND MISS AOKI MAY BOTH GET A SERIES.
SHFF
MURMUR
SHFF
MURMUR
...
I CAN'T WAIT FOR TOMORROW.

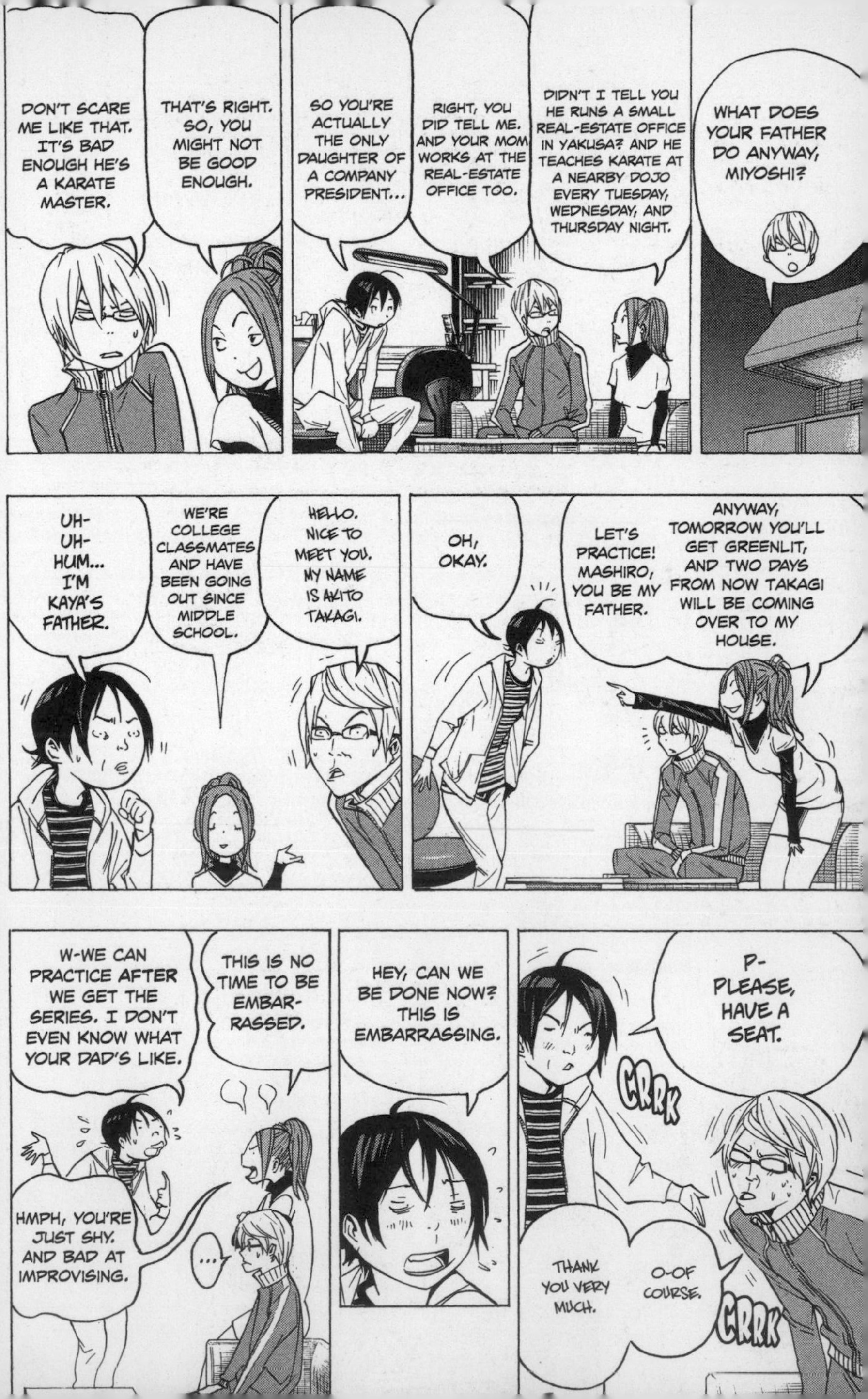

WHAT DOES YOUR FATHER DO ANYWAY, MIYOSHI?
DIDN'T I TELL YOU HE RUNS A SMALL REAL-ESTATE OFFICE IN YAKUSA? AND HE TEACHES KARATE AT A NEARBY DOJO EVERY TUESDAY, WEDNESDAY, AND THURSDAY NIGHT.
RIGHT, YOU DID TELL ME. AND YOUR MOM WORKS AT THE REAL-ESTATE OFFICE TOO.
SO YOU'RE ACTUALLY THE ONLY DAUGHTER OF A COMPANY PRESIDENT...
THAT'S RIGHT. SO, YOU MIGHT NOT BE GOOD ENOUGH.
DON'T SCARE ME LIKE THAT. IT'S BAD ENOUGH HE'S A KARATE MASTER.
ANYWAY, TOMORROW YOU'LL GET GREENLIT, AND TWO DAYS FROM NOW TAKAGI WILL BE COMING OVER TO MY HOUSE.
LET'S PRACTICE! MASHIRO, YOU BE MY FATHER.
OH, OKAY.
HELLO. NICE TO MEET YOU. MY NAME IS AKITO TAKAGI.
WE'RE COLLEGE CLASSMATES AND HAVE BEEN GOING OUT SINCE MIDDLE SCHOOL.
UH-UH-HUM... I'M KAYA'S FATHER.
P-PLEASE, HAVE A SEAT.
CRRK
O-OF COURSE.
THANK YOU VERY MUCH.
CRRK
HEY, CAN WE BE DONE NOW? THIS IS EMBARRASSING.
THIS IS NO TIME TO BE EMBARRASSED.
W-WE CAN PRACTICE AFTER WE GET THE SERIES. I DON'T EVEN KNOW WHAT YOUR DAD'S LIKE.
HMPH, YOU'RE JUST SHY. AND BAD AT IMPROVISING.
...

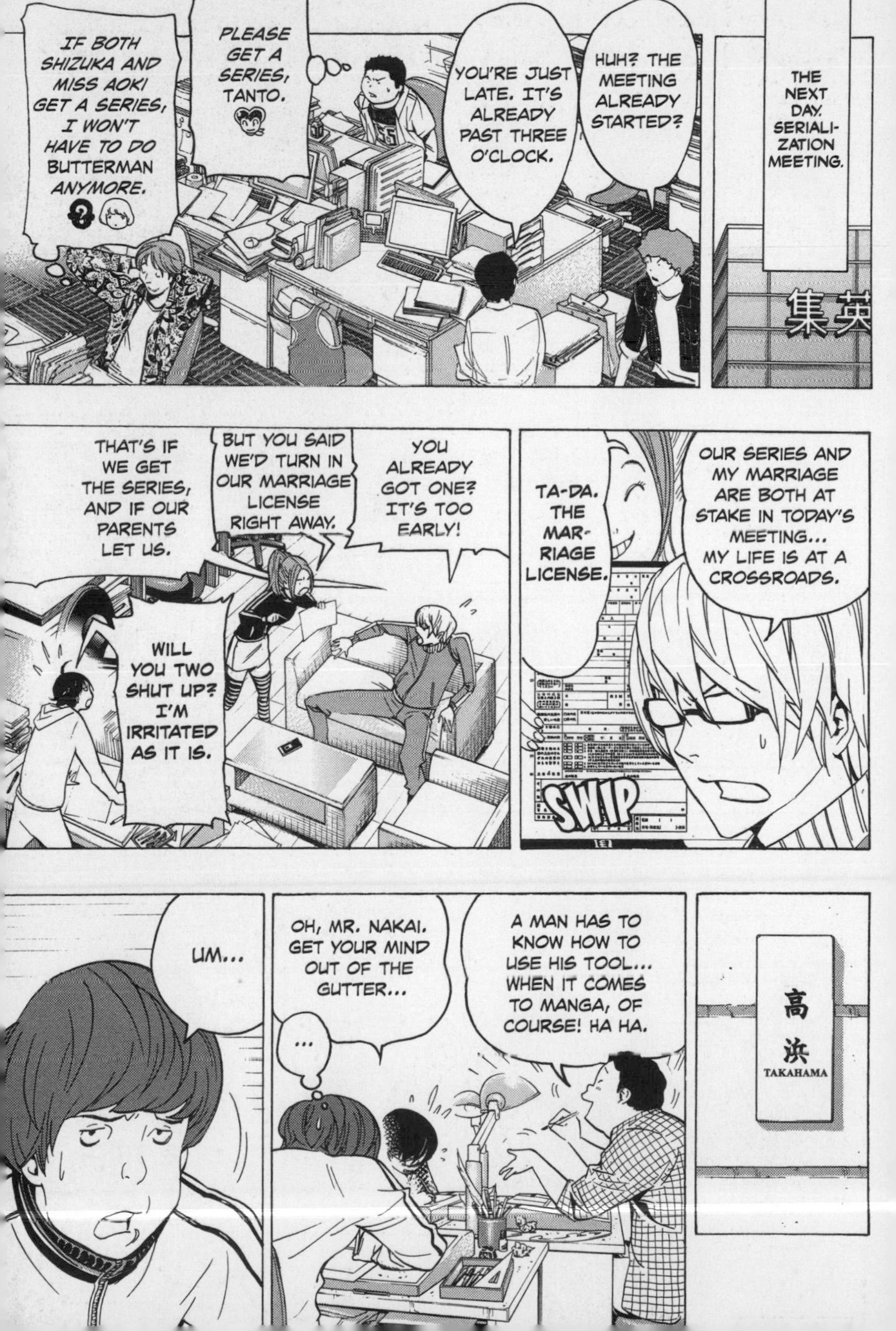

THE NEXT DAY. SERIALIZATION MEETING.
集英
HUH? THE MEETING ALREADY STARTED?
YOU'RE JUST LATE. IT'S ALREADY PAST THREE O'CLOCK.
PLEASE GET A SERIES, TANTO.
IF BOTH SHIZUKA AND MISS AOKI GET A SERIES, I WON'T HAVE TO DO BUTTERMAN ANYMORE.
OUR SERIES AND MY MARRIAGE ARE BOTH AT STAKE IN TODAY'S MEETING... MY LIFE IS AT A CROSSROADS.
TA-DA. THE MARRIAGE LICENSE.
SWIP
YOU ALREADY GOT ONE? IT'S TOO EARLY!
BUT YOU SAID WE'D TURN IN OUR MARRIAGE LICENSE RIGHT AWAY.
THAT'S IF WE GET THE SERIES, AND IF OUR PARENTS LET US.
WILL YOU TWO SHUT UP? I'M IRRITATED AS IT IS.
高浜
TAKAHAMA
A MAN HAS TO KNOW HOW TO USE HIS TOOL... WHEN IT COMES TO MANGA, OF COURSE! HA HA.
OH, MR. NAKAI. GET YOUR MIND OUT OF THE GUTTER...
...
UM...

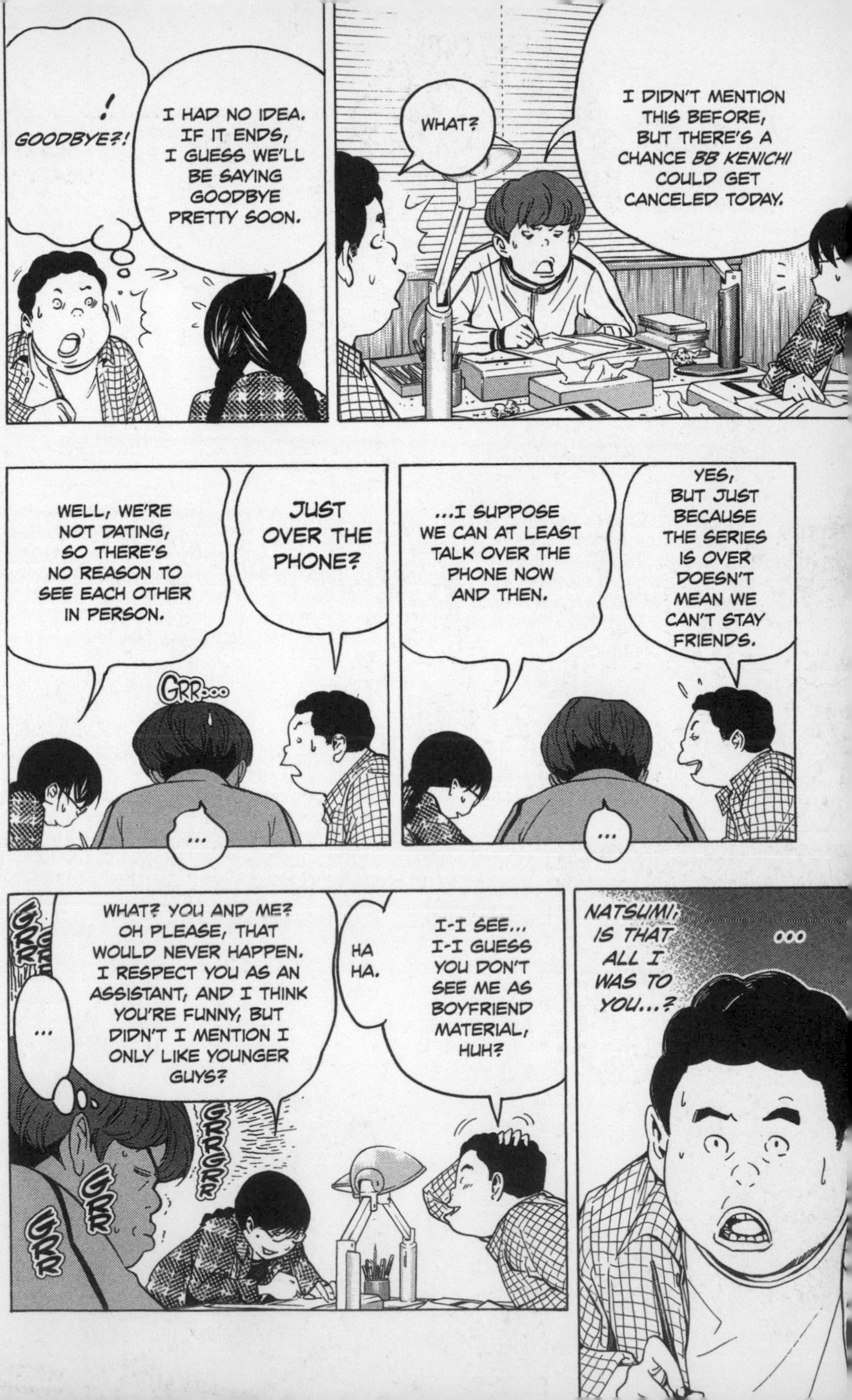
I DIDN'T MENTION THIS BEFORE, BUT THERE'S A CHANCE *BB KENICHI* COULD GET CANCELED TODAY.
WHAT?
I HAD NO IDEA. IF IT ENDS, I GUESS WE'LL BE SAYING GOODBYE PRETTY SOON.
! GOODBYE?!
YES, BUT JUST BECAUSE THE SERIES IS OVER DOESN'T MEAN WE CAN'T STAY FRIENDS.
...I SUPPOSE WE CAN AT LEAST TALK OVER THE PHONE NOW AND THEN.
...
JUST OVER THE PHONE?
WELL, WE'RE NOT DATING, SO THERE'S NO REASON TO SEE EACH OTHER IN PERSON.
GRR...
...
NATSUMI, IS THAT ALL I WAS TO YOU...?
I-I SEE... I-I GUESS YOU DON'T SEE ME AS BOYFRIEND MATERIAL, HUH?
HA HA.
WHAT? YOU AND ME? OH PLEASE, THAT WOULD NEVER HAPPEN. I RESPECT YOU AS AN ASSISTANT, AND I THINK YOU'RE FUNNY, BUT DIDN'T I MENTION I ONLY LIKE YOUNGER GUYS?
...
GRRRGRR
GRR
GRR

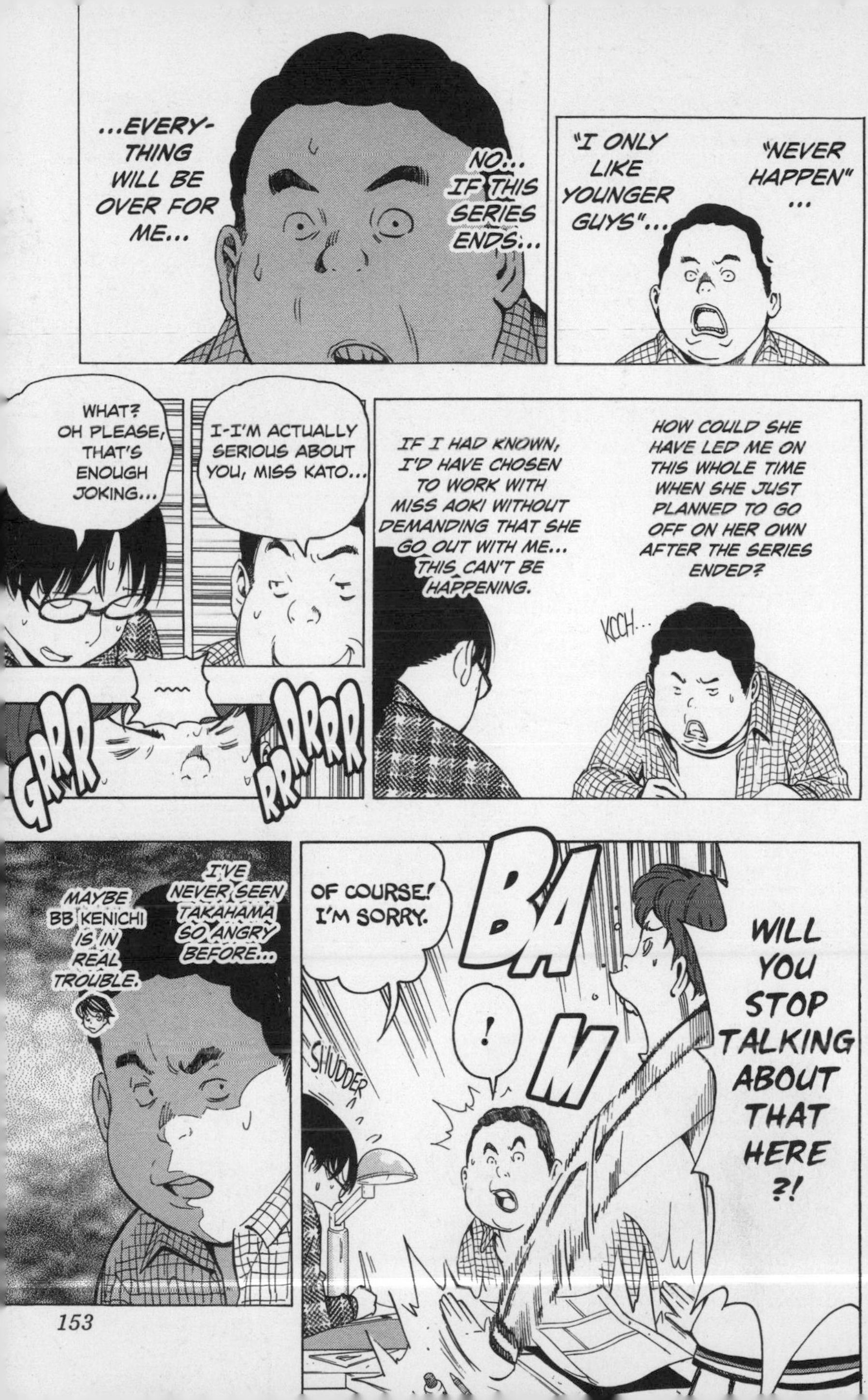
"NEVER HAPPEN" ...
"I ONLY LIKE YOUNGER GUYS"...
NO... IF THIS SERIES ENDS...
...EVERYTHING WILL BE OVER FOR ME...
HOW COULD SHE HAVE LED ME ON THIS WHOLE TIME WHEN SHE JUST PLANNED TO GO OFF ON HER OWN AFTER THE SERIES ENDED?
IF I HAD KNOWN, I'D HAVE CHOSEN TO WORK WITH MISS AOKI WITHOUT DEMANDING THAT SHE GO OUT WITH ME... THIS CAN'T BE HAPPENING.
KICCH...
I-I'M ACTUALLY SERIOUS ABOUT YOU, MISS KATO...
WHAT? OH PLEASE, THAT'S ENOUGH JOKING...
~~~
RRRRRR
GRRR
WILL YOU STOP TALKING ABOUT THAT HERE?!
BAM
!
OF COURSE! I'M SORRY.
SHUDDER
I'VE NEVER SEEN TAKAHAMA SO ANGRY BEFORE...
MAYBE BB KENICHI IS IN REAL TROUBLE.
~~~

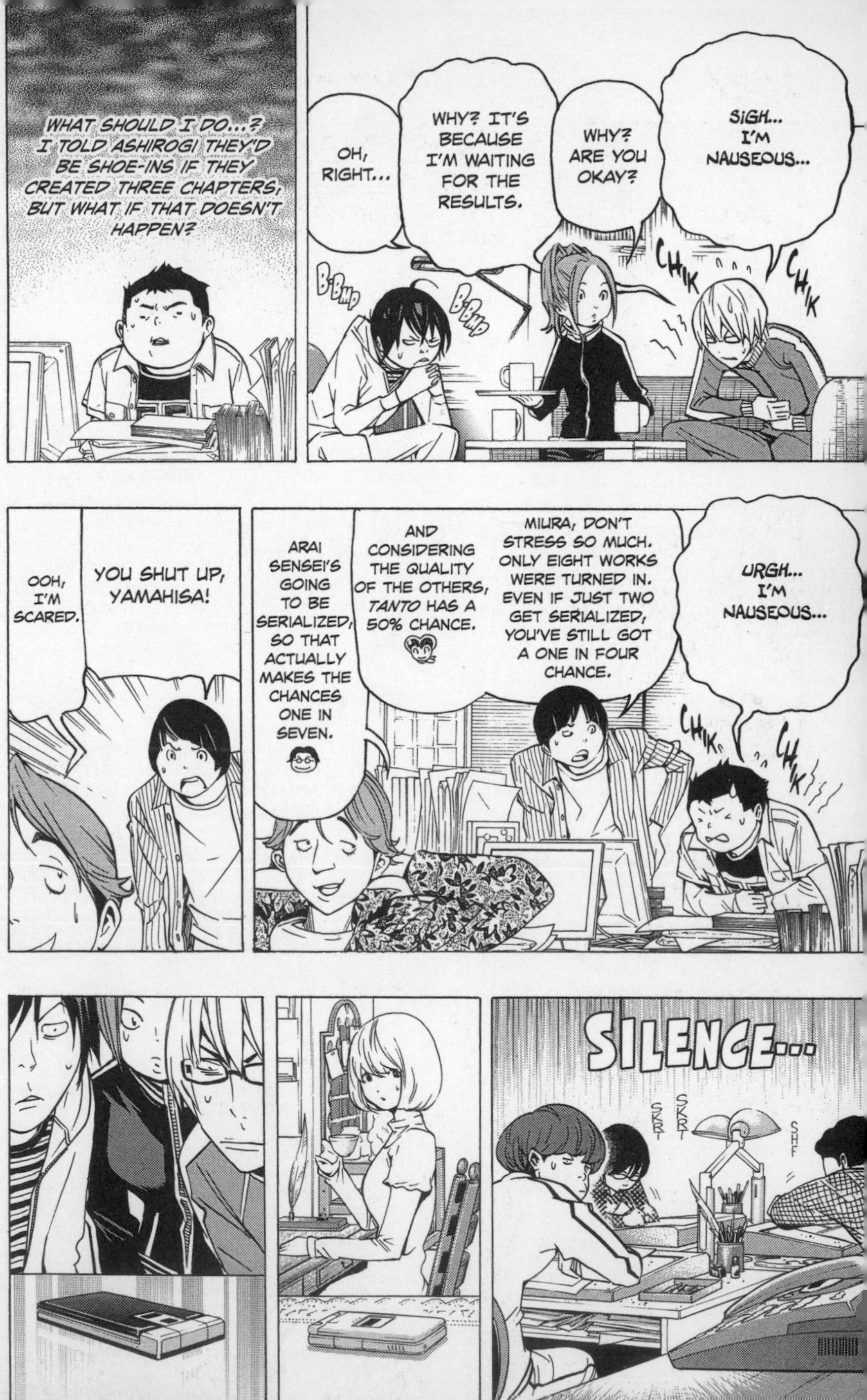
SIGH... I'M NAUSEOUS...
CHIK
CHIK
WHY? ARE YOU OKAY?
WHY? IT'S BECAUSE I'M WAITING FOR THE RESULTS.
B-BMP
B-BMP
OH, RIGHT...
WHAT SHOULD I DO...? I TOLD ASHIROGI THEY'D BE SHOE-INS IF THEY CREATED THREE CHAPTERS, BUT WHAT IF THAT DOESN'T HAPPEN?
URGH... I'M NAUSEOUS...
CHIK
CHIK
MIURA, DON'T STRESS SO MUCH. ONLY EIGHT WORKS WERE TURNED IN. EVEN IF JUST TWO GET SERIALIZED, YOU'VE STILL GOT A ONE IN FOUR CHANCE.
AND CONSIDERING THE QUALITY OF THE OTHERS, *TANTO* HAS A 50% CHANCE.
ARAI SENSEI'S GOING TO BE SERIALIZED, SO THAT ACTUALLY MAKES THE CHANCES ONE IN SEVEN.
YOU SHUT UP, YAMAHISA!
OOH, I'M SCARED.
SILENCE...
SKRT
SKRT
SHF

READ THIS WAY

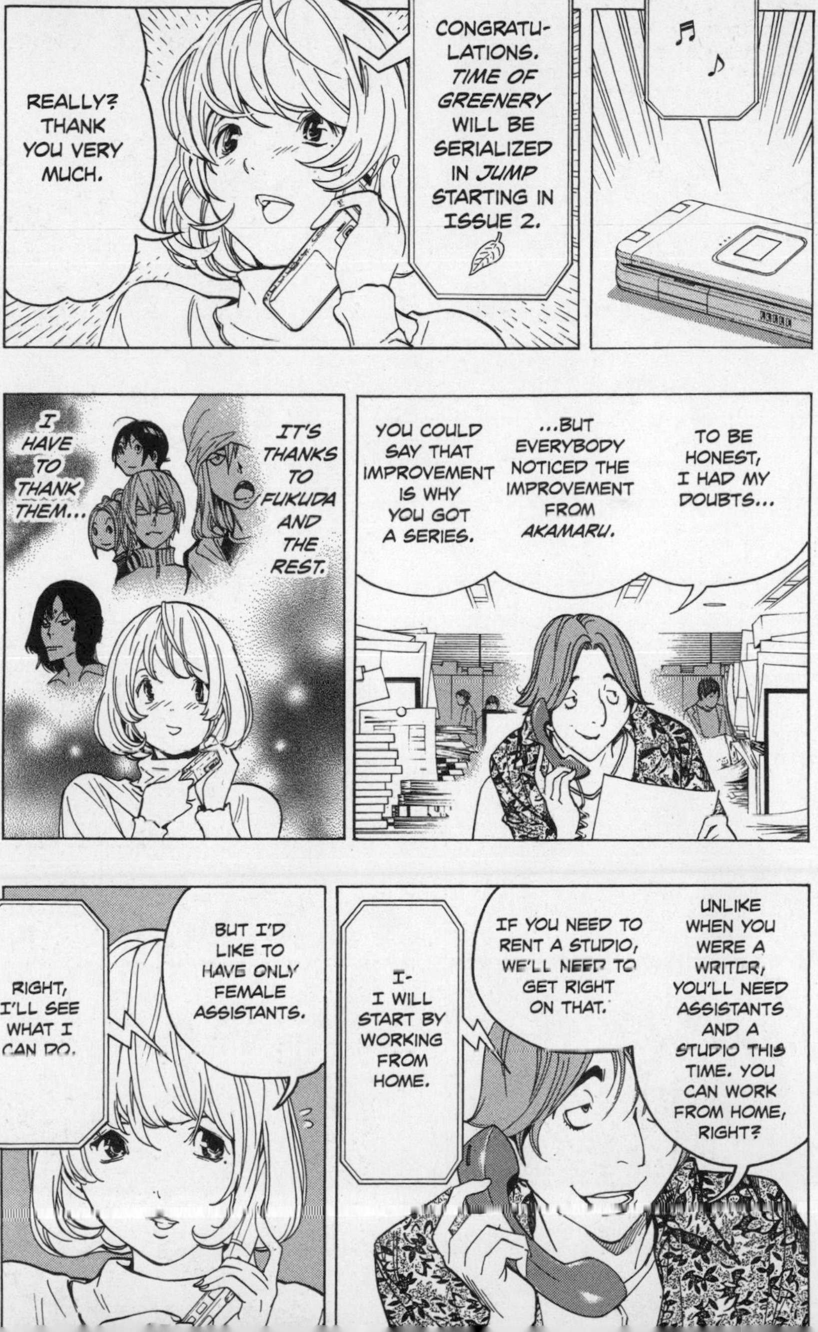
♬ ♪
CONGRATULATIONS. *TIME OF GREENERY* WILL BE SERIALIZED IN *JUMP* STARTING IN ISSUE 2.
REALLY? THANK YOU VERY MUCH.
TO BE HONEST, I HAD MY DOUBTS...
...BUT EVERYBODY NOTICED THE IMPROVEMENT FROM AKAMARU.
YOU COULD SAY THAT IMPROVEMENT IS WHY YOU GOT A SERIES.
IT'S THANKS TO FUKUDA AND THE REST.
I HAVE TO THANK THEM...
UNLIKE WHEN YOU WERE A WRITER, YOU'LL NEED ASSISTANTS AND A STUDIO THIS TIME. YOU CAN WORK FROM HOME, RIGHT?
IF YOU NEED TO RENT A STUDIO, WE'LL NEED TO GET RIGHT ON THAT.
I- I WILL START BY WORKING FROM HOME.
BUT I'D LIKE TO HAVE ONLY FEMALE ASSISTANTS.
RIGHT, I'LL SEE WHAT I CAN DO.

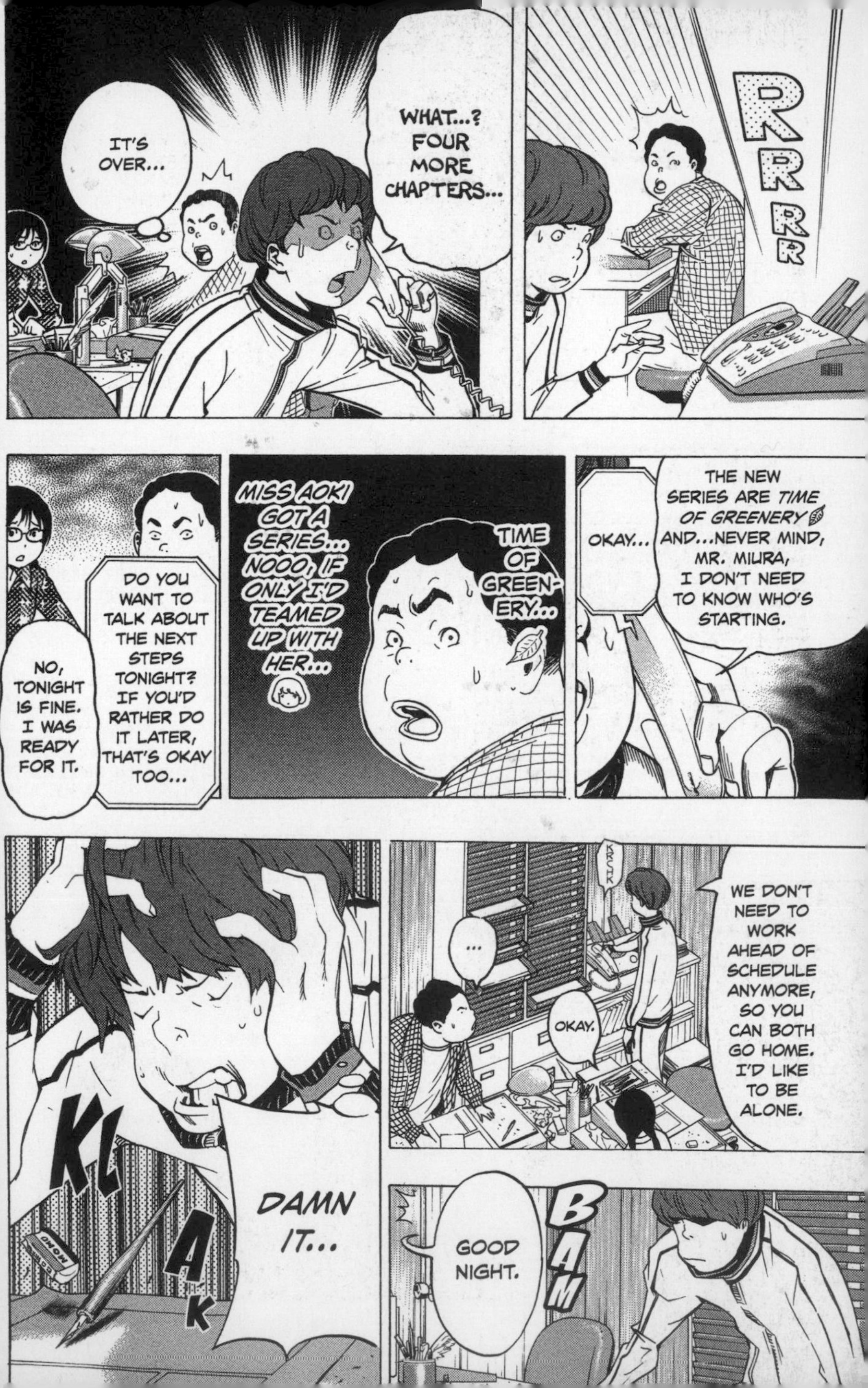
RRRR
WHAT...? FOUR MORE CHAPTERS...
IT'S OVER...
THE NEW SERIES ARE *TIME OF GREENERY* AND...NEVER MIND, MR. MIURA, I DON'T NEED TO KNOW WHO'S STARTING.
OKAY...
TIME OF GREENERY...
MISS AOKI GOT A SERIES... NOOO, IF ONLY I'D TEAMED UP WITH HER...
DO YOU WANT TO TALK ABOUT THE NEXT STEPS TONIGHT? IF YOU'D RATHER DO IT LATER, THAT'S OKAY TOO...
NO, TONIGHT IS FINE. I WAS READY FOR IT.
WE DON'T NEED TO WORK AHEAD OF SCHEDULE ANYMORE, SO YOU CAN BOTH GO HOME. I'D LIKE TO BE ALONE.
KRSHK
OKAY.
...
BAM
GOOD NIGHT.
DAMN IT...
KLAK

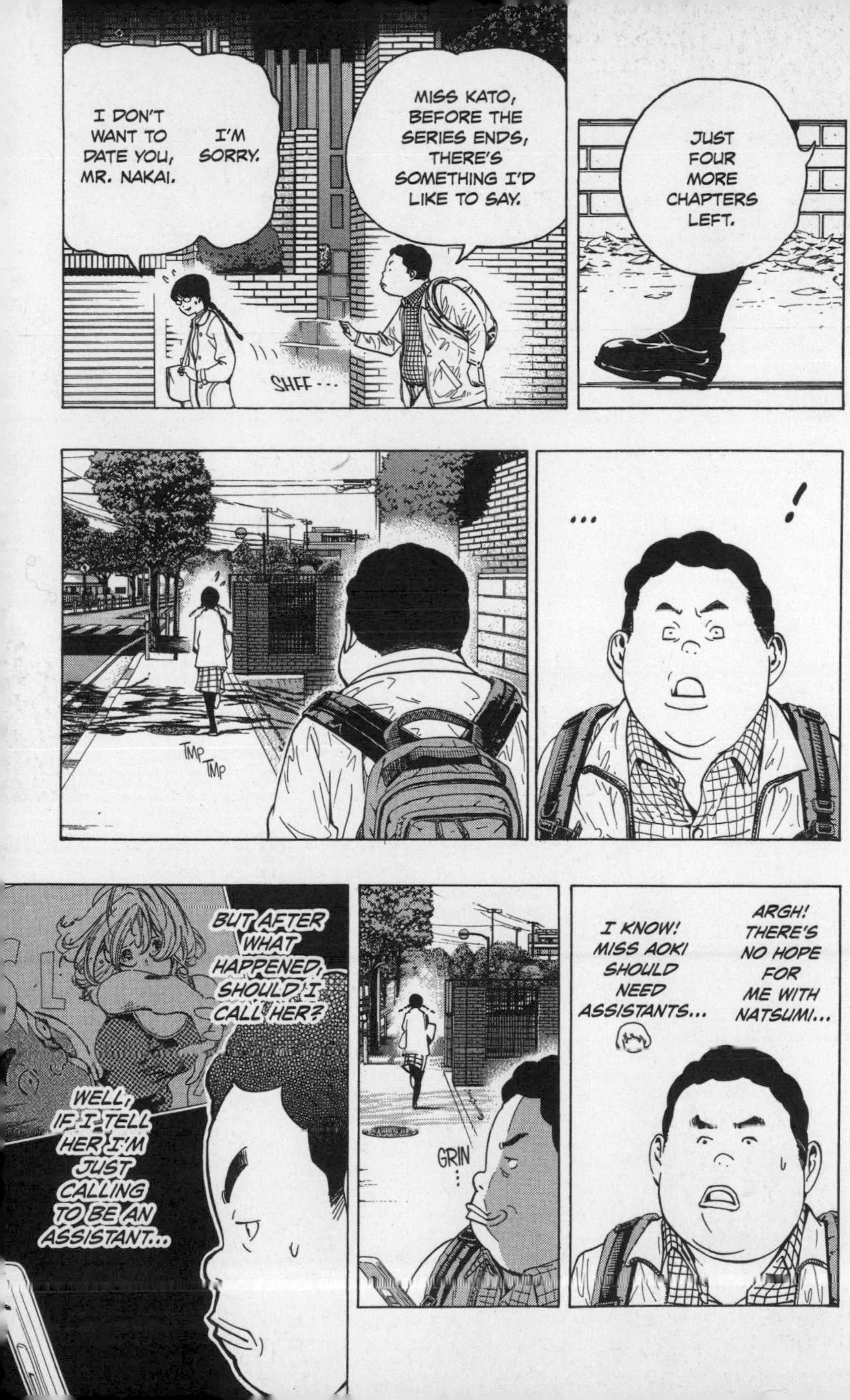
JUST FOUR MORE CHAPTERS LEFT.
MISS KATO, BEFORE THE SERIES ENDS, THERE'S SOMETHING I'D LIKE TO SAY.
I'M SORRY.
I DON'T WANT TO DATE YOU, MR. NAKAI.
SHFF...
...
!
TMP TMP
ARGH! THERE'S NO HOPE FOR ME WITH NATSUMI...
I KNOW! MISS AOKI SHOULD NEED ASSISTANTS...
GRIN...
BUT AFTER WHAT HAPPENED, SHOULD I CALL HER?
WELL, IF I TELL HER I'M JUST CALLING TO BE AN ASSISTANT...

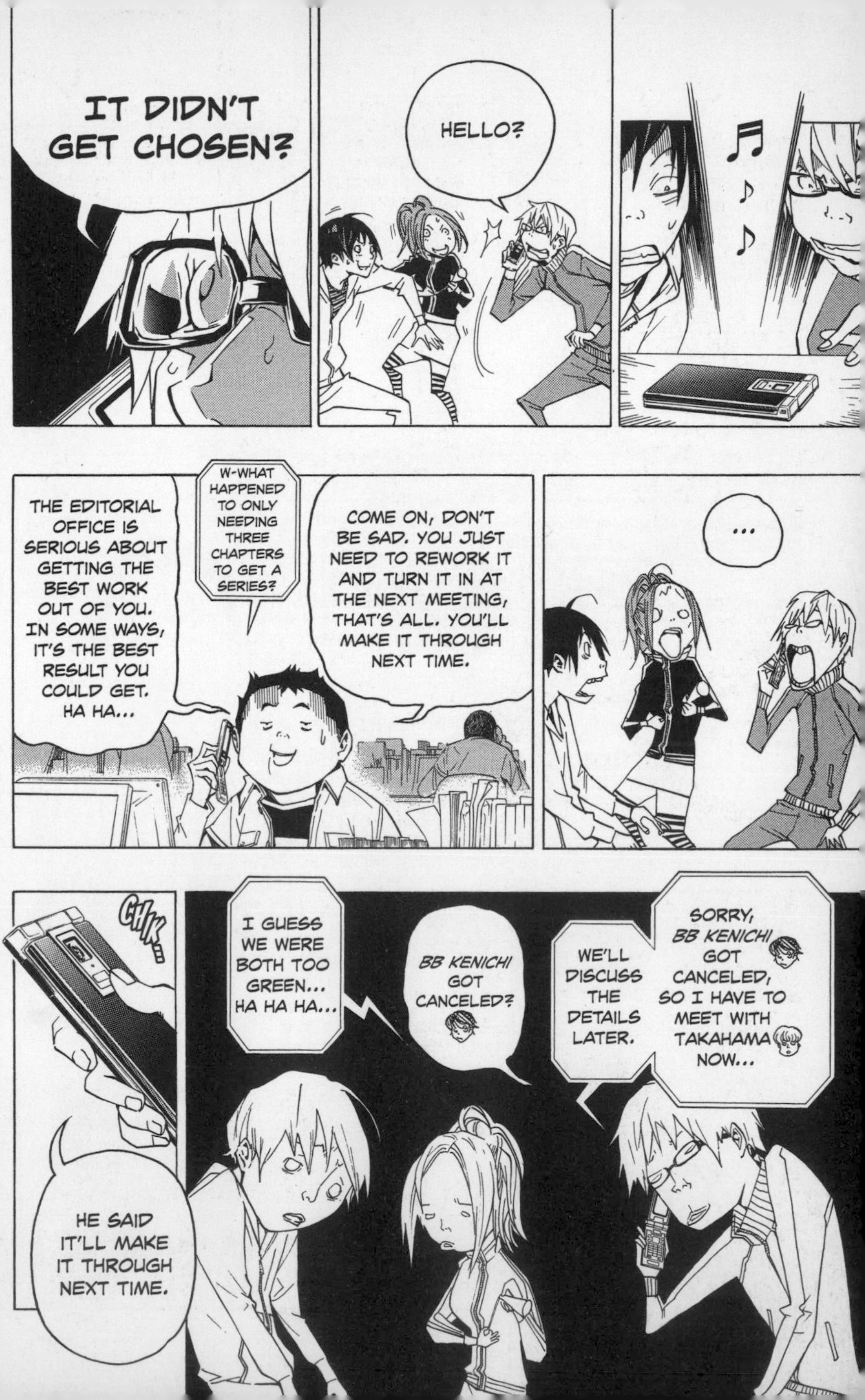
HELLO?
IT DIDN'T GET CHOSEN?
...
COME ON, DON'T BE SAD. YOU JUST NEED TO REWORK IT AND TURN IT IN AT THE NEXT MEETING, THAT'S ALL. YOU'LL MAKE IT THROUGH NEXT TIME.
W-WHAT HAPPENED TO ONLY NEEDING THREE CHAPTERS TO GET A SERIES?
THE EDITORIAL OFFICE IS SERIOUS ABOUT GETTING THE BEST WORK OUT OF YOU. IN SOME WAYS, IT'S THE BEST RESULT YOU COULD GET. HA HA...
SORRY, *BB KENICHI* GOT CANCELED, SO I HAVE TO MEET WITH TAKAHAMA NOW...
WE'LL DISCUSS THE DETAILS LATER.
BB KENICHI GOT CANCELED?
I GUESS WE WERE BOTH TOO GREEN... HA HA HA...
CHIK
HE SAID IT'LL MAKE IT THROUGH NEXT TIME.

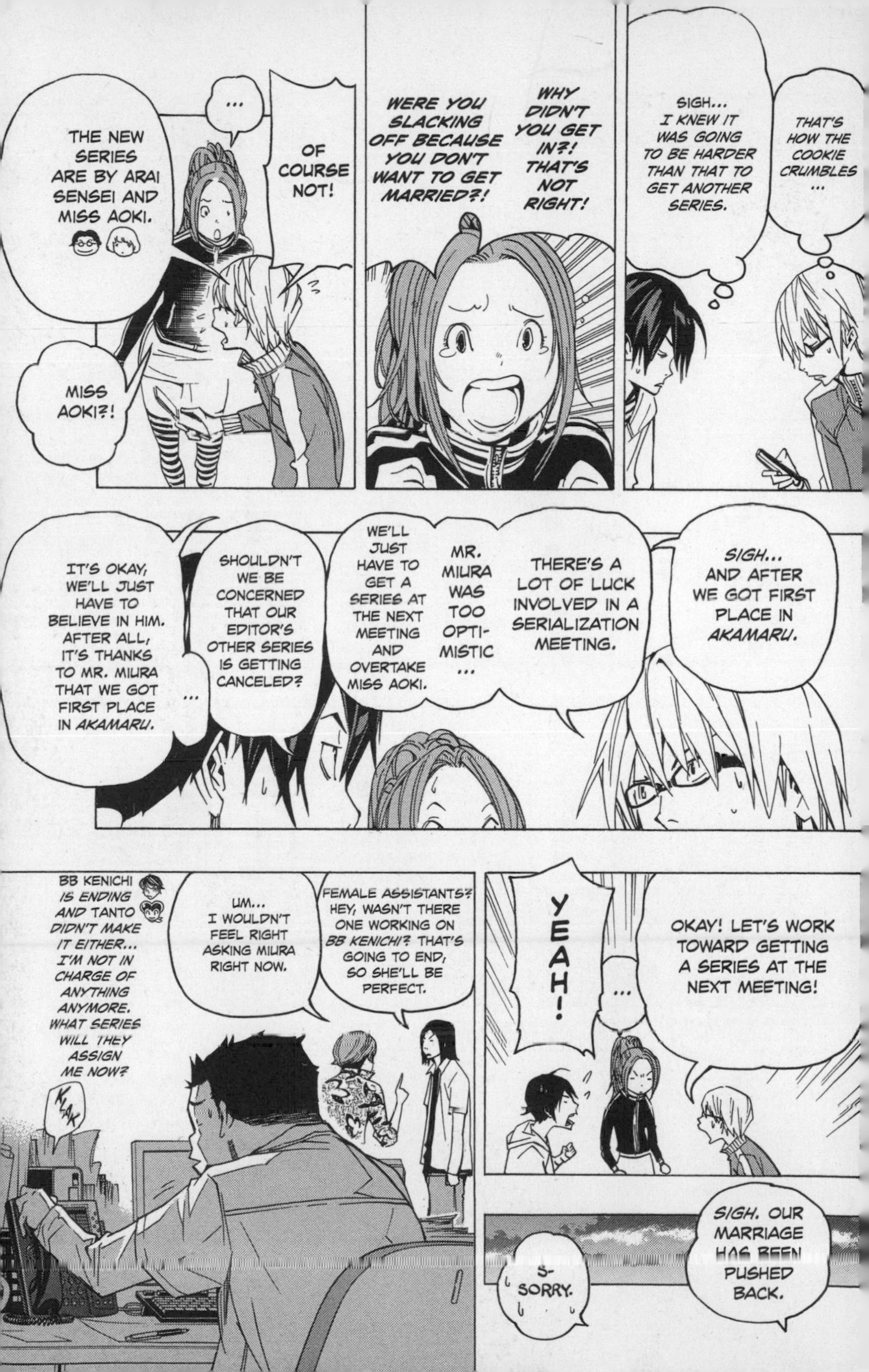

THAT'S HOW THE COOKIE CRUMBLES...
SIGH... I KNEW IT WAS GOING TO BE HARDER THAN THAT TO GET ANOTHER SERIES.
WHY DIDN'T YOU GET IN?! THAT'S NOT RIGHT!
WERE YOU SLACKING OFF BECAUSE YOU DON'T WANT TO GET MARRIED?!
OF COURSE NOT!
...
THE NEW SERIES ARE BY ARAI SENSEI AND MISS AOKI.
MISS AOKI?!
SIGH... AND AFTER WE GOT FIRST PLACE IN AKAMARU.
THERE'S A LOT OF LUCK INVOLVED IN A SERIALIZATION MEETING.
MR. MIURA WAS TOO OPTIMISTIC...
WE'LL JUST HAVE TO GET A SERIES AT THE NEXT MEETING AND OVERTAKE MISS AOKI.
SHOULDN'T WE BE CONCERNED THAT OUR EDITOR'S OTHER SERIES IS GETTING CANCELED?
...
IT'S OKAY, WE'LL JUST HAVE TO BELIEVE IN HIM. AFTER ALL, IT'S THANKS TO MR. MIURA THAT WE GOT FIRST PLACE IN AKAMARU.
OKAY! LET'S WORK TOWARD GETTING A SERIES AT THE NEXT MEETING!
...
YEAH!
SIGH. OUR MARRIAGE HAS BEEN PUSHED BACK.
S-SORRY.
FEMALE ASSISTANTS? HEY, WASN'T THERE ONE WORKING ON BB KENICHI? THAT'S GOING TO END, SO SHE'LL BE PERFECT.
UM... I WOULDN'T FEEL RIGHT ASKING MIURA RIGHT NOW.
BB KENICHI IS ENDING AND TANTO DIDN'T MAKE IT EITHER... I'M NOT IN CHARGE OF ANYTHING ANYMORE. WHAT SERIES WILL THEY ASSIGN ME NOW?
KLAK

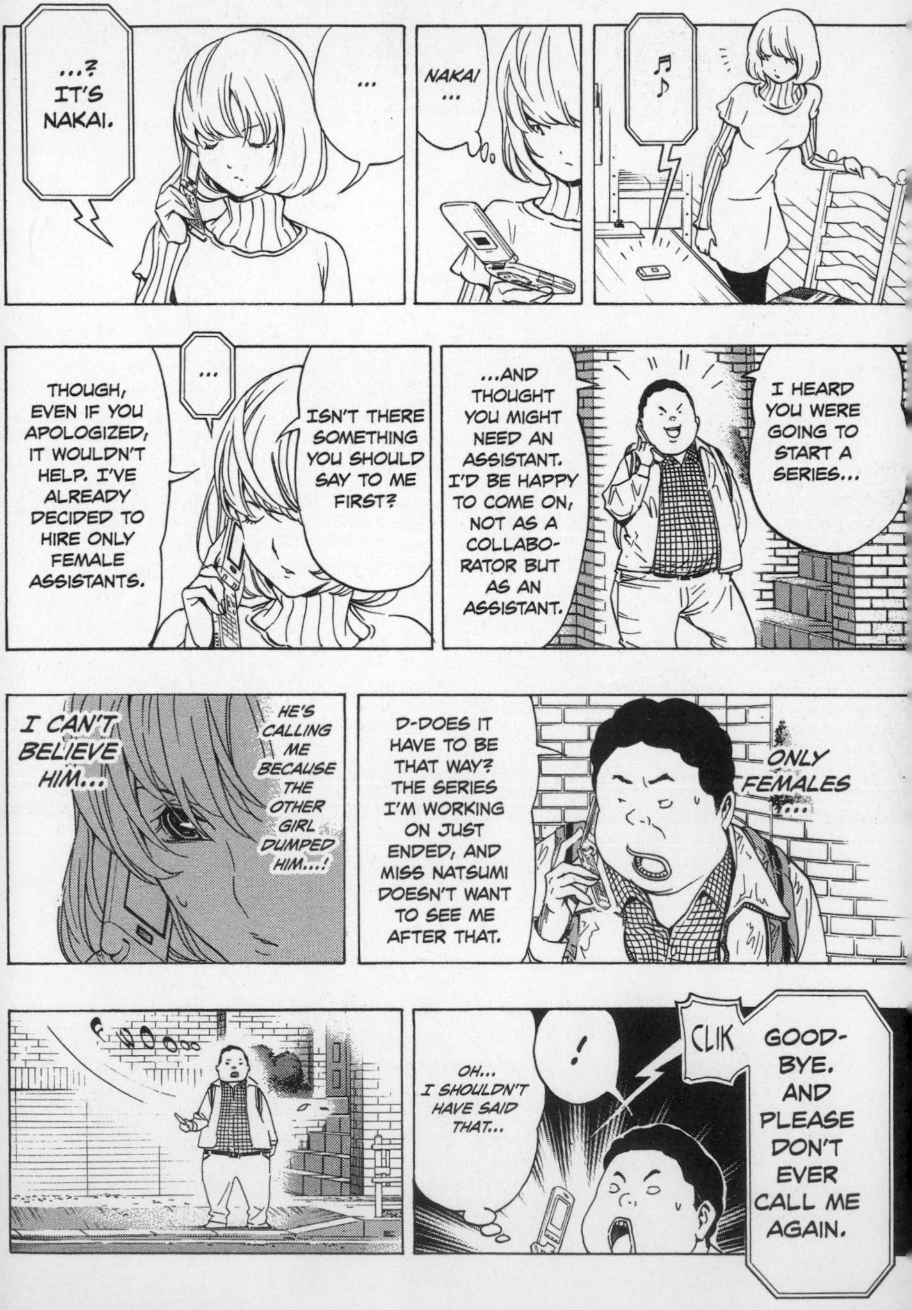
NAKAI ...
...
...? IT'S NAKAI.
I HEARD YOU WERE GOING TO START A SERIES...
...AND THOUGHT YOU MIGHT NEED AN ASSISTANT. I'D BE HAPPY TO COME ON, NOT AS A COLLABORATOR BUT AS AN ASSISTANT.
ISN'T THERE SOMETHING YOU SHOULD SAY TO ME FIRST?
...
THOUGH, EVEN IF YOU APOLOGIZED, IT WOULDN'T HELP. I'VE ALREADY DECIDED TO HIRE ONLY FEMALE ASSISTANTS.
ONLY FEMALES...
D-DOES IT HAVE TO BE THAT WAY? THE SERIES I'M WORKING ON JUST ENDED, AND MISS NATSUMI DOESN'T WANT TO SEE ME AFTER THAT.
HE'S CALLING ME BECAUSE THE OTHER GIRL DUMPED HIM...!
I CAN'T BELIEVE HIM...
GOOD-BYE. AND PLEASE DON'T EVER CALL ME AGAIN.
CLIK
!
OH... I SHOULDN'T HAVE SAID THAT...

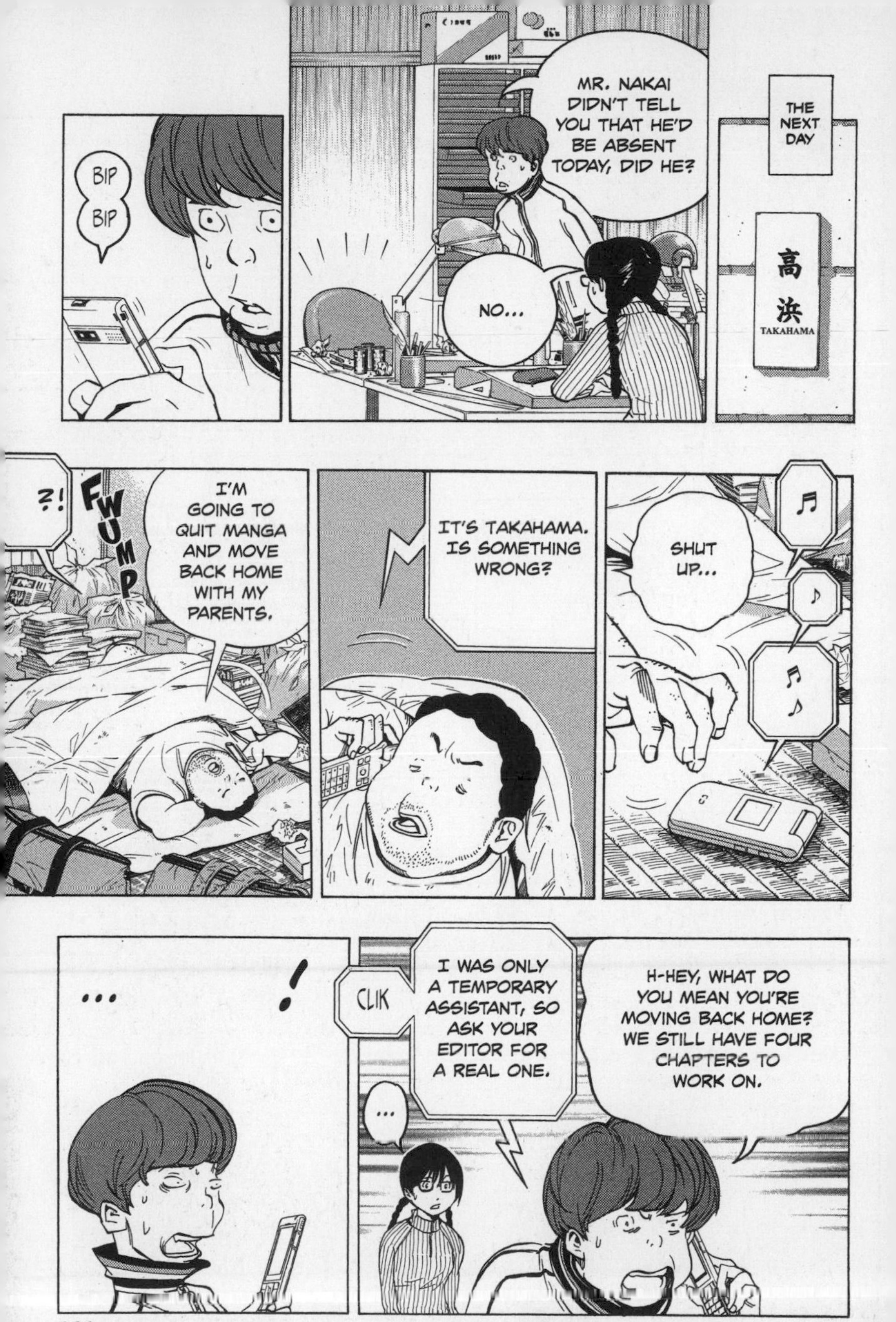
THE NEXT DAY
高浜
TAKAHAMA
MR. NAKAI DIDN'T TELL YOU THAT HE'D BE ABSENT TODAY, DID HE?
NO...
BIP
BIP
♪
SHUT UP...
♪
♪♪
IT'S TAKAHAMA. IS SOMETHING WRONG?
I'M GOING TO QUIT MANGA AND MOVE BACK HOME WITH MY PARENTS.
FWUMP
?!
H-HEY, WHAT DO YOU MEAN YOU'RE MOVING BACK HOME? WE STILL HAVE FOUR CHAPTERS TO WORK ON.
I WAS ONLY A TEMPORARY ASSISTANT, SO ASK YOUR EDITOR FOR A REAL ONE.
CLIK
...
!
...

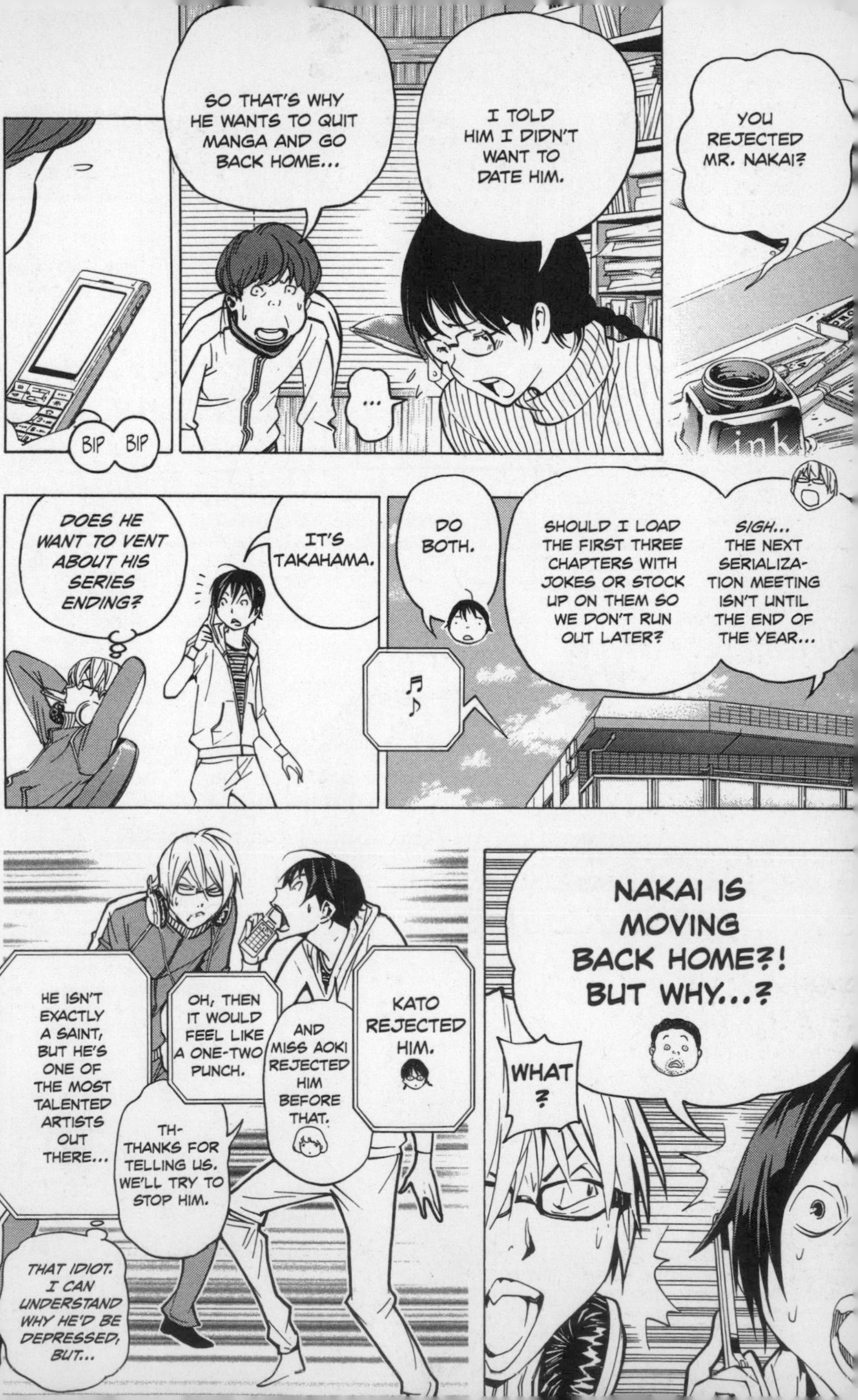
YOU REJECTED MR. NAKAI?
I TOLD HIM I DIDN'T WANT TO DATE HIM.
...
SO THAT'S WHY HE WANTS TO QUIT MANGA AND GO BACK HOME...
BIP BIP
SIGH... THE NEXT SERIALIZATION MEETING ISN'T UNTIL THE END OF THE YEAR...
SHOULD I LOAD THE FIRST THREE CHAPTERS WITH JOKES OR STOCK UP ON THEM SO WE DON'T RUN OUT LATER?
DO BOTH.
♫ ♪
IT'S TAKAHAMA.
DOES HE WANT TO VENT ABOUT HIS SERIES ENDING?
NAKAI IS MOVING BACK HOME?! BUT WHY...?
WHAT?
KATO REJECTED HIM.
AND MISS AOKI REJECTED HIM BEFORE THAT.
OH, THEN IT WOULD FEEL LIKE A ONE-TWO PUNCH.
HE ISN'T EXACTLY A SAINT, BUT HE'S ONE OF THE MOST TALENTED ARTISTS OUT THERE...
TH- THANKS FOR TELLING US. WE'LL TRY TO STOP HIM.
THAT IDIOT. I CAN UNDERSTAND WHY HE'D BE DEPRESSED, BUT...

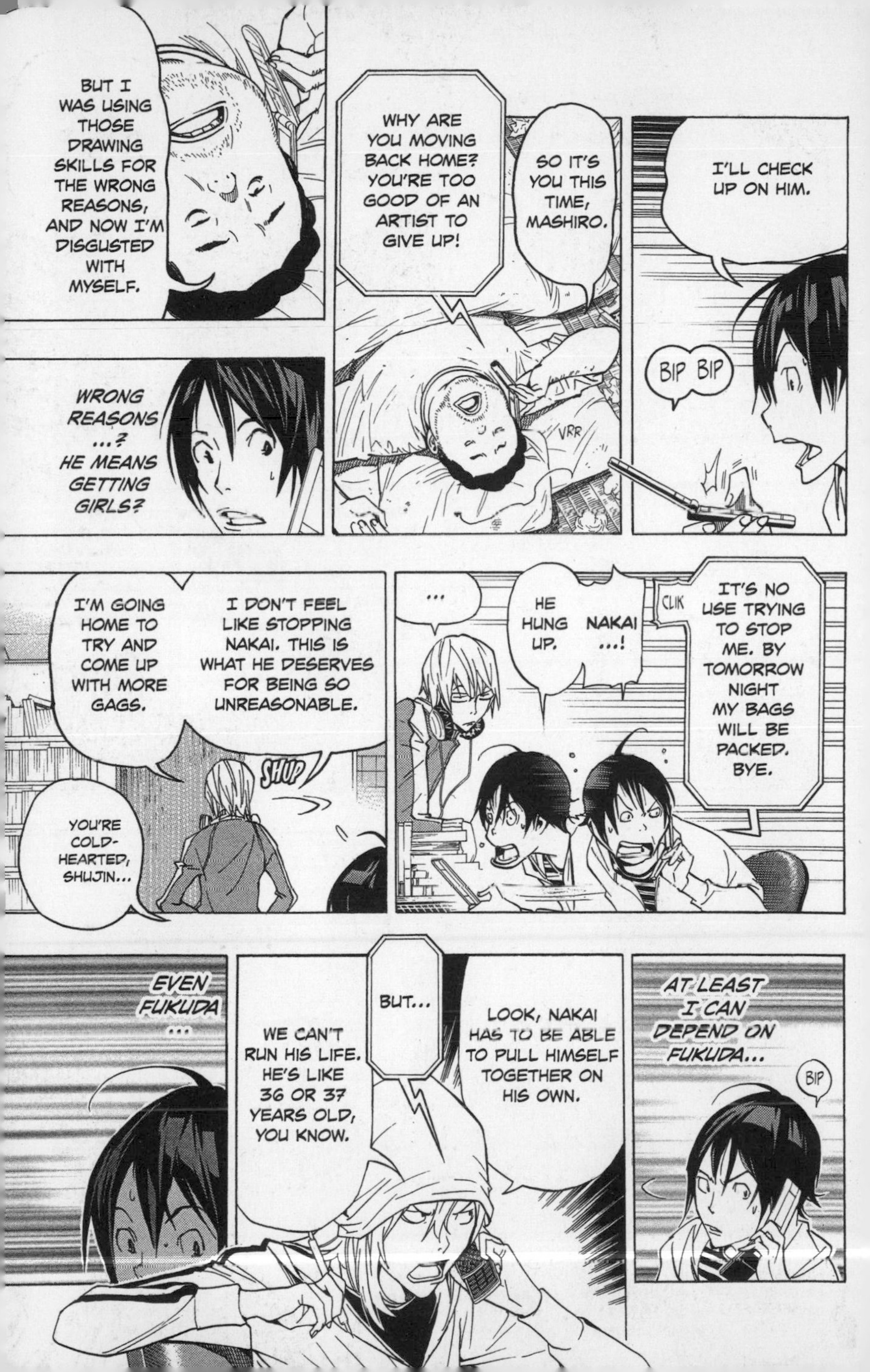
I'LL CHECK UP ON HIM.
BIP BIP
SO IT'S YOU THIS TIME, MASHIRO.
WHY ARE YOU MOVING BACK HOME? YOU'RE TOO GOOD OF AN ARTIST TO GIVE UP!
VRR
BUT I WAS USING THOSE DRAWING SKILLS FOR THE WRONG REASONS, AND NOW I'M DISGUSTED WITH MYSELF.
WRONG REASONS...? HE MEANS GETTING GIRLS?
IT'S NO USE TRYING TO STOP ME. BY TOMORROW NIGHT MY BAGS WILL BE PACKED. BYE.
CLIK
NAKAI...!
HE HUNG UP.
...
I DON'T FEEL LIKE STOPPING NAKAI. THIS IS WHAT HE DESERVES FOR BEING SO UNREASONABLE.
I'M GOING HOME TO TRY AND COME UP WITH MORE GAGS.
SHUP
YOU'RE COLD-HEARTED, SHUJIN...
AT LEAST I CAN DEPEND ON FUKUDA...
BIP
LOOK, NAKAI HAS TO BE ABLE TO PULL HIMSELF TOGETHER ON HIS OWN.
BUT...
WE CAN'T RUN HIS LIFE. HE'S LIKE 36 OR 37 YEARS OLD, YOU KNOW.
EVEN FUKUDA...

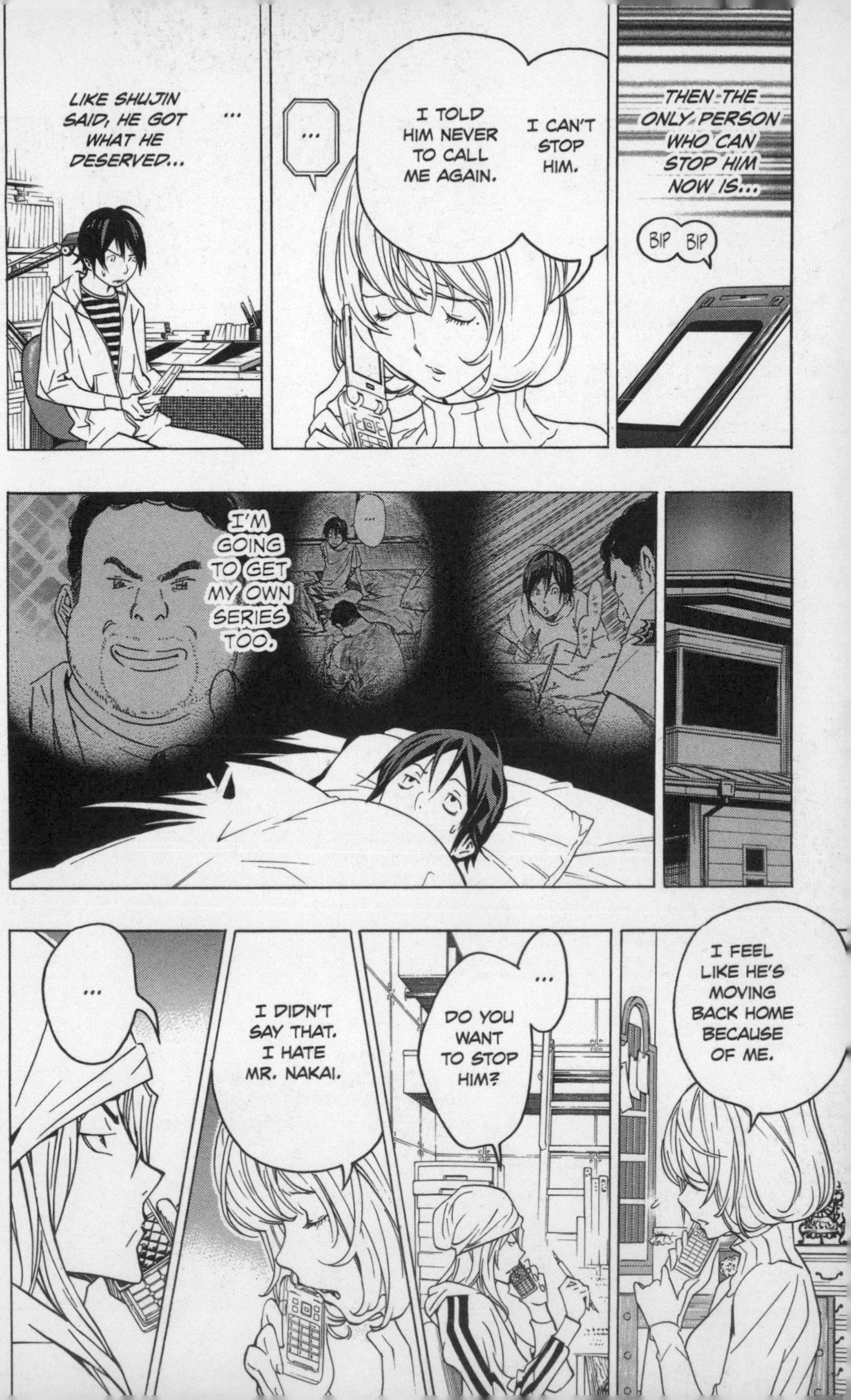
THEN THE ONLY PERSON WHO CAN STOP HIM NOW IS...
BIP BIP
I CAN'T STOP HIM.
I TOLD HIM NEVER TO CALL ME AGAIN.
...
...
LIKE SHUJIN SAID, HE GOT WHAT HE DESERVED...
...
I'M GOING TO GET MY OWN SERIES TOO.
I FEEL LIKE HE'S MOVING BACK HOME BECAUSE OF ME.
...
DO YOU WANT TO STOP HIM?
I DIDN'T SAY THAT. I HATE MR. NAKAI.
...

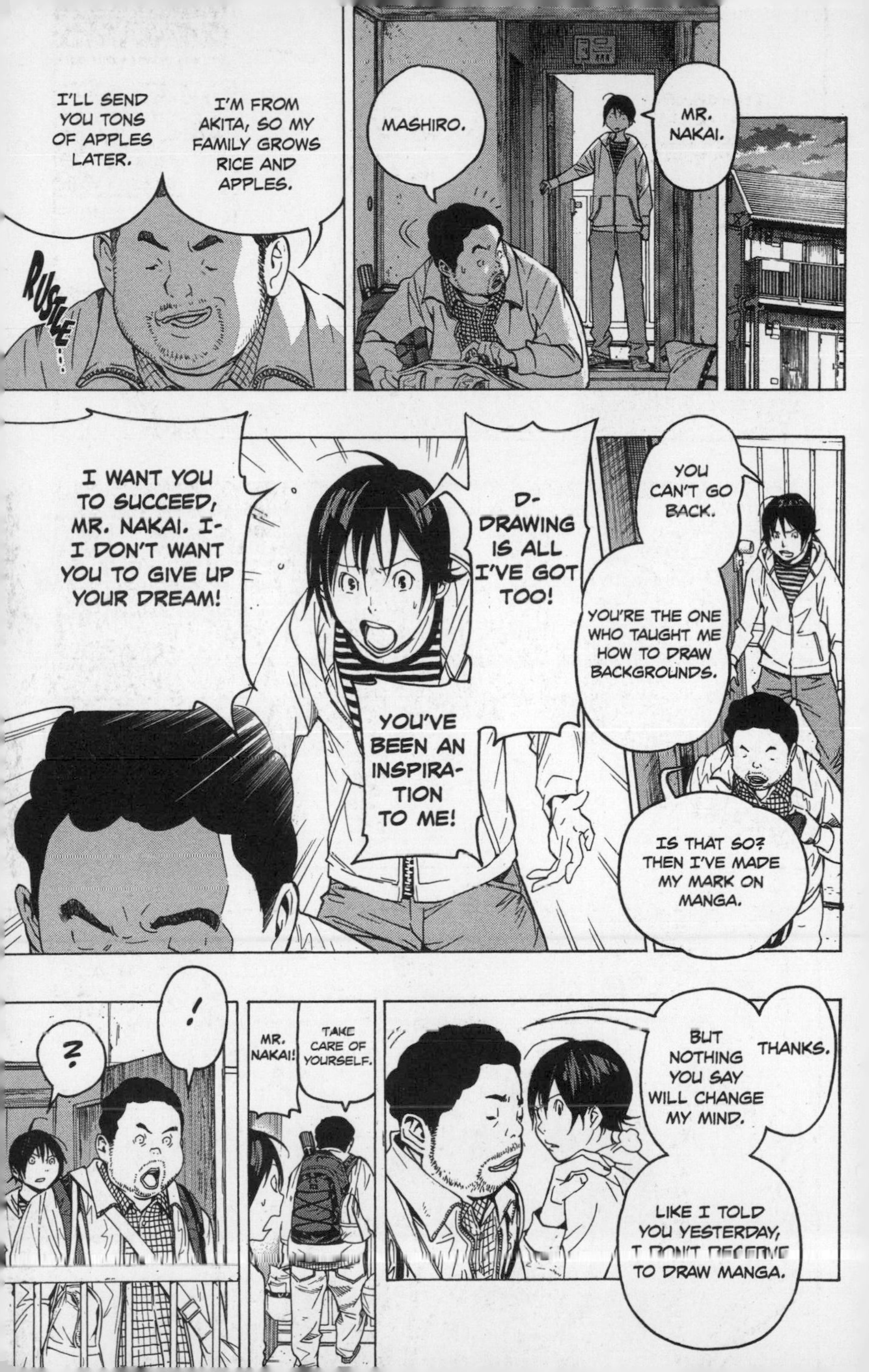
MR. NAKAI.
MASHIRO.
I'M FROM AKITA, SO MY FAMILY GROWS RICE AND APPLES.
I'LL SEND YOU TONS OF APPLES LATER.
RUSTLE...
YOU CAN'T GO BACK.
YOU'RE THE ONE WHO TAUGHT ME HOW TO DRAW BACKGROUNDS.
IS THAT SO? THEN I'VE MADE MY MARK ON MANGA.
D-DRAWING IS ALL I'VE GOT TOO!
I WANT YOU TO SUCCEED, MR. NAKAI. I-I DON'T WANT YOU TO GIVE UP YOUR DREAM!
YOU'VE BEEN AN INSPIRATION TO ME!
THANKS.
BUT NOTHING YOU SAY WILL CHANGE MY MIND.
LIKE I TOLD YOU YESTERDAY, I DON'T DESERVE TO DRAW MANGA.
TAKE CARE OF YOURSELF.
MR. NAKAI!
!
?

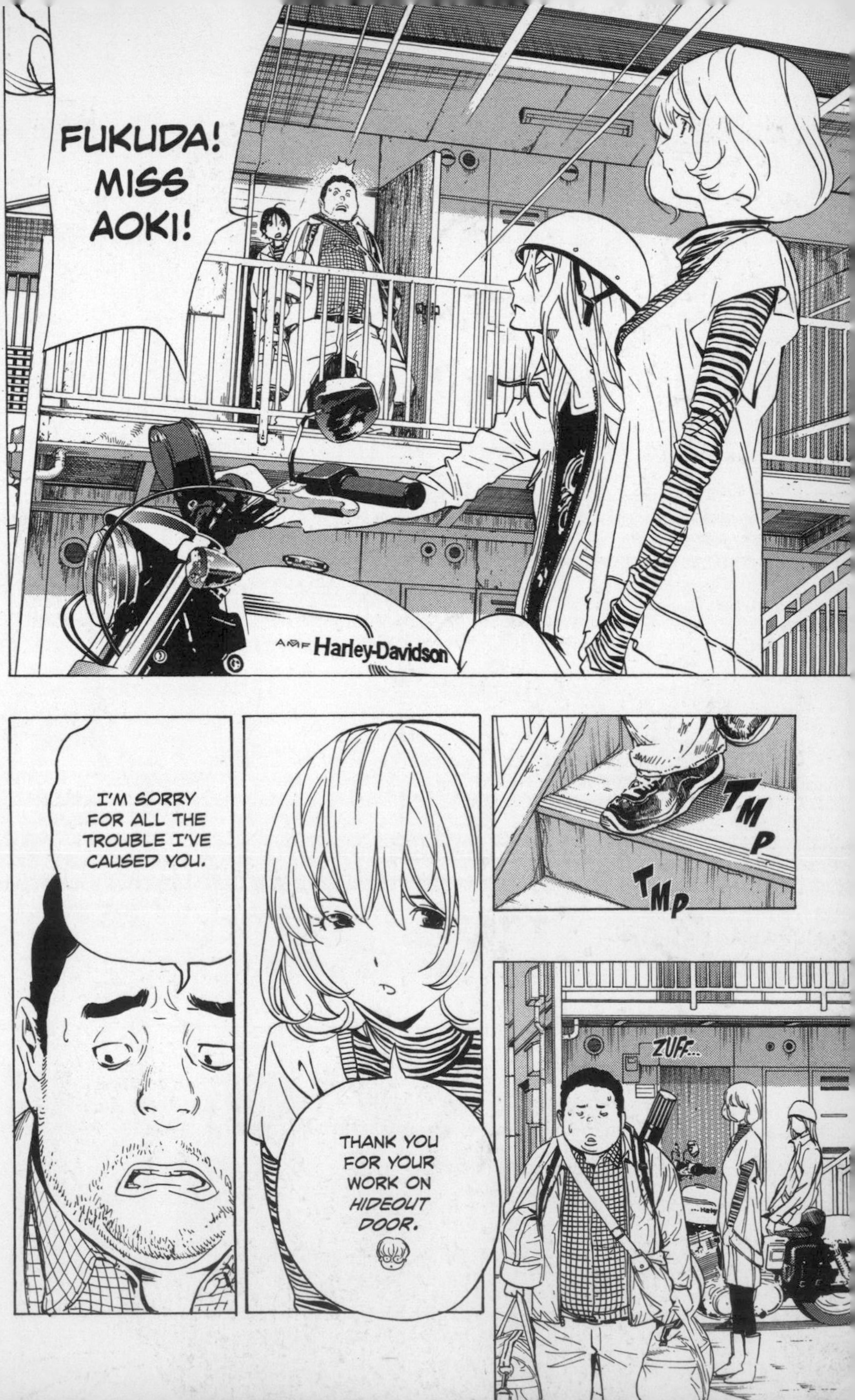
FUKUDA! MISS AOKI!
AMF Harley-Davidson
TMP
TMP
ZUFF...
THANK YOU FOR YOUR WORK ON *HIDEOUT DOOR*.
I'M SORRY FOR ALL THE TROUBLE I'VE CAUSED YOU.

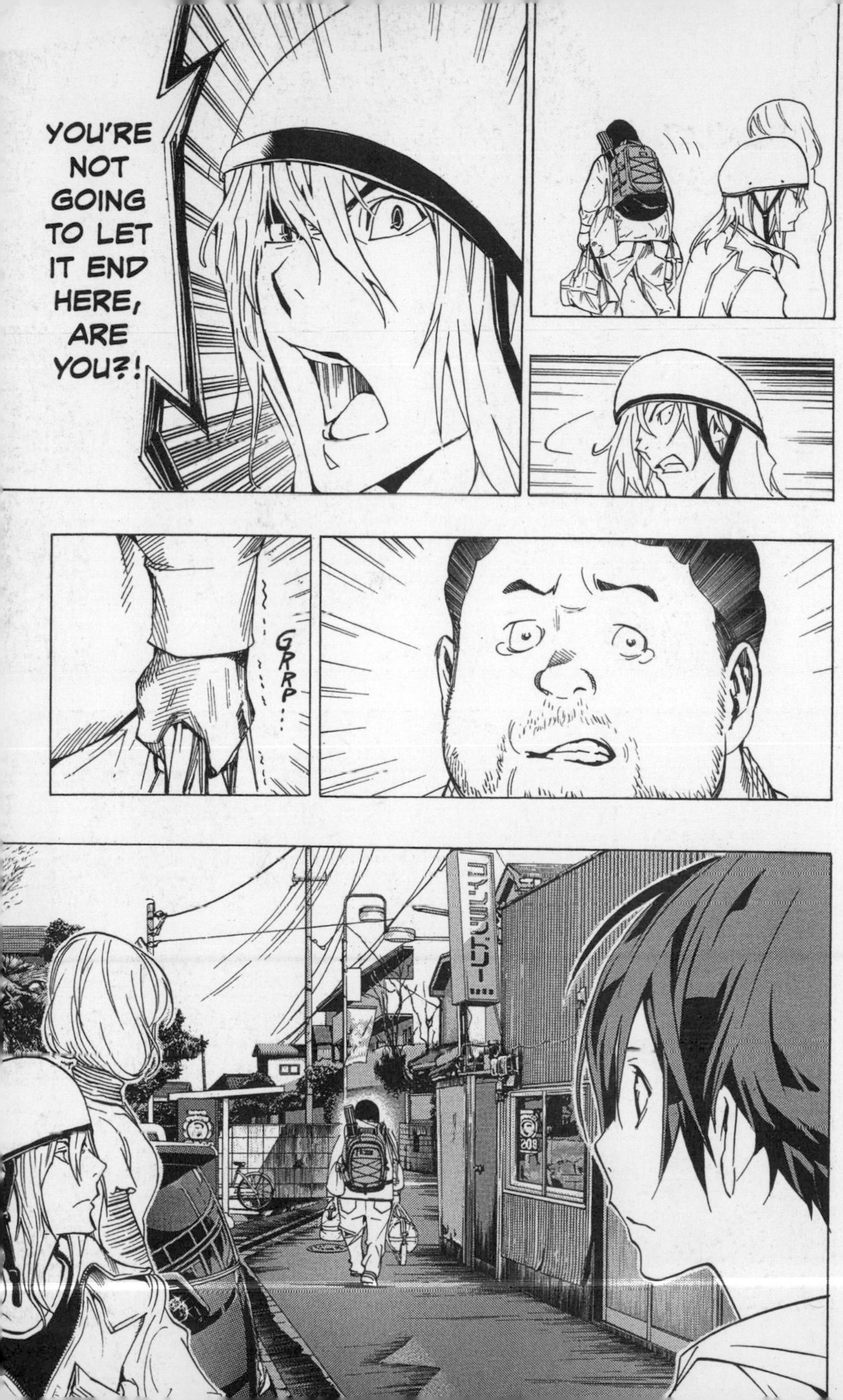
YOU'RE NOT GOING TO LET IT END HERE, ARE YOU?!
GRRP...

OHBA'S STORYBOARD

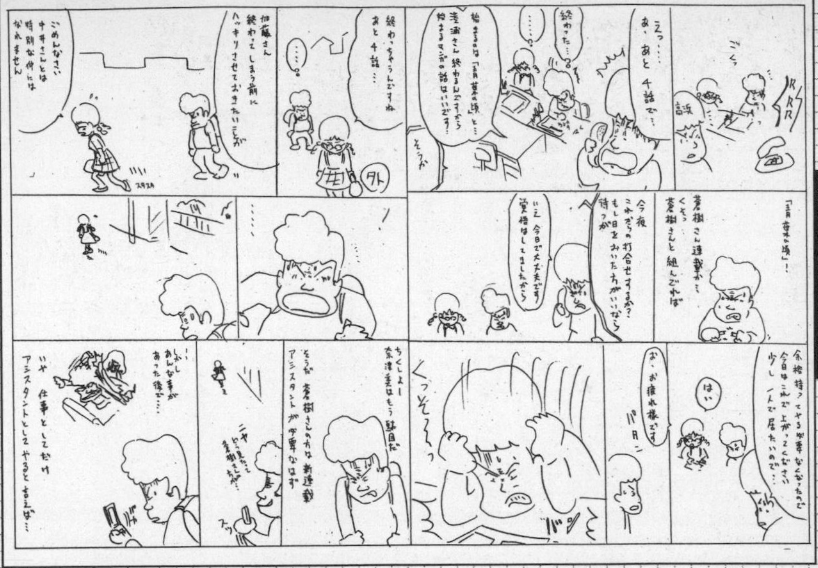
RRR
ごくっ
えっ… あ、あと4話で…
終わった…?
……?
始まるのは「青葉の頭」と… 港浦さん終わるんですから始まるマンガの話はいいです…
そうか
終わっちゃうんですね あと4話…
……。
加藤さん 終わってしまう前に ハッキリさせておきたいことが
ごめんなさい 中井さんとは 特別な仲には なれません
「青葉の頭」!
蒼樹さん連載かよ… くそっ 蒼樹さんと組んでれば
今夜 これからの打合せするか? もし日をおいた方がいいなら待つが
いえ 今日で大丈夫です 覚悟はしてましたから
……
!
余裕持ってやる必要なくなったので今日はこれで上がってください 少し一人で居たいので…
はい
お、お疲れ様です
パタン
くっそ〜っ
ドン
ちくしょー 蒼樹嬢はもう駄目だ
そうだ 蒼樹さんの方は新連載 アシスタントが必要なはず
ニヤ
スッ
しかしあんな事があった後で…
いや 仕事としてだけアシスタントとしてやると言えば…

OBATA'S STORYBOARD

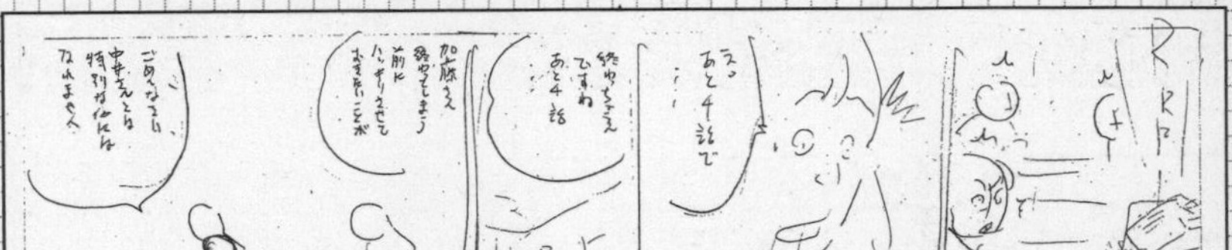

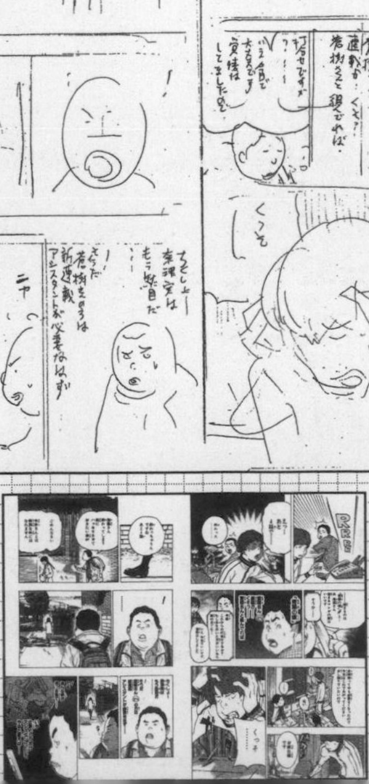

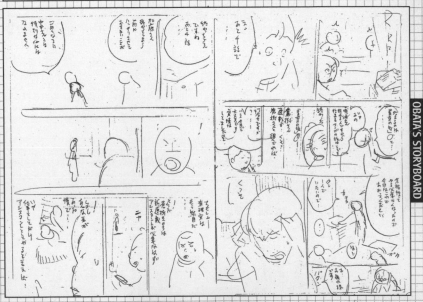

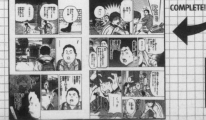

COMPLETE!

※CREATOR STORYBOARDS AND FINISHED PAGES IN JAPANESE

BAKUMAN。 vol.8

"Until the Final Draft Is Complete"

Chapter 69, pp. 156-157

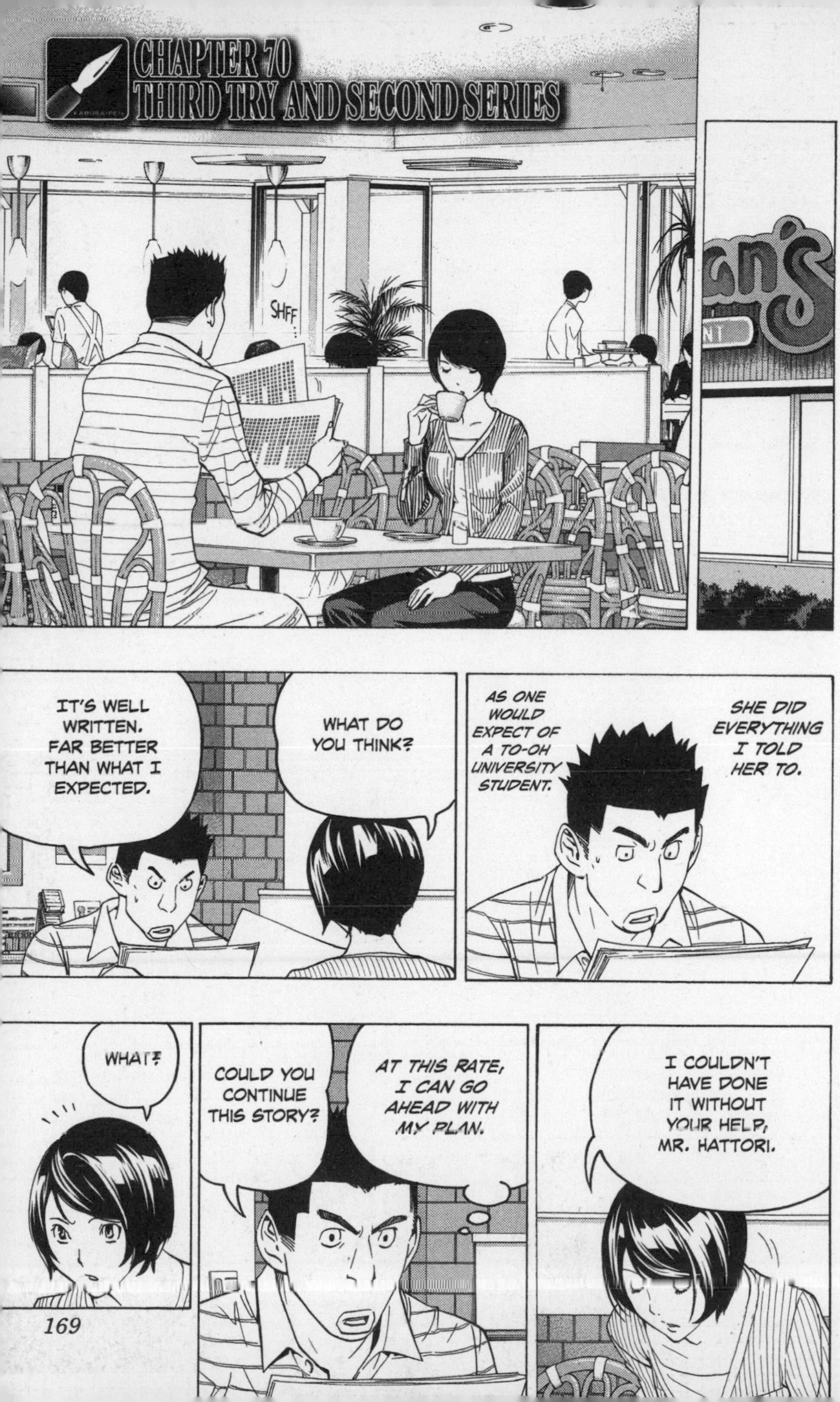
CHAPTER 70
THIRD TRY AND SECOND SERIES
SHFF
SHE DID EVERYTHING I TOLD HER TO.
AS ONE WOULD EXPECT OF A TO-OH UNIVERSITY STUDENT.
WHAT DO YOU THINK?
IT'S WELL WRITTEN. FAR BETTER THAN WHAT I EXPECTED.
I COULDN'T HAVE DONE IT WITHOUT YOUR HELP, MR. HATTORI.
AT THIS RATE, I CAN GO AHEAD WITH MY PLAN.
COULD YOU CONTINUE THIS STORY?
WHAT?

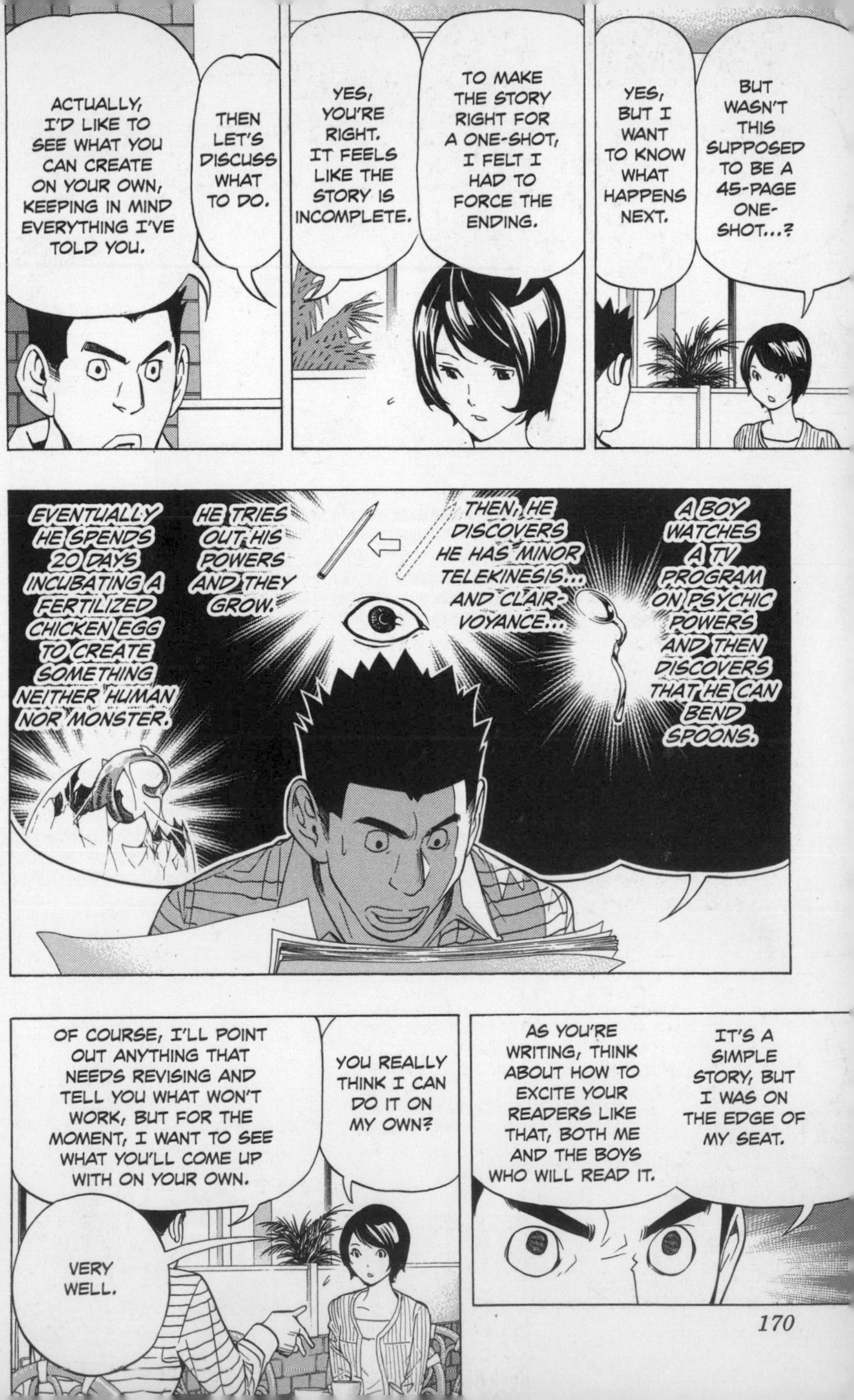
BUT WASN'T THIS SUPPOSED TO BE A 45-PAGE ONE-SHOT...?
YES, BUT I WANT TO KNOW WHAT HAPPENS NEXT.
TO MAKE THE STORY RIGHT FOR A ONE-SHOT, I FELT I HAD TO FORCE THE ENDING.
YES, YOU'RE RIGHT. IT FEELS LIKE THE STORY IS INCOMPLETE.
THEN LET'S DISCUSS WHAT TO DO.
ACTUALLY, I'D LIKE TO SEE WHAT YOU CAN CREATE ON YOUR OWN, KEEPING IN MIND EVERYTHING I'VE TOLD YOU.
A BOY WATCHES A TV PROGRAM ON PSYCHIC POWERS AND THEN DISCOVERS THAT HE CAN BEND SPOONS.
THEN, HE DISCOVERS HE HAS MINOR TELEKINESIS... AND CLAIR-VOYANCE...
HE TRIES OUT HIS POWERS AND THEY GROW.
EVENTUALLY HE SPENDS 20 DAYS INCUBATING A FERTILIZED CHICKEN EGG TO CREATE SOMETHING NEITHER HUMAN NOR MONSTER.
IT'S A SIMPLE STORY, BUT I WAS ON THE EDGE OF MY SEAT.
AS YOU'RE WRITING, THINK ABOUT HOW TO EXCITE YOUR READERS LIKE THAT, BOTH ME AND THE BOYS WHO WILL READ IT.
YOU REALLY THINK I CAN DO IT ON MY OWN?
OF COURSE, I'LL POINT OUT ANYTHING THAT NEEDS REVISING AND TELL YOU WHAT WON'T WORK, BUT FOR THE MOMENT, I WANT TO SEE WHAT YOU'LL COME UP WITH ON YOUR OWN.
VERY WELL.

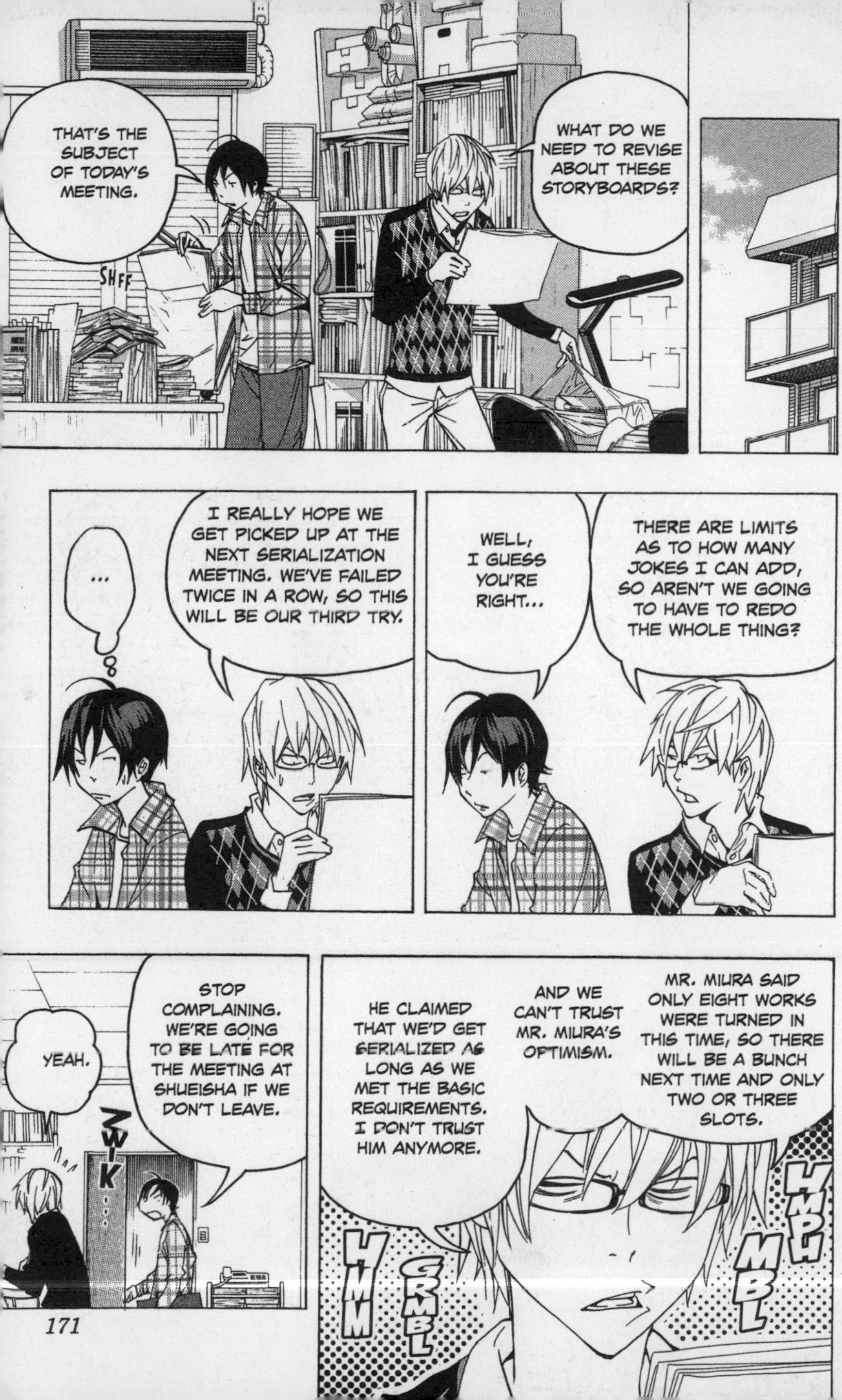
WHAT DO WE NEED TO REVISE ABOUT THESE STORYBOARDS?
THAT'S THE SUBJECT OF TODAY'S MEETING.
SHFF
THERE ARE LIMITS AS TO HOW MANY JOKES I CAN ADD, SO AREN'T WE GOING TO HAVE TO REDO THE WHOLE THING?
WELL, I GUESS YOU'RE RIGHT...
I REALLY HOPE WE GET PICKED UP AT THE NEXT SERIALIZATION MEETING. WE'VE FAILED TWICE IN A ROW, SO THIS WILL BE OUR THIRD TRY.
...
MR. MIURA SAID ONLY EIGHT WORKS WERE TURNED IN THIS TIME, SO THERE WILL BE A BUNCH NEXT TIME AND ONLY TWO OR THREE SLOTS.
AND WE CAN'T TRUST MR. MIURA'S OPTIMISM.
HE CLAIMED THAT WE'D GET SERIALIZED AS LONG AS WE MET THE BASIC REQUIREMENTS. I DON'T TRUST HIM ANYMORE.
HMPH
MBL
GRMBL
HMM
STOP COMPLAINING. WE'RE GOING TO BE LATE FOR THE MEETING AT SHUEISHA IF WE DON'T LEAVE.
YEAH.
ZWIK...

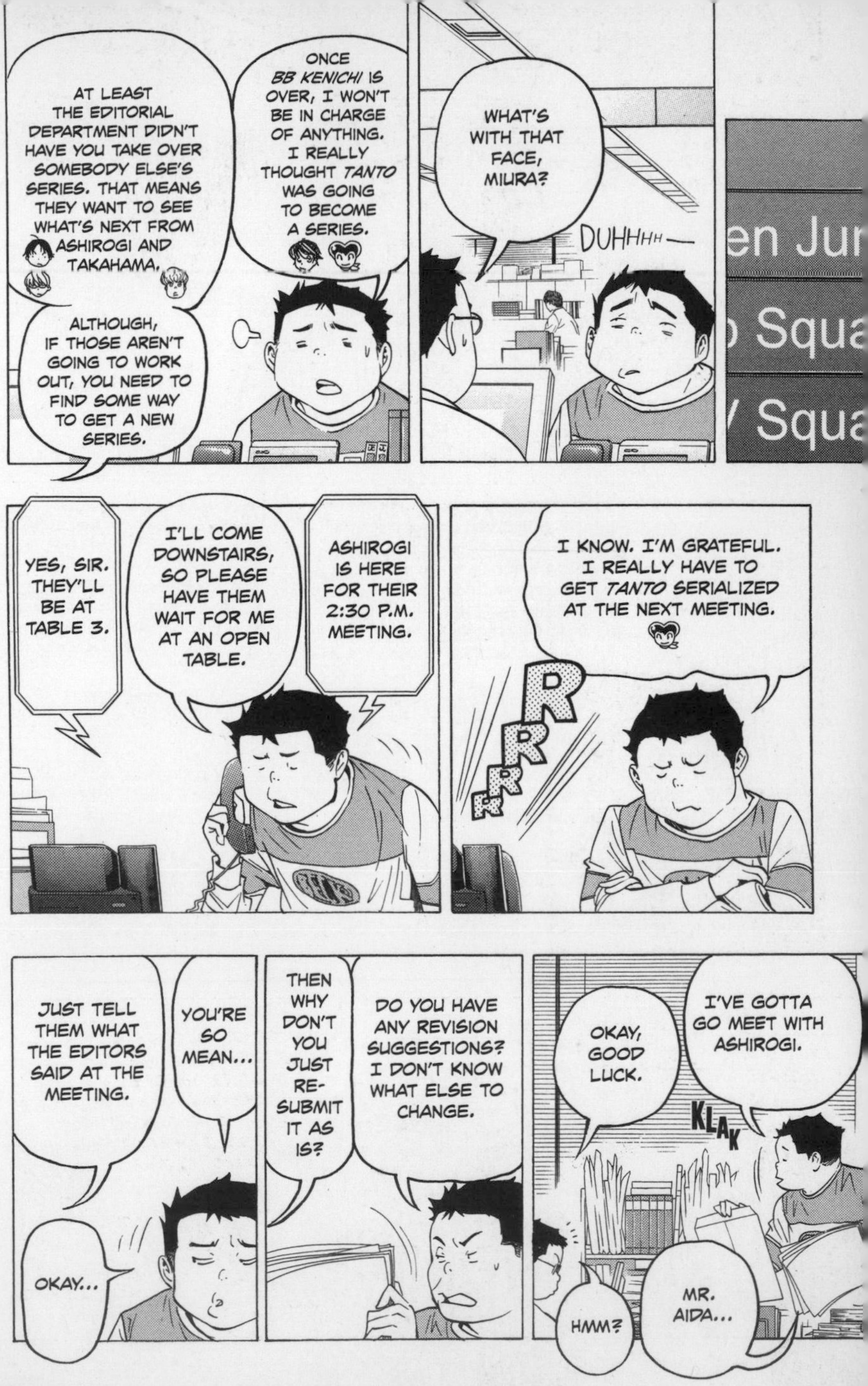
WHAT'S WITH THAT FACE, MIURA?
DUHHHH—
ONCE BB KENICHI IS OVER, I WON'T BE IN CHARGE OF ANYTHING. I REALLY THOUGHT TANTO WAS GOING TO BECOME A SERIES.
AT LEAST THE EDITORIAL DEPARTMENT DIDN'T HAVE YOU TAKE OVER SOMEBODY ELSE'S SERIES. THAT MEANS THEY WANT TO SEE WHAT'S NEXT FROM ASHIROGI AND TAKAHAMA.
ALTHOUGH, IF THOSE AREN'T GOING TO WORK OUT, YOU NEED TO FIND SOME WAY TO GET A NEW SERIES.
I KNOW. I'M GRATEFUL. I REALLY HAVE TO GET TANTO SERIALIZED AT THE NEXT MEETING.
RRRRRR
ASHIROGI IS HERE FOR THEIR 2:30 P.M. MEETING.
I'LL COME DOWNSTAIRS, SO PLEASE HAVE THEM WAIT FOR ME AT AN OPEN TABLE.
YES, SIR. THEY'LL BE AT TABLE 3.
I'VE GOTTA GO MEET WITH ASHIROGI.
OKAY, GOOD LUCK.
KLAK
MR. AIDA...
HMM?
DO YOU HAVE ANY REVISION SUGGESTIONS? I DON'T KNOW WHAT ELSE TO CHANGE.
THEN WHY DON'T YOU JUST RE-SUBMIT IT AS IS?
YOU'RE SO MEAN...
JUST TELL THEM WHAT THE EDITORS SAID AT THE MEETING.
OKAY...

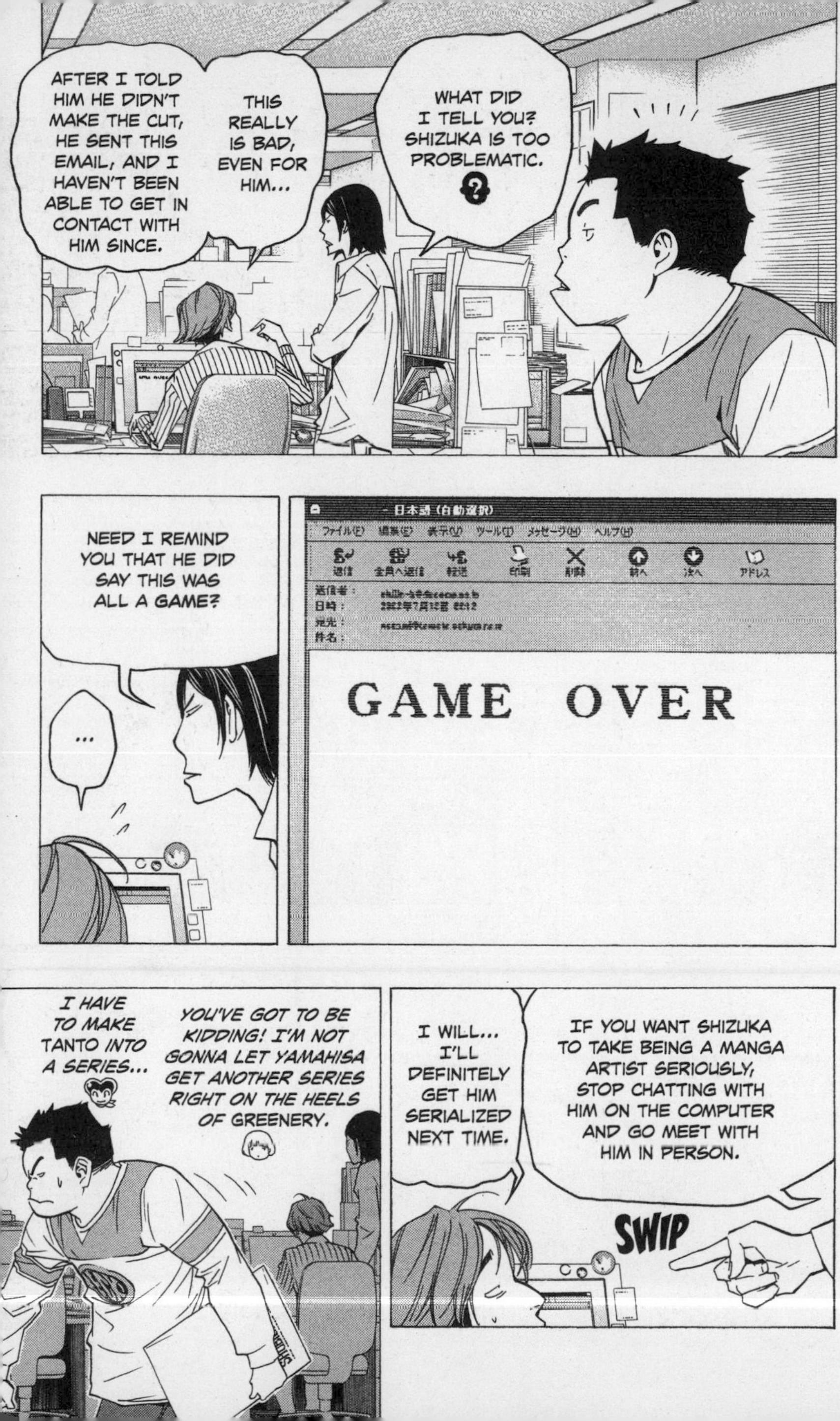
WHAT DID I TELL YOU? SHIZUKA IS TOO PROBLEMATIC.
THIS REALLY IS BAD, EVEN FOR HIM...
AFTER I TOLD HIM HE DIDN'T MAKE THE CUT, HE SENT THIS EMAIL, AND I HAVEN'T BEEN ABLE TO GET IN CONTACT WITH HIM SINCE.
- 日本語 (自動選択)
ファイル(F) 編集(E) 表示(V) ツール(T) メッセージ(M) ヘルプ(H)
返信 全員へ返信 転送 印刷 削除 前へ 次へ アドレス
送信者:
日時:
宛先:
件名:
GAME OVER
NEED I REMIND YOU THAT HE DID SAY THIS WAS ALL A GAME?
...
IF YOU WANT SHIZUKA TO TAKE BEING A MANGA ARTIST SERIOUSLY, STOP CHATTING WITH HIM ON THE COMPUTER AND GO MEET WITH HIM IN PERSON.
I WILL... I'LL DEFINITELY GET HIM SERIALIZED NEXT TIME.
SWIP
YOU'VE GOT TO BE KIDDING! I'M NOT GONNA LET YAMAHISA GET ANOTHER SERIES RIGHT ON THE HEELS OF GREENERY.
I HAVE TO MAKE TANTO INTO A SERIES...

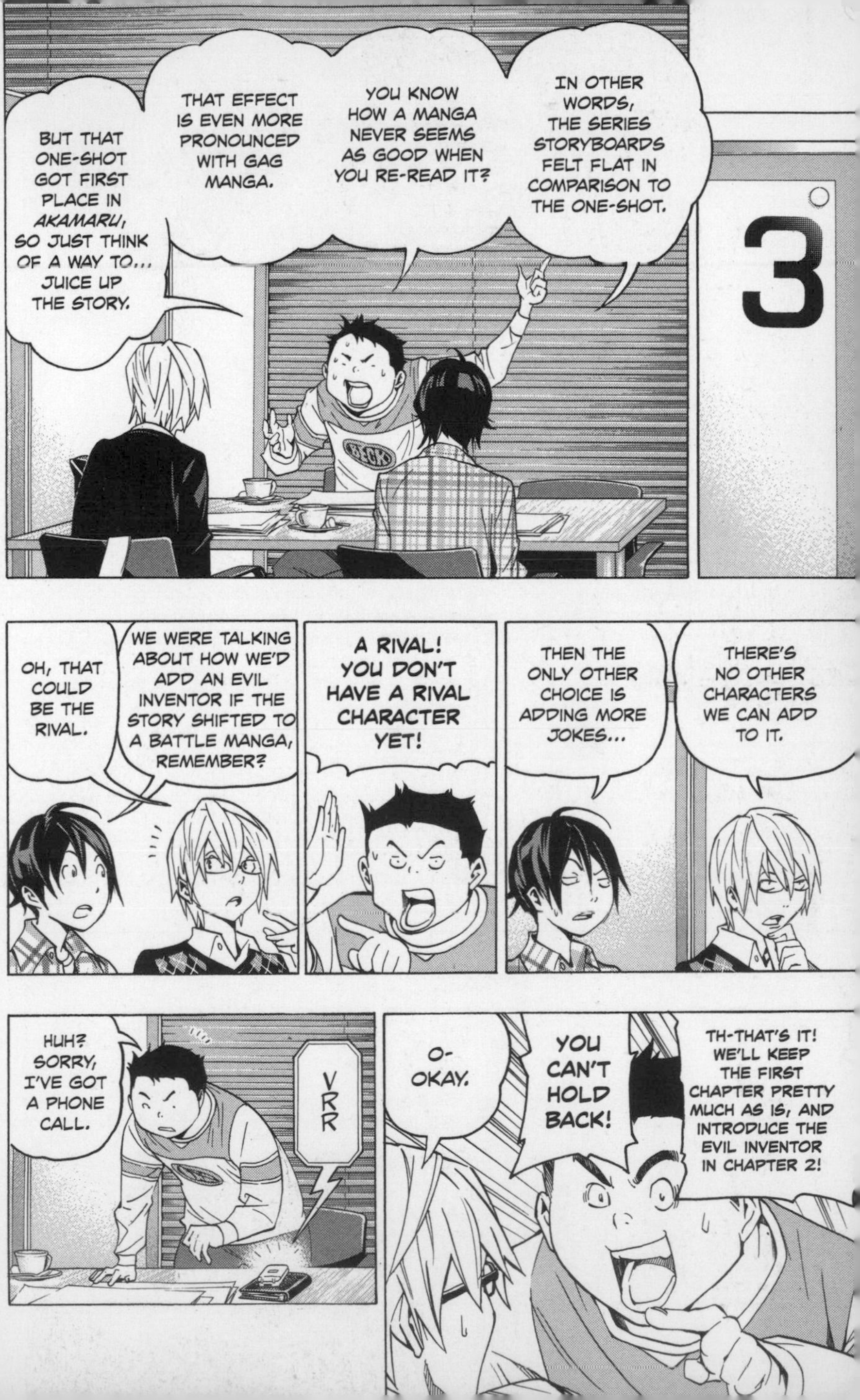
IN OTHER WORDS, THE SERIES STORYBOARDS FELT FLAT IN COMPARISON TO THE ONE-SHOT.
YOU KNOW HOW A MANGA NEVER SEEMS AS GOOD WHEN YOU RE-READ IT?
THAT EFFECT IS EVEN MORE PRONOUNCED WITH GAG MANGA.
BUT THAT ONE-SHOT GOT FIRST PLACE IN *AKAMARU*, SO JUST THINK OF A WAY TO... JUICE UP THE STORY.
3
THERE'S NO OTHER CHARACTERS WE CAN ADD TO IT.
THEN THE ONLY OTHER CHOICE IS ADDING MORE JOKES...
A RIVAL! YOU DON'T HAVE A RIVAL CHARACTER YET!
WE WERE TALKING ABOUT HOW WE'D ADD AN EVIL INVENTOR IF THE STORY SHIFTED TO A BATTLE MANGA, REMEMBER?
OH, THAT COULD BE THE RIVAL.
TH-THAT'S IT! WE'LL KEEP THE FIRST CHAPTER PRETTY MUCH AS IS, AND INTRODUCE THE EVIL INVENTOR IN CHAPTER 2!
YOU CAN'T HOLD BACK!
O- OKAY.
VRR
HUH? SORRY, I'VE GOT A PHONE CALL.

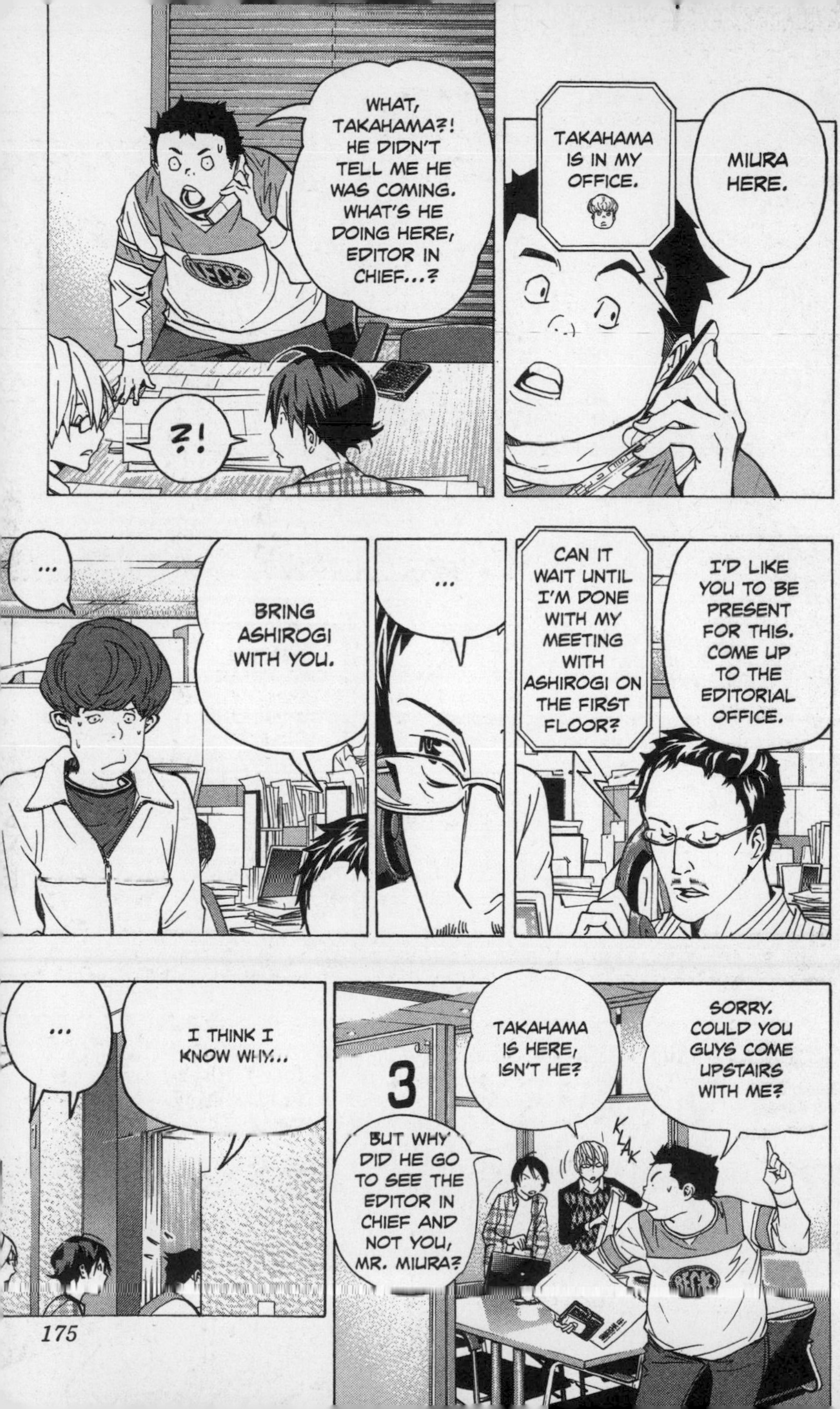
MIURA HERE.
TAKAHAMA IS IN MY OFFICE.
WHAT, TAKAHAMA?! HE DIDN'T TELL ME HE WAS COMING. WHAT'S HE DOING HERE, EDITOR IN CHIEF...?
?!
I'D LIKE YOU TO BE PRESENT FOR THIS. COME UP TO THE EDITORIAL OFFICE.
CAN IT WAIT UNTIL I'M DONE WITH MY MEETING WITH ASHIROGI ON THE FIRST FLOOR?
...
BRING ASHIROGI WITH YOU.
...
SORRY. COULD YOU GUYS COME UPSTAIRS WITH ME?
TAKAHAMA IS HERE, ISN'T HE?
3
KLAK
BUT WHY DID HE GO TO SEE THE EDITOR IN CHIEF AND NOT YOU, MR. MIURA?
I THINK I KNOW WHY...
...

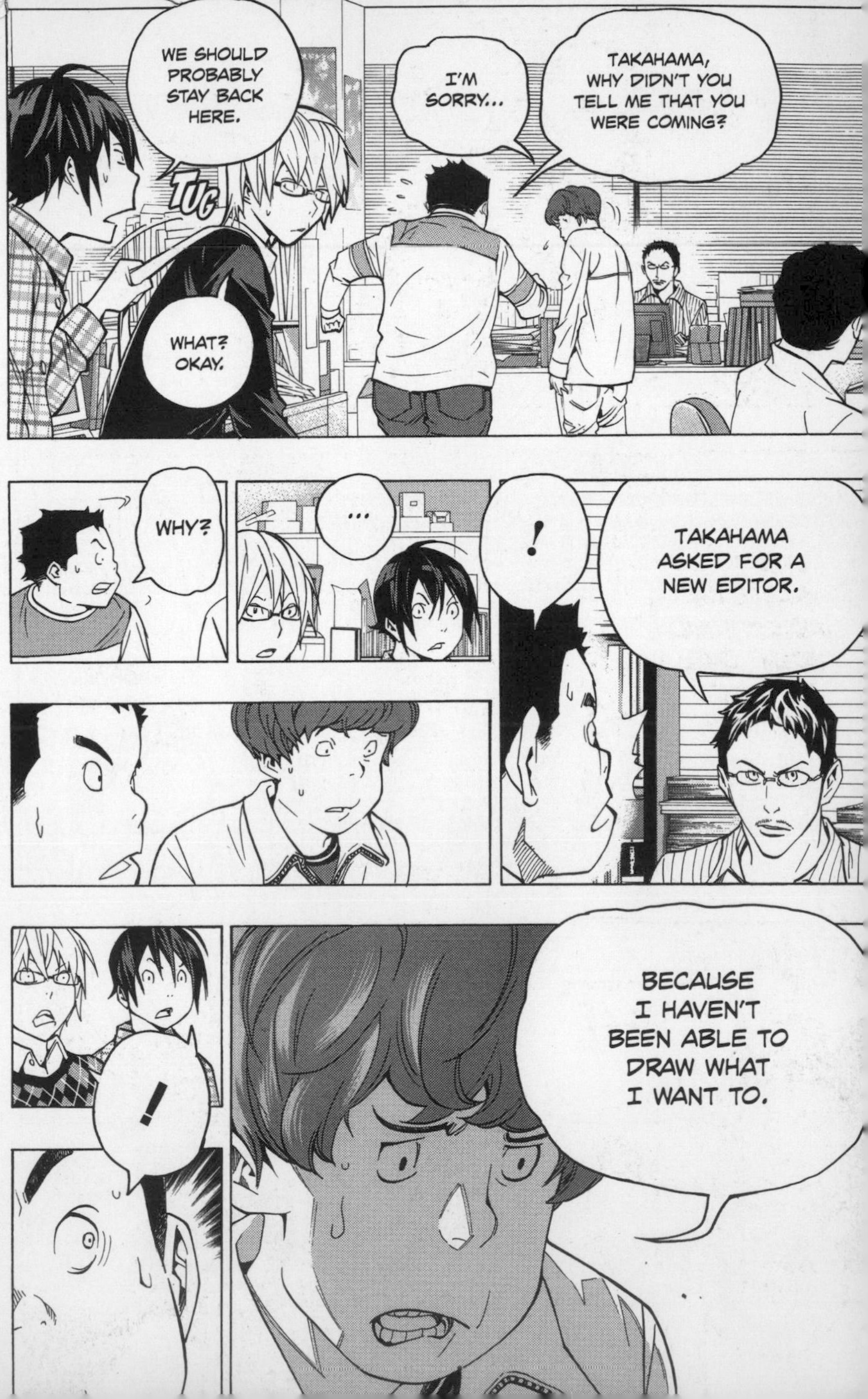
TAKAHAMA, WHY DIDN'T YOU TELL ME THAT YOU WERE COMING?
I'M SORRY...
WE SHOULD PROBABLY STAY BACK HERE.
TUG
WHAT? OKAY.
!
TAKAHAMA ASKED FOR A NEW EDITOR.
...
WHY?
BECAUSE I HAVEN'T BEEN ABLE TO DRAW WHAT I WANT TO.
!

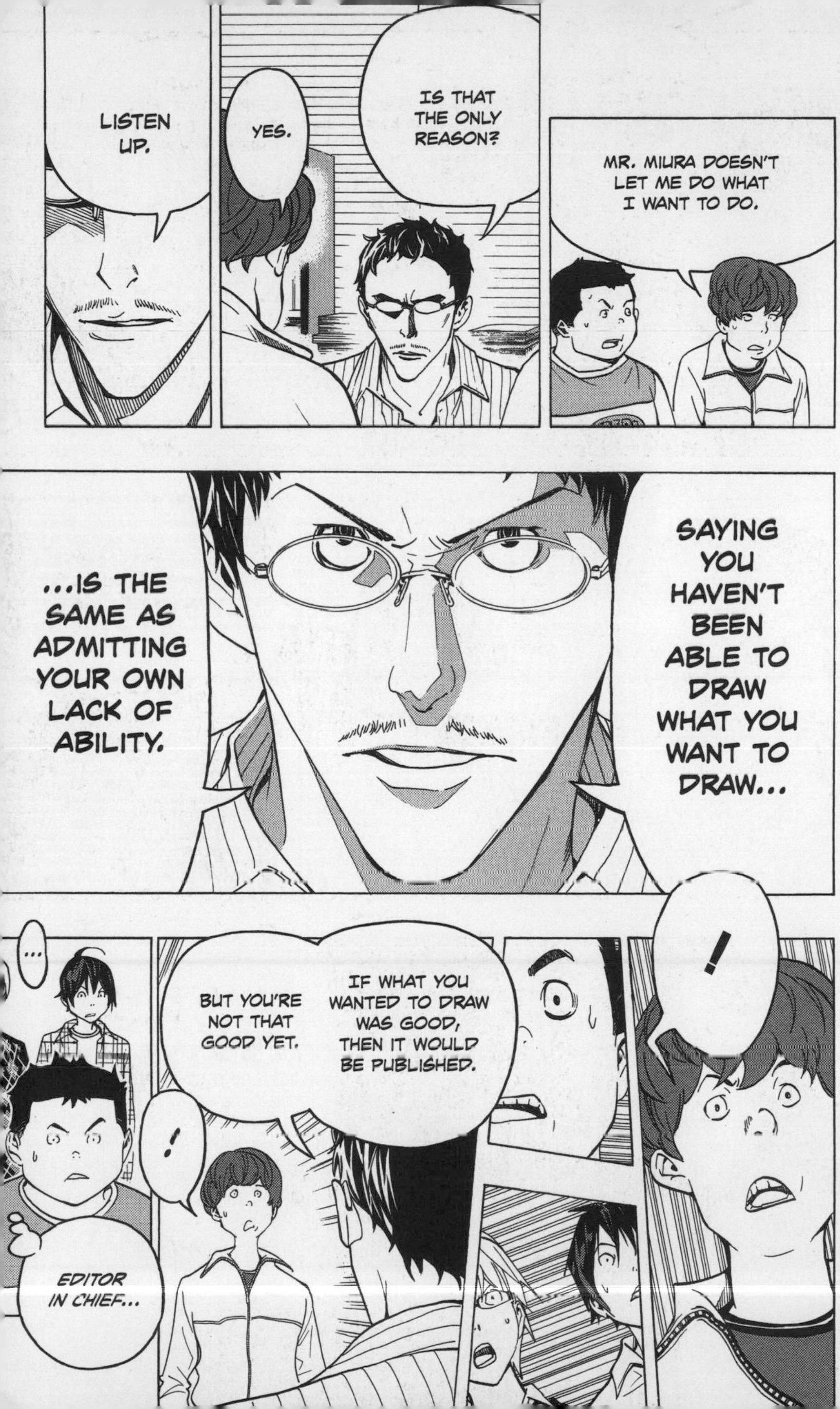
MR. MIURA DOESN'T LET ME DO WHAT I WANT TO DO.
IS THAT THE ONLY REASON?
YES.
LISTEN UP.
SAYING YOU HAVEN'T BEEN ABLE TO DRAW WHAT YOU WANT TO DRAW...
...IS THE SAME AS ADMITTING YOUR OWN LACK OF ABILITY.
!
IF WHAT YOU WANTED TO DRAW WAS GOOD, THEN IT WOULD BE PUBLISHED.
BUT YOU'RE NOT THAT GOOD YET.
!
...
EDITOR IN CHIEF...

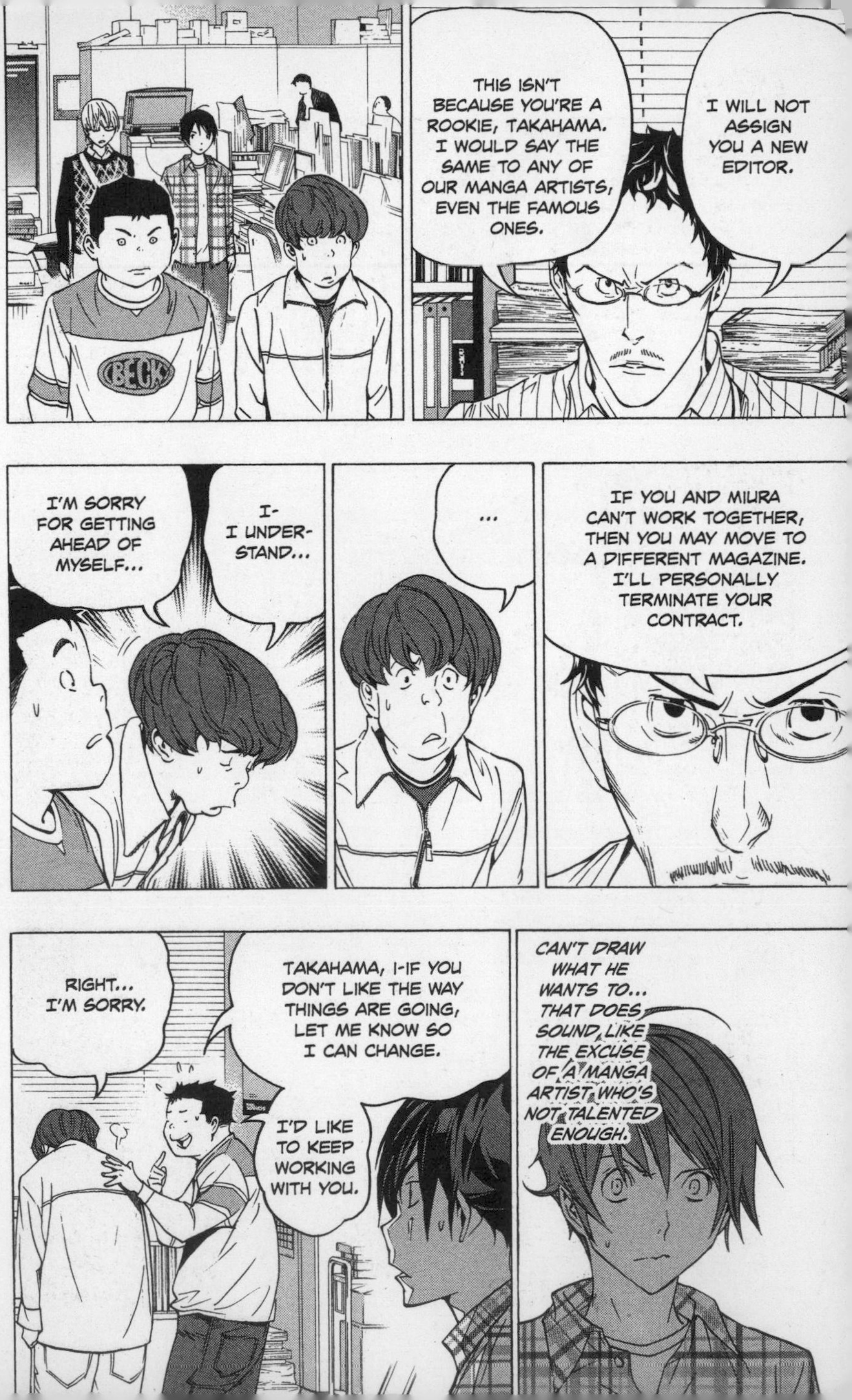
I WILL NOT ASSIGN YOU A NEW EDITOR.
THIS ISN'T BECAUSE YOU'RE A ROOKIE, TAKAHAMA. I WOULD SAY THE SAME TO ANY OF OUR MANGA ARTISTS, EVEN THE FAMOUS ONES.
BECK
IF YOU AND MIURA CAN'T WORK TOGETHER, THEN YOU MAY MOVE TO A DIFFERENT MAGAZINE. I'LL PERSONALLY TERMINATE YOUR CONTRACT.
...
I- I UNDER-STAND...
I'M SORRY FOR GETTING AHEAD OF MYSELF...
CAN'T DRAW WHAT HE WANTS TO... THAT DOES SOUND LIKE THE EXCUSE OF A MANGA ARTIST WHO'S NOT TALENTED ENOUGH.
TAKAHAMA, I-IF YOU DON'T LIKE THE WAY THINGS ARE GOING, LET ME KNOW SO I CAN CHANGE.
RIGHT... I'M SORRY.
I'D LIKE TO KEEP WORKING WITH YOU.

READ THIS WAY

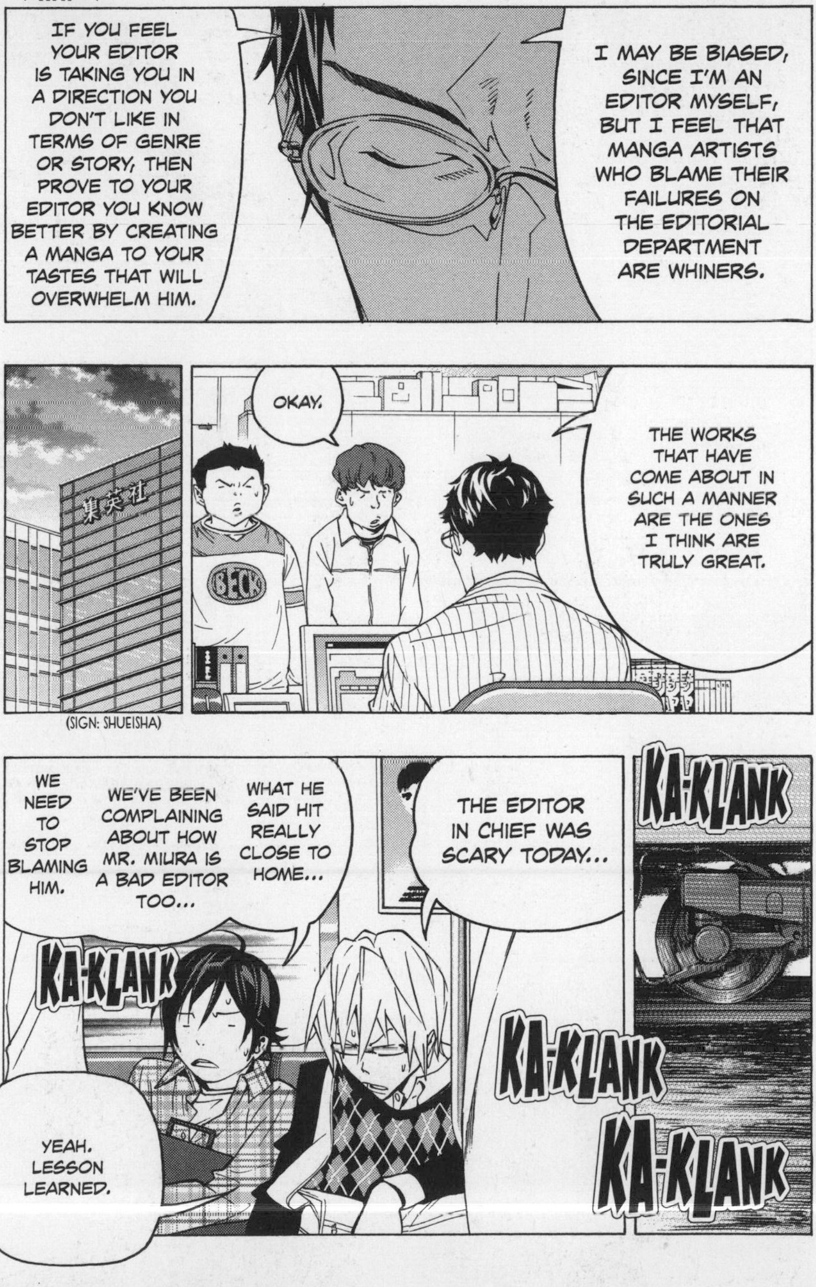
I MAY BE BIASED, SINCE I'M AN EDITOR MYSELF, BUT I FEEL THAT MANGA ARTISTS WHO BLAME THEIR FAILURES ON THE EDITORIAL DEPARTMENT ARE WHINERS.
IF YOU FEEL YOUR EDITOR IS TAKING YOU IN A DIRECTION YOU DON'T LIKE IN TERMS OF GENRE OR STORY, THEN PROVE TO YOUR EDITOR YOU KNOW BETTER BY CREATING A MANGA TO YOUR TASTES THAT WILL OVERWHELM HIM.
THE WORKS THAT HAVE COME ABOUT IN SUCH A MANNER ARE THE ONES I THINK ARE TRULY GREAT.
OKAY.
BECK
集英社
(SIGN: SHUEISHA)
KA-KLANK
THE EDITOR IN CHIEF WAS SCARY TODAY...
WHAT HE SAID HIT REALLY CLOSE TO HOME...
WE'VE BEEN COMPLAINING ABOUT HOW MR. MIURA IS A BAD EDITOR TOO...
WE NEED TO STOP BLAMING HIM.
KA-KLANK
KA-KLANK
KA-KLANK
YEAH. LESSON LEARNED.

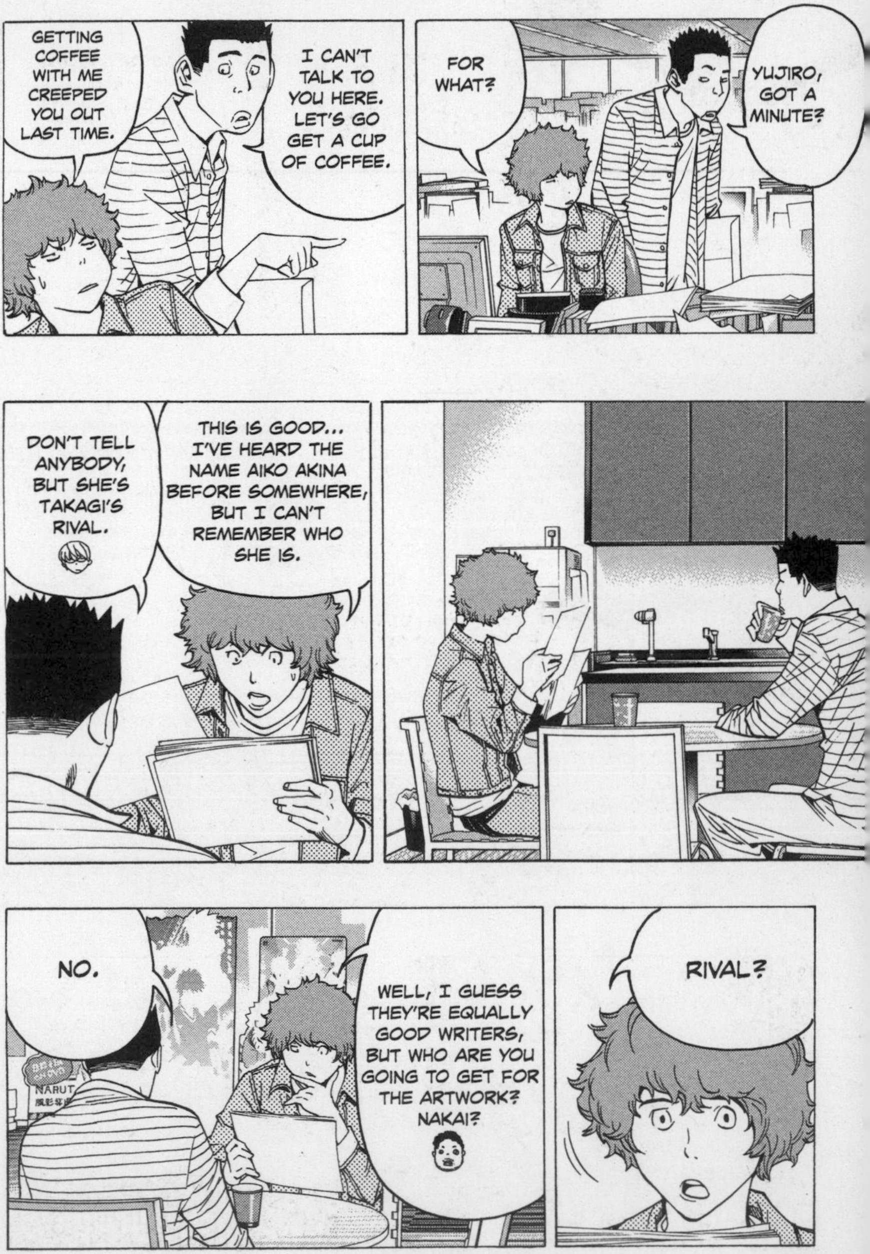
YUJIRO, GOT A MINUTE?
FOR WHAT?
I CAN'T TALK TO YOU HERE. LET'S GO GET A CUP OF COFFEE.
GETTING COFFEE WITH ME CREEPED YOU OUT LAST TIME.
THIS IS GOOD... I'VE HEARD THE NAME AIKO AKINA BEFORE SOMEWHERE, BUT I CAN'T REMEMBER WHO SHE IS.
DON'T TELL ANYBODY, BUT SHE'S TAKAGI'S RIVAL.
RIVAL?
WELL, I GUESS THEY'RE EQUALLY GOOD WRITERS, BUT WHO ARE YOU GOING TO GET FOR THE ARTWORK? NAKAI?
NO.

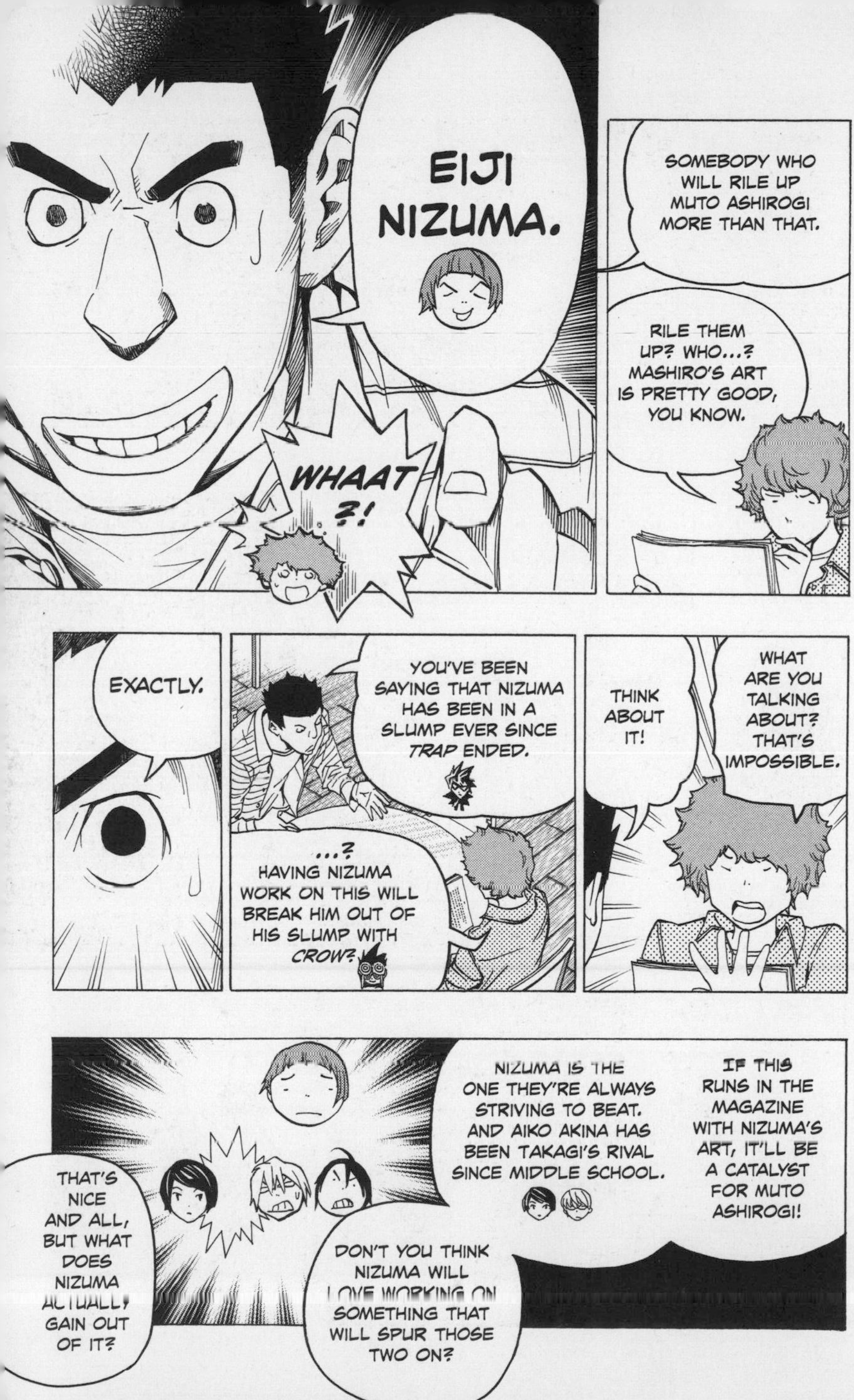
SOMEBODY WHO WILL RILE UP MUTO ASHIROGI MORE THAN THAT.
RILE THEM UP? WHO...? MASHIRO'S ART IS PRETTY GOOD, YOU KNOW.
EIJI NIZUMA.
WHAAT ?!
WHAT ARE YOU TALKING ABOUT? THAT'S IMPOSSIBLE.
THINK ABOUT IT!
YOU'VE BEEN SAYING THAT NIZUMA HAS BEEN IN A SLUMP EVER SINCE *TRAP* ENDED.
...? HAVING NIZUMA WORK ON THIS WILL BREAK HIM OUT OF HIS SLUMP WITH *CROW*?
EXACTLY.
IF THIS RUNS IN THE MAGAZINE WITH NIZUMA'S ART, IT'LL BE A CATALYST FOR MUTO ASHIROGI!
NIZUMA IS THE ONE THEY'RE ALWAYS STRIVING TO BEAT. AND AIKO AKINA HAS BEEN TAKAGI'S RIVAL SINCE MIDDLE SCHOOL.
THAT'S NICE AND ALL, BUT WHAT DOES NIZUMA ACTUALLY GAIN OUT OF IT?
DON'T YOU THINK NIZUMA WILL LOVE WORKING ON SOMETHING THAT WILL SPUR THOSE TWO ON?

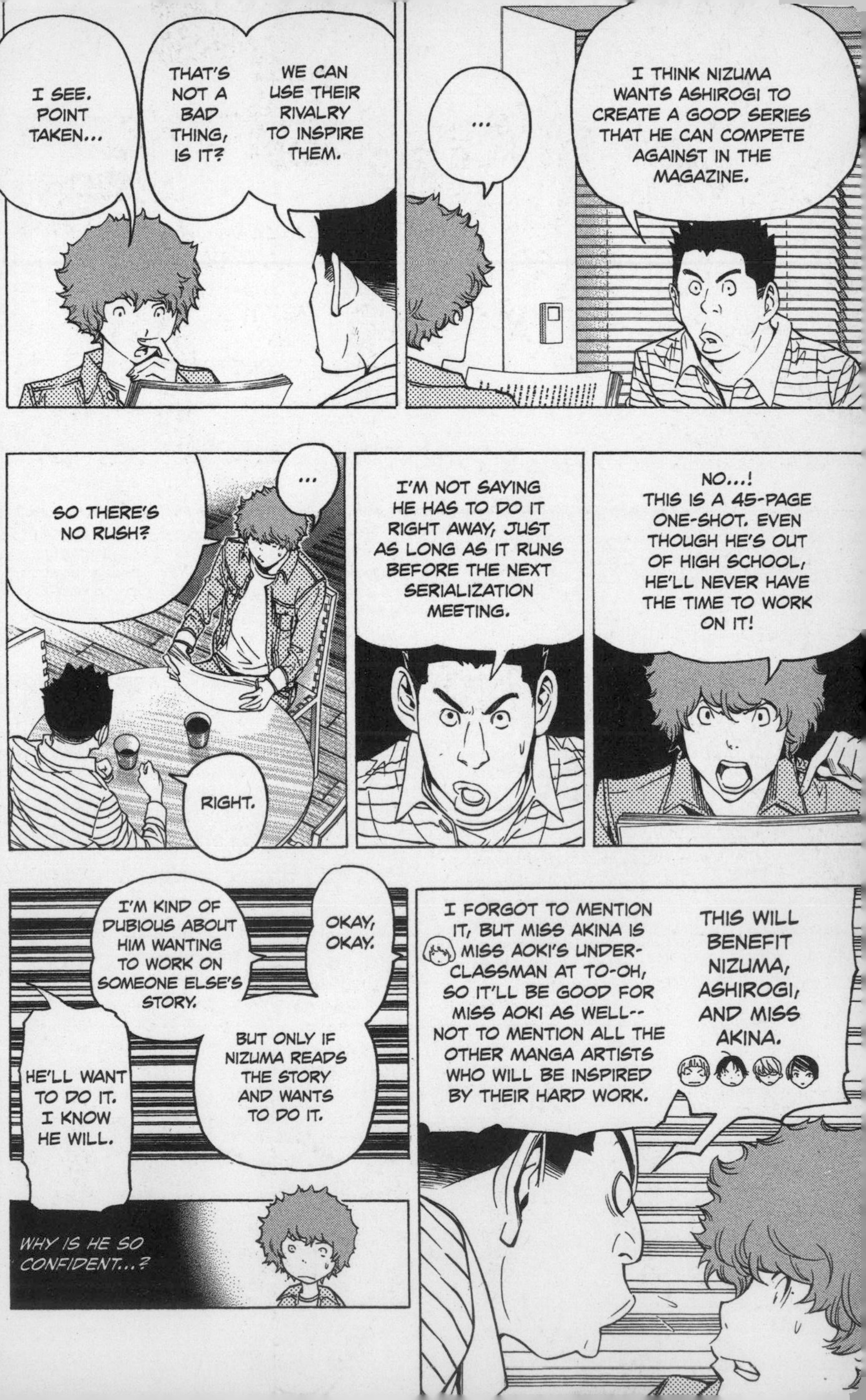
I THINK NIZUMA WANTS ASHIROGI TO CREATE A GOOD SERIES THAT HE CAN COMPETE AGAINST IN THE MAGAZINE.
...
WE CAN USE THEIR RIVALRY TO INSPIRE THEM.
THAT'S NOT A BAD THING, IS IT?
I SEE. POINT TAKEN...
NO...! THIS IS A 45-PAGE ONE-SHOT. EVEN THOUGH HE'S OUT OF HIGH SCHOOL, HE'LL NEVER HAVE THE TIME TO WORK ON IT!
I'M NOT SAYING HE HAS TO DO IT RIGHT AWAY, JUST AS LONG AS IT RUNS BEFORE THE NEXT SERIALIZATION MEETING.
...
SO THERE'S NO RUSH?
RIGHT.
THIS WILL BENEFIT NIZUMA, ASHIROGI, AND MISS AKINA.
I FORGOT TO MENTION IT, BUT MISS AKINA IS MISS AOKI'S UNDER-CLASSMAN AT TO-OH, SO IT'LL BE GOOD FOR MISS AOKI AS WELL--NOT TO MENTION ALL THE OTHER MANGA ARTISTS WHO WILL BE INSPIRED BY THEIR HARD WORK.
OKAY, OKAY.
I'M KIND OF DUBIOUS ABOUT HIM WANTING TO WORK ON SOMEONE ELSE'S STORY.
BUT ONLY IF NIZUMA READS THE STORY AND WANTS TO DO IT.
HE'LL WANT TO DO IT. I KNOW HE WILL.
WHY IS HE SO CONFIDENT...?

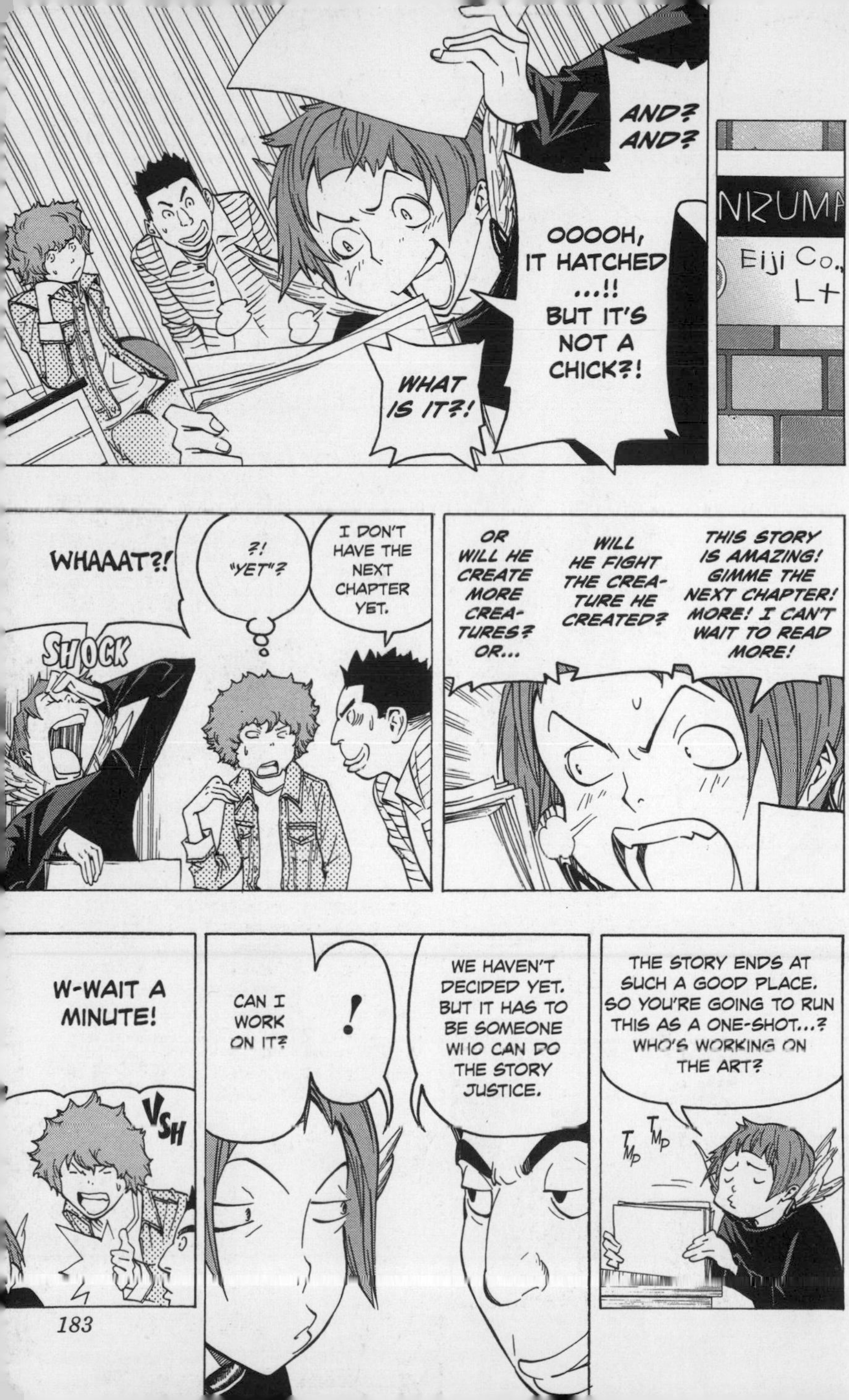
NIZUMA
Eiji Co., Lt
AND? AND?
OOOOH, IT HATCHED ...!! BUT IT'S NOT A CHICK?!
WHAT IS IT?!
THIS STORY IS AMAZING! GIMME THE NEXT CHAPTER! MORE! I CAN'T WAIT TO READ MORE!
WILL HE FIGHT THE CREA-TURE HE CREATED?
OR WILL HE CREATE MORE CREA-TURES? OR...
I DON'T HAVE THE NEXT CHAPTER YET.
?! "YET"?
WHAAAT?!
SHOCK
THE STORY ENDS AT SUCH A GOOD PLACE. SO YOU'RE GOING TO RUN THIS AS A ONE-SHOT...? WHO'S WORKING ON THE ART?
TMP
TMP
WE HAVEN'T DECIDED YET. BUT IT HAS TO BE SOMEONE WHO CAN DO THE STORY JUSTICE.
!
CAN I WORK ON IT?
W-WAIT A MINUTE!
VSH

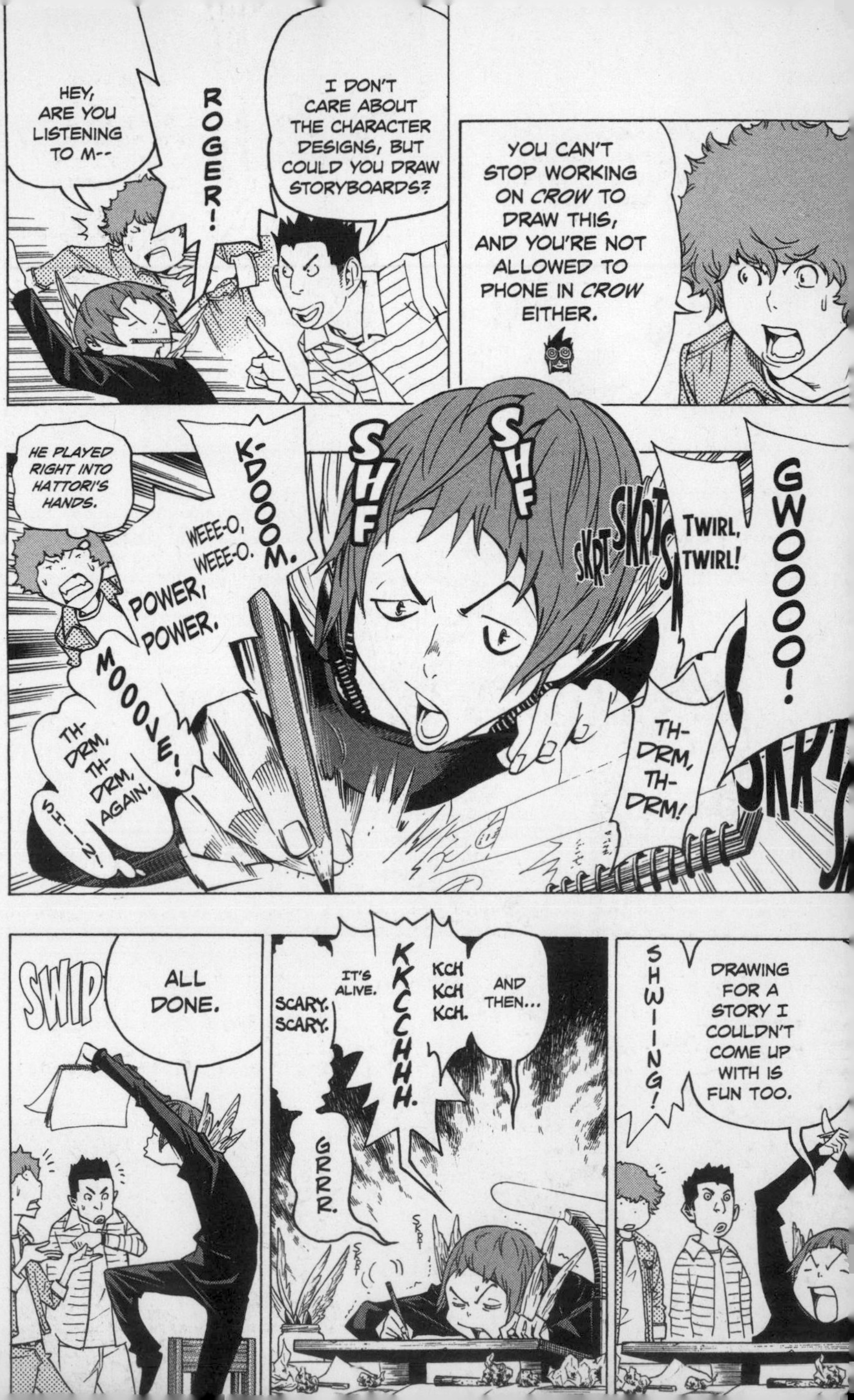
YOU CAN'T STOP WORKING ON *CROW* TO DRAW THIS, AND YOU'RE NOT ALLOWED TO PHONE IN *CROW* EITHER.
I DON'T CARE ABOUT THE CHARACTER DESIGNS, BUT COULD YOU DRAW STORYBOARDS?
ROGER!
HEY, ARE YOU LISTENING TO M--
GWOOOOO!
TWIRL, TWIRL!
SKRT SKRT SKRT
SHF
SHF
TH-DRM, TH-DRM!
K'DOOOM.
WEEE-O, WEEE-O.
HE PLAYED RIGHT INTO HATTORI'S HANDS.
POWER, POWER.
MOOOOVE!
TH-DRM, TH-DRM, AGAIN.
SH--N!
SHWIING!
DRAWING FOR A STORY I COULDN'T COME UP WITH IS FUN TOO.
AND THEN...
KCH KCH KCH.
KKCCHHH.
IT'S ALIVE.
SCARY. SCARY.
GRRR.
ALL DONE.
SWIP

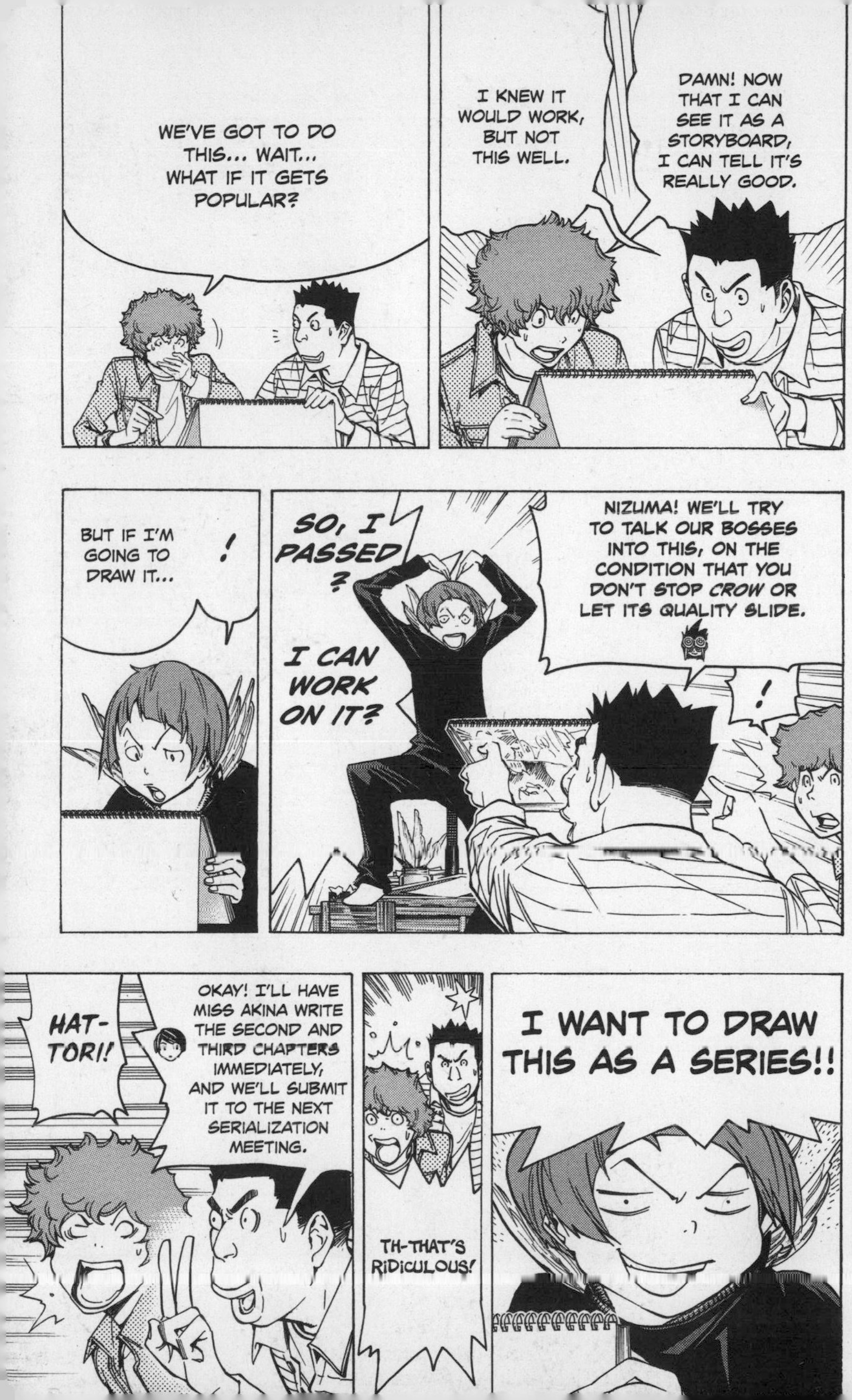
DAMN! NOW THAT I CAN SEE IT AS A STORYBOARD, I CAN TELL IT'S REALLY GOOD.
I KNEW IT WOULD WORK, BUT NOT THIS WELL.
WE'VE GOT TO DO THIS... WAIT... WHAT IF IT GETS POPULAR?
NIZUMA! WE'LL TRY TO TALK OUR BOSSES INTO THIS, ON THE CONDITION THAT YOU DON'T STOP *CROW* OR LET ITS QUALITY SLIDE.
!
SO, I PASSED?
I CAN WORK ON IT?
BUT IF I'M GOING TO DRAW IT...
!
I WANT TO DRAW THIS AS A SERIES!!
TH-THAT'S RIDICULOUS!
OKAY! I'LL HAVE MISS AKINA WRITE THE SECOND AND THIRD CHAPTERS IMMEDIATELY, AND WE'LL SUBMIT IT TO THE NEXT SERIALIZATION MEETING.
HAT-TORI!!

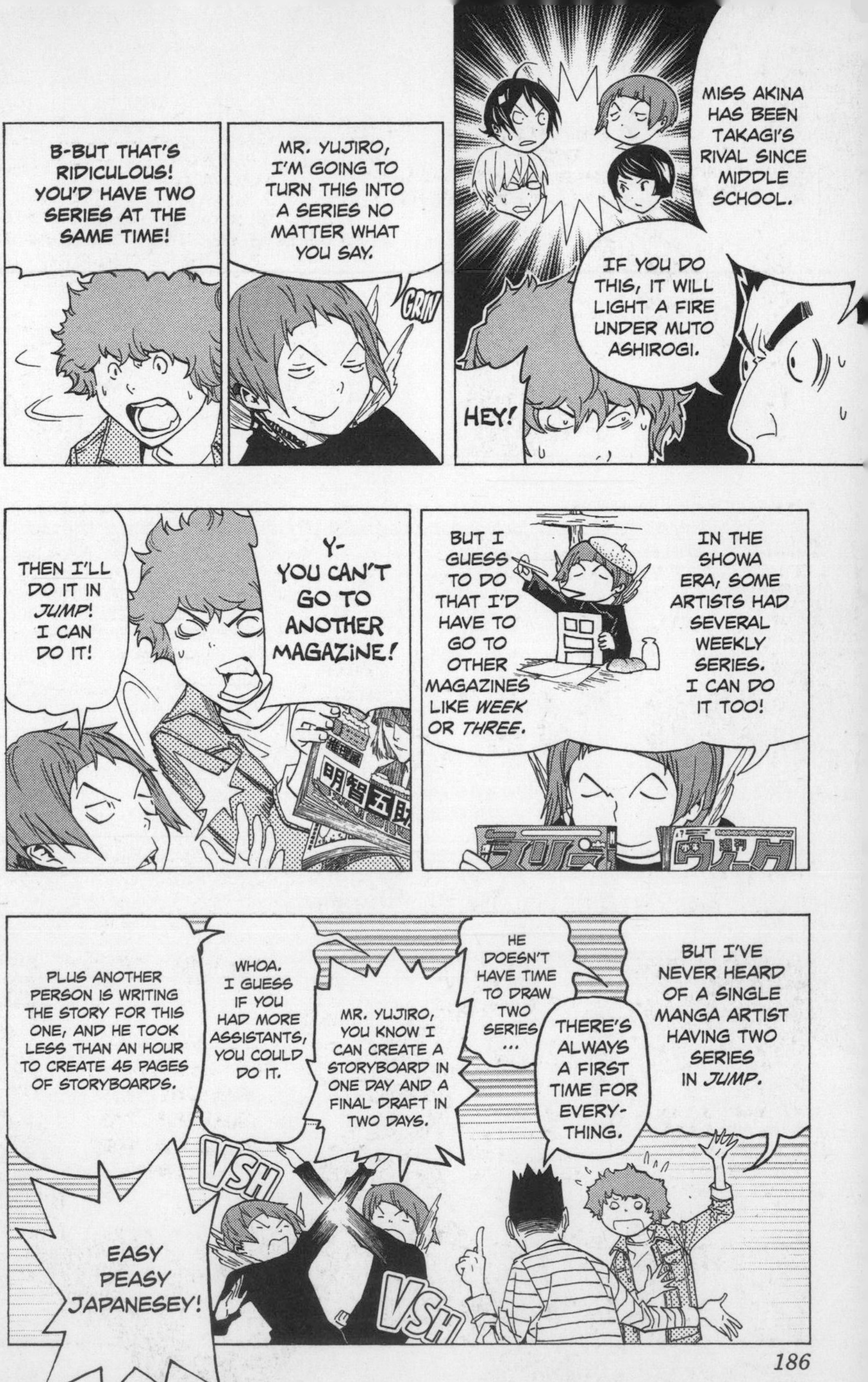
MISS AKINA HAS BEEN TAKAGI'S RIVAL SINCE MIDDLE SCHOOL.
IF YOU DO THIS, IT WILL LIGHT A FIRE UNDER MUTO ASHIROGI.
HEY!
MR. YUJIRO, I'M GOING TO TURN THIS INTO A SERIES NO MATTER WHAT YOU SAY.
GRIN
B-BUT THAT'S RIDICULOUS! YOU'D HAVE TWO SERIES AT THE SAME TIME!
IN THE SHOWA ERA, SOME ARTISTS HAD SEVERAL WEEKLY SERIES. I CAN DO IT TOO!
BUT I GUESS TO DO THAT I'D HAVE TO GO TO OTHER MAGAZINES LIKE *WEEK* OR *THREE*.
Y- YOU CAN'T GO TO ANOTHER MAGAZINE!
THEN I'LL DO IT IN *JUMP*! I CAN DO IT!
BUT I'VE NEVER HEARD OF A SINGLE MANGA ARTIST HAVING TWO SERIES IN *JUMP*.
THERE'S ALWAYS A FIRST TIME FOR EVERY-THING.
HE DOESN'T HAVE TIME TO DRAW TWO SERIES ...
MR. YUJIRO, YOU KNOW I CAN CREATE A STORYBOARD IN ONE DAY AND A FINAL DRAFT IN TWO DAYS.
WHOA. I GUESS IF YOU HAD MORE ASSISTANTS, YOU COULD DO IT.
PLUS ANOTHER PERSON IS WRITING THE STORY FOR THIS ONE, AND HE TOOK LESS THAN AN HOUR TO CREATE 45 PAGES OF STORYBOARDS.
VSH
VSH
EASY PEASY JAPANESEY!

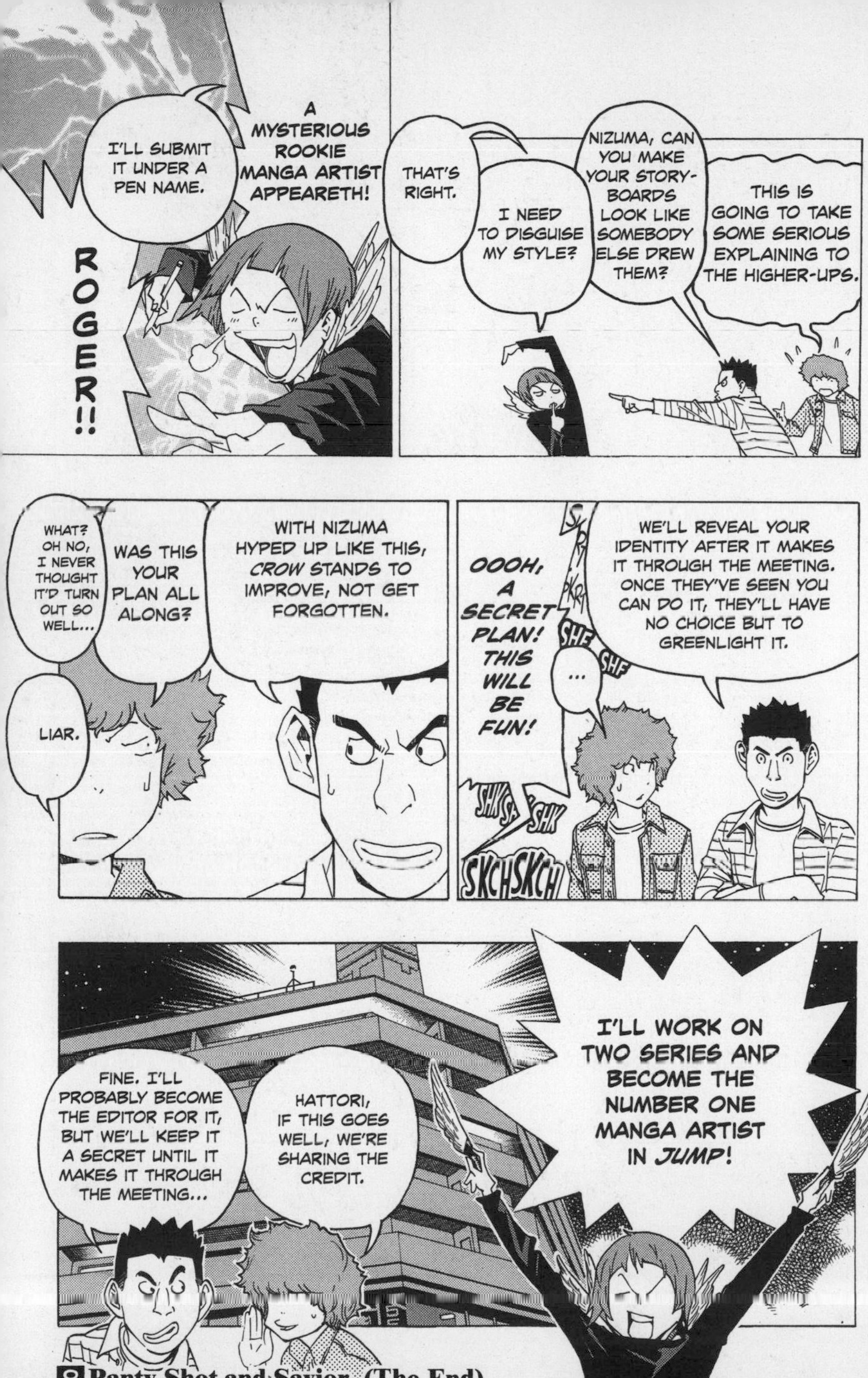
THIS IS GOING TO TAKE SOME SERIOUS EXPLAINING TO THE HIGHER-UPS.
NIZUMA, CAN YOU MAKE YOUR STORY-BOARDS LOOK LIKE SOMEBODY ELSE DREW THEM?
I NEED TO DISGUISE MY STYLE?
THAT'S RIGHT.
A MYSTERIOUS ROOKIE MANGA ARTIST APPEARETH!
I'LL SUBMIT IT UNDER A PEN NAME.
ROGER!!
WE'LL REVEAL YOUR IDENTITY AFTER IT MAKES IT THROUGH THE MEETING. ONCE THEY'VE SEEN YOU CAN DO IT, THEY'LL HAVE NO CHOICE BUT TO GREENLIGHT IT.
...
SHF SHF
OOOH, A SECRET PLAN! THIS WILL BE FUN!
SHK SHK
SKCHSKCH
WITH NIZUMA HYPED UP LIKE THIS, *CROW* STANDS TO IMPROVE, NOT GET FORGOTTEN.
WAS THIS YOUR PLAN ALL ALONG?
WHAT? OH NO, I NEVER THOUGHT IT'D TURN OUT SO WELL...
LIAR.
I'LL WORK ON TWO SERIES AND BECOME THE NUMBER ONE MANGA ARTIST IN *JUMP*!
HATTORI, IF THIS GOES WELL, WE'RE SHARING THE CREDIT.
FINE. I'LL PROBABLY BECOME THE EDITOR FOR IT, BUT WE'LL KEEP IT A SECRET UNTIL IT MAKES IT THROUGH THE MEETING...

8 Panty Shot and Savior (The End)

OHBA'S STORYBOARD

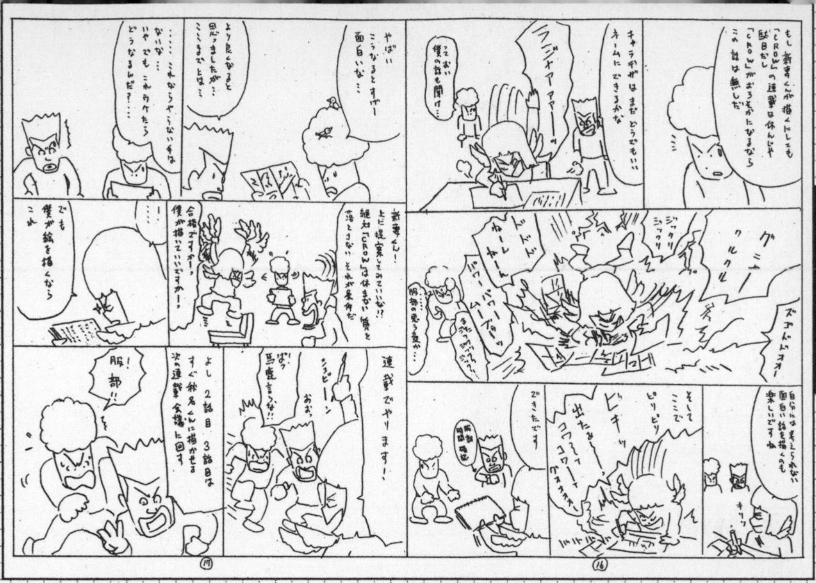
もし新妻くんが描くとしても「CROW」の連載は休んじゃ駄目だし「CROW」がおろそかになるならこの話は無しだ
キャラデザはまだどうでもいい ネームにできるかな
ラジオアアアー…ッ
っておい 僕の話も聞け…
グニャー
クルクル
ズゴドドオオー
ジックリ ジックリ
ドドドド
服部の思う壺か…
自分には考えられない面白い話を描くのも楽しいですね
キリッ
そしてここで
ピリピリ
ビキーッ
出たぁ〜
できたです
やばい こうなるとすげー面白いな…
より良くなると思ってましたが…ここまでとは…
……これならやらない手はないな… いや でもこれウケたらどうなるんだ?…
新妻くん! 上に提案してみていいな!? 絶対「CROW」は休まない 質を落とさない それが条件だ
合格ですか!? 僕が描いていいですか!
でも 僕が絵を描くならこれ
連載でやります!
おお…
ばっ 馬鹿言うな!!
よし 2話目 3話目はすぐ秋名くんに描かせる 次の連載会議に回す
服部!!
16
17

OBATA'S STORYBOARD

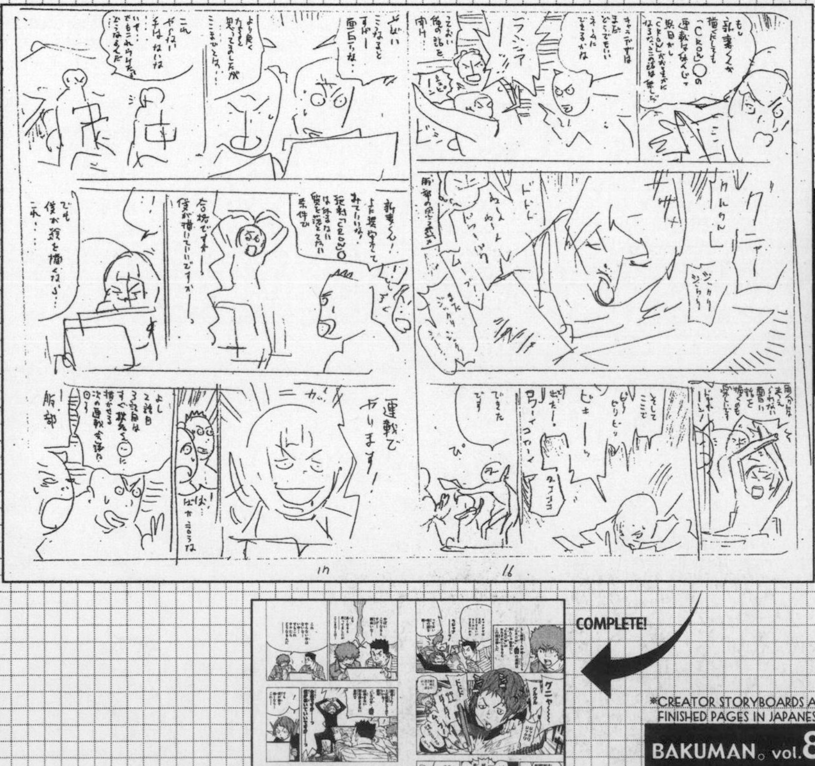
連載でやります!
16
17

COMPLETE!

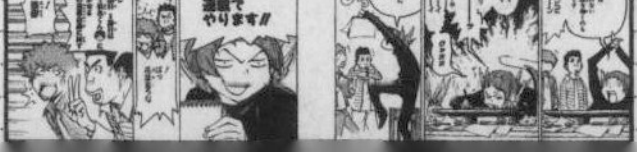

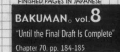

*CREATOR STORYBOARDS AND FINISHED PAGES IN JAPANESE

BAKUMAN。 vol. 8
"Until the Final Draft Is Complete"
Chapter 70, pp. 184-185

BAKUMAN。

SIR WILLIAM STEPHENSON
YOUNG ADULT

In the NEXT VOLUME

Moritaka and Takagi find themselves competing with Eiji once again as they make one final push to win a new series in *Shonen Jump*. Meanwhile, a new rival is emerging as Ryu Shizuka continues to work with his editor to get his series ready for serialization.

Available February 2012

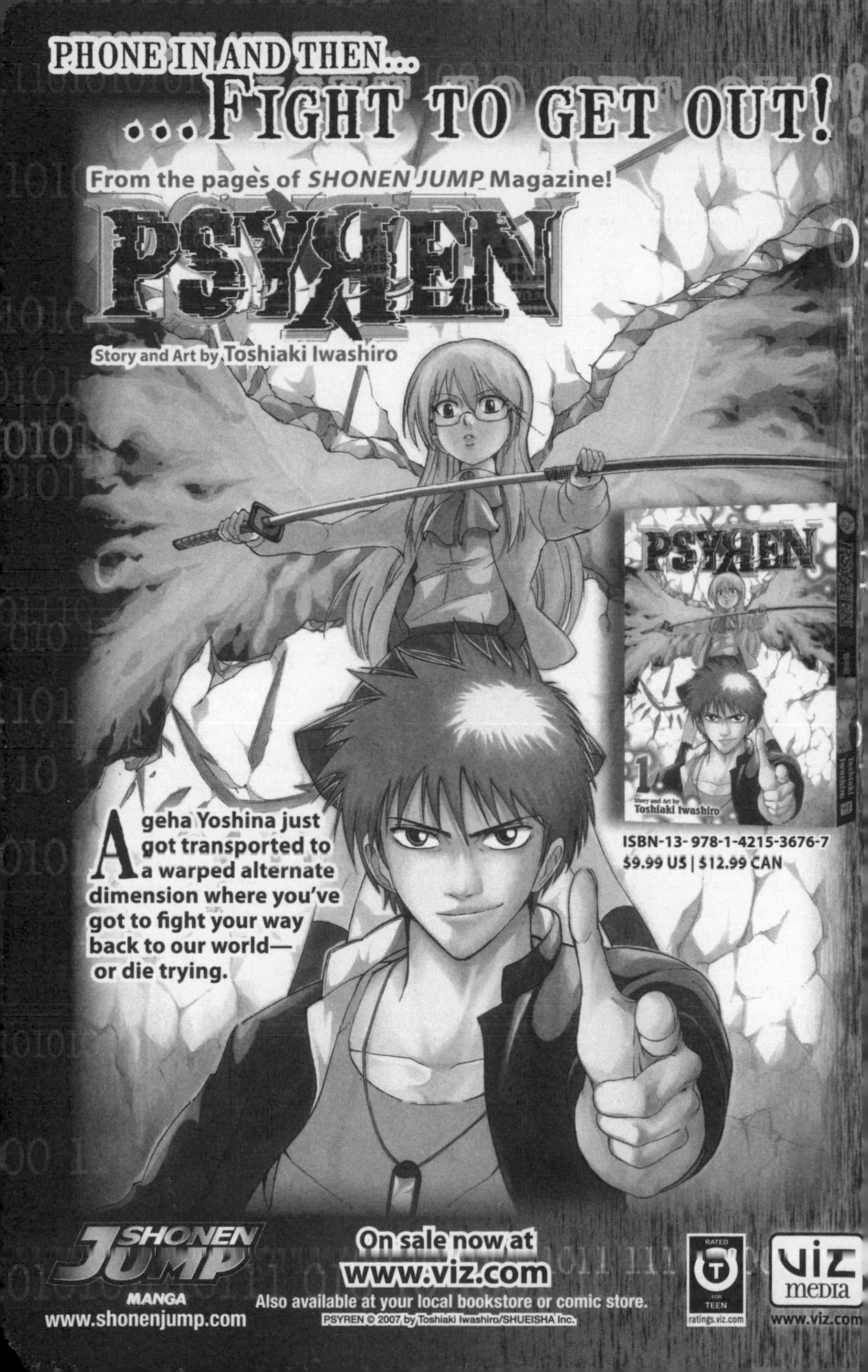
PHONE IN AND THEN...
...FIGHT TO GET OUT!
From the pages of SHONEN JUMP Magazine!
PSYREN
Story and Art by Toshiaki Iwashiro
PSYREN
1
Story and Art by Toshiaki Iwashiro
ISBN-13- 978-1-4215-3676-7
$9.99 US | $12.99 CAN
Ageha Yoshina just got transported to a warped alternate dimension where you've got to fight your way back to our world—or die trying.
SHONEN JUMP MANGA
www.shonenjump.com
On sale now at
www.viz.com
Also available at your local bookstore or comic store.
PSYREN © 2007 by Toshiaki Iwashiro/SHUEISHA Inc.
RATED T FOR TEEN
ratings.viz.com
VIZ media
www.viz.com